While the United States Slept

Also by Nasrollah S. Fatemi:

The Dollar Crisis (with Thibaut de Saint-Phalle and
   Grace O'Keefe)

Diplomatic History of Persia

Multinational Corporations (with Thibaut de Saint-Phalle and
   Gail Williams)

Oil Diplomacy

Problems of U.S. Trade and Balance of Payments

While the United States Slept

Nasrollah S. Fatemi

With a Foreword by Fairleigh S. Dickinson, Jr.

NEW YORK • *Cornwall Books* • LONDON

© 1982 by Rosemont Publishing and Printing Corp.

Cornwall Books
4 Cornwall Drive
East Brunswick, New Jersey 08816

Cornwall Books
69 Fleet Street
London EC4Y 1EU, England

Cornwall Books
Toronto M5E 1A7, Canada

Library of Congress Cataloging in Publication Data

Fatemi, Nasrollah S. (Nasrollah Saifpour), 1910-
  While the United States slept.

  Includes bibliographical references and index.
  1. United States—Foreign economic relations.
2. United States—Commerce. 3. Balance of payments—
United States. 4. United States—Economic conditions—
1971-   . I. Title.
HF1455.F28   337.73   81-65538
ISBN 0-8453-4721-7   AACR2

Printed in the United States of America

This book is dedicated
to Fairleigh S. Dickinson, Jr.,
whose sponsorship and active participation
made this study possible.

Contents

	Foreword	9
	Acknowledgments	15
	Introduction	17
1	The Balance-of-Payments Problem	27
2	U.S Direct Investment Abroad: Foreign Investment in the United States	64
3	International Trade in the United States	88
4	What Price Government Interventions and Shackles?	120
5	The Impact of Taxation on International Trade	144
6	U.S. Economic Growth and Its Problems	178
7	The Transfer of Technology	215
8	The Future of the Developing Nations	242
	Index	305

Foreword

by Fairleigh S. Dickinson, Jr.

In 1961 I first became concerned with what I knew would be an increasing problem for the United States—a currency crisis brought about by the increasing deficit in our balance of payments. The world was quite a different place then. In Europe and Japan, the United States was looked upon as the model of an advanced industrial society that other nations hoped to emulate. Servan-Schreiber's *The American Challenge*, for example, reflects the explicit and implicit respect in which American corporate managers were then held.

I first expressed my forebodings to Thibaut de Saint-Phalle, when we were on our way to Grenoble, France, to negotiate the purchase of a small engineering firm that I felt we needed for our company in New Jersey. I was then and had been for some time chief executive of Becton, Dickinson and Company, a concern founded by my father in 1897. Our sales were less than $30 million a year, and Saint-Phalle was chief financial officer and in charge of the company's foreign operations. In 1981, twenty years later, sales have approached $1 billion, and the company employs more than 20,000 highly trained and dedicated people worldwide, compared with only 4,500 in 1961.

Many years after he had founded the company—in 1941, just after the Great Depression—my father advanced a sum of money to found a small two-year college in Rutherford, New Jersey, which was named after him. It is now Fairleigh Dickinson University, with 21,000 students and four campuses. In 1961 Nasrollah S. Fatemi, who had already had a distinguished career as governor of a province in his native Iran and subsequently as ambassador from Iran to the United Nations, became dean of the graduate school of the university.

In 1961, on returning from Grenoble, I was able to bring Fatemi and Saint-Phalle together and suggest that they collaborate on a study to be published by the university on the problem of the United States balance of payments. In 1963 it was published as *The Dollar Crisis*.

In 1976 Dr. Fatemi brought out *Multinational Corporations*, a study of global corporate power. Now comes this much more ambitious project, which focuses on the changing economic position of the United States in a world context.

When I look at what has happened to the company and to the university, it may seem hard to imagine that the United States has not fulfilled its industrial or educational promise. But the growth of high-technology entrepreneurial enterprise and of the educational base without which it could not develop masks some very serious problems that will affect the economic well-being of our country in the future. This study examines in detail what is happening to our economy as we start to create a postindustrial society. What the author shows is that the United States is now faced with the need to renovate its industrial structure in order to continue employing its citizens, maintaining their standard of living, providing the economic base essential to the maintenance of the country's political power, and ensuring the very survival of our society in the years to come.

It is not solely a problem for the government, even though the power of government has so grown in the past fifty years that we are increasingly inclined to blame it for our ills. It is a situation that will require the best efforts of all of us: of government, business, labor, the press, and the public.

It is clear that there is a strong feeling of uneasiness in our land: a decline of confidence in government as well as in business, a spirit of confrontation between different elements of our society, constant attempts to find someone or something to blame for what we think is amiss in the way our economy is managed. Our sense of identity and of the meaning of our nation seem sometimes to have disappeared.

It is becoming more and more evident that today's corporate leaders are professional managers, business mercenaries who ply their skills for a salary and bonus but rarely for a vision. Lacking a gut feeling for the *Gestalt* of their business, they see managing by the numbers as their only recourse.

Before the merger craze of the 1960s, corporate leaders were, for the most part, autocratic entrepreneurial men who were ready to take risks for what they felt in their guts would pan out. Sarnoff with RCA and the Watsons at IBM illustrate in one succinct sentence what we have lost from a glorious phase: "Edwin H. Land would have grimaced at the idea of doing a discounted cash flow on research for the Polaroid camera."*

The author has attempted to trace this decline of confidence in ourselves in economic terms over the course of the last thirty-year period. In the early chapters he shows how the position of the United States in trade has changed with respect to the rest of the world. In the later ones he brings the focus nearer to home by analyzing in depth how the structure of our society has itself brought about these problems. Finally, he recommends solutions that he believes essential—solutions that will require profound changes in outlook on the part of many of us.

---

*This and the preceding paragraph are taken almost exactly from an extensive article in *Business Week,* June 30, 1980. Massive parts of this article should be commended to the reader for perspective on our economic needs during what is called "The Reindustrialization of America."

I believe this to be an important book, and I am proud of my part in bringing it about. I think it describes accurately the new economic challenge we face as a nation. I equally believe that this next generation of Americans is fully capable of the innovative thinking that enabled my own generation to meet the challenges we faced in World War II and its aftermath.

It is now difficult to escape a growing conviction that the decade that has elapsed since *The Dollar Crisis* was published has seen a watershed in historical affairs, particularly those which most affect the well-being, the minds, and the hearts of the American people. It was impossible in 1962 to look at the relationship of this republic with its allies and the rest of the world with complete equanimity. We might, however, do with ease some things that would correct serious and growing dangers to the nation and to the comity of states. There was a time when deterioration in the economic welfare of this country could be foreseen, and thus remedies could be made available long before the slide produced a genuine crisis. The corrections were simple; the palliatives, relatively pleasant.

In the interval, however, the country slept, largely unaware of the fact that there was a true crisis at our door, not diminishing, but growing ever more dangerous. We had lost a time during which with almost no effort we could establish the strength of this country economically and socially. Our destinies then could be determined by our own options and free choices.

Now many of the options are denied us; many sound courses are closed to us because the seamarks are no longer lighted or because the channels are shoaled. Now, indeed, it would be fair to say that, beyond a mere dollar crisis, we have come to a turning point in history when we must determine with unwonted and uncomfortable precision just what we must do. No longer can we luxuriate in the comfort of a wide margin for error.

Many readers of *The Dollar Crisis* will recall the profound disquietude with which the authors viewed the growing crisis of our dollar, the steadily deteriorating trade imbalances contrary to the best economic interest of the United States. In the years following, Americans contented themselves with the immediate, with the "next quarter," with the political realities seen in the perspective of at most a year or so. During these slumbers not only trade deficits but adverse net balances of trade grew worse at an alarming rate.

It is idle to go over the things of the past. We must look at our situations as it exists and as it may reasonably be anticipated to exist in the 1980s and beyond. Once this is said, however, it is obvious that a review of our affairs in the world order is most timely. The author suggests choices that, while distressingly difficult, in most cases can and must be made. Today wise counsel is seldom available.

With lucidity and thorough analysis, the author has stated the choices available to us and put the importance of each into perspective. Specifically, he has addressed the problem of controlling the dollar in the Eurodollar market and has pointed out how this nation recklessly created a pool of funds, the precise dimensions of which no one really knows, the ownership of which is really unknown, and the future uses of which are obscure.

The author has pointed out that the United States itself must now focus on its own development. It has become painfully obvious that to do otherwise is to do damage that cannot be undone in our time, if ever. Along with these thoughts, there is the question of where the dollar of the American public should be spent.

The author feels that there is a wide lack of perception of the fact that the dollar spent here has a different value from that which is spent overseas. Simplistically, $100 million spent on constructing generating plants in the United States is quite a different thing from $100 million spent for fuel in distant lands.

We have become so imbued with proclaiming the virtues of the Puritan ethic that we strive to extend our own laws to nations that may resent the approaching American presence in the same way we showed our resentment of the British presence at the time of Lord North and King George III. Thus we have extended our morality to the advancement of "proper" conduct abroad. In nations with which we have cordial relations, extending our diplomatic policies to include the concept of business transactions is often resented because it comes as free advice from an unwelcome source. We have perhaps forgotten the experience of our missionaries who found that carrying American enlightenment to islands in the South Pacific was not so completely beneficial as had been hoped.

It is impossible to exaggerate how much our suggested economic activities are resented as denigrating by very proud people, are resented by those who view American business transactions as completely at variance with those between nationals of a different land living under its laws, customs, and sovereignty. This is to suggest that we should live within the standards of countries that permit us to enter. As hosts, they are entitled to determine what our course of conduct should be, to determine that which is proper and that which is not.

Our faults in this regard often abrade our friends greatly; we have forgotten that Machiavelli was not a moralist but a chronicler of his time. We permit ourselves to become conspicuous advocates of various courses of conduct by others at a time when our advocacy has behind it little other than moral strength. Moral strength will doubtless in the long run prove beneficent, but those who so greatly admire the funeral oration of Pericles and his eloquent and poignant advocacy of the city of Athens as "open to the world" fail to remember sometimes that it was the Athenians who lost the war.

Next, it would be remiss not to note that among the incredible strengths that the United States and the American people have is our ability to absorb and indeed to enjoy the most advanced technology. Perhaps in this we have no peer. It may be noted ruefully that at a time of considerable national peril we are far too willing to criticize that which we know best—the most sophisticated techniques of an advanced society. Power generation is a dreary example. We look to simplistic solutions for problems that we have not viewed as part of a whole.

The overview taken in this book comes at a time far past mid-voyage, with lowering visibility, and with the vessel laboring. Its searchlight may be uncomfortable, but it reveals much that is useful, much that brings good tidings to the watch.

The book calls us away from our distractions and to our duty. While we may not all agree with the solutions proposed, they will at least have stimulated our thinking and our realization that something must be done.

This is a time for Americans to rethink these moral, economic, and technological problems and the solutions to them, and to heed the advice of the sardonic and able general of the Roman Republic, Amelius Paulus (ca. 229–160 B.C.), who said:

> Commanders should be counseled chiefly by persons of known talent, by those who have made the art of war their particular study, and whose knowledge is derived from experience, by those who are present at the scene of action, who see the enemy, who see the advantages that occasions offer, and who, like people embarked in the same ship, are sharers of the danger.

FAIRLEIGH S. DICKINSON, JR.

Edgartown
Martha's Vineyard Island
Massachusetts

Acknowledgments

The author is deeply indebted to Fairleigh S. Dickinson, Jr., for his sponsorship and full participation in this study, his valuable advice in the preparation of the book, and his generous financial support of all the research projects of the Graduate Institute of International Studies at Fairleigh Dickinson University.

For their helpful comments and suggestions, I express my thanks to Professor Rikard Lang of the University of Zagreb; to H. E. Mr. Bogdan Lewandowski, under secretary-general of conferences of the United Nations; to Dr. Donald Guertin of Exxon Corporation; to Mr. Robert Krieble of Loctite Corporation; to Mr. Richard Foxen of Rockwell International; and to Professor Z. Milkdashi of Lausanne University.

I am also indebted to the United Nations Library; to the U.S. Department of Commerce, *Survey of Current Business;* the Senate Subcommittee on Banking; the Treasury Department Publication on Taxes; the State Department's Bureau of Public Affairs; the Federal Reserve Board's Report; the Bank for International Settlement; the Bulletin of European Communities; the OECD Monetary Studies; the Federal Reserve of Cleveland; and many other sources and publications that have been used and mentioned in this study.

Finally, thanks are also due to Rita Stollman for editing the manuscript and to Sandra Asdoorian for her assistance.

Introduction

Winston Churchill once said: "Writing a book is an adventure. To begin with, it is a toy and an amusement, and then it becomes a mistress, and then it becomes a master, and then it becomes a tyrant, and the last phase is that just as you are about to be reconciled to your servitude, you kill the monster and fling him about to the public."

This study is the continuation of a work that started twenty years ago under the initiative and sponsorship of Fairleigh S. Dickinson, Jr., chairman of the board of trustees of Fairleigh Dickinson University.

Under Mr. Dickinson's patronage and support, *The Dollar Crisis* was published in 1963, *Problems of U.S. Trade and Balance of Payments* appeared in 1974, and *Multinational Corporations: Their Problems and Prospects* was published in two editions in 1976 and 1978.

This study, the first of two volumes, attempts to deal with the economic problems of a confusing past, a chaotic present, and an uncertain future. It endeavors to explain how the principal actors in this unfolding international drama moved in two different directions, with the Japanese and Western Europeans moving toward economic expansion and exports and the United States neglecting to boost productivity, expand trade, and restrain spending. Eventually this indifference, lack of decision making, and overspending resulted in serious monetary, trade, unemployment, and inflation problems. Finally, the massive 1977–80 U.S. trade deficit of nearly $130 billion signaled to U.S. policymakers that they still had serious problems with the country's trade situation, balance of payments, the rate of national growth, and the stability of the dollar.

An analysis of the unprecedented trade deficit of the past four years indicates that, despite the 23½% decline in industrial oil consumption, in the United States there are serious problems facing our economy, both at home and abroad.

To a significant extent, the current economic and inflationary crisis is the result of such domestic difficulties as the decline in production, the reduction in research and development expenditures, the decrease in capital reinvestment, arbitrary and harmful laws and regulations, and the unfair trade practices of our major trading partners (especially Japan).

The U.S. share of world exports decreased from 20% in 1960 to 10% in 1978. In fact, the trade surplus in categories in which the United States has enjoyed a traditional advantage—manufactured products—fell by more than 60% in 1977, dropping from $12.2 billion in 1976 to $4.8 billion.

Meanwhile, the U.S. nonoil trade surplus during 1977 "suffered a sharp fall of $9 billion."

Even more troubles lie ahead. The 1980 results show little improvement in the trade situation. In fact, the U.S. trade deficit for 1980 could be as large as 1979's.

This high trade deficit coupled with large U.S. expenditures abroad have resulted in an enormous balance-of-payments deficit, a devalued dollar, higher energy prices, and more inflation. And at the time that the United States is plagued by all these economic problems, its markets are flooded with foreign cars (30% of the total cars sold in 1980 were made outside the United States) as well as imported steel, textiles, electronics, and many other foreign-made products.

The current situation leaves the nation's policymakers with the dilemma of either restraining imports or expanding exports. A report of the Senate Budget Committee concludes that continued export expansion is vital to the achievement of domestic economic goals regarding full employment, reduced inflation, and a balanced federal budget.

During the 1970s, the United States had the third worst record in exports among the major OECD nations—surpassing only the United Kingdom and Canada. Japan, meanwhile, continued to outperform the United States in trade despite a large appreciation in the price of the yen; Germany, throughout the decade, maintained its 1970 share in spite of a 60% appreciation of the mark on a trade-weighted basis.

One reason often given for the lagging performance of U.S. exports is increased protectionism overseas. However, nobody explains why increased protectionism has had so little impact on Japanese or German exports of manufactured goods.

The U.S. ratio of exports to imports is alarming. It has declined precipitously during the last decade from 3.84% in 1960 to 1.58% in the 1970s. During the last ten years the U.S. share of technology of intensive commodities has declined by 1.2% while Japan's share has increased by 3.38%.

Since 1970, both Republican and Democratic administrations have neglected the stability of the dollar, which has led to a big loss vis-à-vis the German mark, the Swiss franc, and the Japanese yen. The money managers in Washington have not accepted the fact that domestic prices, international trade, and the stability of the dollar are all interrelated and affect both the political and the economic position of the United States throughout the world. A net importing nation cannot allow its internatioal currency to become weak. What happens to the value of the dollar affects the buyer of gas and oil as well as all other commodities around the world.

One purpose of this book is to explain that given the interdependence of trading relationships, no country—especially a nation whose currency is

Introduction

still the international means of exchange—can ignore the integrity of its currency, its inflation rate, its monetary expansion, and huge gaps in its domestic budget and in its trade balance without affecting other nations.

Beginning with the Vietnam War, the Johnson and Nixon administrations were so involved with the conflict abroad that they neglected the stability of the dollar, the deterioration in trade, the effect of deficit spending on inflation, and the decline in productivity. The Carter administration's initial concern was little better, centering on domestic policy and the creation of new jobs.

In this study I have tried to concentrate on the U.S. balance of payments, its trade relations, and the relevance of its global economic posture, hoping that at this late hour the country would resume its traditional role as the leader of the non-Communist countries.

The economic well-being of the United States is essential to the maintenance of stability and peace at home and abroad. For in this new world, where more than one hundred nations are urging a new economic order, we must constantly remind ourselves that economic chaos in the United States can threaten the progress of development and prosperity everywhere.

Chapter 1 describes the erosion of the U.S. balance of payments since the 1960s. Primarily, it shows how the nation has neglected to put its monetary house in order. Mired in a plethora of regulations, U.S. policymakers have all too often opted for hasty decisions when they needed, instead, to gauge the outcome of their actions on the national interests of the United States.

The achievements of the last decade are not satisfactory. Our balance of payments cannot show a deficit forever. This country is not capable of spending more than $15 billion annually on military expenditures and foreign aid abroad. Can we find an answer to our energy predicament other than by war? How long can we spend one-third of our budget on defense?

Chapter 2 deals with the role of U.S. capital, technology, and management in the economic development of other nations. It also touches on the recent rise in foreign investments in the United States.

Foreign direct investment in the United States has traditionally come from Europe and Canada. Almost two-thirds ($42.8 billion) of the total $52.3 billion in foreign direct investment in the United States at the end of 1979 came from the Netherlands, the United Kingdom, Canada, Germany, Japan, Switzerland, and France. By contrast, direct investment in the United States by the thirteen nations of the Organization of Petroleum Exporting Countries (OPEC) in 1979 was about $401 million.

Historically, foreign portfolio investment (that is, U.S. securities other than U.S. Treasury securities) in the United States has usually exceeded foreign direct investment. These were $61.9 billion and $52 billion, respectively, in 1979. This contrasts sharply with U.S. investment abroad, the bulk of which was direct in 1979—$192.6 billion versus a portfolio investment of $56.7 billion.

Chapter 3 describes the evolution of trade in the United States since the 1960s. It shows how the nation slept during a period when imports increased rapidly and exports remained stagnant. In particular, the chapter deals with the following questions: What is the future of United States trade? Are we truly headed for another $30 billion deficit in the 1980s? Can we find a solution to our disputes with Japan and our other trade partners? Why is it not possible to have a reciprocity arrangement in our trade with Japan? Can we find an answer to the questions raised in the North-South negotiations? Have we an increasing tendency in international trade to emphasize our services and technological know-how rather than our products?

Chapter 4 explains how U.S. business is shackled by laws and regulations that are arbitrary and harmful. A recent survey presented to the Senate Subcommittee on Finance shows many examples of laws, executive actions, and court rulings that impede business, production, and exports. It recommends that these laws and regulations should be revoked or modified. The competitive status of the nation as a whole could benefit from removing the red tape that adds billions of dollars to production costs and interferes with the free flow of trade.

Chapter 5 deals with the taxation system of the United States and the other industrial nations. Although tax-related export incentives are in theory forbidden under international agreements and GATT regulations, massive tax incentives for the promotion of exports have been developed by foreign governments in recent years.

This chapter also explains that our trading partners are striving hard to expand their exports through both tax and nontax incentives. Unfortunately, American exporters in many cases are at a disadvantage. It is imperative for Congress to take a very serious look at the tax laws and other laws that hinder production and strangle exports.

Any tax shackles on corporations have far-reaching consequences for both the home and the host country's trade, investment, balance of payments, employment, and prices. Thus, Congress should know that the formation of a tax policy entails more than just weighing the revenue consequences.

Chapter 6 deals with the problem of productivity, which is the source of great concern throughout the world. Every nation is striving right now to produce more for less and to sell competitively in order to meet its import bills. This concern is perhaps most intense in the United States, where the decline in productivity and increases in the price of energy, raw materials, and wages have produced double-digit inflation. The tragedy is that the

Introduction

United States—which for many decades based its prosperity and high standard of living on high productivity—has experienced a large decline in the past decade both in absolute terms and in comparison with the other industrial nations.

Any increase in productivity, of course, is the result of a more efficient use of labor or capital, improved work habits, a better-trained labor force, a greater dedication to work, a larger investment in new equipment, more funds for research and development, and greater cooperation among government, business, and labor. Very few people realize that a major reason for inflation is the lack of gains in productivity and the best way to alter this situation is to create an awareness of the problem on the part of labor, management, the public, and government. Only by working together can the various sectors solve this problem.

In West Germany, Switzerland, Japan, and most recently in France, the issue of productivity has become the dominant expression of national will. Unfortunately, in the United States very little attention has been paid to this major cause of inflation. There will be no decline in inflation, no stability in our economic situation, and no improvement in our trade competitiveness until and unless we make improvements in productivity a high-priority national goal.

Chapter 7 deals with the transfer of technology. It points out that a technological society is based on order, certainty, and precision; it should be organized by engineers, planners, and innovators, and it should be based on knowledge and discipline.

The transfer of technology is a two-way street that can have a beneficial impact on both home and host countries. Technology is usually transferred (1) through multinational corporations, (2) through international organizations and public agencies, and (3) through multilateral and intergovernmental agreements. These transfers can take many forms, including private foreign investment; turnkey arrangements; supplies of equipment, know-how, and expertise; licensing agreements; and joint-venture agreements.

In transferring technology, consideration should be given to all aspects of its movement, including the technical, social, political, financial, commercial, and administrative. Also, the developing nations should produce their own indigenous research, which should be based on the strengthening of industry and the solving of potential problems resulting from these changes. No country can achieve real development if its machinery and the majority of the workers needed to run it have to come from outside.

It would be impossible to make technology work without a well-balanced program based on the needs of a country. Finally, in the words of the United Nations: "If we are going to solve the major problems facing humanity—overpopulation, air pollution, water pollution, and many others—we need a vast generation and exchange of technology. A free flow of technology contributes in an important way to a rising standard of living both in this country and elsewhere."

Chapter 8 addresses the role of the developing nations, discussing the development process and the sources of capital and funds for development; the management of international debt; the management of petrodollars and the international monetary system; international trade, including the continued reduction of trade barriers and the establishment of trade facilities and other measures to assist the industrialization of developing countries; world commodity markets, the level of prices, and price stabilization; private capital and its advantages with respect to industrial development; ways to avoid sudden default on debts or other unilateral actions that adversely affect creditors or host nations; and the decision-making process for international economic matters and the desire of developing nations for a greater participation in decision making.

To achieve all or some of the above goals, the developing nations have put forth a set of proposals for changing the existing international economic and political institutions. They are talking about a "new economic order" to increase their participation in trade, aid, and investments, as well as their share in the benefits they receive from their natural resources. Whether these specific recommendations serve the interests of the developing nations or the whole world is a matter for study, analysis, discussion, and debate. But in any event, they are likely to plague the relations between the industrial countries and the developing nations in every international arena. They also will cause constant economic instability and tension. It is important, therefore, for both sides to understand the realities, challenges, and problems facing the whole world in the l980s.

The developing countries in the aggregate have a larger trade with the United States than Western Europe. They are also considerable participants in the international financial system as both lenders and borrowers. Their development has reached a point where their cooperation or lack of it will have a great impact on U.S. inflation, employment, liquidity, and economic growth. It is to the interest of both sides to accept the truth that cooperation is no longer a luxury or a matter of charity but rather a matter of simple self-interest. If we do not hang together, we will be hanged separately.

The broader scope of this book deals with international trade, the current exchange-rate system, the balance of payments, government regulations, productivity, and the failure of management and labor to come to grips with the causes of our productivity decline.

A look at the elements affecting productivity and inflation shows that technological innovation and research and development are responsible for 44% of productivity, the education of workers for 12%, better resource allocation for 12%, scale economies for 16%, and tangible capital for 16%.

In 1980 new investments in plant and equipment in terms of "real" dollars was −0.5. For 1981, business plans to increase new plant and equipment spending by 1.5% in real terms. While U.S. productivity has increased very little since 1975, the cost of labor and production and eventually the prices of manufactured goods have increased almost 70%.

If present economic trends in the United States continue, we run the risk of becoming a developing nation—exporting food, raw materials, and arms and importing all kinds of machinery and manufactured goods. In 1979, U.S. agricultural exports increased 40% over 1978, while the U.S. balance of trade in manufactured goods reached a deficit of $23 billion, compared with $22.9 in 1978.

The theme of this book is that a truly effective, long-range national economic policy is needed in the United States. Business growth, productivity, and assistance to exporters and producers have never been given a high priority either by the executive branch or by Congress because policymakers have never understood the close link among exports, inflation, economic growth, and a sound dollar.

This study attempts to show how this linkage increasingly operates within the international community. It is pointed out that the United States has the strongest economy (6% of the world's population is responsible for 35% of the world's gross national product). What the nations' policymakers have ignored is that, thanks to U.S. generosity, the world economic balance has changed. Today we confront determined trade and business adversaries. It is necessary, therefore, that we demonstrate our determination and commitment to a strong export policy, better productivity, and a real cooperation among labor, management, and government.

Finally, it is essential for the peace and stability of the world that the United States reestablish its position in international trade, reduce inflation, increase productivity, restore its economic growth, and regain its leadership of the international economy.

While the United States Slept

1
The Balance-of-Payments Problem
The Breakdown of the Regime of the International Monetary System

No nation was ever ruined by trade or saving.

Benjamin Franklin

A nation's balance of payments is a summary of all the transactions which take place between the nation's business, government, and the total population of the rest of the world. Since it summarizes all sales, expenditures and debt, it must balance.

Norman F. Keiser

The man who will live above his present circumstances is in great danger of living in a little time much beneath them, or as an Italian proverb says: the man who lives by hope will die by despair.

Joseph Addison

Sound economy is a sound understanding brought into action; it is calculation realized; it is the doctrine of proportion reduced to practice; it is foreseeing contingencies and providing against them.

Hannah More

1

One of the most serious economic problems confronting the United States today is the persistent, substantial deficit in the balance of trade and its balance of international payments. While the trade deficit has been plaguing the nation since 1972 (with the exception of the year 1976), the balance-of-payments situation has been deteriorating since fourth-quarter 1945. Much effort has been devoted over the past ten years to studying the problem, tracing its causes, and offering possible solutions. And numerous short-term corrective measures have been taken under the mistaken belief that some one factor—the energy crunch, a lack of trade reciprocity, inflation, or speculation by the Arabs, the Japanese, or the Europeans—is to blame.

So far, however, the balance-of-payments and trade deficits persist because they spring not from some single, easily manageable factor but "from deep-seated causes, and no politician is brave enough and sufficiently knowledgeable to deal with it."[1]

At the heart of the problem lie some basic structural changes in the U.S. domestic economy and in its political and economic relationships with the rest of the world over the past two decades. This study offers a factual analysis of these basic, multiple causes, and it is hoped that a clear presentation of them will lead to private and, particularly, governmental readjustments of a more fundamental and remedial nature than the stopgap measures taken so far.

It is also hoped that this analysis will convince policymakers of the need for immediate, comprehensive action, of the fact that the problem is a chronic one and is apt to turn worse in the near future because of the following scenario: imports are likely to increase even more as the consumption and prices of oil, natural gas, and other raw materials rise; agricultural exports may well turn sharply downward in the aftermath of the trade embargo with the Soviet Union; and government expenditures are likely to increase even further as a larger and larger proportion is spent on defense and on foreign military and economic aid.

In addition, because of the Soviet invasion of Afghanistan and pressure from U.S. allies, we can expect further military expenditures in West Berlin, Germany, Japan, and the Persian Gulf area. This will mean a larger deficit in terms of the U.S. balance-of-payments situation.

But the problem, as indicated earlier, has its roots much farther back than some recent military crisis. Since 1950 this country has been suffering from a chronic condition in its balance of international payments. In every year except 1957 and 1976, total outpayments have exceeded receipts. In fact, from 1950 through 1956, the annual deficit ranged between $300 million and $3.6 billion, with the average shortfall for the seven-year period totaling $1.5 billion.

Following a modest surplus of about $500 million in 1957,[2] the deficit rose sharply to $3.5 billion in 1958 and continued to increase through 1959 and 1960, reaching a peak of $3.9 billion in 1960.

Debt prepayments by foreign governments reduced the adverse balance for 1961 to $2.4 billion. (If these payments had not been made, the 1961 deficit would have amounted to $3.2 billion.) Debt prepayments of $666 million in 1962, plus $470 million in advance payments for military exports, cut the 1962 deficit by nearly $1.2 billion, to a total of $2.2 billion. Without these special transactions, the 1962 deficit would have exceeded $3.3 billion (Table 1.1).

The Balance-of-Payments Problem

In February 1961, President John F. Kennedy sent a message to Congress defining the framework of an external economic policy for the United States. The message pointed to the gold drain of the past three years as the element that had focused attention on a problem that had been smoldering for more than a decade. In effect, he said that the United State would have to take its balance of payments into account when formulating economic policies.

The first steps to be taken, he said, were to improve our general economic situation, improve U.S. technology, increase our productivity, and decrease our marketing costs. The goal was to devise new and superior products under conditions of price stability. While the surplus of exports over imports was substantial at the time, Kennedy noted, it was not large enough to cover total U.S. expenditures for military and diplomatic needs, capital invested overseas by U.S. businesses, and government economic assistance and loan programs.[3]

It was clear that the president was counting on an increasing American export strength to counter future payments pressures. The president's message concluded with a statement of principles that included recommendations that the United States—

1. maintain gold at $35 per ounce;

2. gain control of its balance-of-payments position;

3. expand its exports (a return to protectionism was not the solution; instead, there ought to be a flow of resources from the industrialized countries to the developing countries, and that flow ought to be increased);

4. take the lead in harmonizing the financial and economic policies for growth and stability of the industrialized nations.

The action program proposed by the president was divided into two parts, the first of which was to ease the short-term demand for U.S. reserves by surplus countries. The second part was designed to relieve the basic imbalances in the merchandise and long-term capital accounts.[4]

Despite a record level of exports of American products and all these suggestions, the adverse balance of payments continued for the fifth consecutive year in 1962. This negative balance was accompanied by a further outflow of gold. In the second half of 1962, the U.S. gold stock fell below $16 billion for the first time since before World War II.

Merchandise exports, meanwhile, were close to the $20 billion record set in 1961, with a decline in shipments of industrial materials offset by an increase in foods and finished manufactures. Imports were running high in 1962, but the balance of trade still favored the United States. This, however, was offset by a year-to-year increase in military expenditures, foreign aid, and other public outlays.

The policies adopted by the Kennedy administration were only partially successful, because the decrease in the rate of gold outflow and a reduction in the balance-of-payments deficit for the second consecutive year led policymakers to believe that they had temporarily solved the problem when they had not.

In addition, price trends abroad began to work in favor of the United States; a trade expansion bill passed in 1962 was expected to add to the favorable commercial export surplus; and investments abroad were showing signs of tapering off while the return on those overseas investments was increasing. Meanwhile, some government aid programs were now being designed to ensure that a higher proportion of any money given would be spent in the United States. All these trends, therefore, were lulling policymakers into a false complacency.

Unfortunately, neither the Kennedy administration nor succeeding administrations ever came to grips with the fact that adverse payments balances are closely tied to foreign aid, declining export markets, the maintenance of military bases abroad, and military aid to friendly nations. The permanent solution to the problem was—and still is—to convince such strong trade partners as Germany and Japan to share our enormous military expenditures abroad and to ensure free trade by the elimination of all restrictions.

Thus 1963 did not bring about anything different; in fact, it continued the problems that had been surfacing in previous years. Although the balance of trade continued to be favorable to the United States, it was offset once again by the continuing expansion of government spending. There were signs of a decrease in military expenditures because of a sharp rise in military payments to the United States by its allies. (This reflected agreements with ally nations to purchase more equipment and supplies from the United States to help offset the costs of maintaining U.S. forces in their territories.) And a large proportion of the U.S. deficit was being financed by foreigners holding balances in U.S. commerical banks or in purchases of short-term government bonds. The remainder was financed by a decrease in U.S. monetary-reserve assets—specifically our gold stock, which had declined by almost $3.5 billion since 1960—and an increase in the holding of dollars by the International Monetary Fund (IMF).

In a special message to Congress on July 18, 1963, President Kennedy called for a new revision in his balance-of-payments policy. Citing the reduction in the payments deficit the year before, he credited this to his 1961 priority list. His new message, in effect, ruled out import restrictions, capital controls, and any restrictions on government spending overseas unless it was justifiable on foreign-policy grounds. It also rejected contractionist policies in the domestic economy. Kennedy's pledge to maintain the existing dollar-gold relation, considered in isolation from the rest of his message, was thus a ritualistic gesture only.

Among the new changes he did propose was the imposition of an excise tax on purchase of foreign securities in U.S. money markets. The tax applied to purchase of both new and outstanding securities issued by corporations and individuals,whether purchased in the United States or abroad. Other changes he proposed were increased export expansion efforts, the encouragement of foreign tourism to the United States, a reduction in the foreign-exchange costs of federal expenditures abroad, tax reductions for foreign investors to encourage putting their money in the United States, and an arrangement for a $500 million draw on the IMF. All of these foreign exchange proposals, while steps in the right direction in many instances, did not go far enough or penetrate deep enough to make a real change in the payments problem.

2

Since 1963 the balance-of-payments policies of the United States have been closely related to capital flows and capital markets. A brief description of the structural differences between the capital markets of continental Western Europe and the United States will add some perspective to the capital-flows problem. In brief, the assumption underlying the interest-equalization tax was that developed countries in continental Europe had embarked on ambitious growth programs for which their domestic capital sources were inadequate and would be increasingly so in the future.

This backward development of capital markets added to high interest rates and issue costs in these countries—high interest rates because of excess demand pressures on limited capital funds and because of the premiums demanded by domestic lenders seeking to compensate for a lack of marketability, and high issue costs because of a failure to realize economies of scale and to develop underwriting and distribution facilities.

Following the adoption of the policy recommendations made by President Kennedy in 1963, there was a gradual improvement in the U.S. balance of payments, although reserves were still being drained out of the United States.[5] This brought increasing concern in 1964 about potential inflation as a result of continuing deficits in the balance of payments and military expenditures in Vietnam. While the private sector continued to show a slight excess, government expenditures overseas kept swallowing up any surpluses.

The payments problem and the resulting "gold crisis" continued to worry international monetary authorities throughout 1965. On February 4, French president Charles de Gaulle advocated a return to a full-fledged gold standard on a gradual basis and at a higher price than the $35 per ounce that prevailed at the time. Meanwhile, the U.S. monetary gold stock fell to its lowest level since 1939, and Congress passed a bill to eliminate the 25% gold cover on deposits in Federal Reserve district banks.

President Johnson stated in a 1965 message to Congress that the United States had the world's most productive economy, the largest supply of gold, the best creditor position ($28 billion that was owed to the United States and $51 billion that the United States owed others), and the most favorable trade position. Unfortunately, the year before, the balance-of-payments deficit had been $3 billion.

Therefore, the president announced that he was asking U.S. banks to limit their foreign lending. At the same time, he applied the interest-equalization tax to bank loans of more than a year, and he asked Congress to extend the tax for another two years, to extend it to nonbank credits bearing one- to three-year maturities, and to reduce duty-free exemptions for foreign purchases of U.S. travelers to $50.

Congress complied with his request, and although these measures did not cure the payments problem they at least alleviated the crisis in the short run. In the second quarter, the United States actually had a payments surplus of $82 million in its current account. It was, to be sure, not much, but it was the first surplus since 1957.

Among policymakers there was no agreement on the solution to the payments problem. Early in the year Senator Mike Mansfield said that if the president's moral suasion did not work, "we would have to look at our military forces abroad, our foreign aid, and, of course, our credit policy." Sadly, the United States lost more gold during the year than at any time since 1958, but no one took Mansfield's suggestion to do more about the problem.

The payments deficit continued in 1966, although there were fewer doubts about the strength of the dollar. On a liquidity basis, the deficit was $2.3 billion in 1964, $1.3 billion in 1965, and $1.1 billion for the first three quarters of 1966. On an official-settlements basis, the deficit was $1.5 billion in 1964, $1.3 billion in 1965, and for the first three quarters of 1966 there was a substantial surplus.[6]

But these results were based on a continued decline of the payments balance on trade and services, large inflows of capital attracted by high domestic interest rates, and a number of favorable transactions. It was generally considered that the improvement in 1966 could not be sustained even if, as seemed unlikely, high interest rates were maintained.

On the other hand, if interest rates were reduced, if expenditures in Vietnam continued to mount, and if the balance on trade and services continued to fall, the balance-of-payments surplus could quickly swing into a large deficit. At the end of the year it was not clear what actions the United States might take with respect to interest rates, capital controls, and fiscal policy.

The Balance-of-Payments Problem

The payments deficit continued, in fact, to be troublesome. On the liquidity basis, the deficit was $1.3 billion in 1966 and $2 billion in the first half of 1967. On the official-settlements basis, there was a surplus of $200 million in 1966—due largely to changes in the maturity of foreign investments—followed by an indicated deficit of at least $2.5 billion in the first half of 1967. President Johnson asked for a tax increase of 6% and later raised his request to 10%, but by the end of the year his chances of getting either had become negligible.

It seemed that production had decreased during 1966 and the first half of 1967, not only in the United States but also in Canada, West Germany, and the United Kingdom.

The years 1968 through 1970 showed very little change in the payments situation with the exception of near-record imports in 1968, but the trade balance did maintain a modest $837 million surplus in 1968 and a $700 million surplus in 1969. The other capitalist nations continued to expand their trade at exceptionally high levels through the first half of 1969, despite the longest dock strike in U.S. history, which tied up outgoing and incoming ships from December 1968 to April 1969 in some ports.

In the aggregate, U.S. merchandise exports to foreign subsidiaries and branches of U.S. multinational corporations increased from $7.8 billion in 1966 to $13 billion in 1970, an average gain of 13.5%. In contrast, the imports from affiliates of U.S. companies rose from $5.3 billion in 1966 to $10.9 billion in 1970, an average gain of 17.2%.[7] In 1966, exports to U.S. affiliates accounted for 26.7% of all U.S. merchandise exports, rising to 31% in 1970.[8]

The year 1970 brought about the two largest quarterly balance-of-payments deficits in U.S. history. For the first time since 1893, the nation's foreign trade moved into a deficit position. Even though exports in the first six months of the year rose by 5% over first-half 1970, imports climbed three times as fast. At annual rates, U.S. exports totaled $45.1 billion, leaving a trade deficit of $700 million. In September the trade balance showed a surplus for the first time since March, but there was no evidence that this shift signaled a trend, and, in fact, the balance of payments showed a high deficit of $30 billion. In April President Nixon announced that the embargo on trade with the People's Republic of China, which had been in effect since 1950, was being lifted. In August the president killed the gold-exchange standard, or rather the gold-convertible dollar standard of the postwar years, and allowed the U.S. dollar to float.[9] All the major trading nations, except France, followed suit. In the weeks that followed, most other currencies tended to increase in value relative to the dollar, thus effectively devaluing the U.S. currency.

The currency realignments were officially expected to result in a turnaround in the U.S. balance of payments of between $8 billion and $10 billion a year, but it was recognized that this improvement would take time.

In 1972 the U.S. trade balance was adversely influenced by the strong recovery in domestic economic activity, coupled with sluggishness in most of the Western European economies and in Japan. It was therefore not surprising that the U.S. trade deficit remained uncomfortably high in the first part of the year and that the intended correction became apparent only in the fall and winter. For 1972 the deficit was estimated at about $6 billion, the worst trade result in U.S. history.

During the latter part of 1973, the dollar was devalued by a total of about 30% from its fall 1971 level against the German mark, 25% against the yen, and by smaller amounts against the other leading currencies. On the basis of the volume of U.S. trade with its major trading partners, the overall global dollar devaluation was calculated at about 20% over the two-year period.

The balance-of-payments picture was bound to change noticeably in the wake of all these exchange rate moves, but there were other reasons as well. In 1972 the U.S. economy had been expanding much more rapidly than that of Europe or Canada. In 1973 the U.S. expansion slowed, while most foreign economies were just gaining momentum. The catching up of foreign income and demand growth stimulated U.S. exports, and shortages of foreign agricultural products led to especially impressive gains in U.S. sales of wheat, corn, soybeans, and other footstuffs. Although the overall 1972 trade deficit hit a record $6.4 billion, the trend throughout the year was favorable. By midyear the trade account was in balance and a deficit of only $1 billion to $2 billion was anticipated for the entire year.

The capital accounts performed more erratically. Speculative exchange-market activity at first led to large outflows of liquid dollars, but as the crisis atmosphere evaporated, most of this capital returned to the United States. The reflow would surely have been greater and more rapid had it not been for foreign uncertainty about the nature and effectiveness of U.S. anti-inflationary policies and worries about the political consequences of the Watergate scandal. The poor performance of the U.S stock market ruled out any significant inflows of foreign-portfolio capital. On the other hand, increasing numbers of foreign multinational corporations were taking steps to establish affiliates in the United States, and there were fresh hopes for a better two-way balance in the U.S. foreign direct-investment account with the rest of the world.

Trade deficits and short-term capital outflows produced a large deficit in the official-reserve-transactions account in the first quarter, but later improvements in both accounts put overall payments roughly in balance for the rest of the year. Exports from the United States soared 39% over the same months of the preceding year, in large part as a result of world inflation.

U.S. trade moved into deficit again in 1974 as steep price increases for petroleum and other foreign products caused imports to rise in value faster

The Balance-of-Payments Problem   35

than exports. Imports through July reached an annual rate of $95.8 billion, and exports totaled $94.1 billion. The $1.7 billion annual rate of deficit in the first seven months of 1974 stood in sharp contrast to a $1.3 billion surplus for all of 1973.

The deterioration of trade in current dollars nevertheless masked an improvement as measured in real terms. Over the period of comparison, the quantity of exports advanced strongly, whereas the volume of imports declined.

In the case of petroleum, quadrupling prices produced a nearly $10 billion expansion of imports in the first seven months of 1974 compared with the same period in 1973. At the same time, somewhat less oil was being imported. The Arab embargo on shipments to the United States, imposed during the Mideast War, was lifted in mid-March. The deficit with the petroleum-exporting countries swelled from $425 million in 1973 to about $6.6 billion in 1974, despite a vigorous climb in sales to those nations.[10]

The U.S. surplus with other developing countries jumped sharply. All in all, 1974 can only be described as a year of economic disappointments. Early in the year it had been generally predicted that inflation would decline to a 5% level by December. The economists were somewhat unhappy about this figure, and had feared that it would be reached only at the pain of a fairly flat year in the economy. But they hardly imagined that inflation would climb in 1974 to an annual rate of 12% or that, even as this happened, the economy would plunge toward recession. The recession resulted in both a severe slump and a trade deficit.

In the first half of 1975, U.S. trade shifted back into surplus as imports—with demand weakened by the continuing recession—dropped by 13% from the preceding half. By the third quarter, imports began to rise again, but the faster rate of growth in exports created a rapidly rising surplus. This shift resulted largely from the fact that the severity of the slump in the United States was greater than elsewhere in the world. A sharp decline in U.S. output, reduced consumer spending, a huge liquidation of inventories, and lower prices for some key products all tended to depress imports from every region in the world. U.S. exports to the developed countries, meanwhile, declined from second-half 1974 levels as foreign demand also dropped off as a result of lower production, sluggish consumer purchasing, and a destocking of supplies abroad.

U.S. exports advanced only marginally in 1976 despite a general improvement in foreign economic conditions; in the first seven months of the year, exports were valued at an annual rate of $112.4 billion, about 5% above 1975. On the other hand, imports climbed rapidly by 20% to an annual rate of $115.6 billion. The result was a net deficit of $3.2 billion at a yearly rate. (During 1975, in contrast, the United States had experienced the largest trade surplus in its entire history.)[11]

The heavy growth in purchases from abroad was directly related to a recovery in the U.S. economy that began about the middle of 1975. As consumer and then industrial demand began to pick up and excess inventories were eliminated, it became necessary to increase imports in order to meet rising production requirements and to restock inventories.

As domestic production of petroleum continued to decline and demands for consumer and industrial use increased, imports of foreign oil jumped by the end of July to an annual rate of $30.3 billion, $5 billion above the preceding year. The rise in value in the first seven months resulted partly from increased quantities and partly from the fact that average prices were about 55¢ a barrel higher. The United States became even more dependent on Mideast oil when both Canada and Venezuela, major U.S. suppliers, reduced the quantities available for export.

There was a modest rise in U.S. exports through July, mostly in non-agricultural products. Agricultural exports, meanwhile, rose only 5%, primarily from the increased sales of grain, especially to the Soviet Union.

In 1977 the U.S. exported $120 billion worth of goods, ranging from soybeans and blue jeans to machine tools, computers, and aircraft. But U.S. imports soared to $147 billion and opened up a yawning $27 billion trade deficit.

Two developments that have preoccupied the central banks of the industrial world of late had their roots in this period: currency problems and inflation. The currency problems were brought under control around the end of 1978, only to be followed by destabilization during the first few months of 1979. And U.S. inflation soared during 1979. Both these developments are symptomatic of the deep-rooted trade and payments problems already mentioned.

The sizable changes that took place in U.S. trade balances in 1978 were almost fully reflected in shifts of similar magnitude in the global pattern of current-payments balances. As a result, the distribution of the current-account positions of the major groups of trade partners in 1978 resembled more closely the pre-1974 pattern than the 1974–78 periods. The combined current account of the group of ten countries and Switzerland swung from a $5 billion deficit in 1977 to a surplus of $18 billion in 1978. At the same time, the combined deficit of the other developed countries was reduced to $11 billion. (In 1974 this deficit was close to $20 billion.) In part, this improvement in the developed countries' current position, totaling $35 billion, was at the expense of the United States, the centrally planned socialist economies, and the nonoil developing countries. There also was an unexpected and rapid fall of $22 billion in the oil-exporting countries' current surplus to only $7 billion. Thus in 1978 the oil exporters' surplus temporarily ceased to be the major destabilizing factor in the world's current-payment structure.

While this situation was a combined improvement of $14.3 billion in the

The Balance-of-Payments Problem 37

current position of France, Italy, and Sweden, it was overshadowed by the widening gap between the U.S. current-account deficit and the current-payments surpluses of Germany, Japan, and Switzerland. The aggregate surplus of these three countries rose by $12.1 billion to $30.7 billion in 1978, while the U.S. deficit increased slightly to $16 billion.

The best success story of 1978 occurred in Japan, where not only the real-trade surplus but also the volume of exports to the United States was increased. In 1976 Japan's trade surplus was $9.9 billion. By 1977 and 1978 it had risen to $17.3 billion and $24.7 billion, respectively, while the U.S. trade deficit in the same period totaled $74.6 billion. What saved the United States from this tremendous shortfall was its sizable income from investments and services abroad.[12] The deficit in the U.S. current-account balance in 1977 and 1978, meanwhile, was $16.3 billion and $16 billion, respectively.

As a result of adverse trade and current-account balances in 1977 and 1978, several meetings (including two summit conferences) took place in 1979. As reported in the press, one conference concluded that there were a number of reasons that swift corrective actions might not be possible: "First, the persistence of long-term capital outflows on the scale required may be difficult to ensure. This is partly because of the need to take account of domestic requirements in framing monetary policy and interest rate policy; in addition, large and persistent current-payments imbalances, often with concomitant inflation differentials, may as in 1977–78 give rise to expectations of exchange rate changes that [would] make capital flow out of deficit countries and into surplus countries.

"Secondly, large and persistent current-payments surpluses, even if offset by long-term capital outflows, may over time pose external financing problems for the countries with the counterpart deficits. This consideration applies with particular force to surpluses run by non-OPEC countries at a time when there is again a significant OPEC current payments surplus vis-à-vis the rest of the world."[13]

For the above reasons, it would be wise not to put too much reliance on capital movements, rather than current-account adjustments, as a way of achieving a more stable world balance of trade and balance of payments.

Another monetary development in 1978 was the question of a very large current-payments imbalance within the group of ten countries and Switzerland. The overall U.S. payments deficit was twice as large as its current-account deficit, while in Switzerland net official monetary assets increased by much more than its current surplus. In Germany, also, the reserve gain was not far from the current-account surplus. Only in Japan was the reserve considerably lower, because of long-term capital outflows. This unpleasant situation came to a climax in the last part of 1978, when $16 billion—as much as for the year as a whole—left the country from

October to December. This created a real currency crisis, and the U.S. Treasury Department was forced to resort to market intervention during November and December.

As soon as the market started to settle in the first few months of 1979 and a substantial amount of funds from surplus nations started to flow into the United States, the world was faced with another energy crisis and a 60% increase in the price of oil. The high price of energy accompanied by a 12% inflation rate in the United States played havoc with the U.S. economy and threatened to do the same in the European countries. The collective surplus of the group of ten countries and Switzerland was reduced in 1979, while the surplus of the oil-exporting countries was expected to increase.

With such a scenario facing us, the global pattern of current-payments balances is likely to move back in the near future toward more instability and chaos.

Although the U.S. current-payments deficit, which became very substantial in 1977, was little changed in 1978, the basis of statistical calculation was changed. According to this new system of calculation, the net retained earnings on direct investments are now counted as a credit in the current-account and a debit in the capital account. Under this accounting arrangement, the current balance was in surplus by $4.3 billion in 1976, followed by deficits of $15.3 billion and $16 billion in 1977 and 1978, respectively.

The deficit was very large in fourth-quarter 1977 and first-quarter 1978—when it averaged $27.4 billion at a seasonally adjusted annual rate. The capital account for 1978 showed a large net outflow of private and nonreserve official capital that further aggravated the current-account deficit. Identified net outflows amounted to $26.8 billion, but there was a favorable statistical discrepancy of $11.5 billion, and the official settlement deficit was $31.3 billion.[14] The following two tables show the international current-account transactions for 1977–78 and 1979 and the United States balance of payments, 1976–78.

The 1978 and 1979 quarterly reports of the U.S. balance of payments showed that the situation was very stormy and unstable. Reflecting the dollar crisis of 1978, the major variations occurred in the capital account and statistical discrepancy categories. Because the statistics no longer distinguished long-term from short-term flows through U.S. banks, it was no longer possible to treat the banks' short-term positions—which exclude movements in the deposits of foreign official institutions—as a financing item.

The first-quarter 1978 dollar was generally very weak, and the banks were not lenders abroad. This created a crisis on a scale comparable only to that which led to the final collapse of the Bretton Woods System in early 1973. It also brought about a sharp decline in the price of the dollar against all other major currencies of the world, with the exception of the Canadian

International Current-Account Transactions

Countries & areas	Trade balance (f.o.b.)			Services & transfers			Current balance		
	1977	1978	1979	1977	1978	1979	1977	1978	1979
	in billions of U.S. dollars								
BLEU*	− 1.4	− 1.2	− 3.3	0.7	0.3	− 0.5	− 0.7	− 0.9	− 3.3
Canada	2.5	3.0	3.4	− 6.6	− 7.6	− 7.7	− 4.1	− 4.6	− 4.3
France	− 2.4	1.5	− 1.3	− 0.5	2.2	2.8	− 3.0	3.7	1.5
Germany	19.8	25.6	17.3	− 15.5	− 16.7	− 23.1	4.3	8.9	− 5.8
Italy*	− 0.1	2.9	− 1.0	2.6	3.3	6.1	2.5	6.2	5.1
Japan*	17.3	24.6	2.0	− 6.4	− 8.1	− 10.6	10.9	16.5	− 8.6
Netherlands*	− 0.1	− 0.9	− 1.2	0.7	− 0.5	− 1.1	0.6	− 1.4	− 2.3
Sweden	0.3	2.6	0.9	− 2.4	− 2.9	− 3.4	− 2.1	− 0.3	− 2.5
Switzerland*	− 0.1	0.2	− 2.2	3.5	4.2	4.7	3.4	4.4	2.5
United Kingdom	− 3.9	− 2.9	− 6.9	3.6	4.7	1.9	− 0.3	1.8	− 5.0
United States	− 30.9	− 33.8	− 29.5	16.8	20.3	29.2	− 14.1	− 13.5	− 0.3
Group of Ten & Switzerland	1.0	21.6	− 21.8	− 3.6	− 0.8	− 1.7	− 2.6	20.8	− 23.5
Australia	1.0	0.1	2.5	− 3.6	− 3.9	− 4.6	− 2.6	− 3.8	− 2.1
Austria*	− 3.9	− 3.1	− 3.9	0.9	1.6	2.0	− 3.0	− 1.5	− 1.9
Denmark*	− 2.7	− 2.4	− 3.4	1.0	0.9	0.4	− 1.7	− 1.5	− 3.0
Finland	0.5	1.2	0.6	− 0.7	− 0.6	− 0.9	− 0.2	0.6	− 0.3
Greece*	− 3.2	− 3.5	− 5.2	1.9	2.2	2.9	− 1.3	− 1.3	− 2.3
Ireland*	− 0.8	− 1.0	− 2.2	0.5	0.7	0.6	− 0.3	− 0.3	− 1.6
Israel	− 2.2	− 2.8	− 3.0	1.7	1.8	1.8	− 0.5	− 1.0	− 1.2
New Zealand*	0.2	0.6	0.7	− 0.8	− 1.0	− 1.2	− 0.6	− 0.4	− 0.5
Norway	− 4.0	− 0.5	0.1	− 1.0	− 1.6	− 1.3	− 5.0	− 2.1	− 1.2
Portugal	− 2.5	− 2.4	− 2.4	1.0	1.6	2.6	− 1.6	− 0.8	0.2
South Africa*	2.5	3.8	6.2	− 2.0	− 2.3	− 2.5	0.5	1.5	3.7
Spain*	− 6.2	− 4.0	− 5.5	4.0	5.6	6.5	− 2.2	1.6	1.0
Turkey	− 3.5	− 1.9	− 2.3	0.1	0.4	0.9	− .	− 1.5	− 1.4
Yugoslavia*	− 3.6	− 3.5	− 5.3	2.0	2.2	1.9	− 1.6	− 1.3	− 3.4
Other developed countries	− 28.4	− 19.4	− 23.1	5.0	7.6	9.1	− 23.4	− 11.8	− 14.0
Total developed countries	− 27.4	2.2	− 44.9	1.4	6.8	7.4	− 26.0	9.0	− 37.5
Oil-exporting countries	62	42	112	− 36	− 42	− 49	26	0	63
Other developed countries	− 10	− 20	− 33	− 1	− 5	− 5	− 11	− 25	− 38
Total developed countries	52	22	79	− 37	− 47	− 54	15	− 25	25

*Services and transfers account figures for these countries exclude undistributed income from direct investment.

dollar. And it happened while all major currencies were floating, thus disproving the theory that whatever the shortcomings of the floating rates, they had at least one virtue—namely, that they did not allow exchange crises to occur. The obvious conclusion to be drawn from the analysis of the dollar crisis of 1978 is that neither the pegged nor the floating systems can work properly when there is a loss of confidence in a currency.

U.S. Balance of Payments, 1976–78

Items	1976	1977	Year	1st quarter	2nd quarter	3rd quarter	4th quarter[1]
			in billions of U.S. dollars				
Current transactions							
Mdse. exports (f.o.b.)	114.7	120.6	141.9	30.8	35.3	36.5	39.3
Mdse. imports (f.o.b.)	124.1	151.7	176.0	42.7	43.2	44.5	45.6
Trade balance	− 9.4	− 31.1	− 34.1	− 11.9	− 7.9	− 8.0	− 6.3
Invest income, net[2]	15.9	17.5	19.9	4.8	4.6	4.9	5.6
Other services & transfers, net	− 2.2	− 1.7	− 1.8	− 0.5	− 0.1	− 0.6	− 0.6
Services & transfers	13.7	15.8	18.1	4.3	4.5	4.3	5.0
Current balance	4.3	− 15.3	− 16.0	− 7.6	− 3.4	− 3.7	− 1.3
Capital transactions[3]							
U.S. government	0.8	− 2.0	− 1.8	− 0.1	− 1.5	− 1.1	− 0.9
Direct investment[4]	− 7.3	− 8.9	− 9.8	− 4.2	− 2.1	− 0.5	− 3.0
Portfolio investment	− 5.7	− 1.2	0.2	− 0.1	0.3	0	0
Flows reported by U.S. banks, n.i.e.	− 7.6	− 4.1	− 14.8	− 5.7	2.2	1.3	− 12.6
Other identified capital flows	− 22.3	− 17.7	− 26.8	− 11.8	− 0.6	0.6	− 15.0
Statistical discrepancy	9.3	− 0.9	11.5	4.6	9.1	− 1.6	− 0.6
Capital balance	− 13.0	− 18.6	− 15.3	− 7.2	8.5	− 1.0	− 15.6
Overall balance[5]	− 8.7	− 33.9	− 31.3	− 14.8	5.1	− 4.7	− 16.9
of which, changes in:							
U.S. official reserve assets	2.5	0.2	− 0.9	− 0.2	− 0.4	− 0.1	− 0.2
U.S. liabilities to foreign official agencies[3]	− 11.2	− 34.1	− 30.4	− 14.6	5.5	− 4.6	− 16.7

[1]Quarterly data seasonally adjusted.
[2]Including net retained earnings on direct investment.
[3]Because of definitional differences, some of the capital-account totals, and U.S. liabilities to foreign official agencies, are not identical to those published by the U.S. authorities.
[4]Including the reinvestment of net retained earnings on direct investment.
[5]Excludes valuation adjustments.

In the face of such turmoil, the Carter administration in 1978 again resorted to temporary solutions. On August 28 reserve requirements on funds borrowed abroad were abolished. This measure, coupled with the Treasury's intervention in the market, temporarily reversed lending in the third quarter. But the biggest change came in the fourth quarter, when U.S. banks reported net outflows of $12.6 billion, which was more than accounted for by additional dollar claims on foreigners, mainly in November and December. Moreover, if it had not been for the first issue of deutsche mark–denominated "Carter notes" to German residents, the net outflow in the fourth quarter would have been $1.6 billion larger. "Part of this outflow may have been purely seasonal," stated the Bank for

International Settlements, "but it is likely that much of it represented a response to the increased readiness of the U.S. authorities to intervene in foreign exchange markets to support the dollar, which enabled unwilling holders of dollar assets to cover their exchange risk without fear of triggering a large and costly fall in the dollar."[15]

The current-account deficit was in fact larger in 1978 than in 1977. The following table shows the seasonally adjusted quarterly movements of the U.S. balance of goods and services during 1977 and 1978, both in current dollars:

In Billions of Dollars at Current Prices

	1977					1978			
Year	First Quarter	Second Quarter	Third Quarter	Fourth Quarter	Year	First Quarter	Second Quarter	Third Quarter	Fourth Quarter
−11.1	−8.5	−5.9	−7.0	−23.2	−12.0	−24.1	−5.5	−10.7	−7.6

While the trade deficit decreased after fourth-quarter 1977 and first-quarter 1978, many people inside and outside the administration were disappointed that the subsequent improvement was less than might have been expected. The striking point in this analysis is that since the middle of 1977 there has not been any significant increase in net exports in spite of the depreciation of the dollar. It is also noteworthy that between second-quarter 1977 and fourth-quarter 1978, unit labor costs in U.S. manufacturing fell by 11½% relative to the other industrial nations.[16]

The recent evolution of the U.S. balance of payments and balance of trade would become clearer if we compare the recent currency depreciation and related developments with those of 1971–73, as shown in the table on page 42.

As the facts and figures point out, the early benefits of the 1971–72 dollar devaluation were responsible for better employment in this domestic economy but no improvement in the trade balance. In contrast, the 1973 depreciation had no impact on employment but helped the export of goods from the U.S.

So far, the aftereffects of the 1977–78 depreciation, which was 9%, has been disappointing. The increase in capacity utilization has been much smaller than in 1972, while U.S. exports in proportion to gross national product have decreased. Moreover, business-cycle developments in other countries have added to the nation's deficit problems. As a result, the most recent devaluation has solved no problems and, in some aspects, has caused the situation to deteriorate.

At the beginning of 1970, it was expected that the current deficit for the year would be roughly halved to between $8 billion and $10 billion. This

UNITED STATES: EFFECTS OF DOLLAR DEPRECIATION

Year and size of depreciation

No. of quarters after beginning of depreciation	Change in capacity utiliza. in mfg.	Volume of net ex.	Change in capacity utiliza. in mfg.	Volume of net ex.	Change in capacity utiliza. in mfg.	Volume of net ex.
1	+1.5	−0.20	+1.5	+0.31	−0.1	−0.70
2	+4.0	−0.48	+2.1	+0.58	−1.1	0.72
3	+5.9	−0.36	+3.4	+0.87	+1.2	−0.11
4	+7.2	−0.12	+2.2	+1.16	+2.4	−0.27
5	+10.3	−0.10	−0.1	+1.34	+3.5	−0.21
6	start of 2nd episode (see next column)		—	+1.37	+3.7	−0.30
7			−0.3	+1.37		
8			−7.1	+1.61		

SOURCE: Bank for International Settlements—4/1/78–3/31/79

expectation was dashed as a result of further increases in oil prices and a runaway inflation. Both these events prevented any improvement in the U.S. current account in 1979.

It is interesting to note that the balance-of-payments developments in 1978 in the three major surplus countries—Japan, Germany, and Switzerland—were strongly influenced by the sharp decline of the dollar. "All three countries experienced sizable increases in their current account surpluses arising out of terms-of-trade improvements that more than offset reduction in the volume of their net exports," says the Report of the Bank for International Settlements. "In addition, all three received massive inflows of short-term capital, so that additions to their net official reserves were even larger than in 1977, as the monetary authorities intervened heavily to moderate the upward movement of their exchange rates."[17]

The year 1979 ended with a trade deficit of $29.5 billion and a current-account deficit of $0.3 billion compared with $13.5 billion in 1978. This decline in the current-account deficit was the result of $37.7 billion in income on U.S. direct investment abroad. Receipts from petroleum affiliates were particularly strong, thus saving the United States from another substantial balance-of-payments deficit.

The dollar was more stable, on the average, than in 1978. On a trade-weighted basis, from the end of 1978 to the end of 1979, the dollar depreciated 1% against the currencies of the ten industrial countries. However, underlying the relative stability there were wide changes: a 23% appreciation against the yen, a 9% depreciation against the pound sterling, a 5% depreciation against most Western European currencies, and a 1% depreciation against the Canadian dollar.

In the early months of 1979 there was a reflux of funds from Germany, Switzerland, and Japan back into the dollar. Substantial dollar sales by German and Swiss monetary authorities, and purchases of marks by the United States, helped to limit the dollar's appreciation in March and April. Western Europe and the OPEC nations evidently considered the petroleum price increases a less serious problem for the United States than for Japan and the Western European countries.

This perception changed in early summer when inflation in the United States accelerated and the trade deficit increased. As a result, the dollar declined against most European currencies during the summer months. By August the price of gold, silver, and other commodities had risen substantially. Despite a tightening of monetary policy in Washington, the price of the dollar continued deteriorating until, at the end of September, the revaluation of the mark alleviated pressure on the U.S. currency.

When on October 6 the Federal Reserve implemented its new tight monetary policy, the dollar strengthened against the European currencies and the yen. In November the sale of mark-denominated U.S. Treasury notes gave the dollar another "shot in the arm." However, the crisis was intensified by the holding of American hostages in Teheran and the freezing of Iranian government assets in the United States, and by mid-November the result was a weakening of the dollar. By December 1979 the dollar had lost even more ground, and U.S. monetary authorities were forced to call for higher interest rates and tightened credit restrictions.

The significant market intervention by the U.S. throughout 1979 resulted in an increase of $1.1 billion in official-reserve assets. This was partly due to the sale of mark- and franc-denominated Treasury notes.

Foreign official assets in the U.S. declined by $15.2 billion in 1979 compared with a $33.8 billion increase in 1978. This decline resulted from large decreases in the first half of 1979 when Germany, Japan, and Switzerland intervened to limit depreciation of their currencies, and in the fourth quarter when the Japanese authorities again intervened.

U.S. banks reported $26.1 billion in claims abroad, reflecting sustained economic expansion in the other industrial countries and foreign-government borrowing to pay for oil imports.

These withdrawals and outflows were partly offset by the increases in assets placed in the United States by OPEC members in the second half of the year. Also, a substantial share of the financing for U.S. bank lending abroad and in the United States was obtained from offshore branches of U.S. banks in the Caribbean and England. Thus in 1979 the reported liabilities of U.S. banks increased by $37.4 billion, compared to $19.2 billion in 1978.

Receipts of income on U.S. direct investment abroad totaled $37.7 billion, which helped improve the balance of payments in 1979. However, according to the report of the U.S. Department of Commerce, a record discrepancy in accounts makes it difficult to interpret current and capital transactions during 1979. "The statistical discrepancy has tended to be large during periods of international economic, financial, and political uncertainty. [The statistical discrepancies, errors, and omissions in reported transactions were $28.7 billion in 1979.] In 1979 the exceptional 23% appreciation of the dollar against the Japanese yen and differences in balance-of-payments methodology and accounting between the United States and Japan may have contributed to the large positive statistical discrepancy attributable to Japan."[18]

It is too early to foresee the impact of the 100% increase in the price of oil on the industrial nations because of so many uncertain factors—the new energy policy in the United States, the cooperative conservation policy of the industrial nations, the stability of the dollar, the attempt to bring U.S. inflation under control, and the trade between oil consumers and producers.

A survey of OPEC nations indicates that, under normal trade relations, U.S. agricultural and industrial exports and services to the OPEC countries could easily absorb 50% of the export earnings of the major oil-producing countries. But with domestic restraints in the United States, this country's share of trade with the OPEC nations is much smaller than that 50%.

The U.S. exchange crisis of 1978 took place in response to a balance-of-payments disequilibrium and large trade deficits. The relationship between the dollar and the other major currencies was significantly altered as a consequence, in real as well as in nominal terms. A study of the exchange rate of the dollar vis-à-vis other currencies shows that the dollar continues to move in a direction generally consistent with the reduction of the U.S. current-account imbalance. Thus the mark and the yen, the currencies of the two countries with the largest surplus in 1978, appreciated far more rapidly during 1978 at the expense of the dollar, the currency of the country with the largest trade deficits. "Exchange rate influences," observes a U.S. Department of Commerce Report, "on relative cost and price movements, and thus on competitive positions in international trade, were correspondingly more pronounced and began in the first half of 1978 to have a perceptible effect on trade volumes."[19]

In retrospect, it is clear that the lack of attention paid export problems, expenditures abroad, and inflation for the past two decades has resulted in the depreciation of the dollar and the decline of its purchasing power against virtually all major currencies.

Thus, the crisis of 1978, like those of 1959, 1968, and 1972, was treated with palliatives rather than with surgery. The governments of the United States, West Germany, Japan, and Switzerland announced a package of

The Balance-of-Payments Problem 45

coordinated policy measures designed to correct a chronic malady that instead needed bitter medicine for its cure. These suggestions were an abridged edition of pronouncements, promises, and plans that had been repeatedly announced since 1958 by Republican as well as Democratic administrations in the United States. Unfortunately, little had been achieved over all these years for the simple reason that none of the U.S. proposals ever dealt directly with the causes of so much chaos—such structural problems as the trade deficit, declining productivity, military expenditures in Germany and Japan, inflation, and government regulations detrimental to trade exports.

As the previous pages show, the period since the November 1978 announcement has witnessed the same ups and downs as during previous currency-patching occasions. After the dollar's short recovery in the first and second quarters of 1979 against the Western European currencies, and an 18% appreciation against the yen, the dollar began sliding backward in July. By September the dollar had depreciated against every currency except the Canadian dollar and the yen.

By the end of 1979 the U.S. had the highest interest rates in the industrialized world, a 13% inflation rate, and a very weak currency. This serious situation caused so much concern in international monetary circles that the International Bank for Settlements, in its 1979 report, warned the world:

> Two series of developments have preoccupied the central banks of the industrial world in the past year: currency unrest brought under control around the end of 1978 and followed by *some* stabilization during the first few months of 1979, and, more recently, signs of a generalized resurgence of inflation. The currency unrest is a reflection of earlier major imbalance and, in particular, of the *huge U.S. balance-of-payments deficits*. Preoccupation with exchange markets and price trends will continue to shape domestic and international monetary policies in ways which may have far-reaching consequences not only for the countries directly concerned but for the entire world economy.[20]

There are two facts that deserve careful consideration in the analysis of this crisis. The first is that it happened while all the major currencies were floating—not freely, admittedly, but floating nevertheless. It thus contrasted sharply with the crisis of 1971 and early 1973, both of which took place under the regime of pegged rates. At that time many economists—and even some central bankers—had come to believe that floating rates, whatever their shortcomings, had at least one virtue—namely, that they did not allow exchange crises to occur. Experience with floating rates since 1973 has brought about a progressive revision of their views, culminating in the reaction of the U.S. authorities to 1978's events. This included not only a sharp depreciation of the dollar but also hectic exchange-rate fluctuations and a situation in which market participants simply formed themselves without counterparts.

The immediate and obvious conclusion to be drawn from the analysis of exchange-rate development in 1978 is that neither the pegged nor the floating system can work properly when there is a loss of confidence in the internal and external value of the main international reserve and trading currency (the dollar).

Flexible exchange rates have not prevented the United States from incurring massive deficits in the current account, nor have they ameliorated the condition of the U.S. balance of trade and payments.

The main reason that flexible exchange rates have not helped the U.S. trade and current-account position is that too much emphasis was placed on using exchange rates as a means to adjust the balance of payments without the appropriate domestic fiscal and monetary measures' being taken. Since the United States did not take appropriate domestic measures to moderate rises in relative prices and costs, to eliminate excessive domestic demand, and to maintain proper differentials in interest rates, flexible rates of the dollar did nothing but add to inflation without improving the trade deficit of the balance-of-payments position.

Some economists believe that flexible rates helped out three trade competitors—Germany, Japan, and Switzerland—to adjust their economies to the oil price increase. These three nations, as a result of the declining dollar vis-à-vis their currencies, were greatly benefited. To Switzerland alone the fivefold increase in the price of oil has meant a 40% decrease in the price of imported oil. The same thing happened in Germany. The question is: When is the United States going to wake up and stop decline in productivity and the dollar, deficit in trade, and the balance of payments?

The report of the Bank for International Settlements points out that whatever the exchange-rate system, neither the United States nor the world can live with a large and persistent U.S. current-account deficit. This is because the U.S. situation differs sharply from that of any other country in several respects: first, in the dollar's role as a reserve and grading currency, which means that a substantial amount of dollar-denominated financial assets are held outside the U.S.; second, in the complete freedom that Americans have enjoyed since January 1974 with regard to external capital transactions; third, in the fact that the total amount of dollars held by residents and nonresidents represents a large proportion of the world money supply. As a result, the dollar rate has become particularly sensitive to decisions taken by holders of liquid portfolios to diversify into, or out of, other currencies. Therefore, a loss of confidence in the dollar because of a large current-account deficit is likely to lead to a disorderly and excessive appreciation elsewhere—not to mention its impact on the price of oil and other commodities.[21]

The Balance-of-Payments Problem 47

In October 1979, at a meeting of the International Monetary Fund and the World Bank, monetary officials and private bankers from 136 countries agreed that there was a disarray in the exchange markets and that its cause was the weakness of the dollar and chaos in Washington. The message issued by those assembled as the leaders of the non-Communist world stated that the United States had a duty to be more economically responsible and responsive and that it had to terminate its policies of deficit spending, trade deficits, and military expenditures abroad. Instead, the statement said, the United States should adhere to economic discipline both internally and externally. At the meeting, participants also pointed out that the quick fixes of the seven years between 1972 and 1979 had failed and that the twin economic rescue missions of November 1978 did not succeed because all the promises to reduce spending, control inflation, and restrain military expenditures abroad were never fulfilled.

Commenting on the meeting, the *New York Times* and the *Wall Street Journal* stated that the world was asking the United States to accept stronger medicine, to do something tangible about the trade deficit and inflation.[22] Unfortunately, however, the new trade agreements and all the bilateral negotiations with Japan and the other nations have so far produced no real results: the U.S. trade deficits for 1979 and 1980 did not decline, military expenditures abroad did not decrease, and inflation was and is still as rampant as ever. Now the message is loud and clear that it is up to the United States, not the rest of the world, to act to counter the weakness of the dollar.

The present dollar decline and trade chaos cannot be solved without an understanding of their origins and the devastating consequences of the government waste, negligence, and mistakes of the past two decades.

The administration and the media are prone to put the blame for inflation, the dollar decline, and international monetary chaos on the increase in oil prices in 1973. They may be partly correct, but they ignore the fact that much of the trouble started with the Vietnam War.

An objective analysis of the international economic system between 1969 and 1979 shows that the causes of the present economic chaos are found in three interdependent areas: monetary crises, U.S. trade deficits, and the high cost of energy. All three areas enjoyed some degree of stability until the end of the decade of the 1960s. It started to weaken during the Vietnam War and became more pronounced in the U.S. balance-of-payments and trade deficits. It gave rise to inflation, destroyed the norms and regulations of the Bretton Woods Agreement, and eventually increased the price of oil 400%.

During the decade of the 1960s the international monetary regime, despite tolerable balance-of-payments deficits in the United States, was explicit, formally institutionalized, and comparatively stable. Governments belonging to the International Monetary Fund were responsible for maintaining official par value for their currencies. During the period of Bretton Woods, the rules were largely followed; parity changes for major currencies were few and of minor consequence.[23] Even the U.S. government, in response to a large deficit in its overall balance-of-payments liquidity, was forced to introduce an interest-equalization tax in 1963 and voluntary capital controls in 1965. But unfortunately the war in Vietnam, military expenditures abroad, and the lack of attention by the United States to exports and trade with Japan and Western Europe undermined confidence in the dollar. As a result of this loss of confidence, a plan called Special Drawing Rights (SDRs), designed to provide a source of international liquidity to serve in lieu of dollars, was created. This reform did not succeed because the conditions that it was meant to produce never materialized. Rather than eliminating its deficits, the United States let its balance of payments on current accounts deteriorate sharply in the last half of the sixties. The increased military spending abroad, the Vietnam War coupled with a large fiscal deficit, and the inflationary momentum forced the Nixon administration in August 1971 to suspend the convertibility of the dollar into gold. The Smithsonian Institution Agreement following the Bretton Woods regime, reached in December 1971 to restore fixed exchange rates, collapsed under the pressures of monetary expansion in the United States and of broad and large continuing American deficits, which reached a total of $50 billion during the years from 1970 to 1973.[24]

The collapse of the international monetary regime in 1971–73 was connected directly with American economic policy. Years of balance-of-payments and budget deficits, along with heavy expenditure for military and economic aid abroad and fighting an unpopular and costly war, produced a lack of confidence and resulted in difficulty in maintaining the value of the dollar at the old exchange rates.

"World import and export prices, measured in dollars," according to economist Robert Triffin, "rose by less than 1% a year in the 1960s but by more than 6% a year from 1970 through 1972, and by as much as 30% in the last 12 months *before* the explosion of oil prices in the fall of 1973. This was not unconnected, to say the least, with the enormous and mounting U.S. deficits abroad which flooded the world monetary system, doubling world reserves from the end of 1969 to the end of 1972, increasing them as much in this short span of three years as in all previous centuries in recorded history."[25]

Foreign dollar claims on the U.S. government and banks increased from $49 billion to $85 billion between 1969 and 1972. At the same time, international monetary reserves increased from $79 billion to $159 billion, and foreign reserves of dollars and Eurodollars jumped from $20 billion to $81 billion.

In 1963, in *The Dollar Crisis*,[25] it was pointed out that U.S. resources were not inexhaustible and that it was high time that Germany and Japan

The Balance-of-Payments Problem

supported the local expenses of the American troops protecting their territory. Since 1954 the United States has spent a stunning $2.4 trillion in building a colossal military machine, in arming and equipping foreign governments, in rebuilding Western Europe and Japan, and in assisting 145 nations with money and technology. While Japan now spends an average of less than 1% of its GNP on defense, and Germany less than 4% since World War II, the United States has diverted nearly 10% to military expenses at home and abroad. As Sentor Frank Church put it:

> The emphasis on military spending has also resulted in much of our national research being directed to this purpose. While only about 5% of the Japanese R&D Budget is earmarked for defense and 25% of Germany's, over 70% of our Government's R&D Budget goes for military or aerospace projects.
> Since 1946, we have spent some $200 billion for such assistance, spread among *145* foreign governments. Some of this money has been put to good use rebuilding Western Europe and bringing a measure of humanitarian relief to certain impoverished lands. But so often, this money has gone not for need development but in futile efforts to prop up anti-Communist governments which were too repressive or too corrupt to survive on their own.[27]

The following table shows the results of thirty years of military expenditures, foreign aid, and inflationary explosions of international liquidity in billions of dollars.

	End 1969	End 1972	End 1977	Mid-1978	Mid-1978 % of 1969
I. Foreign Dollar Claims	78	146	363	373	478
A. On U.S. Government and Banks	49	85	210	221	451
B. On Foreign Branches of U.S. Banks	29	61	153	152	524
II. International Monetary Reserves	79	159	319	330	418
A. Foreign Exchange	33	104	244	256	776
1. Dollars & Eurodollars	20	81	197		985
2. Other Currencies	7	15	27		386
3. Other	7	8	22		314
B. Other: World Monetary Gold, SDR Allocations, and IMF Loans and Investments	46	55	75	75	163
III. Commercial Banks Foreign Liabilities in:	121	217	658	700	579
A. Dollars and Eurodollars	94	157	481		512
B. Other Currencies	27	60	177		656

SOURCES: These rough estimates are derived from various tables published by the *International Monetary Fund* in its *International Financial Statistics and Annual Reports*, by the *Federal Reserve Bulletin*, and by the *Bank for International Settlements* in its *Annual Reports* and quarterly releases on Eurocurrency and other international banking developments. They are not fully comparable, owing particularly to the different definition (*Foreign Affairs* [Winter 1978–79]) of "foreign" liabilities in U.S. and European reporting. Following the usual practice, detailed figures are shown in rounded-off billions of dollars. At the end of June 1980 West Germany's currency reserves totaled $53.9 billion, France's $29.5 billion, Italy's $23.6 billion, Britain's $23.2 billion, Japan's $23.2 billion, and Switzerland's $18.3 billion. The U.S. showed a currency reserve of $23 billion. What a change! In 1949 the U.S. reserve of gold at $36 an ounce was $24.6 billion. In 1980 it dropped to $11.6 billion.

There are no exact figures for official and private dollar and Eurodollar holdings, but a conservative estimate puts the total at well above $700 billion. Half of this sum consists of liabilities of the U.S. government and U.S. banks and their branches abroad. The other half constitutes the liabilities of foreign commercial banks.

The continued foreign expenditures of the United States, coupled with the cost of the Vietnam War and the fourfold increase in oil prices in the fall of 1973, have piled up an enormous indebtedness in foreign dollar balances, which rose from $78 billion in 1969 to about $390 billion by the end of 1978. This accumulation led to the dollar's decline to one-half of its previous value vis-à-vis German marks, Swiss francs, and the Japanese yen.

ECONOMIC GROWTH, DEFENSE SPENDING[28]

Economic Growth = annual compound rate of growth in gross national product, 1960–77.
Defense Spending = percent of GNP devoted to defense, 1961–77.

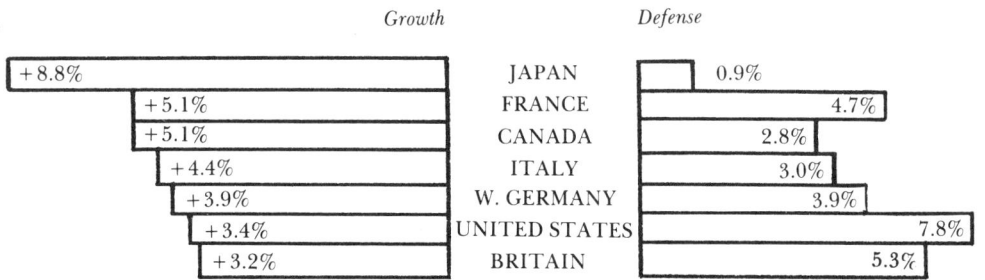

SOURCE: World Bank, U.S. Arms Control Agency.
[28]*New York Times*, October 15, 1980, p. D2.

The world economy in 1977, 1978, and 1979 operated under the converging influence of three depressive factors: the deficit in the U.S. balance of payments, the high price of energy, and the persistent inflationary disturbances inherited from the late 1960s and early 1970s. All three of these factors exerted a restraining influence on government policies, while the climate of uncertainty generated by them affected business decisions and perhaps even consumer behavior. The result has been a renewed slowdown in the growth of output and imports in some industrial nations.

Considering that the global oil surplus actually declined in 1977 and in the first part of 1978, and that many countries have achieved a better balance in their external payments and have managed to reduce imports

The Balance-of-Payments Problem

and inflation, this evaluation might seem rather paradoxical. But if one looks beneath the surface, there is a close interrelationship between the shrinking oil surplus, the improved balance-of-payments situation in a number of countries, the slowdown of inflation, and the unsatisfactory growth of imports of the major industrial nations except the United States.

On the other hand, while the actual and potential costs of energy have put constraints on expansion in a number of countries, continued cost inflation has exerted a strong inhibiting influence on the growth of imports and domestic demands—even in Germany and Japan, where big surpluses dominated the balance of payments. The United States thus represents an exception, with its increase in both its imports and its balance-of-payments deficit.

The result of a new economic policy of expanding exports and restraining imports by most industrial countries except the United States was an impressive improvement in their balance of payments in 1977 and 1978. Thus the most worrisome economic development of those years was the stubborn persistence of payments surpluses in West Germany[29] and Switzerland, and particularly the increase in Japan's surplus from $3.7 billion in 1976 to $11 billion in 1977.[30] The volume of Japanese imports of goods and services increased by only 2% against a 10.4% rise in exports.

In Japan and West Germany, meanwhile, there has been pressure for more exports and fewer imports. The long-awaited upturn in fixed investment failed to materialize, expenditures on personal consumption and imports tapered off, and the governments concentrated on accumulating more surpluses at the expense of the United States.

Owing to the upswing in the U.S. economy, business, consumer, and mortgage credits have all risen, while in Germany and Japan credit plans and spending are still mainly under the influence of the government.

The record current-payments deficit of the United States has been accompanied by substantial capital and short-term bank outflows, so that the 1978 deficit of $34 billion had to be financed by additions to the foreign official holdings of dollars. At the same time, the size of the U.S. deficit has lightened the financing burdens of other deficit countries. With a few notable exceptions, other developed countries have had easy access to international capital markets both for private and official borrowing. Similarly, the nonoil developing countries have continued to be large-scale market borrowers, although with further declines in their current external credits in 1980 they have become, on balance, a liability to the international banking system.

3

The doubling of the price of oil in 1979 created a new problem both for the United States (whose oil bill in 1980 was $70 billion) and other oil-consuming nations. How much of this new flow of money is going into international trade and development? How great is the flow? Is the world witnessing the creation of a new international currency? Who controls it? What is its meaning? These questions are very important to both the United States and the rest of the world. From the incomplete knowledge at hand we understand that during the first six months of 1980 the amount of petrodollars flowing into Eurocurrency is very large. It grows every year as additional billions from Saudi Arabia, Kuwait, and Libya enter the American and European markets.

So far, the owners of surplus petrodollars have been positive and reasonable in the recycling of their money. Direct assistance and aid has been given to Muslim countries and other African and Asian nations. Saudi Arabia and Kuwait and the United Arab Emirates have participated in the International Monetary Fund program to increase funds available to be used for development loans. These and other positive steps have enabled less fortunate nations to import oil and, at the same time, to continue their development plans.

What about the future? It is estimated that the surplus of four countries—Saudi Arabia, Kuwait, United Arab Emirates, and Libya—for 1980 could be close to $100 billion. A large portion of these surplus funds will go into securities in developed countries. At current interest rates of 14% in the United States, the amount of interest alone can cause serious future problems to the balance of payments of the United States. This trend may be the cause of some anxiety, but what should concern us most is that the bulk of the surplus dollar that will go to the large Eurodollar banks located in London. These banks in turn "recycle" the money deposited with them—that is to say, lend it out to their clients all over the world. These new clients are mostly developing nations that would rather borrow from private commercial banks than from the International Monetary Fund. The Eurocurrency banks ask few questions from their customers and their loans are not conditional upon making unpopular decisions so as to avoid similar balance-of-payments problems and waste in the future.

The owners of the petrodollars deposit their money generally for six months, but the banks lend their money to the developing nations for five years or more, with high interest rates.

So far, according to the U.S. Department of the Treasury, from 1974 through 1979, $225 billion was loaned or invested by the OPEC nations. The lion's share ($84.5 billion) went to the Eurocurrency market, which parceled it out to borrowers all over the world. The United States received $45.5 billion; the less-developed nations' share was $43.25 billion. The IMF and the World Bank received $8.75 billion, and the amount loaned to other countries totaled $53.25 billion. Up to the end of 1979 the Euromarket and the American banks handled the OPEC surpluses with remarkable ability and efficiency. But with the revolution in Iran and the doubling of the price of oil in less than six months, the world is now faced with $100 billion surplus in 1980 alone. It is hoped that, with the stable oil price, conservation, and increase of expenditures in the OPEC countries, this surplus could be cut to $80 billion in 1981. Furthermore, the oil-surplus nations have been both reasonable and conservative in the recycling of their cash. In September 1980 the Saudi Arabian Monetary Agency (SAMA) granted Germany $4.95 billion deutsche mark balance-of-payments credit. Even smaller industrial nations have little trouble borrowing at relatively reasonable rates.

But the destiny of the poor countries in the future is in the hands of the oil-producing nations and international bankers. The total amount of debts of the development nations is close to $300 billion, compared with $100 billion in 1974. In many cases, the banks already question the creditworthiness of the borrowers. As the debt burdens of some non-oil-producing countries increase, according to J. William Middendorf, "a crisis of financing may surface in a major way next year. It is bound to happen that one of these debtor countries will come to the market to reschedule its debts and the market will say, 'No.' "[31]

But Middendorf's counterparts in Citicorp believe that this kind of pessimism is unfounded. Alarming as the developing nations' debt figures may look in the aggregate, the bulk of the United States banks' loans to the developing nations is concentrated in seven countries. Mexico and Venezuela are rich, and are oil exporters; Argentina is virtually self-sufficient; South Korea and Taiwan are expanding their exports by 10% every year; Brazil and the Philippines are now going through austerity programs, making sure that their credit remains good.

Whichever view proves right, one point seems acceptable to all the bankers: the poor countries need more loans than the commercial banks are able to supply. The shortfalls, which would amount to between $14 to $30 billion by 1983–84, has to be covered by aid from OPEC and industrial nations.

Without loans and aid, the growth in the developing nations would be reduced to 1%—low enough to cause political upheavals. If this disastrous situation is to be avoided, the poor countries will have to borrow heavily from the banks or seek aid from the oil-producing and industrial countries. In either case, the rich nations must subsidize the poor.

Why should rich nations help Third World countries? For the same reasons that the United States gave assistance to Western Europe and Japan:

1. Humanitarianism. More than a billion of the world's people live in abject poverty, "a condition so limited by malnutrition, illiteracy, disease,

high infant mortality, and low life expectancy as to be beneath any rational definition of human decency. These people lie at the very edge of survival and any downward adjustment means total disaster."[32]

2. Commercial and political interests. In 1979 the non-OPEC developing countries accounted for $48 billion of the U.S. exports, or one-quarter of the total exports of this country. This was higher than the total exports to the European community. It represented about one million jobs for the American workers.

3. Impact on the banking system. The Third World nations are responsible for 50% of the profits of many commercial banks. Any default by a debtor country will create a substantial rise in the commercial banks' "nonperforming" assets. But, according to C. Fred Bergsten, former Assistant Secretary of the Treasury for International Affairs, the banks would attempt to avoid any slowdown with their debtors. Even if a country were not able to meet its commitments, a rescheduling plan could be arranged. Furthermore, the economic interests of the OPEC nations and the security and strategic interests of the industrial nations force them to come to the aid of the defaulting country.

When Zaire asked for rescheduling of its debts, the United States and other Western governments—worrying about the survival of the Mobutu regime, and the loss of the cobalt and copper mines of the country—rushed to the aid of the Zaire government. They saved Zaire from bankruptcy by extending the debts and pouring more money in order to keep Mobutu in power. The same thing happened in the case of Turkey. Western nations put together an aid package totaling $1.16 billion and rescheduled almost $3 billion in debts. In addition, the IMF approved a $1.6 billion loan. The object of all these efforts was to save Turkey from chaos and bankruptcy.

In the same way, it is natural for the oil-producing nations to look for stability and seek prosperity throughout the world. These nations now have as much at stake as the industrial nations, the banks and the international institutions. The bulk of official Arab investment still remains in dollar deposits and relatively safe, short-term instruments, such as Treasury bills and government bonds. Sixty percent of the surplus oil money belongs to Saudi Arabia, Kuwait, and the United Arab Emirates.[33]

The Kuwaiti International Investment Company has developed a bond market, including some issues denominated in Kuwaiti dinars that protect investors from foreign devaluations. The Kuwaiti's company issued $2.3 billion in 1980. It is at present among the world's top fifteen bond-issuing houses. The Kuwaitis, who call themselves modern Rothschilds, have also branched out into direct and equity investments. They own 14% of Daimler-Benz, 10% of Volkswagen shares, and real estate and hotels in

The Balance-of-Payments Problem

England, the U.S. Sun Belt, and France. The Arab investors complain that they have been slandered and maligned by different groups in New York, Chicago, and the West Coast of the United States. As a result of these hysterical attacks, Arab investors attempt to steer clear of long-term investments. A spokesman for Saudi Arabia, referring to charges in the United States, contends: "We are not sure that some people in the United States would welcome our sincere efforts for investments and cooperation. Therefore, we try to invest our money where it is welcomed."

As far as aid is concerned, the OPEC countries' record is outstanding. As a percentage of GNP, the aid supplied by the Arab countries alone is over 4%. Between 1974 and 1979 the Arab contribution exceeded $26 billion in nonmilitary aid. That is three times as much as any other nation has donated.

Many economists and money managers believe that the surplus OPEC money is manageable, provided that the industrial nations seriously start discussions on a long-term price-and-production formula for oil, and price stability for their manufactured products.

At present, the IMF has about $20 billion to lend. It is getting pledges from oil-producing nations and other members for another $15 billion to be loaned to the poor nations. In addition, the IMF is negotiating for a loan of $25 billion from Saudi Arabia, Kuwait, and the United Arab Emirates at commercial rates.

Furthermore, in order to reduce the financial burden of the developing African countries, the four African members of the Organization of Petroleum Exporting Countries decided at a special meeting on November 10, 1980, to set aside 4% of their overall oil output for developing African countries. Total oil production of the four countries—Algeria, Libya, Nigeria, and Gabon—is close to 5 million barrels a day. The 200,000 barrels set aside is likely to exceed the oil supplies that the African oil-importing nations normally got from Iran and Iraq. This new arrangement would not affect existing bilateral oil agreements with developing countries in other continents. The other members of OPEC also announced in their meeting of mid-December 1980, in Bali, Indonesia, they would take similar measures to help developing countries on other continents to offset losses in oil supplies resulting from the war.[34]

4

The implications of a widely fluctuating and shaky dollar are not only of vital concern to OPEC members, but are of serious importance to the viability and efficiency of the international monetary system. "The drop in dollar value aggravates U.S. inflation and has a rather slow beneficial effect on America's balance-of-payments." The weak dollar also has been responsible for the flight of capital from the United States and the reduction in private investments. "Add above all, a failing dollar upsets the whole fragile fabric of the present international monetary system."[35]

The present unhappy dollar situation is chiefly the result of billions in foreign aid, military expenditures, the Vietnam War, huge oil imports, decline in productivity, a balance-of-trade gap of more than $100 billion since 1971, a mammoth budgetary deficit for two decades, and high inflation.

The immediate measures that are likely to enhance world confidence in the dollar would seem to be the United States' continued pursuit of expansion of exports, determined market intervention to smooth out disorderly currency rates, increasing the United States' capability for market intervention as a kind of psychological underpinning of the dollar-support policy, and above all a clear turnabout of the inflationary forces in the United States. In the long run, however, the real hope for dollar stability and OPEC's cooperative attitude would be: (1) coordination of policies among the major industrial countries to ensure conservation and search for other sources of energy; (2) orderly noninflationary growth under free market conditions; and (3) an accommodative arrangement between OPEC and major oil consumers with respect to recycling of oil revenues and protection of the dollar's purchasing power.

"Improvement in basic underlying conditions," according to an IMF report, "is a contributor to great stability of exchange markets and such stability, in turn, is considered extremely important for the health of the world economy."[36]

As Paul Volcker, chairman of the Federal Reserve System, observes: "Once serious doubt comes to be cast on that future value [of the dollar], trading can become dominated by that consideration, losing touch with current purchasing power and competitive considerations.

"There are symptoms of just that sort of development today, and they are profoundly disturbing given the sheer magnitude of the dollar's role as the preeminent international money and the inflationary consequences of excessive depreciation."[37]

In the following chapters ways and means of how to cope with problems plaguing the American economy are explored.

Notes

1. Nasrollah S. Fatemi, Thibaut de Saint-Phalle, and Grace O'Keefe, *The Dollar Crisis* (Cranbury, N.J.: Fairleigh Dickinson University Press, 1963), p. 1.
2. U.S. gold holdings on December 31, 1949, stood at $24.6 billion. By December 31, 1979, they had dropped to $11.6 billion (their lowest level.)
3. President John F. Kennedy's message to Congress, February 6, 1961.
4. Ibid.
5. Alvin M. Saton, "Balance of Payments Positive and Negative Effects," manuscript, 1978.
6. Ibid.
7. See Nasrollah Fatemi, Thibaut de Saint-Phalle, and Gail Williams, *Multinational Corporations* (Cranbury, N.J.: A. S. Barnes, 1978).
8. Ibid.
9. President Nixon's announcement of August 1971.
10. U.S. Department of Commerce, *Statistical Abstracts*, 1978.
11. Ibid., 1977.
12. See *Report of the Bank for International Settlements*, June 11, 1979.
13. Ibid.
14. Ibid.
15. *Report of the Bank for International Settlements*, Forty-ninth Annual Report, June 1979.
16. Ibid.
17. Ibid.
18. U.S. Department of Commerce, *Survey of Current Business*, March 1980.
19. Ibid.
20. *Report of the Bank for International Settlements*, Forty-ninth Annual Report, June 1979.
21. Ibid.
22. *New York Times* and *Wall Street Journal*, October 8 and 9, 1979.
23. Alfred E. Eckes, Jr., *A Search for Solvency: Bretton Woods and International Money System, 1941–1971* (Austin: University of Texas Press, 1975).
24. Benjamin J. Cohen, *Organizing the World's Money* (New York: Basic Books, 1977).
25. See Robert Triffin, *Foreign Affairs* (Winter 1978–79), pp. 269–85.
26. Nasrollah Fatemi, Thibaut de Saint-Phalle, and Grace O'Keefe, *The Dollar Crisis* (Cranbury, N.J.: Fairleigh Dickinson University Press, 1963).
27. Senator Frank Church, speech at the University of Utah, December 12, 1978.
28. *New York Times*, October 15, 1980, p. D2.
29. The balance-of-payments surplus of West Germany for 12 months of 1978 was $9.6 billion, compared with $2.18 billion in 1977.
30. Japan's gold and foreign exchange reached a record high of $33 billion in December 1979, after gaining $10.0 billion in 1978.
31. In *Fortune* magazine, November 17, 1980.
32. Robert McNamara, President of the World Bank, Annual Report October 1980.
33. In 1979 oil-exporting countries held 1,135 tons of gold worth over $25 billion.
34. *New York Times*, November 10, 1980.
35. *Foreign Affairs*, "OPEC and the Dollar Dilemma" (July 1978).
36. Report to meeting of International Monetary Fund, April 30, 1978.
37. Paul Volcker's remarks at Adelphi University, October 1978.

TABLE 1.1

U.S. Balance of International Payments
1950–62

	1950	*1951*	*1952*	*1953*	*1954*
Current account: (in millions of dollars)					
Merchandise exports	+10,117	+14,123	+13,319	+12,281	+12,799
Merchandise imports	−9,108	−11,202	−10,838	−10,990	−10,354
Trade balance	+1,009	+2,921	+2,481	+1,291	+2,445
Services, receipts	+3,690	+4,621	+4,673	+4,474	+4,778
Services, payments	−2,344	−2,501	−2,374	−2,956	−2,935
Balance on services	+1,346	+2,020	+1,799	+1,518	+1,843
Overall balance on current account	+2,355	+4,941	+4,280	+2,809	+4,288
Private capital account:					
U.S. foreign investments, net	−1,265	−1,048	−1,160	−383	−1,622
Foreign long-term investments in U.S. net[1]	+90	+243	+212	+178	+240
Balance on capital acct.	−1,175	−305	−948	−205	−1,332
U.S. government account:					
Military expenditures abroad	−576	−1,270	−2,054	−2,615	−2,642
Military transactions[2]	—	—	—	+192	+182
Grants, economic aid	−3,484	−3,035	−1,960	−1,837	−1,647
Loans, net[3]	−156	−156	−420	−218	+93
Pensions and other transfers	−79	−71	−128	−141	−129
Total government outflow	−4,295	−4,532	−4,562	−4,619	−4,143
Other:					
Private remittances	−444	−386	−417	−476	−486
Balance on recorded transactions	−3,559	−782	−1,647	−2,491	−1,723
Unrecorded transactions	−21	+477	+601	+339	+173
Total net receipts (+) or payments (−)	−3,580	−305	−1,046	−2,152	−1,550
Settlement items:					
Gold and convertible currencies: purchases (−), sales (+)	+1,743	−53	−379	+1,161	+298
Liquid liabilities, total: increase (+), decrease (−)	+1,837	+358	+1,425	+991	+1,252

[1] Also includes foreign commercial credits and other nonliquid capital.
[2] Receipts from military transactions which, prior to 1953, were included in merchandise exports and services.
[3] New loans minus repayments on earlier loans. The loan repayment for 1962 alone was $660 million.

1955	1956	1957	1958	1959	1960	1961	1962[4]
+14,280	+17,379	+19,390	+16,282	+19,915	+20,566		
+11,527	−12,804	−13,291	−12,952	−15,310	−14,723	−14,514	−16,193
+2,753	+4,575	+6,099	+3,312	+972	+4,736	+5,401	+4,373
+5,324	+6,055	+6,716	+6,503	+6,892	+7,219	+7,745	+8,610
−3,367	−3,875	−4,245	−4,474	−4,925	−5,417	−5,462	−5,800
+1,957	+2,180	+2,471	+2,029	+1,967	+1,802	+2,283	+2,810
+4,710	+6,755	+8,570	+5,341	+2,939	+6,538	+7,684	+7,183
−1,255	−3,071	−3,577	−2,936	−2,375	−3,882	−3,953	−3,051
+394	+653	+487	+22	+863	+335	+733	+975
−861	−2,413	−3,090	−2,914	−1,512	−3,547	−3,220	−2,076
−2,901	−2,949	−3,216	−3,435	−3,107	−3,048	−2,947	−3,006
+200	+161	+375	+300	+302	+335	+406	+638
−1,901	−1,733	−1,616	−1,616	−1,633	−1,664	−1,851	−1,872
−310	−629	−958	−971	−353	−1,105	−926	−1,124
−141	−135	−159	−182	−216	−214	−235	−243
−5,053	−5,285	−5,574	−5,904	−5,007	−5,696	−5,553	−5,607
−444	−530	−543	−540	−575	−628	−643	−681
−1,648	−1,478	−637	−4,017	−4,155	−3,333	−1,732	−1,181
−503	−543	−1,157	−488	−412	−592	−628	−1,000
−1,145	−935	+520	−3,529	−3,743	−3,925	−2,360	−2,181
+41	−306	−798	+2,275	+731	+1,702	+742	+907
+1,104	+1,241	+278	+1,254	+3,012	+2,223	+1,618	+1,274

[4]Preliminary
SOURCES: U.S. Department of Commerce, Office of Business Economics, *Balance of Payments Statistical Supplement, 1963*; *Survey of Current Business*, March 1963, p. 22.

TABLE 1.2
FOREIGN COMMERCE AND AID
U.S. International Transactions: 1965 to 1977

[In millions of dollars. Minus sign (−) denotes debits. The account definition has been changed to include reinvested earnings on foreign investments and historical data have been revised accordingly. See also *Historical Statistics, Colonial Times to 1970*, series U 1–25]

Type of Transaction	1965	1970	1972	1973	1974	1975	1976	1977
Exports of goods and services[1]	41,090	65,659	77,197	109,853	146,086	155,655	171,274	183,214
Merchandise, excl. military[2]	26,461	42,469	49,381	71,410	98,306	107,088	114,604	120,585
Transfers under U.S. military agency sales contracts	830	1,501	1,163	2,342	2,952	3,919	5,213	7,079
Travel and transportation	3,826	5,988	7,071	8,821	10,788	11,666	13,740	14,513
Miscellaneous services	2,533	3,950	4,888	5,584	6,499	7,623	8,384	8,938
Income on U.S. investments abroad[2 4]	7,441	11,751	14,694	21,697	27,541	25,359	29,244	32,100
Transfers of goods and services under U.S. military grants, net	1,636	2,713	4,492	2,818	2,207	373	194	—
Imports of goods and services	−32,801	−60,005	−79,321	−99,087	−137,182	−132,595	−161,913	−193,727
Merchandise, excl. military[2]	−21,510	−39,866	−55,797	−70,499	−103,649	−98,041	−124,047	−151,644
Direct defense expenditures	−2,952	−4,855	−4,784	−4,629	−5,032	−4,795	−4,901	−5,745
Travel and transportation	−5,106	−8,011	−10,099	−11,907	−13,893	−14,188	−15,985	−17,557
Miscellaneous services	−1,146	−1,760	−2,099	−2,399	−2,524	−3,006	−3,670	−4,189
Income on foreign investments in U.S.[3 4]	−2,088	−5,516	−6,544	−9,655	−12,084	−12,564	−13,311	−14,593
U.S. military grants of goods and services, net	−1,636	−2,713	−4,492	−2,810	−1,818	−2,207	−373	−194
Unilateral transfers (excl. military grants), net	−2,854	−3,294	−3,854	−3,881	−7,186	−4,615	−5,022	−4,708
U.S. Government grants	−1,808	−1,736	−2,173	−1,938	−5,475	−2,894	−3,145	−2,776
U.S. Govt. pensions, private remittances, other transfers	−1,046	−1,558	−1,681	−1,943	−1,711	−1,721	−1,878	−1,932
U.S. assets abroad, net (increase/capital outflow (−))	−5,718	−9,340	−14,461	−22,823	−34,712	−39,444	−50,608	−34,650
U.S. official reserve assets, net	1,222	2,477	32	209	−1,434	−607	−2,530	−231
U.S. Govt. assets, other than official reserve assets, net	−1,605	−1,589	−1,568	−2,644	366	−3,470	−4,213	−3,679
U.S. loans and other long-term assets	−2,463	−3,293	−3,819	−4,638	−5,001	−5,936	−6,943	−6,445
Repayments on U.S. loans[5]	874	1,721	2,086	2,596	4,826	2,475	2,597	2,720
U.S. foreign currency holdings and U.S. short-term assets, net	−16	−16	165	−602	541	−9	133	47
U.S. private assets, net	−5,335	−10,228	−12,925	−20,388	−33,643	−35,368	−43,865	−30,740
Direct investments abroad[4]	−5,010	−7,589	−7,747	−11,353	−9,052	−14,244	−11,614	−2,215
Foreign securities	−759	−1,076	−618	−671	−1,854	−6,235	−8,852	−5,398
U.S. claims on unaffiliated foreigners reported by U.S. nonbanking concerns	341	−596	−1,054	−2,383	−3,221	−1,357	−2,030	−1,700
U.S. claims reported by U.S. banks, n.i.e.[6]	93	−967	−3,506	−5,980	−19,516	−13,532	−21,368	−11,427
Long-term	−232	155	−1,307	−933	−1,183	−2,357	−2,362	−751
Short-term	325	−1,122	−2,199	−5,047	−18,333	−11,175	−19,006	−10,676
Foreign assets in the U.S., net (increase/capital inflow (+))	740	6,357	21,696	18,663	34,677	15,550	36,969	50,869
Foreign official assets in the U.S., net	132	6,907	10,705	6,299	10,981	6,907	18,073	37,124
Other foreign assets in the U.S., net	607	−550	10,991	12,364	23,696	8,643	18,897	13,746
Direct investments in U.S.[4]	415	1,464	949	2,800	4,760	2,603	4,347	3,338
U.S. Treasury securities	−131	81	−34	−214	697	2,590	2,783	563
U.S. securities other than U.S. Treasury securities	−358	2,189	4,507	4,041	378	2,503	1,284	2,869
U.S. liabilities to unaffiliated foreigners reported by U.S. nonbanking concerns	178	2,014	815	1,035	1,844	319	−507	257
U.S. liabilities reported by U.S. banks, n.i.e.[6]	503	−6,298	4,754	4,702	16,017	628	10,990	6,719
Long-term	241	23	149	227	9	−280	231	373
Short-term	262	−6,321	4,605	4,475	16,008	908	19,759	6,346
Allocations of special drawing rights	—	867	710	—	—	—	—	—
Statistical discrepancy (sum of above items with sign reversed)	−457	−244	−1,966	−2,725	−1,684	5,449	9,300	−998

—Represents zero. [1]Excludes transfers of goods and services under U.S. military grant programs. [2]Excludes exports of goods under U.S. military agency sales contracts identified in Bureau of the Census export documents, excludes imports of goods under direct defense expenditures identified in Census import documents, and reflects various other adjustments (for valuation, coverage, and timing) of census statistics to a balance of payments basis. [3]Consists of interest, dividends, and branch earnings. [4]Includes reinvested earnings of foreign incorporated affiliates of U.S. firms, or of U.S. incorporated affiliates of foreign firms. [5]Includes sales of foreign obligations to foreigners. [6]Not included elsewhere.

SOURCE: U.S. Bureau of Economic Analysis, *Survey of Current Business*, June 1978.

TABLE 1.3

INTERNATIONAL CURRENT-ACCOUNT TRANSACTIONS[1]

Countries and areas	Trade balance (f.o.b.)			Services and transfers			Current balance		
	1977	1978	1979	1977	1978	1979	1977	1978	1979
	in billions of US dollars								
BLEU*	−1.4[2]	−1.2[2]	−3.3[2]	0.7	0.3	−0.5	−0.7	−0.9	−3.8
Canada*	2.5	3.0	3.4	−6.6	−7.6	−.7	−.1	−4.6	−4.3
France	−2.4	1.5	1.3	−0.6	2.2	2.8	−3.0	3.7	1.5
Germany	19.8	25.6	17.3	−15.5	−16.7	−23.1	4.3	8.9	−5.8
Italy*	−0.1	2.9	−1.0	2.6	3.3	6.1	2.5	6.2	5.1
Japan*	17.3	24.6	2.0	−6.4	−8.1	−10.6	10.9	16.5	−8.6
Netherlands*	−0.1	−0.9	−1.2	0.7	−0.5	−1.1	0.6	−1.4	−2.3
Sweden	0.3	2.6	0.9	−2.4	−2.9	−3.4	−2.1	−0.3	−2.5
Switzerland*	−0.1	0.2	−2.2	3.5	4.2	4.7	3.4	4.4	2.5
United Kingdom	−3.9	−2.9	−6.9	3.6	4.7	1.9	−.3	1.8	−5.0
United States	−30.9	−33.8	−29.5	16.8	20.3	29.2	−4.1	−13.5	−0.3
Group of Ten and Switzerland	1.0	21.6	−21.8	−3.6	−0.8	−1.7	−2.6	20.8	−23.5
Australia	1.0	0.1	2.5	−3.6	−3.9	−4.6	−2.6	−3.8	−2.1
Austria*	−3.9	−3.1	−3.9	0.9	1.6	2.0	−3.0	−1.5	−1.9
Denmark*	−2.7	−2.4	−3.4	1.0	0.9	0.4	−1.7	−1.5	−3.0
Finland	0.5	1.2	0.6	−0.7	−0.6	−0.9	−0.2	0.6	−0.3
Greece*	−3.2	−3.5	−5.2	1.9	2.2	2.9	−1.3	−1.3	−2.3
Ireland*	−0.8	−1.0	−2.2	0.5	0.7	0.6	−0.3	−0.3	−1.6
Israel	−2.2	−2.8	−3.0	1.7	1.8	1.8	−0.5	−1.0	−1.2
New Zealand	0.2	0.6	0.7	−0.8	−1.0	−1.2	−0.6	−0.4	−0.5
Norway	−4.0	−0.5	0.1	−1.0	−1.6	−1.3	−5.0	−2.1	−1.2
Portugal	−2.5	−2.4	−2.4	1.0	1.6	2.6	−1.5	−0.8	0.2
South Africa*	2.5	3.8	6.2	−2.0	−2.3	−2.5	0.5	1.5	3.7
Spain*	−6.2	−4.0	−5.5	4.0	5.6	6.5	−2.2	1.6	1.0
Turkey	−3.5	−1.9	−2.3	0.1	0.4	0.9	−3.4	−1.5	−1.4
Yugoslavia*	−3.6	−3.5	−5.3	2.0	2.2	1.9	−1.6	−1.3	−3.4
Other developed countries	−28.4	−19.4	−23.1	5.0	7.6	9.1	−23.4	−11.8	−14.0
Total developed countries	−27.4	2.2	−44.9	1.4	6.8	7.4	−26.0	9.0	−37.5
Oil-exporting countries	62	42	112	−36	−42	−49	26	0	63
Other developing countries	−10	−20	−33	−1	−5	−5	−11	−25	−38
Total developing countries	52	22	79	−37	−47	−54	15	−25	25
Centrally planned economies[4]	−1	−6	0	.	.	.	.	.	.

*Services and transfers account figures for these countries exclude undistributed income from direct investment.

[1]On a transactions basis, except for Greece and New Zealand. [2]Imports and exports partly c.i.f. [3]OPEC countries, plus Bahrain and Oman. [4]Eastern European countries, the Soviet Union and China; partly estimated; based on customs data.

SOURCE: Bank for International Settlements; *Fiftieth Annual Report 1 April 1979–31 March 1980*, p. 94.

TABLE 1.4

Aggregate Current-Account Transactions of OPEC Countries, 1973–79*

Items	1973	1974	1975	1976	1977	1978	1979
	in billions of US dollars						
Exports (f.o.b.)	40	121	113	137	151	146	217
	(100)	(98)	(87)	(100)	(100)	(96)	(97)
Imports (f.o.b.)	−21	−38	−59	−71	−89	−104	−105
	(100)	(139)	(194)	(231)	(265)	(277)	(244)
Trade balance	19	83	54	66	62	42	112
Services and private transfers, net	−12	−14	−19	−26	−31	−37	−43
Official transfers, net	−1	−2	−4	−4	−5	−5	−6
Current account	6	67	31	36	26	0	63
of which:							
Countries with a relatively low absorptive capacity	5	40	24	29	24	10	36
Countries with a relatively high absorptive capacity	1	27	7	7	2	−10	27

Note: Figures in brackets are volume indices (1973 = 100).
*Members of the Organization of Petroleum Exporting Countries (Algeria, Ecuador, Gabon, Indonesia, Iran, Iraq, Kuwait, Libya, Nigeria, Qatar, Saudi Arabia, United Arab Emirates, Venezuela) plus Bahrain and Oman.
SOURCE: Bank for International Settlements, *Fiftieth Annual Report, 1st April 1979 31st March 1980*, p. 85.

TABLE 1.5

Rate of Economic Growth, Defense Spending

	1970	1975	1976	1977	Yearly Rate Sept.-Dec. '77	Jan.-March '78
I. Current Account	2	18	4	−15	−28	−27
II. Net Capital Outflows (other than under III)	5	14	12	18	11	13
III. Official Reserves and Bank Assets (I-II)	−3	4	−8	−33	−39	−41
A. U.S. Assets	−2	14	24	12	35	24
1. Bank Loans	1	14	21	11	35	23
2. Official Reserves	−3	1	3	—	—	−1
B. U.S. Liabilities (−) to	−2	−10	−32	−44	−74	−65
1. Private Holders	6	−3	−14	−7	−11	−2
2. Official Holders:	−8	−7	−18	−37	−62	−65
OPEC	...	−7	−10	−7	−4	−7
Other	...	—	−8	−30	−58	−55
IV. Dollar Depreciation (−) since May 1970, vis-à-vis:						
10 major currencies	−1	−15	−13	−19	−19	−22
Swiss Franc	—	−39	−43	−54	−54	−57
Mark	−7	−28	−35	−42	−42	−44
Yen	—	−15	−13	−33	−33	−33
Pound	—	+19	+41	+26	+26	+29

TABLE 1.6

ELEMENTS IN THE WORLD BALANCE OF PAYMENTS BY COUNTRY GROUP
1971, 1976, 1977, AND 1978

			(Billions of dollars)	
Item and country group	1971	1976	1977	1978
Exports f.o.b.				
World	348.9	985.1	1,121.8	1,285.6
Market economies	315.2	900.0	1,022.0	1,171.0
Developed	253.0	647.5	735.0	876.1
Developing	62.2	252.5	287.8	295.4
Oil-exporting countries	23.3	138.9	152.1	145.5
Other	38.9	113.6	135.0	148.9
Centrally planned economies	33.7	85.0	98.9	114.2
Imports c.i.f.				
World	362.5	1,008.5	1,154.1	1,333.3
Market economies	329.8	916.3	1,053.2	1,216.7
Developed	262.5	702.0	793.8	909.9
Developing	67.2	214.4	259.4	306.7
Oil-exporting countries	12.9	67.8	89.6	104.9
Other	54.3	146.6	169.8	201.8
Centrally planned economies	32.7	92.1	100.9	116.6
Balance of trade				
World	−13.5	−23.4	−32.4	−47.7
Market economies	−14.5	−16.3	−30.4	−45.2
Developed	−9.5	−54.5	−58.8	−33.8
Developing	−5.0	+38.1	28.4	−11.3
Oil-exporting countries	10.4	71.1	62.6	41.6
Other	−15.4	−33.0	−34.1	−52.9
Centrally planned economies	1.0	−7.1	−2.0	−2.5
Changes in international reserves				
Market economies	40.4	30.5	60.4	42.9
Developed	35.2	9.2	38.4	45.9
Developing	5.2	21.3	22.0	−3.0
Oil-exporting countries	3.5	9.3	10.8	−15.5
Other	1.7	12.0	11.2	12.5
Net changes in other balance-of-payments items				
Market economies	54.9	46.9	90.8	88.1
Developed	44.7	63.7	97.2	79.7
Developing	10.2	−16.8	−6.4	8.3
Oil exporting countries	−6.9	−61.8	−51.7	−57.0
Other	17.1	45.0	45.3	75.4

SOURCE: World Economic Survey 1978, United Nations, New York, 1980, p. 22.

In the most difficult financial position are the developing countries that are not oil exporters, and particularly those among them which are becoming considerable consumers of oil but not yet so developed to be able to improve their bargaining position at the world market.

Declining rate of growth. According to an analysis of the relevant U.N. expert teams, published in the "World Economic Survey 1978," the decade of the seventies started with higher rates of growth as compared with the performance after 1973. This is valid for both developed market economies and the centrally planned economies. Toward the end of the decade, the latter group of countries has shown even poorer performance.

2
U.S. Direct Investment Abroad: Foreign Investment in the United States

Commerce links all mankind in one common brotherhood of mutual dependence and interest.
James A. Garfield

Commerce and investment are the equalizers of the wealth of nations.
Gladstone

1

Before the balance-of-payments problem can be thoroughly understood, two more areas must be explored: U.S. direct investment abroad and foreign investment in the United States.

In 1946 the U.S. government undertook the major task of rebuilding the war-torn nations of Western Europe and Japan. It was generally considered that the 1946 loan to Britain and France, the Marshall Plan, and the special fund for reconstructing Japan would provide ample assistance for the repair, rehabilitation, and recovery of industry and trade in Western Europe and Japan. By 1950, industrial output in most of these countries was at the same level as in 1938. Furthermore, the multilateral trade accords negotiated in Geneva (1947) and Annecy (1949) seemed to signal a reduction in the barriers to world commerce.

But the sudden sharp devaluation of the pound sterling, and the weakness of the French franc in September 1949, brought into the open the need to reassess the economic situation of Western Europe and to find a means for furnishing further fundamental assistance. U.S. corporations, with their vast capital, technology, managerial skill, and productive capacity, represented the only source of help at the time to Western Europe and Japan.

The real difficulty was that U.S. assistance through the Marshall Plan

American corporations were induced to invest and establish manufacturing facilities in foreign countries by the following realities at home:

1. Foreign nations' tariffs, import quotas, and currency controls, especially before 1960, severely limited foreign markets for U.S. companies.

2. Direct investment abroad meant reduced transportation costs for locally produced goods and substantially lower production costs.

3. Excess capacity in most of the durable goods industries in the United States led many firms to look abroad for more attractive investment opportunities.

4. Foreign trade barriers. The creation of a European Economic Community, and desire to benefit from the expanding European markets.

5. The international role of the U.S. dollar, and restriction on convertibility of other currencies in Europe and Japan.

6. Patent laws that, in some countries, require firms to manufacture locally in order to obtain patent protection and to achieve the legal status necessary to assert infringement claims.

7. Lower corporate income taxes and more generous depreciation allowances abroad.

What Are the Characteristics of the Multinational Corporation?

To deal with a phenomenon as complex and as heterogeneous as multinational corporations, it is necessary to simplify, although practices vary greatly and it may sometimes be misleading to generalize from specific companies or specific industries.

However, and in spite of the broadness of this definition and the pitfalls inherent in any generalization, it is possible to single out some common denominators characterizing the multinationals, regardless of their field of activity. These specific features apply to (1) the enterprise or corporation, (2) its mode of operations, and (3) its usual economic environment.

The characteristics that apply to the enterprise lie in its particular structures and, conventionally, although not necessarily, in its size.

The outstanding feature of the enterprise is its central direction or control. Regardless of the number of branches, subsidiaries or affiliates of a multinational, its operations are basically initiated, coordinated, and managed from its center or headquarters.

This characteristic (which distinguishes the multinationals from, e.g., an international holding company) and its effects on the sovereignty of the host country are at the core of the present discussion on the role and impact of multinationals.

and other governmental plans had reached a point of diminishing returns. The decline of Britain's economic position, and Western Europe's need to finance large import surpluses even with Marshall Plan aid, caused a continuing disequilibrium in the trade account. Britain, Western Europe, and Japan were no longer able to finance their large imports of capital goods. This situation confronted the United States with a number of significant policy issues, such as: (1) If the rest of the world could not regain its economic health, what would happen to the U.S. surplus in agricultural and manufactured goods? (2) What would be the future of Western Europe and Japan without stable political and economic institutions? This concern was significantly heightened as the Soviets' aggressive intentions in Eastern Europe and the Middle East became apparent. Communism was seen as a great threat to the development of stable and free democratic systems in Western Europe.

The U.S. government, in an unprecedented and generous program (the Marshall Plan), attempted to find answers to these questions by alleviating the economic problems of Western Europe. This was useful as an emergency response to the challenge but not sufficient to have any lasting effect. To continue the momentum, it was argued, a massive capital infusion into Europe was needed. This infusion of capital goods was to be supplied by U.S. corporations, which would also help hold up the postwar demand level in the U.S. domestic economy. In the long run, the rebirth of the European and Japanese economies also held the promise of a greater expansion of world trade.[1]

The U.S. motivation in establishing the Marshall Plan and the private investment policy in Europe and Asia is still being debated: "It is enough for our purposes here," wrote the *New York Times*, "to record that the United States undertook a major problem—economic, political and military—designed to aid the U.S. economy in its transition to peacetime production, and forestall any plans by the Soviet Union to directly, or indirectly, absorb the countries of Western Europe."[2]

In fact, it was this strategy of private investment abroad that planted the first seeds of today's multinational corporations. To clarify the factors underlying investment decisions at the time, it is helpful to classify direct investments abroad by the following functional categories: investments designed to develop foreign sources of raw materials and semimanufactures for American industry; investments designed to promote the distribution and sale in foreign markets of goods produced in the United States; investments designed to provide services in foreign countries, including direct investments in public utilities, transportation and communications, hotels, and various other service industries; and investments in foreign manufacturing enterprises.

What were the incentives for the multinationals? Aside from the pressures and promises of the Truman and Eisenhower administrations,

The extent of central management versus decentralization may vary according to the enterprise and there may be more or less autonomy of branches and affiliates, but there is an invariable characteristic to all multinationals—the existence of a financial and operational link between headquarters and all affiliates. Each operating unit is linked by financial ties allowing the transfer of funds between them and headquarters. Such transfers range from equity investment, dividends, repayments, and loans, to intracompany pricing arrangements.

Typically, the multinational has a large number of branches, affiliates, and production or supply centers in many countries. This introduces the element of size of the firm. Three hundred multinational enterprises—among the largest in the world—have affiliates in twenty or more countries.

There is no universally accepted minimum size, and therefore the number of enterprises in the world considered to qualify as multinationals varies. A comparison between gross national product of countries and gross annual figures of multinationals shows that of the one hundred largest economic units in the world, fifty are national states and fifty multinationals. More than two hundred multinationals have surpassed the $1 billion U.S. level of annual sales. The largest among them is Exxon, whose total sales exceed $110 billion.

A typical mode of operation and of expansion is more difficult to characterize, because it varies according to the sector, or sectors, of industry, in which multinationals operate. Economic theory distinguishes, e.g., three types of operations, according to which the multinational (1) has developed to obtain supplies of raw materials or intermediate goods in a "backward vertical operation," (2) advances new or protects existing markets in an extension of its sales functions—a "forward vertical operation," and (3) operates horizontally within a given sector.

However, some multinationals defy any such classification, having expanded for multiple motives in a wide variety of industrial sectors and economic activities.

Ownership

Whole or majority ownership of affiliates is the prevailing pattern. Multinationals normally prefer retaining full ownership of newly established subsidiaries. In fact, at least 80% of U.S. firms' affiliates and 75% of U.K. affiliates are either wholly owned or majority controlled.

However, corporations are increasingly asked by host countries to undertake operations together with nationals or the government itself of the host country. The result is a variety of joint-venture relations.

The market environment in which multinationals operate is generally oligopolistic. The most typical example is oil, but this also applies, e.g., to computer technology, to the motorcar industry, and, to a growing extent, to the pharmaceutical industry.

A further characteristic of multinationals is that they originate and have their headquarters in the developed market economies—U.S.A., U.K., the EEC countries, Sweden, Switzerland, and Japan (eight of the ten largest multinationals are based in the United States).

The country where the headquarters of the enterprise is located (incorporated) indicates the "nationality" of the enterprise and its origin: very few multinationals have "dual" nationality, i.e., headquarters—e.g., Unilever, Royal Dutch/Shell.

Although the study of multinationals covers different ground from the study of direct foreign investment, it is sometimes difficult to draw a strict dividing line between the two subjects. Direct investment into foreign countries is one element of the multinationals' activity and as such is shown in the statistics of both private capital exporting and importing countries. Government and UN financial-flow figures therefore include the multinationals' investments in overall "private foreign investment" data. This is particularly true for the developing countries, where, because there is a lack of systematic data to provide any quantitative description and breakdown on the multinationals' activity, it can only be assumed that direct private-investment figures coincide with the inflow of capital originating from multinationals.

Areas of Activity

The sectors in which multinationals operate and the very characteristics and the reasons for their growth and expansion are closely interlinked; hence it is difficult to establish a cause-effect relationship. A look at the one hundred, two hundred, or five hundred largest enterprises shows the same pattern as to the industrial areas in which multinationals operate; this, however, neither explains why multinationals are absent from sectors like cotton or textile nor does it prove that any manufacturing enterprise can be typically or untypically an affiliate of a multinational outfit.

The internationalization of finance since the postwar era, the free convertibility of currencies, and the adherence of most developing countries to few monetary zones have promoted the rapid growth of the international banking network: concentration, mergers of large banks, establishment of branches in developing countries, in all free markets—and increasingly in centrally planned countries. But although banks and insurance companies are generally not considered in studies on multinationals, they have comparable characteristics and are essential elements in the world economy in which multinationals operate.

The sector most clearly dominated by multinationals is that of petroleum; companies have grown both through vertical integration—from extraction and refining, to distribution—and horizontally—into processing, derivations, and petrochemicals to the "frontiers" of chemical industry. (It is, however, not foreseeable whether the present structure, extraction-to-distribution pattern, and form of ownership in the oil industry will continue. Technology is standardized and readily available, and the growing, recent political awareness of the relative scarcity of oil, a new flexibility of its price according to the market laws, and the principle of sovereignty over natural resources may initiate rapid changes.)

Concentration on specific industrial activities varies according to the country of origin of the enterprise; it also depends on whether the main concern of the enterprise is to assure the supply of raw material, to secure markets, or to acquire manpower. This distinction applies in a very generalized sense to all areas of activities of the multinationals of the United States, European countries, and Japan.[3]

The Impact on the American Economy

The effects of direct investment abroad on the U.S. economy and its political system are not easily measured. The process has established a vast complex of enterprises abroad that churn out a constant stream of new goods and services. In many direct and indirect ways it has altered the structure of international transactions as well as that of domestic economics. It has created new jobs, new markets, mass production, mass consumption, and a new system of management. It also has internationalized capital and production and established a new world economy.

Since the 1950s the multinationals have become the most reliable vehicles for reallocating national resources, in the developing nations as well as in the industrialized ones. They have created a market for the raw materials of the developing countries, accelerated industrial growth and the transfer of technology, and helped raise the living standard in many nations.

"The internationalization of production," states the U.S. Department of Commerce, "brought about by the development of the multinational corporation is regarded by many analysts as the most important event to have occurred in many years, and very likely its ultimate impact would be on a par with the Industrial Revolution of the Eighteenth Century."

From the late 1950s through the 1960s, U.S. corporations invested heavily in overseas operations, especially in Europe, moving from servicing foreign markets by exports to investing directly in manufacturing plants abroad. In 1958 U.S. foreign investments were $27.4 billion. Ten years later those investments totaled $65 billion, having grown steadily about 10% a year. So great was the increase, in fact, that Servan Schreiber, a member of the French National Assembly, warned that the growing U.S. presence was undermining the economic sovereignty of Europe.

American corporations also moved into developing countries, particularly in Latin America. In 1970 U.S. foreign investment in the developing nations amounted to more than $19 billion—$11 billion of that in Latin America.

By the end of 1979 total foreign investments of U.S. corporations had reached $192.6 billion, a 15% increase over 1978, and nearly $50 billion of that was invested in the developing nations. (An increasing proportion of the investment in those developing countries was in manufacturing rather than in the traditional area of new materials.)

Direct investment income increased 50%, to $37.8 billion. Petroleum affiliates accounted for almost 60% of the increase. Fees and royalties increased 6%, to $5 billion. The increase was primarily in royalties, licenses, fees, and dividends. In the industry category, 20% of the position was in petroleum, 44% in manufacturing, and 36% in other industries. By area, 72% was in developed countries, 24% in developing nations, and 4% fell into the "international and unallocated" category.

U.S Direct Investment at the End of 1979[4]

Canada	$41.0	billion
Europe	$81.0	"
Japan	$ 5.7	"
South Africa	$ 1.7792	"
Latin America Republics and Rest of Western Hemisphere	$36.8	"
Other Foreign Nations	$20.6	"
International Organizations	$ 8.8	"

Despite the significant progress and large returns from foreign investments so far, there is reason to believe that the growth in this area will be slower in the future. After their "invasion" of foreign economies in the 1960s, U.S. firms seem to be beating a retreat now. Though this is by no means a hasty retreat and has not been convincingly reflected as yet in the statistics, it is important to examine its causes.

The basic premise of U.S. government policy toward foreign investment was to let market forces prevail so that global economic efficiency and welfare were maximized. The government even encouraged foreign investment by U.S. firms via tax credits and deferrals on income generated abroad and other measures. But of late certain government policies have put a crimp in the relatively free climate for direct foreign investment (DFI).[5]

An example of this new encroachment was the SEC investigations of corrupt practices by U.S. corporations abroad. In light of revelations of alleged bribery of government officials by Lockheed Corporation and similar cases, legislation forbidding these practices has been enacted. Because of such legislation, businessmen are now leery about establishing operations in countries where corruption is rampant.[6]

Congress probed again into the affairs of U.S. multinationals over the Arab attempt to force a boycott of Israel. Firms that acquiesced to Arab pressure were reprimanded, and more legislation was passed.

The growing concern for human rights has prompted additional legislation restricting the activities of U.S. multinationals. A limited number of proposed investments by U.S. firms in countries where human rights are grossly violated have been discouraged by the State Department, and these companies have been denied guarantees and financing from the Export-Import Bank.

Congress is also under pressure from labor unions, which claim that DFI amounts to "exporting" U.S. jobs. Without discussing the "runaway industry" argument at length, it should be mentioned that there are certain congressmen, particularly those with blue-collar constituencies, who are sympathetic to the demands of labor to restrict DFI and "preserve" U.S. jobs.

The assertion is not being made here that the measures taken by the U.S. government in the above cases are either justified or unjustified. What is important is that these pieces of legislation make up a confusing patchwork of regulations. This confusion, and the prospects for further regulation, can deter a businessman from risking capital for foreign investment overseas.

The regulation of multinational activities by host country governments has also contributed to the changing climate for U.S. DFI. This is particularly true in the case of developing countries. U.S. firms face much tougher contract negotiations and stiffening restrictions on their investments, particularly in Latin America.[7] The Andean countries have been especially strict in formulating guidelines for foreign investments in their countries. In addition to individual and regional efforts to control the multinationals, the United Nations also offers information and expertise to help less-developed countries (LDCs) deal with multinationals. It also seems likely that the United States will at some time in the near future pass a set of internationally recognized guidelines for direct foreign investment, delineating the responsibilities of multinationals and their host countries. If there has been a heyday for U.S. foreign investments, when aggressive businessmen wangled lucrative deals for subsoil rights or for millions of acres of banana trees, that day has certainly passed.

Beyond the tighter DFI regulations in developing countries, potential investors are now wary about the possibility of outright nationalization. This is of particular concern to companies whose direct investment abroad would involve an expensive initial investment, such as in the extractive industries or in heavy manufacturing.

Fears of nationalization have already deterred investors in Indonesia. There, companies with investments already in place have cut back on their operations, and in the case of some U.S. firms—including Phillip Morris, R. J. Reynolds, and three small oil companies— have cut their losses (or expected losses) entirely and left their investments behind for fear that the situation would deteriorate further.[8] Similar fears have also caused U.S. businessmen with investments in Quebec quite a bit of concern because of the growing support for Rene LeVesque's separatist and nationalist movement.[9]

The Difficulties of Joint Ventures

Another factor contributing to the slowdown in foreign investments by U.S. firms is the reluctance of U.S. businessmen to relinquish partial control of their overseas operations. Generally, U.S. firms prefer to manage their foreign plants by themselves and maintain full control. They feel uncomfortable with joint-venture arrangements with the host country. Evidence of this can be found in the dealings between several large U.S. firms and a Brazilian company, Compania Vale do Rio Doce (CVRD). Brazil needed U.S. technology for a large metal-processing plant, but it wanted to maintain some control of the enterprise through a joint-venture arrangement. After considering such an arrangement for an aluminum smelter, Reynolds Metal Company decided not to invest, partly because of its unwillingness to yield some management control to its Brazilian partners. U.S. Steel Corporation actually went ahead and invested with CVRD in an iron-ore project, but after a time the company sold off its holdings, in part because of disagreements with CVRD about control.[10]

U.S. businessmen have had similar difficulties elsewhere with joint ventures, even in Japan, where such projects can be rather appealing to both parties: the Japanese partner gets U.S. technology, while the U.S. partner gets access to the Japanese domestic market. But some of these partnerships, such as that between Sterling Drug and Niigata Engineering Company, have broken up over control disputes.[11] It seems clear that as host countries attempt to exert more control over DFI by outside firms via joint-venture arrangements, U.S. businessmen must either become more accommodating to joint control or else withdraw from foreign operations.

Rising Labor Costs in Europe

U.S. foreign investments have been concentrated largely in Western Europe. In the 1960s' rush of U.S. investment, "le défi Americain," the Europeans felt particularly threatened by the onslaught. DFI in Europe still constitutes a significant portion of U.S. investments abroad—more than $81.4 billion of a total U.S. DFI position of about $192.6 billion at year-end 1979. But according to one analyst, "the bloom is pretty much off the investment rose in Europe as far as American business is concerned."[12] Although DFI in certain sectors is increasing, notably in petroleum, food, transportation, and services, U.S. investment in Europe is generally diminishing.[13]

One reason for this waning interest in Europe is the increased cost of labor. Labor costs are rising at a faster rate than in the United States, and in some areas they are absolutely higher. Even when wages are significantly lower in Europe, the fringe benefits enjoyed by European workers boost the total bill. And European labor costs rise even higher when the current slowdown in productivity is taken into account.

2

Foreign Direct Investment in the United States

Foreign direct investment in the United States at the end of 1979 reached $52.2 billion. It rose 23% following a similar increase in 1978. Equity and intercompany account inflows in 1979 rose 13%, to $6 billion, following a very large increase in 1978. Inflows in both years helped finance the acquisition of several major U.S. companies and expansion of existing U.S. affiliates. The increase reflected continuing confidence in the U.S. economic expansion, rising borrowing costs, and a weakness of the dollar vis-à-vis other currencies.

The return on investments in 1979 rose 43%, to $6 billion, and the rate of return increased to 12.7%, from 10.% in 1978. Contrary to the media's false propaganda, direct investment in the United States did not come primarily from the Arab or OPEC countries, but from Western Europe, Canada, and Japan. Seven countries had positions in excess of $1.8 billion, and together these countries accounted for 90% of the total direct foreign investment in the United States:[14]

(1)	Netherlands and Netherlands Antilles	29%
(2)	United Kingdom	20% +
(3)	Canada	13%
(4)	Germany	8%
(5)	Switzerland	7%
(6)	Japan	7%
(7)	France	5%

The thirteen members of the Organization of Petroleum Exporting Countries together accounted for less than 1% of the total direct investment in the United States, and their position was mostly in real estate and manufacturing.

By industry, 40% of the foreign position investment in the United States was in manufacturing, 22% in trade, 19% in petroleum, 7% in insurance, and 12% in "other" industries. More than one-third of the position in manufacturing was in chemicals, and about one-half of the position in "other" industries was in finance.

About $900 million, or 2% of the position, was in real estate. This sum covers only that part of U.S. real estate owned by foreign parents. Direct investment in an affiliate in another industry, which may *hold* real estate, is classified in the industry of that affiliation.[15]

Ninety-four percent of the foreign direct investment in the United States at the end of 1979 was in incorporated U.S. affiliates, and 6% in unincorporated U.S. affiliates:

Foreign Direct Investment Position in the United States at the End of 1979

All Areas	$52.2
Canada	$ 6.9
Europe, minus England	$26.6
United Kingdom	$ 9.3
Japan	$ 3.4
Others	$ 5.8

In 1979 foreign investment in the United States increased by $9.7 billion. It consisted of equity and intercompany account inflows of $6 billion, reinvested earnings of $3.7 billion, and a small negative valuation adjustment.

There were several reasons for such large direct investments:

1. The rise in the U.S. interest rate, reflecting continued economic expansion. As the cost of borrowing rose in the United States, U.S. affiliates of foreign corporations relied more on funds from their foreign parents and on reinvested earnings, and less on funds borrowed in the U.S. financial markets.

2. Measures taken by the Federal Reserve to stem further depreciation of the dollar against the yen and the Western European currencies.

3. New developments in world economic and political situations which made the United States an attractive place for foreign investments—including the strong rise in U.S. output in the 1974–75 recession, the depreciation of the dollar, the decline in U.S. costs of production compared with those of Japan and Western Europe, and the political stability of the United States compared with the rest of the world.

By origin of foreign parent, the seven industrial countries with the largest positions together accounted for 93% of the additional investment: the Netherlands and Antilles accounted for 31%, the United Kingdom 18%, Japan for about 9%, Germany for 14%, Canada for 9%, and Switzerland and France for 4% each.[16] For the seven countries combined, the addition for 1979 was twice as large as the average increase in 1975–77, with only France and Switzerland investing smaller sums.

By industry, the increases for 1979 were widespread: manufacturing accounted for nearly 30%, petroleum for 22%, trade for 20%, and insurance for 71%. The additions in petroleum and insurance were mainly accounted for by existing U.S. affiliates. The additions in manufacturing largely reflected acquisitions of U.S. companies; the additions in trade were accounted for by expanded activities of existing U.S. affiliates and by the acquisitions of other U.S. companies.

The increase in net purchases of capital stock was aided by the depreciation of the dollar, which reduced U.S. equity prices in terms of a number of foreign currencies. In a few cases foreign parents acquired U.S. companies directly. In many other cases acquisitions of U.S. companies were made by existing U.S. affiliates.

By industry, the increase in petroleum mainly went to existing U.S. affiliates of Netherlands parents; in manufacturing, the increase was largely for acquisitions of U.S. companies in the food, metals, and transportation-equipment industries by United Kingdom, Netherlands, and German parents; in trade, most acquisitions were made by Japanese corporations.

The income of foreign corporations in the United States increased 43% to $6 billion, following a 40% increase in 1978.[17]

All of these statistics indicate that while U.S. firms are withdrawing from direct investment abroad, non-U.S. firms are showing an increased interest in direct investment in the United States. As the wave of U.S. investment recedes from foreign shores, a wave of European, Japanese, and Canadian DFI is arriving. Since 1970 the amount of foreign investments in the United States has nearly tripled. According to the Commerce Department, DFI in the United States stood at $52.2 billion at year-end 1979, compared with $42.4 billion at the end of 1978. Although this figure is small compared with the $192.6 billion worth of U.S. direct investment abroad, it illustrates the fact that foreign investment in the United States has increased markedly over a short period of time.

Obviously, the big lure to foreign businessmen is the potential of the U.S. market, which has the largest mass purchasing power of any market in the world. But that does not explain why businessmen abroad have turned to direct investment here, rather than servicing the American market via exports. The answer is twofold: some foreign businesses are investing directly for aggressive reasons, to expand out of the smaller European markets; other firms are investing as part of a defensive strategy, in order to protect their existing market shares in the United States.

Firms investing in the United States as part of an aggressive strategy are challenged by the opportunity for growth in the U.S. market and believe they can compete successfully with American firms on their own turf. Bosch of Germany is one such company pursuing this aggressive stance; it has already purchased several U.S. companies producing products similar to its own (automobile ignition and lighting systems), and it built its own plant in South Carolina in 1974.[18]

In expanding into the U.S. market, most foreign investors have preferred to acquire an existing firm and keep its management in place rather than build a plant from scratch and import managers from the parent company. This pattern of investment allows the foreign firm to benefit from the American managers' familiarity with the U.S. market. Acquisition of established firms is especially important in the case of consumer goods, where the foreign investor purchases an established marketing network and a brand name, e.g., Baskin-Robbins Ice Cream, Calgon Bath Oil Beads, and Clorox Bleach.

For foreign companies that have already established a market share in the United States via their exports, investing in U.S. competitors is a good defensive strategy. As industrial productivity rose abroad in the late 1960s and 1970s, especially in Japan, countries exporting to the United States initially began improving their sales services here. The product quality and design of foreign goods were also improved and became more attractive in the U.S. marketplace. Thus, for the Japanese and European firms that had a head start over American firms in producing energy-efficient goods, the 1973 oil price rise and the subsequent concern for energy efficiency represented boons.[19] The popularity among U.S. consumers of small gas-saving foreign cars is a case in point. And similar biases have surfaced with railroad cars, as American buyers began looking to Fiat for an energy-efficient product, and with airplanes, as U.S. carriers began looking at the smaller, cheaper European Airbus.

However, that carefully established foreign market share in the United States is now being threatened. One quite obvious reason is the decline in the value of the U.S. dollar. Whereas foreign-produced goods had an advantage because of an overvalued dollar, lower production costs, and some slim profit margins in the early 1970s, that advantage has slowly dissolved. The falling value of the dollar has made exports to the United States more expensive and hence less competitive.

The growing dissatisfaction in the United States over our huge trade deficit has also given foreign firms an impetus to invest directly in the U.S. Congress and the administration have been under heavy pressure from certain industries to prevent foreign dumping: the textile industry, for instance, has been particularly vocal in asking for relief from foreign imports, and the steel industry has successfully pressured for an "orderly marketing arrangement" to curtail dumping of Japanese and European products.

Foreign businessmen are thus afraid of being closed out of the market by higher import duties, voluntary quotas, and other nontariff barriers. To get around these potential barriers, Japanese textile manufacturers are often investing directly in the United States.[20] Japanese television makers have already pursued this strategy successfully. Honda has a motorcycle plant in this country and is now considering building cars in the United States, as are Datsun, Toyota, and Renault.[21] Volkswagen has already started producing its Rabbit model at its plant in Pennsylvania.

Besides the attractive size of the American market, foreign businessmen have expressed confidence in the basic strength of the U.S. economy. Despite the immediate difficulties of inflation and recession, they believe that the prospects for a strong recovery over the long term are good.[22] To quote an associate of European financier Baron Lambert, "The Baron is less interested in Europe these days. He thinks the future is in the U.S."[23] And an analysis by Morgan Guaranty Trust Company describes foreign investors as "bullish on America." In fact, the stable business environment offered by the United States is the most important factor in the decision of foreign firms to invest directly in this country. They are drawn by a relatively nondisruptive relationship between labor and management, a state of political stability, and a belief by most Americans in the basic advantages of the market system.

In contrast, labor costs in Europe have been steadily rising for several years, as unions have demanded higher wages and more benefits,[24] and—of greater concern to European businessmen—there is a growing militancy in the labor movement abroad. The situation in Britain is particularly acute. Strikes have severely disrupted the economy, and union pressure contributed to the demise of both the Callaghan government and the Tory government that preceded it. Now the unions are demanding representation on corporate boards of directors. Looking at the relations between labor and management in the United States, foreign businessmen are understandably envious.

The U.S. political environment is also attractive to foreign investors. Despite ceaseless government intervention, the market system here is unfettered in comparison to some European social welfare states. Although the people of these nations enjoy the benefits of redistributed income and state-provided services and subsidies, high tax rates that act as disincentives to capital investment and entrepreneurship are taking their toll in reduced efficiency and overall output. By contrast, the United States is still free from nationalization and state socialism. "America is a haven for growth and opportunity."[25]

All this is augmented by the appreciation of most foreign currencies against the dollar, the depressed state of the stock market, and the growth of a foreign banking network in this country.

In a pattern similar to that followed by foreign manufacturers and industrialists, foreign banks have been rushing into the United States in the last few years. According to the Federal Reserve Board, the total assets of foreign banks in May 1978 were $98.6 billion, up from $24.4 billion in November 1972. At year-end 1972 foreign banks had 54 branches, subsidiaries, or agencies of some kind in the United States. By May 1978 they had 176 such facilities here.[26] Of the top five foreign banking investors in the United States, two are Japanese, one is French, one is Canadian, and one is a European group venture.[27]

As a foreign company moves into the U.S. market, its home bank will often follow in order to service the subsidiaries and affiliates. This may make it somewhat easier for the foreign firm to finance its U.S. investments, since American banks generally prefer to provide financing for American firms, with which they are familiar.[28]

However, foreign banks do not come to the United States solely to do business with foreign firms; they also try to offer credit and other services to American firms at very competitive rates in order to win their commercial loan business.

3

The issue of U.S. corporate investment abroad generates the most controversy over its effect on domestic employment. U.S. labor unions can produce reams of data showing that it costs American jobs via the "runaway industry" argument. Business can produce equally impressive statistics proving that American foreign investment actually increases employment. They argue that by building an assembly plant overseas, a U.S. firm actually increases its exports of intermediate goods to the foreign subsidiary and will, therefore, take on more workers at home to produce those export goods. This argument between labor and management tends to go on ad infinitum.

A study by Thomas Horst at the Brookings Institution offers convincing evidence that neither the labor nor the management position is precisely correct.[29] He shows that the actual effect of DFI on U.S. jobs depends on the reasons for the particular investment, the type of operation established overseas, and the nature of the domestic industry. For example, if an American firm invests overseas in order to establish an assembly operation, exports of components from the U.S. plant are likely to increase. If, on the other hand, the firm establishes a full product manufacturing operation, exports are likely to decrease and jobs may be lost to American workers. If those foreign-made products are then exported back into this country and effectively compete with American-made products, even more jobs may be lost.

Horst also draws attention to the fact that, in some cases, if a firm does not invest abroad it will lose its export market entirely. This possible loss of foreign-market share may be the result of an inability to provide adequate overseas sales or service operations or to make adaptations in a product for local conditions overseas. It may also be the result of increased restrictions on the import of assembled products by the foreign country. "Whether employment and the balance of trade benefit or whether they suffer depends on the nature of the investment," Horst says in his book. "Both historical and case study literature reveal the heterogeneous economic circumstances in which foreign investment takes place and the variety of possibilities that could have happened had the investment not been made."[30] Given these conclusions that no definitive correlation among foreign investment, exports, and employment can be established, it is thus difficult to determine what effect the slowdown in U.S. investments abroad will have on employment in this country.

However, the effect of direct investment by foreign nations in this country can generally be considered beneficial, a positive step toward the maximization of global welfare. Foreign investments in the U.S. have the effect of creating more competition in the marketplace, a desired condition in a free-market system. They facilitate the transfer of technology into the United States. And they give the American consumer a greater choice of goods, again a desired goal in our market economy.

The effects of foreign investment may be illustrated by an examination of Japanese direct investment in the television industry in the United States. Japanese producers of television sets have been shifting away from servicing the U.S. market through exports in favor of establishing plants within the country. In 1978, 1.2 million sets were produced by Japanese manufacturers operating in the United States, and this figure is expected to double by 1983.[31] Matsushita purchased Motorola in 1974 and plans to replace most of its Japan-made imports with Quasar television sets made in its new Chicago factory. Sanyo had similar plans for servicing the American market with its 75% share of Warwick Electronics. Sony, meanwhile, started with an assembly operation in its newly acquired San Diego plant in 1972, using 30 workers to turn out 10,000 units per year. By 1977 the company had moved into integrated production and was employing 1,200 workers and producing 400,000 television sets per year—some 60% of Sony's sales in the United States.[32] Toshiba now has plans to build a plant in Tennessee to produce television sets for the U.S. market. Hitachi has joined with General Electric Company to form General Television of America. This arrangement brings together Hitachi's technology and G.E.'s facilities to establish a broad marketing network in America.[33]

The most important reason for the influx of Japanese investments has been the possibility of further import restrictions by U.S. authorities. Voluntary quotas and other barriers have already set limits on the quantity of Japanese television sets that can be imported into this country. A 1977 voluntary marketing arrangement now limits Japanese television imports to 1.75 million sets. Yet, imports were nearly 3 million sets. By establishing operations in the United States, behind the import barriers, Japanese producers are thus able to circumvent such restrictions. As restrictions tighten still more, the Japanese-owned plants in this country are expected to shift from simple assembly operations into more integrated production, utilizing additional American-made components.

The Japanese DFI strategy has met with considerable success. As the figures cited show, production of Japanese TV sets in the United States has jumped markedly over a period of a few years, proof that the companies involved have successfully maintained their market share. Quasar, in fact, has gained an additional 2% of the market since its takeover by Matsushita.[34]

The one area where the effects of foreign investment in the United

States have been viewed in a less favorable light is in real estate, particularly farmland. These "flurries of incipient xenophobia"[35] are the result of the special significance that Americans attach to land. Thus real estate is viewed as something more than an economic asset; farmland and the lifestyle associated with it represent basic values to most Americans.

The extent of foreign investment in American real estate is difficult to assess. Real estate purchases are often conducted through local agents, and foreign buyers prefer to remain anonymous. There is evidence of foreign interests in American office buildings, especially in the Southeast, Southwest, and West. Foreign-owned high rises in Houston have attracted particular attention.[36] It is unclear, though, whether all the talk and the high visibility of some foreign investments are matched by actual investment.

A study of U.S. farmland purchased by foreigners was conducted by the General Accounting Office in response to a request from the Senate Agriculture Committee. The study examined all farm purchases in 148 counties in 10 states over the course of an 18-month period. The analysis concluded that foreigners had purchased more than 248,000 acres out of 3 million that changed hands. These purchases by foreigners tended to be concentrated in a few counties.[37] The acreage was larger, on average, than that purchased by local buyers. Although American farm groups had increased concern about foreigners bidding up the price of farmland and making it inaccessible to local farmers, the GAO study concluded that foreign buyers had not consistently paid more for land than American buyers were paying for similar property.[38]

There also was fear that foreign ownership of farmland would adversely affect local communities and the food supply system. The GAO report, however, found that the foreign-owned farms usually retained local farmers to operate them and that the farms remained part of the local business communities. The land thus continued to be run as a productive venture and improvements were made in many cases. From the data presently available, it appears that foreign investment in farmland has had no adverse effect on the United States.[39]

The motive for foreign investment in farmland is similar to that for foreign investments in U.S. industry. Foreigners are attracted by a strong, stable economic and political climate. Purchases of U.S. farmland thereby represent a secure investment that will appreciate steadily.

4

U.S. Policy toward Foreign Investments by U.S. Firms

An analysis of present U.S. policy toward investments by U.S. firms reveals that the administration does not have a coherent, consistent policy toward foreign investments. The regulations that do apply constitute a patchwork of narrow policies with little coordination between them or the agencies administering them. Responsibility for implementing the various regulations is spread out among the Departments of State, Treasury, and Commerce, and numerous other government agencies.

Basically, there are three primary areas in which U.S. policy pertains to foreign investment by American firms: taxation, insurance against noncommercial risk, and expropriation.[40]

The Internal Revenue Code contains provisions for tax credits and tax deferrals for U.S. corporate income generated in overseas operations. The premise of these credits and deferrals is that U.S. corporations should not be taxed twice on earned income—once by the government of the foreign country where the direct investment is located, and again by the United States.

The Export Credit Insurance provides insurance against noncommercial risks for U.S. companies with overseas investments. These risks would include, for example, the threat of war on currency nonconvertibility. The objective of the insurance is to relieve some of the risk assumed by U.S. companies doing business abroad and thereby to encourage the global expansion of business.

Attempts to provide guarantees against expropriation of U.S. firms by foreign governments have also been undertaken by Congress. The Hickenlooper Amendment to the Foreign Assistance Act prohibits the disbursement of foreign aid to any country that has expropriated property of a U.S. firm without fair, prompt, and adequate compensation. The Hickenlooper Amendment has been applied in only one instance, and it has since been revised to allow more flexibility in its application. Unfortunately, it is now an awkward diplomacy tool, tying foreign policy to the interests of American business.

More recently, Congress has addressed itself to, among other issues, the bribery of government officials by U.S. businessmen, the participation of U.S. firms in the Arab boycott of Israel, the activities of U.S. firms in countries with poor human rights records, and labor charges against "runaway industries" (see chapter 4).

These are several other areas in which foreign investment is affected by U.S. official policy, though in a less direct fashion. Federal antitrust laws apply to the foreign subsidiaries of U.S. corporations. Overseas subsidiaries are also covered by regulations pertaining to negotiations between labor and management as established in the National Labor Relations Act. Of course, American trade and monetary policy, and the administration's economic policy in general, will also indirectly affect direct investments abroad by U.S. firms.

All these regulations make up what has been characterized as an "electic ad hoc approach" to foreign investments abroad.[41] This confusing morass has hurt U.S. interests all over the world.

The official U.S. policy on direct investment by foreigners in the United States is also founded on the premise that unfettered, free-market forces will maximize global economic efficiency and welfare. "Accordingly, the basic policy toward foreign investors in the U.S. is to grant them national treatment, that is to freely admit and to treat them on the basis of equality with domestic investors in their U.S. operations.[42]

There are no special federal incentives to encourage foreign investments in the United States. Certain states, however, have successfully attracted investments through tax breaks, financing aid, and other measures. These states have been concerned about the devastating effects that ailing major industries can have on communities whose livelihoods depend on that industry. For example, the closing of a textile plant in South Carolina may put most of the community's population out of work. In these situations, direct investment by a foreign business via the establishment of a factory represents a revitalization of the community, and local and state officials have gone to great lengths to attract that kind of foreign investments.

There are a few federal barriers to foreign investment in the United States, though. Foreign business is prohibited from participating in the atomic energy industry, the hydroelectric power industry, radio broadcasting, mining on federal lands, domestic air transport, and coastal and internal shipping. With these exceptions, foreign firms operating in the United States are treated as domestic firms, subject to antitrust legislation, tax laws, and Securities and Exchange Commission disclosures where applicable.

For a time, the operation of foreign banks was the one exception to the U.S. policy of treating foreign operations the same as domestic ones. The foreign banks were not subject to all of the domestic regulations on branching and interstate operations, FDIC surety deposits, or Federal Reserve Board controls. In September 1978, after the federal and domestic banks argued that this put the foreigners at a distinct advantage, this situation was remedied with the passage of the International Banking Act (PL 95-369), which places foreign banks operating in the United States on an equal footing with U.S. domestic banks.

In any consideration of the regulation of foreign investments, it should be kept in mind that the amount of foreign business in America is less than one-quarter the amount of investment by U.S. firms abroad. If discriminatory action were taken by the United States against foreign firms, foreign governments could quite easily retaliate against American firms in their own countries. Evidence from the direct foreign investments now in the United States indicates that the present policy of treating foreign enterprises on the same basis as domestic enterprises should be maintained.

TABLE 2.1

Comparison of Combined Total Assets of the Ten Largest Foreign- and U.S.-Based Nonpetroleum Industrial Companies

(Ranked by 1976 Sales)

	Combined Total Assets			
	1965	1970	1973	1976
		(In billions)		
Ten largest foreign-based companies:				
Combined total assets	$ 15.6	$ 33.2	$ 54.0	$ 76.2
Percentage increase over 1965	—%	113%	246%	388%
Ten largest U.S.-based companies:				
Combined total assets	$ 45.1	$ 65.9	$ 89.4	$113.6
Percentage increase over 1965	—%	46%	98%	152%

TABLE 2.2

Home Countries for Top 500 non-U.S. Industrials

Europe (EEC)

Netherlands		10
Luxembourg		1
Belgium		9
U.K.		87
France		46
Germany		67
Italy		14
Denmark		4
	Total	241*

Europe (Other Europe)

Spain		12
Norway		6
Austria		5
Finland		6
Sweden		25
Switzerland		14
	Total	68**

*includes also 1 "Britain-Ned.," 1 "Britain-Italy," "Ned.-Britain"

South America

Brazil		7
Chile		1
Mexico		2
Venezuela		2
	Total	12

Canada   39

Japan   117

TABLE 2.3

U.S. DIRECT INVESTMENT ABROAD—DIRECT INVESTMENT POSITION AND INCOME, BY COUNTRY, 1970 TO 1977, AND BY SELECTED INDUSTRIES, 1977

[In millions of dollars. Minus sign (−) denotes decrease. See also *Historical Statistics, Colonial Times to 1970*, series U 41-46]

Country	Direct Investment Position (at yearend)							1977, prel.			Income[2]						1977, prel.		
	1970	1973	1974	1975	1976	Total[1]	Man-u-fac-turing	Petro-leum	Fi-nance, insur-ance	1970	1973	1974	1975	1976	Total[1]	Man-u-fac-turing	Petro-leum	Fi-nance, insur-ance
All areas	75,480	101,313	110,078	124,050	136,396	148,782	65,604	30,887	19,972	8,169	16,542	19,156	16,615	18,999	19,851	7,326	5,481	3,095
Developed countries	51,819	72,214	82,895	90,695	100,398	108,047	53,364	24,854	9,668	4,577	10,052	10,418	9,509	11,461	11,889	6,018	2,086	1,280
Canada	21,015	25,541	28,404	31,038	33,932	35,398	16,658	7,722	3,700	1,518	2,844	3,394	3,412	3,837	3,341	1,344	992	307
Europe[3]	25,255	38,255	44,652	49,305	55,139	60,591	31,926	5,491	2,401	5,751	5,713	4,989	6,169	7,125	4,165	822	848	
Euro. Econ. Commun. (EEC)[4]	20,104	30,919	35,323	38,773	43,215	47,539	27,520	5,473	3,481	1,919	4,426	4,042	3,620	4,755	3,755	582	607	
Belgium and Luxembourg	1,546	2,512	2,945	3,306	3,558	4,155	2,498	452	435	158	426	375	270	263	360	308	−119	95
Denmark and Ireland	571		1,160	1,295	1,632	1,888	1,025	514	32	45	131	165		267	259	222	−45	8
France	2,643	4,295	4,902	5,743	5,947	6,093	4,138	913	204	237	585	383	657	484	378	312	−7	14
Germany	4,313	7,650	7,971	8,726	10,497	11,003	6,993	2,238	993	588	1,415	1,079	956	1,945	1,609	1,388	16	102
Italy	1,464	2,212	2,680	2,679	2,934	2,969	1,964	606	99	85	225	205	90	664	301	267	−42	41
Netherlands	1,550	2,352	3,127	3,097	3,509	4,010	2,011	1,233	192	180	413	753	540	842	909	290	454	52
United Kingdom	8,016	11,040	12,537	13,927	15,137	17,420	8,872	5,311	1,525	626	1,278	1,081	936	1,414	1,802	967	325	297
Other Western Europe[3]	5,151	7,336	9,329	10,532	11,924	13,052	3,889	364	2,010	483	1,277	1,671	1,369	1,414	1,508	410	239	241
Japan (incl. Okinawa)	1,482	2,671	3,319	3,339	3,797	4,082	1,889	1,549	148	228	514	393	233	417	512	299	76	67
Australia, N. Zealand, So. Africa	4,067	5,746	6,520	7,013	7,530	7,976	3,428	1,657	329	430	943	919	875	1,038	911	210	196	58
Developing countries[6]	19,192	22,904	19,848	26,288	28,884	33,706	12,239	3,014	8,759	2,941	5,840	7,927	6,703	7,047	7,756	1,308	3,362	1,787
Latin American Republics[7]	11,104	13,527	14,597	16,394	17,125	18,729	9,331	1,768	2,295	1,206	2,000	2,297	2,155	1,906	2,241	904	369	350
Mexico, Panama, and other Central America	3,644	4,506	5,141	5,811	5,617	6,124	2,733	190	1,052	264	609	820	926	370	647	221	35	121
Argentina	1,022	1,144	1,138	1,154	1,366	1,505	930	223	91	109	71	47	103	246	273	70	139	26
Brazil	1,526	2,885	3,760	4,579	5,416	5,956	3,935	364	564	208	426	464	657	731	681	362	60	115
Chile	758	643	287	174	179	187	52	(D)		81	6	20	(Z)	22	15	5	9	(Z)
Colombia	584	608	617	648	654	706	436	71	93	43	46	90	53	79	92	68	5	9
Peru	744	859	900	1,221	1,364	1,409	157	328		74	90	47	−88	46	76	−4	31	(Z)
Venezuela	2,241	2,051	1,804	1,506	1,779	917	223	151	395	623	573	344	262	310	157	61	12	
Other Western Hemisphere	1,858	2,957	4,931	5,773	6,809	9,009	623	1,611	5,783	215	512	848	1,067	1,573	1,672	108	220	1,146
Other Africa[8]	2,427	2,376	2,233	2,414	2,775	2,783	266	1,520	76	522	668	1,029	534	610	586	29	461	12
Middle East[9]	1,545	226	−6,432	−4,040	−3,730	−3,083	193	−4,378	153	711	1,730	2,092	1,643	1,941	1,891	10	1,607	85
Other Asia and Pacific	2,260	3,818	4,519	5,747	5,904	6,267	1,826	2,493	453	287	931	1,660	1,304	1,017	1,387	257	706	195
International and unallocated[6]	4,469	6,196	7,335	7,067	7,114	7,029	(X)	3,019	1,546	650	650	811	404	492	205	(X)	34	28

D Withheld to avoid disclosure of data of individual companies. X Not applicable. Z Less than $500,000. [1]Includes industries not shown separately. [2]Equals sum of interest, dividends, earnings of unincorporated affiliates, and reinvested earnings. [3]Includes Mediterranean possessions and countries. Excludes Eastern Europe. [4]As of Jan. 1, 1973, United Kingdom, Denmark, and Ireland became members of EEC. For consistency, data for all years are shown on same basis. [5]Excludes Okinawa. [6]Shipping companies operating under flags of convenience, primarily Panama and Liberia, included in "International and unallocated." [7]Includes countries not shown below. [8]Includes Egypt and all other in Africa except South Africa. [9]Includes Bahrain, Iran, Israel, Jordan, Kuwait, Lebanon, Oman, Qatar, Saudi Arabia, South Yemen, Syria, Trucial States, Oman, and Yemen. Negative position occurs when U.S. parent company's liabilities to the foreign affiliate are greater than its investment in the foreign affiliate.

SOURCE: U.S. Bureau of Economic Analysis, *Survey of Current Business*, August 1978, and supplement titled *Revised Data Series on U.S. Direct Investment Abroad, 1966–76*. 1978 Results—43.3 billion.

TABLE 2.4

FOREIGN DIRECT INVESTMENT IN THE UNITED STATES—VALUE, BY AREA AND INDUSTRY: 1950 TO 1978

Area & Industry	1950	1955	1960	1965	1970	1973	1974	1975	1976	1977	1978 prel.
All areas	3,391	5,076	6,910	8,797	13,270	20,556	25,144	27,662	30,770	34,595	40,833
Petroleum	405	853	1,238	1,710	2,992	4,792	5,614	6,213	5,921	6,573	7,885
Manufacturing	1,138	1,759	2,611	3,478	6,140	8,231	10,387	11,386	12,619	14,030	16,289
Finance & Ins.	1,065	1,499	1,810	2,169	2,256	3,414	2,723	3,152	2,943	4,544	5,179
Trade, wholesale & retail	(NA)	(NA)	634	748	994	3,117	4,387	4,844	6,123	7,237	8,884
Canada	1,029	1,542	1,934	2,388	3,117	4,203	5,136	5,352	5,907	5,650	6,166
Petroleum	56	196	203	208	190	426	547	596	676	710	782
Manufacturing	468	711	932	1,219	1,836	2,319	2,905	3,061	3,386	3,077	3,323
Finance & Ins.	153	179	246	370	324	293	311	341	422	367	457
Europe	2,228	3,369	4,707	6,076	9,554	13,937	16,756	18,584	20,162	23,754	27,895
Petroleum	349	657	1,028	1,478	2,777	4,079	4,714	5,478	4,999	5,523	6,630
Manufacturing	669	1,040	1,611	2,167	4,091	4,790	6,109	6,673	7,426	9,267	10,905
Finance & Ins.	870	1,272	1,504	1,724	1,805	2,086	1,829	2,088	2,637	3,076	3,492
United Kingdom	1,168	1,749	2,248	2,852	4,127	5,403	5,744	6,331	5,802	6,397	7,370
Petroleum	95	204	339	511	1,220	1,212	1,502	(D)	602	486	484
Manufacturing	337	510	722	839	1,391	1,551	1,792	1,833	1,964	2,305	2,930
Finance & Ins.	554	836	953	1,176	1,141	1,198	854	932	1,211	1,425	1,568
Netherlands	334	613	947	1,304	2,151	4,017	4,698	5,347	6,255	7,830	9,767
Petroleum	226	411	639	887	1,311	(D)	(D)	(D)	(D)	(D)	5,073
Manufacturing	44	127	213	328	652	997	1,213	1,345	1,500	2,237	2,842
Switzerland	348	522	773	940	1,546	1,420	1,949	2,138	2,295	2,651	2,844
Manufacturing	204	282	427	590	1,147	922	1,222	1,308	1,357	1,769	1,917
Finance & Ins.	147	223	300	303	351	313	263	365	(D)	486	538
Other Europe	377	485	739	980	1,731	3,097	4,366	4,768	5,810	6,876	7,914
Petroleum	28	42	50	80	246	(D)	(D)	494	(D)	(D)	1,065
Manufacturing	84	121	249	410	901	1,319	1,882	2,187	2,605	2,956	3,216
Finance & Ins.	135	176	209	209	255	426	442	445	(D)	592	697
Japan	134	165	269	{118	229	152	345	591	1,178	1,755	2,688
Other Areas				214	370	2,264	2,907	3,135	3,523	3,436	4,081

SOURCE: U.S. Bureau of Economic Analysis, *Foreign Business Investments in the United States*.

TABLE 2.5
International Transactions—Reserve Assets
U.S. BALANCES ON INTERNATIONAL TRANSACTIONS, BY AREAS AND SELECTED COUNTRIES: 1975 TO 1977

[In millions of dollars. Balances by area have some shortcomings due to statistical discrepancies including errors, omissions, and incorrect area attributions. Minus sign (−) denotes debits]

Area or Country	1975, Balance on—			1976, Balance on—			1977, Balance on—		
	Merchandise trade[1]	Goods and services	Current account	Merchandise trade[1]	Goods and services	Current account	Merchandise trade[1]	Goods and services	Current account
All areas	9,047	23,060	18,445	−9,353	9,361	4,339	−31,059	−10,514	−15,221
Euro. Econ. Community[2]	6,341	3,700	3,823	7,195	5,393	5,443	4,414	2,734	2,853
United Kingdom	1,144	254	258	947	23	−21	901	604	545
Belgium-Luxembourg	1,280	1,299	1,291	1,889	1,883	1,875	1,697	1,841	1,832
France	962	1,204	1,164	1,005	1,118	1,072	530	726	680
Germany	−306	−2,014	−1,684	−192	−949	−616	−1,412	−2,904	−2,471
Italy	464	290	170	533	490	350	−250	−421	−570
Netherlands	2,727	2,519	2,509	3,134	2,893	2,881	2,736	2,628	2,615
Other Western Europe	2,779	2,161	1,867	1,689	1,521	1,165	1,490	1,241	827
Eastern Europe	2,515	2,662	2,596	3,226	3,423	3,351	1,786	1,998	1,936
Canada	1,827	6,809	6,673	−139	5,931	5,794	−1,371	4,896	4,752
Latin Amer., other W. Hem.	931	5,276	4,604	−361	4,789	4,032	−252	2,604	1,842
Japan[3]	−1,690	−1,178	−1,220	−5,335	−5,359	−5,402	−7,984	−8,091	−8,134
Australia and South Africa[4]	1,266	2,518	2,494	1,441	3,132	3,104	988	2,542	2,510
Other Asia and Africa	−4,922	1,441	−1,721	−16,760	−8,937	−12,311	−26,476	−17,334	−20,414
International and unallocated	—	−329	−671	−309	−532	−838	−654	−1,104	−1,394

—Represents zero. [1]Adjusted to balance of payments basis; excludes exports under U.S. military sales contracts and imports under direct defense expenditures. [2]Includes Denmark, Ireland, European Atomic Energy Community, European Coal and Steel Community, and European Investment Bank, not shown separately. [3]Includes Ryukyu Islands. [4]Includes New Zealand.
SOURCE: U.S. Bureau of Economic Analysis, *Survey of Current Business*, June 1978.

U.S. RESERVE ASSETS: 1960 TO 1978
[In millions of dollars. As of end of year or month]

Type	1960	1965	1970	1972	1973	1974	1975	1976	1977	1978, June
Total	19,359	15,450	14,487	13,151	14,378	15,883	16,226	18,747	19,312	18,864
Gold stock[1]	17,804	13,806	11,072	10,487	11,652	11,599	11,598	11,719	11,706	
Special drawing rights	—	—	851	1,958	2,166	2,374	2,335	2,395	2,629	2,804
Convertible foreign currencies	—	781	629	241	8	5	80	320	18	84
Reserve position in IMF[2]	1,555	863	1,935	465	552	1,852	2,212	4,434	4,946	4,270

—Represents zero.
[1]Includes gold in Exchange Stabilization Fund; excludes gold held under earmark at Federal Reserve banks for foreign and international accounts. [2]International Monetary Fund.

U.S. LIABILITIES TO FOREIGNERS, BY AREAS AND COUNTRIES: 1975 TO 1978

[In millions of dollars. As of end of year or month. Represents liabilities as reported by banks in the U.S. "Foreigners" refers to international and regional organizations, foreign governments, central banks, and other official institutions, as well as banks, organizations, and individuals domiciled abroad and foreign subsidiaries and offices of U.S. banks and commercial firms]

Area or Country	1975	1976	1977	1978, May	Area or Country	1975	1976	1977	1978, May
Total	95,590	110,659	126,168	137,028	Latin American and Caribbean[1]	15,028	19,132	23,670	24,804
Europe[1]	44,072	47,076	60,295	62,932	Bahamas	1,874	2,770	3,596	3,324
France	7,726	4,876	5,269	6,275	British West Indies	1,311	1,877	3,998	3,961
Germany, F. R.	4,543	6,241	7,239	9,537	Venezuela	3,309	3,118	2,929	3,299
Italy	1,059	3,182	6,857	6,364					
Netherlands	3,407	3,003	2,869	2,993	Asia[1]	22,384	29,766	30,488	35,495
Switzerland	8,476	9,460	12,343	12,516	Japan	10,207	14,363	14,616	19,999
United Kingdom	6,867	10,018	14,125	11,606	Middle East oil-exporting countries[2]	7,355	9,360	8,979	7,842
					Other	5,488	4,310	3,832	3,908
Canada	2,919	4,659	4,607	6,620	Int'l and regional[3]	5,699	5,714	3,274	3,179

[1]Includes countries not shown separately. [2]Bahrain, Iran, Iraq, Kuwait, Oman, Qatar, Saudi Arabia, and United Arab Emirates. [3]Excludes Bank for International Settlements, which is included in Europe.
SOURCE: Board of Governors of the Federal Reserve System, *Federal Reserve Bulletin*, monthly.

Notes

1. Douglas C. Abbott, Canadian minister of finance, September 1949.
2. *New York Times,* October 31, 1949.
3. The author is indebted to the United Nations documents concerning multinational corporations.
4. U.S. Department of Commerce, *Survey of Current Business* (August 1980).
5. H. Mulmgren, *Multinational Business* (New York, 1978).
6. *Business Week,* April 18, 1979.
7. T. H. Moran, *Multinational Corporations, and the Politics of Dependence* (Princeton, N.J.: Princeton University Press, 1974).
8. *Business Week,* April 18, 1977.
9. *Wall Street Journal,* January 24, 1977.
10. *Business Week,* August 22, 1977.
11. *Wall Street Journal,* November 8, 1976.
12. S. S. Katz, *European Community* (November–December 1976).
13. R. Waldeman, *European Community* (November–December 1976).
14. U.S. Department of Commerce, Bureau of Economic Analysis, *Survey of Current Business,* August 1980.
15. Ibid.
16. Ibid.
17. Income consists of foreign parents' share in the net income (after deduction of U.S. income taxes) of their U.S. affiliates, plus net interest payments on intercompany accounts, less withholding taxes on dividends and interest.
18. *Business Week,* August 29, 1977.
19. L. G. Franke, *Harvard Business Review* (November–December 1978), pp. 98–99.
20. *Oriental Economist* (June 1977), p. 8.
21. *European Community* (July–August 1978), pp. 10–14.
22. Ibid., p. 22.
23. *Business Week,* February 21, 1977, p. 102.
24. *Wall Street Journal,* March 3, 1977, p. 1.
25. *European Community* (July–August, 1978), p. 20.
26. *Morgan Guaranty Survey* (September 1978), p. 14.
27. *Forbes,* September 15, 1976.
28. W. Gundlach, *Euromoney* (September 1976), p. 72.
29. Horst and Moran, *American Multinationals and American Interests* (Washington, D.C.: Brookings Institution, 1978).
30. Ibid., p. 96.
31. *Business Week,* May 8, 1978, p. 86.
32. *Oriental Economist* (July 1977), pp. 10–11.
33. *Business Week,* May 8, 1978, pp. 86–88.
34. *Wall Street Journal,* October 19, 1978, p. 1.
35. *Morgan Guaranty Survey* (September 1978), p. 13.
36. *Business Week,* September 6, 1976, pp. 62–66.
37. U.S. General Accounting Office, *Foreign Investment in U.S. Agricultural Land—How It Shapes Up* (July 1979), p. ii.
38. Ibid., p. vi.
39. Ibid., p. 88.
40. Bergsten,
41. U.S. Department of Commerce, *Foreign Direct Investment in the United States* (October 1975–77).

3
International Trade of the United States

> There is nothing so useful to man in general, nor so beneficial to particular societies and individuals, as profitable trade. This is the alma mater at whose plentiful breast all mankind is nourished.
>
> John Fielding
>
> I ask you to protect the rights and interests of labor generally; in the first place by allowing no free imports from countries which meet you with countervailing duties and do not accept principles of reciprocity.
>
> Benjamin Disraeli

1

The largest component in the U.S. balance of international payments is foreign trade. For this reason, shifts and trends in the trade balance will have significant effects on the overall U.S. balance-of-payments position. In order to determine more precisely the effect these changes in exports and imports of goods have had on the U.S. balance-of-payments deficit, this chapter presents a brief survey of the trends in the U.S. trade balance over the past two decades.

The emphasis will be on the latter part of this period, during which the United States ran a persistent trade deficit. The focus will be on the broad trends. Detailed statistics can be found at the end of the chapter.

Throughout the 1950s and into the 1960s, the United States maintained a consistent trade surplus. The size of this surplus ranged from $7.8 billion in 1957 down to $2.4 billion in 1959 and back up to $6.8 in 1964. These fluctuations can be ascribed largely to changing business conditions abroad. As foreign economies weakened, U.S. exports fell, as those economies regained strength, U.S. exports increased. By contrast, the U.S. economy grew consistently and demand for imports increased steadily as a result of this economic growth.

It is toward the end of the 1960s that a significantly weakening U.S. trade position can be detected. The United States maintained a trade surplus of about $3.8 billion in 1967, but this dwindled to $660 million by 1969.

This deterioration can be explained by two principal factors: First, U.S.

trade deficits with Japan, West Germany, and Canada increased significantly. By 1968 the United States was running a deficit with Japan alone that exceeded $1 billion.

Second, the United States was encountering more competition in world markets. The Japanese and West Germans increased their percentage of world trade while the U.S. percentage dropped from 17.5% in 1964 to 14.2% in 1971.

A recession in the United States in 1970 caused a sharp decline in imports and a subsequent trade surplus. But the revival of the U.S. economy in 1971 brought with it a renewed surge in imports and a $2.8 billion trade deficit.

During 1973 the United States ran moderate surpluses with most countries, but these were more than offset by a $1.4 billion deficit with Japan, a $2.6 billion deficit with Canada, and a $1.6 billion deficit with West Germany. In fact, deficits with these three countries plagued the U.S. balance-of-trade position throughout the 1970s (see Table 3.1).

The persistent deficit with Canada can be ascribed in large part to imports of automobiles and automobile parts under the 1965 Canadian-U.S. Automotive Agreement. This pact created free trade in automotive products between the two countries and allowed U.S. manufacturers to integrate production on both sides of the border.

The explanation for the trade deficit with Japan can be found in several factors. Of those factors contributing to increased imports, the role of MITI is significant. This ministry acts to coordinate business and government export policies. The effectiveness of MITI in encouraging exports is often compared to the ambivalent or discouraging effects of U.S. government export policies.[1]

A second reason for the consistent increase in Japanese exports to the United States is the faster growth in Japanese productivity relative to the United States. The growth in U.S. productivity was slow throughout the 1970s and actually fell in 1979. In Japan, by contrast, productivity made marked gains throughout the decade.

A third factor accounting for the growing Japanese surplus with the United States involves superior planning. The automobile industry provides an example of Japanese management's perceiving and responding to a shift in the preferences of American consumers. Japanese manufacturers firmly established themselves in the U.S. small-car market before U.S. manufacturers began building their own small cars.

The Japanese have built up their trade surplus with the United States not only by increasing exports but also by restricting imports. The Japanese have erected import barriers, particularly of the nontariff variety. Pointing to safety and health regulations, government procurement policies, and other restrictions, U.S. manufacturers have complained of the difficulty of penetrating the Japanese market.

In response to the U.S. trade deficit in 1971 and the rush by foreign holders of dollars to convert their U.S. currency into gold and stronger currencies, the Nixon administration undertook remedial action. In August 1971 the United States suspended the convertibility of the dollar into gold. This had the effect of "unpegging" the dollar from a fixed price denominated in gold ($35 per ounce), and allowed its value to "float" relative to the other major currencies. By late 1971 the dollar had fallen by about 9%. It was hoped that this would make imports to the United States more expensive and also make U.S. exports more competitive in world markets.

Other measures designed to improve the trade balance included a 10% surcharge on all imports to the United States. A 90-day wage-and-price freeze was imposed to quell inflation; it was expected to curb imports and expand exports.

Despite these measures, the U.S. trade deficit increased in 1972 to $6.4 billion. No improvement was registered until the following year, when the United States was able to generate a $900 million surplus. In 1974 this small surplus was lost, and the trade balance slipped back to a $5.4 billion deficit. Most of this shortfall was again accounted for by sizable deficits with Canada, West Germany, and Japan for the same reasons discussed above. The steep OPEC oil price rise also contributed to the problem, with the amount paid by the U.S. for imported petroleum and petroleum products increasing more than threefold to $24 billion.

In 1975 the United States regained a surplus in the balance-of-trade account, largely due to the marked increase of exports to the OPEC countries. These newly rich countries, especially Iran and Saudi Arabia, were spending their money in the United States and other industrialized countries to satisfy their growing demands for capital and consumer goods and military equipment. Iranian and Saudi Arabian purchases of military equipment surpassed $5 billion. Because of the small populations of most of the Arab OPEC nations, however, their ability to "recycle" their oil revenues by making purchases in the industrialized countries was limited.

This inability of the OPEC nations to spend all their oil revenues on imports has led to their running large trade surpluses. In 1976 the United States ran a $12.1 billion deficit in trade with the OPEC nations, in addition to another annual deficit with Japan of $5.4 billion and with Canada of $2.1 billion. The net trade deficit of the U.S. that year was $9.4 billion.

In 1977 the United States experienced the largest trade deficit in its history, $31 billion. Despite a decline in the value of the dollar, this deficit increased to over $42.36 billion in 1978 and $40.37 billion in 1979.[2] This enormous deficit can be ascribed to a number of factors. For one, the U.S. economy continued to expand at an inflationary rate, while our principal trading partners grew more slowly and managed to keep inflation under control. This caused imports to the United States to rise relative to exports to those other countries.

In the absence of an effective energy policy, imports of petroleum continued to increase. The bill for imported petroleum and petroleum products in 1978 and 1979 was $40 billion and $60 billion respectively.

The devaluation of the U.S. dollar has had little lasting effect on the U.S. balance-of-trade deficit. In Japan, for example, which is highly dependent upon imported raw materials, the devalued dollar has made imports of oil much cheaper. This, of course, has lowered the cost of production and the price of Japanese goods for export. So despite a devalued dollar, the Japanese have been able to maintain their U.S. market. The OPEC members have also countered the devaluation of the U.S. dollar. As the value of the dollar has declined, they have simply charged more for their oil.

This sudden deterioration in the merchandise trade balance, as already mentioned, resulted in part from the increase in Japanese and West German exports to the United States and in part from the development of strong competition in foreign markets. Consequently, the United States steadily lost its share of total world exports from 17.5% in 1964 to 10% in 1978. This figure includes government and military exports as well.

2

In a detailed study, the *International Economic Policy* contends that the roots of the present dollar decline and trade deficit should be sought in the evils of the 1960s. From 1964–65 to 1968–69, the merchandise deficit increased by a staggering $6 billion in round numbers.[3]

The tables at the end of the chapter show eleven export items that experienced the worst deterioration in their trade balances, either through a loss of surplus or a worsening deficit. These items contributed $4.6 billion, or 88% of the trade balance's total between the two periods.

Cereals and meats contributed more than $700 million to the deterioration. Grain exports declined from 1964–65 to 1968–69, as the EEC Common Agricultural Board's policy of increased levies prevented growth in U.S. exports. Meat exports held steady, but imports of meat into the United States grew by 8%. Exports of poultry declined in absolute value because of restraint policies of the EEC Common Agricultural Board.

During the 1964–70 period, exports of agricultural products also declined. A moderate increase in 1971 was helped by the sale of $185 million worth of grain to the Soviet Union.

The fact that these agricultural exports declined—despite great demand in Japan and Western Europe—is in large measure the result of Japan's import restrictions and its centralized procurement practices. It is also the result, in particular, of the EEC Common Agricultural Board's policy of variable levies, which counteract the price advantage of many U.S. agricultural exports.

Considering only foods, fodder, and beverages, the United States lost nearly $1 billion of the surplus it had enjoyed in the mid-1960s and realized small deficits ranging from $0.3 billion to $0.5 billion in the latter part of the decade.

The problem of energy also dates back to this period. Oil price increases contributed $500 million to the trade deficit from 1964–65 to 1968–69, and even more before the oil crisis of 1973. The deficit for petroleum and coal in 1971 surpassed $2 billion as demands for energy resources outstripped the available U.S. supply. Raw-material imports increased at a rapid pace before 1973, but nobody could foresee that by 1980 U.S. oil imports would reach $70 billion.

Textiles, yarns, and fabrics, clothing, and footwear together contributed almost $1 billion to the trade deterioration between 1964–65 and 1968–69, as productive capabilities in these essentially low-technology, labor-intensive industries developed abroad. Also, the rapidly rising cost of U.S. domestic production yielded price advantages to these imports.[4]

The same trouble has developed in all U.S. consumer goods other than food. Trade in this area shifted from a $500 million deficit in 1960 to a $5.7 billion deficit in 1971, with the growth of imports far exceeding U.S. imports. (Many of the items included among consumer goods have a low-technology content and require large quantities of relatively unskilled labor, such as that available outside the United States. Other items, such as electronics, require large quantities of highly trained labor for detailed assembly—and much of this has been supplied by Japan, Taiwan, and South Korea.)

Automobile imports from Japan, Canada, and Germany have been the second largest cause of the deteriorating trade balance. Despite a large steady growth of exports of aircraft and aircraft parts, automobile imports created a $700 million deficit in 1968–69.

The 1965 Canadian-U.S. Automotive Agreement created free trade in automobiles and parts between the two countries—but it also resulted in an unfavorable shift in the balance of automobile trade with Canada. By 1971 auto manufacturers had integrated their production on both sides of the border to the extent that the United States was importing cars and parts from Canada in the amount of $1.4 billion more than it was exporting. Meanwhile, American consumers shifted their preference toward smaller automobiles, opening the gates to Japanese and German imports. These events were in no way helped by the benign negligence of Detroit, the undervalued yen, or the vigorous government-industry export expansion efforts in both Japan and Germany.

At the same time that the Japanese and the Germans were flooding American markets with their cars, U.S. auto exports were effectively destroyed by a lack of planning on the part of the automobile industry, by quotas, and by currency regulations and tariff barriers in many countries. By 1971 U.S. auto exports had expanded to $4.4 billion, from $1.3 billion in 1960, but most of this expansion was in exports to Canada under the Automotive Agreement; exports outside Canada grew to only $1.2 billion in 1971, from $866 million in 1960, far less than the $2.8 billion growth in imports.[5]

While it is true that American car makers have consistently paid little attention to changing consumer tastes and the quality of their products both in the United States and abroad, another reason for the decline in their sales has been discriminatory higher tariffs (11% in the EEC nations vs. 3% in the United States), road taxes that rise as car weights or engine displacements rise, foreign quotas, and a variable tariff rate that ranges from 17.5% to 30% for larger automobiles in Japan. These devices have made import sales of American autos in Germany and Japan almost impossible.

To everyone's surprise, imports of iron, steel, and nonferrous metals added another $1 billion to the U.S. deficit between 1964 and 1969. At a time when the steel industry was working at 70% of capacity, the United States was importing more than $1 billion worth of foreign steel and metals. The reasons for this were, and still are, the following:

1. The U.S. gates are open. There are no quotas or restrictions on imports, and our tariffs are lower than those of other countries.

2. In the late 1960s American wages and fringe benefits were much higher than wages in Western Europe and Japan.

3. Imports of iron and steel have also grown because, in contrast to the aging plant and equipment in the United States, the Japanese and German industries have extensively rebuilt with more efficient and modern machinery.

4. The German and Japanese industries have also received preferential investment incentives, and they have been encouraged to hold down export prices to allow expanded sales abroad.

Electrical machinery, including both industrial equipment and household electrical equipment, contributed $362 million to the trade-balance deterioration. However, between 1968 and 1969, U.S. exports with the rest of the world improved except in Japan, where a $700 million deficit wiped out the nation's small net gain in trade elsewhere. This situation was essentially the result of two causes: electronic equipment imports from

Japan soared as Japanese manufacturers dumped their goods on the U.S. market at a very low price (Japanese radios and televisions, for instance, were sold at a cheaper price in the United States than they were in Japan); and U.S. exports to Japan—such as computer and generating equipment—were restricted through quotas, import licensing requirements, and a campaign of "buy only Japanese products."[6]

The one area in which U.S. exports enjoyed rapid growth was capital goods. Here the United States recorded a surplus balance of $18 billion in 1970 and $7.7 billion in 1971, despite restrictions and monetary fluctuations. In the areas of capital goods and computers, the good performance was attributable to the preponderance of "high technology" products. These technology-intensive items, requiring large research and development outlays, needed both skilled labor and large capital. Since at that time only the United States was equipped for the R&D required for such products, every nation depended on our technology-intensive exports, enabling the United States to accumulate a small but steady surplus in this area.

The surplus from technology-intensive manufactured products, together with the surplus from agricultural products, offset the deficits on raw materials and low-technology goods in 1968–70. However, this was a short-lived blessing, because the export of high-technology capital equipment increases the long-term efficiency of foreign competitors. To some extent, the serious deterioration of U.S. trade today is the result of earlier sales of technology and capital goods to other nations.

The Critical Years

The year 1971 introduced a $2.9 billion deficit in the United States and a monetary crisis in the rest of the world. (When we calculate the deficit of 1971, the real deficit in commercial trade alone, unassisted by government grants and loans, would be $6.2 billion.)

In early 1971 the total foreign reserve of dollars continued to rise as many U.S. and foreign banks began to convert their dollars into foreign currencies. The improvement in the U.S. economy, the increase of imports into the United States, and restrictions on foreign imports in Germany and Japan led to a burgeoning of the U.S. merchandise trade deficit and liquid capital flows from the United States. The protectionist policy of Germany in 1971 was to increase central bank reserves in that country from $7.5 billion to $16.5 billion. The same thing happened in Japan, France, Switzerland, and other Western European nations. As long as there was a surplus in the U.S. trade balance, the country could pay a part of government expenses. But with the huge deficit in commercial merchandise and an increase in U.S. military expenditures abroad, U.S. liabilities in 1971 exceeded $20 billion.

The deficits of 1971 and 1972 created a panic, and the Nixon administration tried to find some way to encourage American exports and discourage imports. In August 1971 President Nixon announced his New Economic Policy (NEP).[7] It closed the U.S. gold sales window and thereby suspended the convertibility of the dollar, and it established a 10% cut in foreign aid, an import surcharge, and a ninety-day wage-and-price freeze. Nixon also suggested sharing the burden of defense with our NATO partners and opening new trade negotiations.

In contrast to the year 1973, in which the United States had a small surplus, 1974 produced a deficit of more than $3 billion. While trade with Canada, Japan, Taiwan, West Germany, Venezuela, and Iran showed a deficit of close to $9.5 billion, the United States enjoyed a trade surplus with Mexico, the Netherlands, Brazil, France, Belgium, Austria, South Africa, and Switzerland.

The oil crisis and a fourfold increase in the price of oil added to the United States problems; but fortunately, in 1975, because of a large amount of orders from the OPEC countries, the United States enjoyed a surplus of $9 billion. The year 1976 produced a deficit of $9.4 billion—more than half, $5.4 billion, with Japan.

In 1976 U.S. export growth was 7.5%, while Japan and West Germany enjoyed 22.8% and 12.3%, respectively. At the same time the increase in U.S. imports was twice that of Japan's import increase and 40% more than Germany's. As a result, Japan and West Germany showed a balance-of-payments surplus of $9.2 billion and $18.1 billion, respectively, while the United States produced a $9.4 billion deficit in its merchandise trade balance.

In the current account balance, the U.S. deficit was $1.4 billion, Canada's was $4.9 billion, England's $3.2 billion, France's $6 billion, and Italy's $2.2 billion. Only Japan and Germany showed a surplus of $3.5 and $4 billion, respectively.

In the export-import area, the United States in 1976 had surpluses of $12.5 billion in agriculture and $16 billion in manufactured products, but deficits of $2.45 billion in motor vehicles, $1.4 billion in steel, $3.7 billion in textiles and footwear, $2.6 billion in consumer electronics, $29.1 billion in fuels, and $4.4 billion in minerals and metals.

Trade balances in general in 1976 showed deficits of $5.1 billion with Japan, $2.1 billion with Canada, and $12.1 billion with the OPEC nations; but there was a surplus of $2.15 billion with the Soviet Union, $549 million with Eastern Europe, $7.4 billion with the European Community, and $1.1 billion with the developing countries.

In 1977 the U.S. merchandise trade balance was in deficit by $31.2 billion—the largest in history—compared with $9.3 billion in 1976. Growth in U.S. economic activities increased imports by 22%, to $151.7 billion. Total trade volume increased 13%, the GNP increased 4.9%, and industrial production increased 5.6%. In contrast, industrial growth in other countries was 2.5% both petroleum and nonpetroleum imports contributed to the huge U.S. trade deficit. Petroleum imports increased 29% to $44.7 billion. Trade volume, meanwhile, rose 19% to a record daily rate of 9.2 million barrels, compared with 7.8 million barrels in 1976. Domestic petroleum consumption increased 5%.

Nonpetroleum imports increased 20% to $107 billion. The surprising discovery in this analysis is the large increases in imports of automobiles, steel, textiles, and consumer goods that were available in the United States. At a time when the steel and automobile industries were using only 70% of their productive capacity and were laying off workers, foreign firms were aggressively promoting exports of their goods to the United States.

Exports in 1977 increased 5% to $120.5 billion, while the volume increased less than 1%. Agricultural exports increased 5% to $24.4 billion; volume increased by only 2% compared with 12% in 1976. Nonagricultural exports rose 5% to $96.1 billion; here, the increase was the result of higher prices, since volume actually declined 1%. Exports of industrial supplies and consumer goods increased in both value and volume. However, the growth in the volume of these exports was slower in 1977 than in 1976. Exports of automotive products and capital goods increased in value and declined in volume. The volume of capital goods exports declined in 1977 because of trade difficulties with the Soviet Union, the other socialist countries, and the Arab nations. Machinery exports posted a small increase in volume for the first time since 1975.

The increase in the U.S. trade deficit thus reflected a deterioration in bilateral trade with the industrial nations and the increase in petroleum imports. In the case of the trade deficit with the industrial nations, the decline reflected a policy of restraining U.S. imports and taking advantage of the United State's failure to protect itself against foreign products. In 1977, therefore, the U.S. deficit with Japan was $8.1 billion, the deficit with Canada $1.7 billion, and the deficits with Western Europe $6.2 billion. The surplus with Eastern Europe narrowed to $1.5 billion, less than half of the 1976 level. U.S. exports to the Soviet Union were hampered by the Jackson amendments, forbidding the status of "most favored nation" to the Soviet Union.

The principal cause of the slow growth of U.S. trade in 1977 was sluggish domestic demand in the industrial countries and government restraints on U.S. imports. This was the case not only in countries where the petroleum crisis had created a deficit in their balance of payments but also in two surplus nations, Germany and Japan, where there was plenty of room for expansion by more imports. As a result, the industrial nations' total production and imports—which in 1976 had increased by 9% and 13.5%, respectively—dropped to annual rates of about 5% in the first half of 1977 and 2% in the second half. At the same time, the volume of import growth was only 3.5% in real terms.

The country-by-country pattern of imports and export growth, however, was quite different. There were only three major surplus economies, with the only stimulus coming from the United States. Beginning in 1976, U.S. imports increased by 13%, and the trade deficit reached $14.6 billion. In 1977 the U.S. trade deficit was $31.2 billion, the same year that the two surplus nations, Japan and Germany, restricted imports to only 4.5% and 3.5%, respectively.

Only Austria, Ireland, Portugal, Switzerland, Venezuela, Iran, Saudi Arabia, Kuwait, Indonesia, and Yugoslavia were able to generate more imports. Even Canada, France, and the United Kingdom held their demands back in order to fight inflation and their balance-of-payments deficits. The result was that the EEC nations, with $395.7 billion in exports, purchased only $382.0 billion worth of imports. Japan, at the same time, finished 1977 with $80.5 billion in exports and $70.7 billion in imports, a surplus of $9.5 billion. In Italy and Sweden imports actually fell by 5% and 2%, respectively. The sharpest decline, 20%, took place in South Africa.

Although the imports of oil-producing nations increased by 17% in 1977, this too was lower than the 1976 increase. The growth of import demand in non-oil-producing countries was less than 1%.

The trade balance of the Soviet Union and other socialist nations showed a deficit both in 1976 and 1977. Their exports reached $92 billion in 1976 and $107 billion in 1977. Their imports showed figures of $102 billion and $114 billion, respectively. In 1977 both the Soviet Union and the socialist nations of Eastern Europe reduced their imports from industrial countries to a total $29 billion, compared with $33.32 billion in 1976. Meanwhile, Chinese imports from the West rose by 9% in 1977 to $4.5 billion.

In 1978 the export growth of all the countries, except Germany and Japan, was weaker as a result of the sluggish world economy. In the non-oil-exporting countries export growth fell from 12% in 1976 to 5% in 1977. Even the exports of the oil-producing countries dropped after a 14% increase in the previous year.

As for the socialist countries, their exports increased in value by 16% in 1977 to $107 billion. Most of the increase in trade from the Soviet Union and the other socialist countries was to the developing nations, while those to developed countries showed little change.

The countries that showed significant export increase in 1977 were South Africa, with a 15% rise, and Canada, Finland, Ireland, Spain, and the United Kingdom, with increases of between 9% and 12.5%. Among the three surplus countries—Japan, Germany and Switzerland—the only nation showing a rapid export growth was Switzerland with 12% growth. Countries that suffered greatly from the lack of export growth were the

United States, Sweden, Australia, Norway, the Netherlands, and Greece.[8]

Although increases in petroleum prices were a dominant factor of the U.S. trade deficit in 1978 and 1979, there were other factors that affected trade patterns.

Substantial dollar depreciation against most major currencies in 1978 increased the competitiveness of some U.S. exports to many countries, but the rise in the price of imports neutralized this advantage both in 1978 and 1979. Also, the average real growth among the six major trading partners remained about 4%, while growth in the U.S. slowed from 4.4% to 2.3%, serving to moderate the rise in U.S. spending for imports. It was because of these factors that despite a huge increase in the 1979 oil bill, the U.S. merchandise trade deficit declined to $40.37 billion from $42.36 billion in 1978.[9]

Nonagricultural exports increased 31%, almost twice the 1978 increase. Agricultural exports increased 18% to $35.4 billion after a 23% increase in 1978. Petroleum imports increased 42%, nearly all of the rise the result of higher prices, compared with a 6% decline in 1978, all in volume terms.

About one-half of the total import increase in 1979 was accounted for by petroleum, which increased 42%, to $60 billion. The average number of barrels imported daily was 8.81 million in 1979, compared with 8.72 million barrels in 1978. The small increase in volume in 1979 went into inventories, which raised petroleum reserves 1% above 1978.

Nonpetroleum imports in 1979 increased 14%, to $151.5 billion. Imports of most major consumer goods increased at a slower rate than in 1978. The slowdown in consumer goods, from a 33% increase in 1978 to 6% in 1979, largely reflected a sharp decline in imports of consumer electronic products—particularly color television sets, many of which were being assembled in the U.S. by Japanese affiliates. Automotive imports from the rest of the world—mainly Japan—rose 15%, meanwhile, following a 46.1% rise in 1978. Total sales of imported autos increased 17% to 2.33 million units, in contrast with a 10% decline in domestic auto sales to 8.34 million units. Steel imports increased to $7.8 billion. Nonpetroleum industrial supplies remained the leading commodity category in terms of growth, accounting for about two-fifths of the rise in nonpetroleum imports.[10]

Nonagricultural exports increased 31% in dollar terms, to $146.7 billion; the volume increase was 11%. There were increases in all major commodity categories in 1979, with particularly strong increases in capital goods. About $12 billion of the total $84.5 billion nonagricultural export rise was accounted for by capital goods, which had also risen strongly in 1978. Deliveries of wide-bodied passenger aircraft and spare parts for older planes increased 45% above 1978 deliveries. Chemical exports increased 40% over 1978, especially to Asia, Western Europe, and Latin America.

Agricultural exports reached $35.4 billion, 18% over 1978. Nearly one-third of the increase was due to higher shipments to Socialist countries and the Soviet Union in the last half of 1979. Exports to the Soviet Union of corn, wheat, and soybeans reached 19.1 million metric tons, compared with 13.6 million in 1978. In 1979 the United States became the Soviet Union's second largest trading partner in the West, behind West Germany, largely because of American sales of agricultural goods.[11]

Trade by Area in 1979

By area, the United States' trade balance with developed countries shifted from a deficit of $11.4 billion to a surplus of $1.3 billion. The surplus with European nations increased $9.7 billion. The deficit with Japan was still very high, close to $9 billion. The deficit with Canada reached $2.4 billion. The exports to non-oil-producing developing countries grew faster than trade with developed countries. As a result, the deficit with developing nations was $3 billion, the lowest since 1976. Because of the loss of $3 billion worth of trade with Iran and the increase in the price of oil in the second part of 1979, the deficit with the OPEC nations reached $30.5 billion, compared with $18.4 billion in 1978.

The trade deficit of 1979 was neutralized by the receipt of $37.7 billion in income on U.S. direct investment abroad. This was an increase of $12.1 billion over 1978. Receipts from petroleum affiliates were particularly strong. Most of the price increases for crude and refined petroleum were passed on to the American affiliates, whose income increased significantly. New legislation relating to taxation or inventory profits in England resulted in a large one-time boost in the earnings of American affiliates. A marked rise in the price of minerals in the developing nations also increased the profit of the multinationals.

Unfortunately, 1980 results for U.S. trade are not very encouraging. They show a $36.36 billion deficit.

This large deficit has occurred despite a 7.6% increase in exports and a 17.6% decline in oil volume. In 1980 the U.S. trade deficit with the OPEC nations increased, while the trade deficit with Japan changed very little.[12]

A look at the export policy of the other industrial nations shows that they give all kinds of assistance and priorities to their exports that the United States does not. The following table shows the merchandise exports of the major trading nations and the extent to which their governments provide supports, aid, and guarantees:

	1977 Exports (Billions of Dollars)	Percentage of Exports Supported by Government Credits or Guarantees
Japan	$81 billion	42%
Britain	$57 billion	34%
France	$65 billion	30%
Germany	$119 billion	12%
United States	$120 billion	7%
Canada	$43 billion	6%

While Western Europe and Japan have resorted to the following devices for export encouragement, the United States has done very little either to encourage American exporters or to discourage unnecessary imports to the United States:

1. Low-interest-rate loans to exporters;

2. Tax reductions, subsidies, and rebates;

3. Mixed financing packages that combine export credit with low-interest aid loans;

4. Inflation insurance offered to exporters by government credit agencies to offset rising production costs on fixed-price sales;

5. Financing of the local costs of projects in addition to credits for imported equipment.

At present, very little aid is given to U.S. exporters. The U.S. Chamber of Commerce contends that for the last 200 years this country has paid lip service to exports instead of doing something to foster them.

The U.S. trade imbalance has progressively worsened in recent years. Exports are not rising so rapidly as imports. The U.S. share of world exports of manufactured goods fell in 1979 and 1980 to the lowest level since 1973, and the Department of Commerce reports that only 10% of U.S. manufacturers are exporters.[13]

It is not only the United States government that has neglected exports; manufacturers and labor unions are also guilty of not working toward a plan for improving exports and productivity. Exports have never been a prime consideration for the very reason that until 1970 neither profits nor jobs depended on them. Both groups prospered without having to cope with the different ways of doing business around the world.

Businessmen understandably blame the failure to expand their exports on the government. They complain that instead of helping them the government is hampering their efforts. As major hindrances to exports, they cite taxation of income earned overseas; legislation governing corporate dealings with Arab nations, the Soviet Union, China, and Cuba;

the application of antitrust laws outside the United States, and a lack of interest by or help from the Export-Import Bank.

In answer to these complaints, the Department of Commerce, while accepting some responsibility for the lack of progress, states that corporate directors are often reluctant to spend the time and money required to establish a beachhead abroad and to gradually expand their market share at the expense of short-term profitability.

What the United States is facing today is not a lack of resources or entrepreneurship, but one of good management. At this time the country is in need of a major collective, innovative effort led by the administration to get the nation out of its current economic morass. Whatever decision is made must be tailored to the new world economic situation and must be supported by government, management, and labor. The United States can no longer enjoy economic stability and dominance by collective mismanagement, collective avoidance of the issues, or warmed-over policies from the 1950s and 1960s. Five times since 1960, administrations, both Democratic and Republican, have come up with halfhearted, unrealistic, and impractical plans to stop the imbalance in our balance of payments, to stabilize the dollar, to improve productivity, and to reduce inflation. None of these plans has been successful, and whatever action one now suggests can only succeed if we come up with plans based on the economic needs and interests of the United States, rather than on the petty politics of Congressmen who are striving to get votes in their districts.

Since 1970 imports have gone up almost six times, from $39.8 billion to $211.5 billion, while exports have increased by less than four times. It is that large trade deficit that is causing the present dollar instability.

While it may be good politics to blame the oil-producing nations for the increase in imports, the reality is that during first-quarter 1978 the trade deficit with Japan and West Germany surpassed the petroleum deficit. A large proportion of the imports from Japan and Germany was finished manufactured goods, such as steel, automotives, electronics, and textiles. Those goods accounted for 70% of total imports and a deficit of close to $4.6 billion. Yet at the same time, imports of crude oil fell in 1978 by 6%.

In the administration's 1980 plan for promoting exports there were additional tax incentives to exporters, exceptions to antitrust laws, more liberal income-tax policies for American citizens working abroad, and expanded credit from the Export-Import bank. Unfortunately, this package, even if it is approved and implemented, is another halfhearted palliative. There can be no permanent solution unless the United States convinces Japan and our Western European trade partners that trade is a two-way system. Either all the partners have to accept and abide by a free-trade system, or the United States should reciprocate and close its borders to unwanted products.

Thus correction of the U.S. deficit will not be possible if the protectionist barrier erected by our trade partners continues to rise. Excessive import restraints are not only unfair to the United States but self-defeating in the long run. If the United States has to continue its present policy of trade, it must be allowed to export more so that it can stabilize the dollar and pay for its imports.

The five-year propaganda of blaming petroleum imports as a cause of the trade deficit has created a benign-neglect atmosphere on the part of both business and the administration. While it is true that the energy crises of 1973 and 1979 have had a great impact on the economic situation, it is misleading to place on petroleum imports the sole responsibility for the massive swing from surplus to deficit in our trade balance.

In fact, among the ten major categories of U.S. foreign trade, machinery and transport equipment traditionally register the highest dollar volume. At present the category also ranks as the largest export and import component. And in 1978 the United States ran an $8.9 billion surplus in these goods. Despite such impressive statistics, however, these goods have contributed substantially to the worsening situation. From 1975 to 1978 the annual surplus in such trade was reduced by $13.3 billion, making it the third largest contributor—behind oil and automobiles—to the negative swing in the overall balance of trade.

Mineral fuel accounts for 50% of the trade deficit. Even if the cost of fuel imports had not increased at all in the three years between 1975 and 1978, the United States would still be running a massive record trade deficit of $18.6 billion in 1978. Although the first six months of 1978 witnessed a decline in petroleum imports, the price increases of 1979 have created chaos and resulted in a much larger deficit in 1980.

Manufactured goods classified chiefly by material make up the third largest trade category. They include steel, mill products, paper products, textiles, nonferrous metals, metal containers, and gem diamonds. Between 1975 and 1978 this category experienced the third largest negative swing in trade balance, $12.1 billion, and in 1978 it was running a $15.9 billion deficit, the second largest contributor to the overall trade deficit. More than 40% of this shortfall resulted from the import of more than 20 million tons of steel mill products, which have increased 60% since 1975.

Food and livestock, the second largest export category, had the second largest surplus in 1975, but since that time import growth has outpaced export totals, shrinking the surplus and generating an adverse movement of $2.5 billion in the trade balance.

Crude inedible materials except fuels have provided a surplus in the last three years. Soybeans, logs and lumber, raw cotton, wood pulp, metal ores, and metal scrap are some of the major items included. Trade in this area was in surplus by $1.4 billion between 1975 and 1978, the only substantial improvement in any category.[14]

International Trade in the United States 103

The trade deterioration of recent years has reflected the import expansion side of U.S. business and the stagnation of exports. The growth rate of U.S. imports in four years (1975–78) was 76%, while the increase in exports during the same period was only 38%.[15]

On the export side, 1977's $58 billion value increase concealed a static volume. While agricultural exports edged up to $24.4 billion, the $85 billion in nonagricultural exports was due entirely to higher prices; their volume remained below the peak reached in 1974. The U.S. government maintains that the poor performance of U.S. exports over 1977–79, when world trade in manufactured goods expanded by 10%, is difficult to explain. But to find the answer one need only look at the incentives that Japan and other nations present to their exporters, the restraints they have imposed on their importers, and the shackles that our own Congress and government bureaucracy have placed on U.S. exporters. The United States currently has embargoes on trade with Cuba, Vietnam, Cambodia, North Korea, Iran, and Afghanistan; and it has export controls and restrictions on trade with Eastern Europe, Soviet Union, Libya, China, Syria, South Africa, Iraq, Algeria, and several other nations.

In 1978 more than 350 license applications covering hundreds of millions of dollars were denied, and more than 1,300 applications had not been cleared by the end of the year.

The American gates are open to all kinds of imports, but American exporters are limited by the import restrictions of Japan and Western Europe, by limitations on export financing, by laws and regulations that represent only the vested interests of external and internal pressure groups, and by delays and uncertainties.

Despite all the statements and promises by the administration during 1978, 1979, and 1980, U.S. imports continued to rise rapidly and the trade deficit for those years was close to $120 billion.[16]

The Japanese surplus trade with the United States has been rising every year since 1973. In 1976 it was $5.3 billion; in 1977 it exceeded $8.1 billion; and by 1978 Japanese cars, television sets, cameras, and other products were arriving in this country at a level nearly $10 billion higher than the value of American products entering Japan. By 1979 it reached $9 billion, and this represented nearly one-third of the total trade deficit of the United States.

In Germany the earlier decline of the current-account surplus in 1979 came to a halt, and net long-term exports again assumed sizable proportion. In 1976 Germany's exports increased 13½%, followed by 5% in 1977, while imports increased only 4½%.

West Germany recorded a trade surplus of $21.9 billion in 1978, its largest since 1974. The country's exports rose by $153 billion ($12 billion more than U.S. exports in 1978), and imports reached $131 billion. Also in

1978 West Germany's current-account surplus doubled to about $8.7 billion. All of these rising annual surpluses came during a period when the mark rose about 15% against the dollar.

The 1978 result of world pressure on Germany has had very little effect; the nation has become the world's largest exporter but has done very little to increase its imports. The Carter administration attempted to spur world growth, although stimuli measured by Japan and Germany have not succeeded.

The U.S. trade deficit with West Germany is partly the result of the German government's reluctance to encourage more rapid economic growth. It is understandably fearful about expanding the German economy too rapidly, and repeating the ominous hyperinflation of the 1920s.

But the effect of this slower economic growth in West Germany and the resulting lower demand for imported goods should not be overestimated. Although the growth of GNP in West Germany was slower than that of the U.S., throughout most of the 1970s this was because of its slower recovery from the recession of 1974. By 1979 the nation's rate of economic growth exceeded that of the United States.

To explain the persistent U.S. trade deficit with West Germany, it is necessary to examine more than comparative growth rates. An analysis of the domestic rates of household consumption in the two countries shows that West German households spend a smaller proportion of their incomes on consumption than do American households. In other words, West Germans save more than Americans. The saving rate in West Germany has generally exceeded that of the United States by 7% to 9%. Part of the explanation for this phenomenon can be found in the higher real-interest rates on savings accounts in West Germany. (The real interest rate is equal to the nominal interest rate minus the rate of inflation.) Although nominal interest rates between the two countries do not considerably differ, inflation in West Germany has been significantly lower than in the United States. Therefore real interest rates and real income in West Germany have been higher than those in the United States, and this can be expected to cause West Germans to save a higher proportion of their incomes.[17]

In addition to the higher real interest rates in West Germany, there appears to be a psychological difference between West Germans and Americans in their attitudes toward savings. And what this higher rate of savings among West German households means is that proportionately less money is being spent on goods and services. Less household consumption means less consumption of imported goods.

Besides the slow rate of imports of U.S. goods into West Germany, there are two major factors that contribute to the consistently strong increase in West German goods sold in the United States: superior product innovation and a strong orientation toward exporting.

The West German advantage in product innovation is very evident in the case of energy-saving products. Because of higher energy costs in West Germany relative to the United States and a greater dependence on imported petroleum, the emphasis in West Germany has been on products that save energy. In the United States, the emphasis has tended to be on products that are energy-intensive and save labor instead. Thus, as the cost of energy has increased precipitously in the United States, West German products have become more attractive to American customers.

The West German government has also provided more support of civilian R&D over the years than the U.S. government. In addition, the West German government has directed its efforts at industries that could be competitive in world markets. Thus it has supported the nation's high-technology industries (aircraft, nuclear power, and electrical engineering among them), rather than such declining enterprises as textiles or steel, where it recognized that efforts to use subsidies and import barriers were not economically feasible.

The export orientation of West German firms is a second significant factor contributing to the growth of exports to the United States. Top management is usually closely involved with a firm's export efforts, among small- and medium-sized firms as well as among the larger ones. These companies understand that continued growth depends on sales throughout the European Community and in the United States.

West German banks help even further by working closely with the nation's manufacturers to develop markets abroad. The West German government also encourages this export orientation by offering fewer inhibitions to exporting than the United States and by stressing a greater degree of cooperation with business on trade and economic issues. For example, the West German government's antitrust policy does not apply outside of West Germany and the EEC.

In sum, the U.S. trade deficit with West Germany can be seen as the result of three complementary factors: first, consumption and the demand for imports to West Germany are lower than the demand for imports to the United States; second, West German products, especially those with energy-saving qualities, have an edge over American products; and third, West German manufacturers are highly motivated to sell those products in the United States.

Besides all these factors, special characteristics of the German and the Japanese economies have insulated domestic companies from the effects of the resulting rise in their currencies. Both countries practice protectionism in their imports and all kinds of encouragement of exports.

In Japan a deeply embedded institutionalized chain of trading companies, import restrictions, and protectionism has effectively locked out imports from getting any real market share. In West Germany a combination of positive effects of the dollar's fall, restricted imports, and the tenacity of German exporters and the German government has protected domestic companies.

"The decline of the dollar led to considerable cost benefits for domestic production," according to Martin Grüner, West German state secretary of the Ministry of Economics. "Imported raw materials denominated in dollars have fallen in price, and manufacturers have benefited from some lowered costs."

But the primary factor in the trade imbalance is that the U.S. gates have been left open and obstacles put in the way of American exports, while the Japanese and Germans have closed their gates and made it their first priority to maintain larger foreign-market shares even at the cost of profits and government subsidies.

In response to pressure from some members of Congress and the business community, the Carter administration promised the following measures:

1. increasing direct assistance to United States exporters;

2. reducing domestic and foreign barriers to exports and securing a more equitable international trading system for all exports.

Direct assistance to U.S. exporters will be provided through the Export-Import Bank.

According to a statement made in 1978 by then President Carter,

> During the past two years the administration has increased Eximbank's loan authorization five-fold from $700 million in FY 1977 to $3.6 billion for FY 1979. I intend to ask Congress for an additional $500 million for FY 1980, bringing Eximbank's total loan authorization to $4.1 billion. These authorizations will provide the Bank with the funds necessary to improve its competitiveness in a manner consistent with our international obligations, through increased flexibility in the areas of interest rates, length of loans, and the percentage of a transaction it can finance. . . .
> The Small Business Administration will channel up to $100 million of its current authorization for loan guarantees to small business exporters to provide seed money for their entry into foreign markets. . . .
> The Office of Management and Budget *will* allocate an additional $20 million in annual resources for export development programs of the Departments of Commerce and State to assist U.S. firms, particularly small and medium-sized businesses, in marketing abroad through:
> A computerized information system to provide exporters with prompt access to international marketing opportunities abroad;
> Risk sharing programs to help associations and small companies meet initial export marketing costs; and assistance to firms and industries with high export potential and intensified short-term export campaigns in promising markets.
> Agricultural experts are a vital component of the U.S. trade balance.

Over the past ten years, the volume of U.S. firm exports has doubled and the dollar value has nearly quadrupled. However, this multifaceted agricultural export policy will be strengthened by:

An increase of almost $1 billion (up from $750 million in FY 1977 to $1.7 billion in FY 1978) in the level of short-term export credits;

An increase of almost 20 percent in the level of funding support for a highly successful program of cooperation with over sixty agricultural commodity associations in market development;

Efforts in multilateral trade negotiations to liken the treatment of agricultural and non-agricultural products;

Aggressive pursuit of an international wheat agreement to insure our producers a fair share of the expanding world market.

Direct financial and technical assistance to U.S. firms should encourage them to take advantage of the increasing competitiveness of our goods in international markets.

Equally important will be *the reduction* of government imposed *disincentives* and barriers which unnecessarily inhibit our firms from selling abroad.

President Carter also promised to direct the heads of all executive departments and agencies to report to him the factors that might have possible adverse effects on the United States trade balance. The Departments of Commerce, State, Defense, and Agriculture also received instruction, at this late date, "to take export consequences fully into account when considering the use of export controls of foreign policy purposes. Weight will be given to whether the goods in question are also available from countries other than the United States."

Furthermore, President Carter referred to the Foreign Corrupt Practice Act and Antitrust Law, and added that he was "hopeful that American business will not forgo legitimate export opportunities because of uncertainty about the application of these statutes."

In conclusion, he emphasized that his administration was sick and tired of witnessing so many barriers presented to the American exporters by foreign nations:

Trade restrictions imposed by other countries inhibit our ability to export. Tariff and especially non-tariff barriers restrict our ability to develop new foreign markets and expand existing ones. We are now working to eliminate or reduce these barriers through multilateral trade negotiations in Geneva.

U.S. export performance is also adversely affected by the excessive financial credit and subsidies which some of our trading partners offer to their own exporters.

At this stage international agreements are essential to assure that American exporters do not face unfair competition....

Increasing U.S. exports is a major challenge—for business, for labor, and for government. Better export performance by the United States would spur growth in the economy. It would create jobs. It would strengthen the dollar and fight inflation.[18]

It is encouraging that, at this late hour, President Carter did recognize the difficulties facing American businessmen and exporters. These difficulties are still very serious, and there are no short-term, easy solutions to these problems. Unless President Reagan, his administration, the Congress, and the business community give the U.S. trade deficit the high-level, sustained attention it deserves, the world could face total economic chaos.

To remove barriers to American products in Japan and Germany, the president must be determined to fight for the rights of American exporters and for reciprocity in trade.

After so many years of talk, and promises by both Japan and Germany, the United States is still spending close to $7 billion for their defense and is plagued by a large trade deficit with those two countries. "The American exporters complain that they are still all but shut out of the Japanese markets, and more and more of the American consumers who buy the goods that the Japanese export seem to agree." Pollster Louis Harris found that a strong 64% majority is persuaded that the United States is being shortchanged on trade by Japan as well as by other countries. Today, many Americans firmly believe that if Japan is not prepared to open up its market we should shut down ours.[19]

"High up on the list of American complaints is the sluggishness with which Japan has moved to live up to the trade agreement that was concluded with the United States in January (1978). That pact pledged Japan to cut tariff walls and quotas with the aim of bringing U.S.-Japanese trade back into balance by 1980. But there have been few signs that the promises are being kept, and trade hassles with the Japanese are still as bad as ever."[20]

The United States is blamed for the weakness of the dollar when it is forgotten that a major cause of the weakness of the dollar is the defense expenditures of the last thirty years in Germany and Japan coupled with U.S. trade deficit of the last five years. "What is really needed to restore the dollar's health is quick and dramatic relief from Japanese imports. In trade the Japanese have done nothing for us."[21]

Japan's huge trade surplus with the United States is growing bigger all the time. The excess of Japanese imports to the United States over American exports to Japan reached $12 billion in 1978, $10 billion in 1979 and $9 billion in 1980.

These huge imbalances cost American workers 500,000 jobs, adding fuel to the fire of inflation, and they are the main cause of the weakness of the dollar.

The Japanese concede that there are still some restrictions on American products but they also blame the American exporters for "not wanting to take the time and trouble involved in exports." American businessmen, complain Japanese officials, lack aggressiveness in exports and are looking for cheap products for imports.

Many American officials and foreign diplomats also accuse American businessmen and exporters of not wanting to take the time and trouble involved in expanding exports and restraining imports. "In contrast to U.S. businessmen," Frank Weil, Assistant Secretary of Commerce, stated, "the Japanese gigantic bureaucracy is biased against foreign manufactured goods. It is true that there are few restrictions but most of them have been replaced by something different; a mentality on the part of the average Japanese businessman that says that 'I have been told for a hundred years I should not import. I can make it here.' It is a sort of conditioned reflex."[22]

According to Norman Glick, a member of the U.S. Commerce Department, "The Japanese have protection in depth. As soon as you peel away one layer, you find another." This protection shows itself in many ways. Government agencies in Japan, which spend close to $5.2 billion a year, have been under orders to buy national products, and when the government does not want to buy foreign, wholesalers and industrial buyers steer clear of imports as well.

American exporters are also hampered by Customs red tape and Japan's multilayered, complex distribution system, that giant wholesale trading house which can set the price of imported goods so high that they fall into the luxury, low-sales category. Despite the drop in the dollar, the price of American goods imported to Japan has not dropped, because wholesale houses simply reap the benefits. General Motors can distribute its Cadillac Seville directly at $15,000, but the Japanese, by adding taxes and profits, sell it at $30,000.

The middleman can also effectively block the import of products that compete with domestic producers. The case of Zenith's Nevin, which attempted to enter the Japanese TV market, is a good example.

All the studies and research documents indicate that the United States is a great loser in her trade with Japan and some other industrial nations. This fact puts the future of trade relation between the countries into a rather different perspective. Whatever the roots of American exporters' complaints, one thing is clear: there are barriers, obstacles, and difficulties created by both the United States and foreign nations. The result is that the United States is supplying a smaller part of what Japan and other nations do in fact take in, and receives more than her share of foreign-made and unnecessary products. The United States, thanks to these barriers, has lost its share as supplier to her trade partners in each category of manufactured imports. Japan has expanded beyond expectation her imports to the United States. Japan has been doubly protected, thanks to American generosity, from foreign products and investment—first, by our allowing Japan to continue her own system of protectionism and controls and then also by the indifference the U.S. government and consumers have shown by allowing all kinds of Japanese imports to the United States.

The result has been a disaster. American technology has nurtured competitors who now enter or threaten U.S. markets, "And as a final irony, technology which might have been a lever to enter the Japanese market has been surrendered, and with it the advantage that might have made entry successful."[23]

In addition, the businessmen contend that the U.S.-Japan trade imbalance is intolerable. If Japan desires to import to the United States she must be prepared to purchase more American products. Last year Japan's total surplus came from her trade with the United States. In 1974 Japan required 82% of her total export income to pay for imports of raw materials, food, and fuel. By 1977, however, this proportion declined to 68%. For the United States, which in contrast to Japan produces 60% of the fuel and most of the raw materials and food, the bill for these three items in 1974 was 53% of total exports, but in 1977 the bill was 55%, and in 1980 it would be close to 65%. While Japan expanded exports and restricted imports, in the United States the opposite policy was followed.

Unfortunately, so far all the talk and efforts have produced unsatisfactory results because for two decades different administrations have ignored the seriousness of the energy shortage, the trade problem, the large military expenditures in Germany and Japan, and expanding foreign aid, which have produced the present international trade and monetary disaster and decline, and devaluation of the dollar.

TABLE 3.1

U.S. Balance of Trade with West Germany, Japan, and Canada
(in billions of U.S. dollars)

	1970	1971	1972	1973	1974	1975	1976	1977	1978
U.S. Balance with:									
West Germany	−0.4	−0.8	−1.4	−1.6	−1.4	−0.2	0.1	−1.2	−3.0
Japan	−1.2	−3.2	−4.0	−1.4	−1.8	−1.9	−5.4	−8.0	−11.0
Canada	−2.0	−2.3	−2.5	−2.6	−2.3	−0.4	−2.1	−3.8	−6.1
All countries	2.6	−2.3	−6.4	0.9	−5.4	9.0	−9.4	−30.9	−34.2

TABLE 3.2

U.S. Net Balance by Selected Products
(millions of dollars)

	1964–65 Average	1968–69 Average	Deterioration	% of Total Deterioration of U.S. Trade Balance
Meat & Meat Preparations	−247	−625	−377	7.2%
Cereal & Cereal Preparations	2,604	2,243	−361	6.9%
Petroleum	−1,565	−2,006	−440	8.4%
Textile Yarn & Products	−186	−441	−256	4.9%
Nonmetallic Minerals	−276	−541	−265	5.1%
Iron & Steel	−357	−1,136	−779	14.9%
Nonferrous Metals	−609	−971	−361	6.9%
Electric Machinery	1,123	761	−362	6.9%
Transportation Equipment	2,082	1,396	−686	13.1%
Clothing	−359	−779	−412	7.9%
Footwear	−142	−429	−287	5.5%
NET BALANCE	2,068	−2,528	−4,586	87.7%

Source: OECD, *Trade by Commodities, Series C.*

TABLE 3.3

WORLD TRADE

in billions of US dollars (volume index 1975 = 100)

Areas	Exports (f.o.b.)				Imports (c.i.f.)			
	1976	Year	1977 1st half	1977 2nd half	1976	Year	1977 1st half	1977 2nd half
Developed areas								
Western Europe								
EEC	324.8	375.7	183.5	192.2	341.4	382.0	192.1	189.9
Other countries	78.4	86.9	42.0	44.9	106.9	118.8	58.6	60.2
Total	403.2	462.6	225.5	237.1	448.3	500.8	250.7	250.1
	(111.4)	(117.1)	(116.7)	(117.5)	(113.2)	(116.1)	(117.7)	(114.4)
United States	115.0	120.2	61.1	59.1	129.6	151.7	77.8	78.9
Canada	40.3	43.2	21.8	21.4	40.3	42.0	21.8	20.2
Japan	67.2	80.5	37.4	43.1	64.8	70.7	35.1	35.6
Other countries	26.2	29.5	14.3	15.2	27.0	28.0	13.9	14.1
Total Developed Areas	651.9	736.0	360.1	375.9	710.0	798.2	399.3	398.9
	(111.0)	(115.8)	(115.1)	(116.5)	(113.5)	(117.5)	(119.0)	(116.0)
Developing areas								
Oil-exporting countries	137	148	74	74	70	89	43	46
	(114.0)	(112.0)			(122.5)	(143.0)		
Other areas	114	133	65	68	139	151	73	78
	(112.0)	(117.5)			(102.5)	(103.0)		
Total Developing Areas	251	281	139	142	209	240	116	124
	(113.0)	(114.5)	(112.5)	(117.0)	(108.5)	(115.0)	(111.5)	(118.0)
Centrally planned economies	92	107	50	57	102	114	58	56
Grand Total	995	1,124	549	575	1,021	1,152	573	579
	(111.5)	(115.5)	(114.5)	(116.5)	(112.5)	(117.0)	(117.5)	(116.5)

TABLE 3.4

20 LEADING UNITED STATES FOREIGN-TRADE CUSTOMERS

		U.S. Exports to: 1974	1973	U.S. Imports from: 1974	1973
1	Canada	$19,932,000,000	$15,104,000,000	$22,282,000,000	$17,715,000,000
2	Japan	10,679,000,000	8,313,000,000	12,455,000,000	9,676,000,000
3	West Germany	4,986,000,000	3,756,000,000	6,428,000,000	5,345,000,000
4	Mexico	4,855,000,000	2,937,000,000	3,386,000,000	2,306,000,000
5	Britain	4,574,000,000	3,564,000,000	4,021,000,000	3,656,000,000
6	Netherlands	3,979,000,000	2,859,000,000	1,453,000,000	934,000,000
7	Brazil	3,089,000,000	1,916,000,000	1,705,000,000	1,189,000,000
8	France	2,942,000,000	2,263,000,000	2,305,000,000	1,732,000,000
9	Italy	2,752,000,000	2,119,000,000	2,593,000,000	2,002,000,000
10	Belgium-Luxem.	2,285,000,000	1,623,000,000	1,681,000,000	1,273,000,000
11	Australia	2,157,000,000	1,439,000,000	1,042,000,000	1,067,000,000
12	Spain	1,899,000,000	1,319,000,000	899,000,000	762,000,000
13	Venezuela	1,768,000,000	1,033,000,000	4,679,000,000	1,787,000,000
14	Iran	1,734,000,000	772,000,000	2,132,000,000	347,000,000
15	South Korea	1,546,000,000	1,237,000,000	1,460,000,000	974,000,000
16	Taiwan	1,427,000,000	1,170,000,000	2,108,000,000	1,784,000,000
17	Israel	1,206,000,000	962,000,000	282,000,000	269,000,000
18	South Africa	1,160,000,000	746,000,000	609,000,000	377,000,000
19	Switzerland	1,150,000,000	960,000,000	900,000,000	817,000,000
20	Singapore	988,000,000	684,000,000	553,000,000	467,000,000

SOURCE: U.S. Department of Commerce.

TABLE 3.5

Official Export Support in Several Major Trading Countries[a]

(millions of U.S. dollars)

Country	Insurance and Guarantee Authorizations	Direct and Discount Loan Authorizations	Overall Volume of[b] Support
Canada			
1975	911	1137	2048
1976	1339	718	2057
France			
1975	19626	7326	19626
1976	21920	7595	21920
Germany			
1975	7950	1252	7950
1976	10387	1544	10387
Italy			
1975	4596	2859	4596
1976	3306	1451	3306
Japan			
1975	25968	2377	25968
1976	32034	3266	32034
United Kingdom			
1975	9645	1402	9645
1976	10519	1152	10519
United States			
1975	3744	3813	7557
1976	4800	3489	8289

[a]Source: *Report to the U.S. Congress on Export Credit Competition and the Export-Import Bank of the United States* (July 1977).

[b]For the European countries and Japan, overall volume figures are the same as insurance and guarantee volume statistics because official as well as private portions of direct official credits are insured in these countries.

TABLE 3.6

U.S. MERCHANDISE TRADE BALANCE BY AREA 1965–71

(millions of dollars)

Area	1965	1966	1967	1968	1969	1970	1971
United Kingdom	214	−24	162	−116	−87	302	−122
European Economic Community		1,296	1,015	150	1,045	1,718	520
Other Western Europe[1]	2,470	642	404	301	478	879	412
Eastern Europe	7	21	20	15	54	150	182
Canada	642	801	448	−435	−799	−1,676	−1,880
Latin Amer. & Other West. Hem.	−122	38	18	137	318	581	323
Japan	−388	−634	−345	−1,110	−1,390	−1,246	−3,214
Austr., New Zea., & So. Africa	623	336	474	460	295	456	552
Other Asia & Africa	1,400	1,590	1,826	1,274	746	946	348
Int'l. Organ. & Unallocated	−118	−140	−162	−52	0	0	0
All Areas	4,942	3,927	3,859	624	660	2,110	−2,879

SOURCE: Survey of Current Business, June 1969, 1970, 1971, March 1972.

NOTE: Details may not add to totals due to rounding.

[1]Prior to 1966, EEC and other Western Europe data combined.

TABLE 3.7

WORLD PRODUCTION: ANNUAL GROWTH RATES BY COUNTRY GROUP 1971–78
(percentage change from preceding year)

Item and country group	Average 1971–78	1976	1977	1978
Gross domestic product				
Sum of country groups	4.3	5.5	4.2	3.9
Developed market economy	3.4	5.3	3.6	3.6
Developing countries	5.8	5.7	5.9	4.0
Centrally planned economy	5.8	5.9	5.0	4.2
Agricultural production				
Sum of country groups	2.5	1.8	2.6	3.4
Developed market economy	2.2	0.9	2.7	2.6
Developing countries	2.5	1.8	3.4	2.5
Centrally planned economy	2.4	4.7	3.0	3.6
Industrial production				
Sum of country groups	5.0	8.0	5.2	4.2
Developed market economy	3.2	8.2	4.0	4.2
Developing countries	6.2	8.0	4.7	4.6
Centrally planned economy	7.0	5.6	6.1	5.2
Changes in international reserves				
Market economies	40.4	30.5	60.4	42.9
Developed	35.2	9.2	38.4	45.9
Developing	5.2	21.3	22.0	−3.0
Oil-exporting countries	3.5	9.3	10.8	−15.5
Other	1.7	12.0	11.2	12.5
Net changes in other balance-of-payments items				
Market economies	54.9	46.9	90.8	88.1
Developed	44.7	63.7	97.2	79.7
Developing	10.2	−16.8	−6.4	8.3
Oil-exporting countries	6.9	−16.8	−51.7	−57.0
Other	17.1	45.0	45.3	75.4

SOURCE: World Economic Survey 1978, United Nations, New York, 1980, pp. 18, 22.

TABLE 3.8

WORLD TRADE: ANNUAL GROWTH RATES BY COUNTRY GROUP 1971–78
(Percentage change from preceding year)

Item and country group	Average 1971–78	1976	1977	1978
Quantum of exports				
Market economies	6.1	11.4	3.4	5.3
Developed	6.5	11.2	4.7	5.8
Developing	4.6	13.9	−0.7	3.6
Oil-exporting	1.3	14.6	−1.0	−3.5
Other	7.3	15.9	2.0	9.1
Centrally planned economy	7.8	7.9	8.7	3.5
Quantum of imports				
Market economies	5.6	11.8	4.9	3.4
Developed	5.2	13.2	4.4	4.9
Developing	7.2	8.7	4.9	2.3
Centrally planned economy	8.8	6.7	3.9	7.2
Unit value of exports				
Market economies	12.6	1.9	8.7	9.3
Developed	11.3	—	8.3	13.0
Developing	17.9	6.1	12.1	0.8
Oil-exporting countries	28.2	6.0	10.4	...
Other	11.8	6.0	17.0	...
Unit value of imports				
Market economies	12.6	0.9	8.7	9.3
Developed	12.5	1.4	7.9	10.3
Developing	13.1	1.3	10.2	7.6
Exports f.o.b.				
World	348.9	985.1	1,121.8	1,285.6
Market economies	315.2	900.0	1,022.8	1,171.4
Developed	253.0	647.5	735.0	876.1
Developing	62.2	252.5	287.8	295.4
Oil-exporting countries	23.3	138.9	152.1	145.5
Other	38.9	113.5	135.9	148.9
Centrally planned economies	33.7	85.0	98.9	114.2
Imports c.i.f.				
World	362.5	1,008.5	1,154.1	1,333.3
Market economies	329.8	916.3	1,053.2	1,216.7
Developed	262.5	702.0	793.8	909.9
Developing	67.2	214.4	259.4	306.7
Oil-exporting countries	12.9	67.8	89.6	104.9
Other	54.3	146.6	169.8	201.8
Centrally planned economies	32.7	92.1	100.9	116.6
Balance of trade				
World	−13.5	−23.4	−32.4	−47.7
Market economies	−14.5	−16.3	−30.4	−45.2
Developed	−9.5	−54.5	−58.8	−33.8
Developing	−5.0	+38.1	28.4	−11.3
Oil-exporting countries	10.4	71.1	62.6	41.6
Other	−15.4	−33.0	−34.1	−52.9
Centrally planned economies	1.0	−7.1	−2.0	−2.5

SOURCE: World Economic Survey 1978, United Nations, New York, 1980, p. 21.

TABLE 3.9

Imports into U.S. of Petroleum and Petroleum Products

	in billions of dollars
1960	1.55
1965	2.22
1970	3.08
1973	8.17
1974	25.45
1975	26.48
1976	34.00
1977	44.54
1978	42.11
1979	60.21
1980* (est)	80.70*

Based on FAS transactions.

SOURCE: U.S. Department of Commerce

*For the first six months of 1980 oil imports amounted to $40.2 billion compared with $24.5 billion in 1979. While consumption was down, the United States was importing almost twice as much oil in 1980 as the year before in dollar terms. If further price increases occur during the year, as happened in the final quarter of 1979, the cost of imported oil could reach $100 billion.

Notes

1. Japan's automobile exports to the United States rose in February 1980 to 34% above February 1979; 42% of Japan's total automobile exports are to the United States. In terms of dollars, the United States pays $12 billion for Japanese cars. *(New York Times,* March 28, 1980.)

2. Department of Commerce, *Survey of Current Business,* March 1980. Also see *Wall Street Journal,* "U.S. Trade Gap," March 28, 1980 and March 2, 1981. The trade figures are based on calculations for imports, using the so-called C.I.F. method, which includes cost, insurance, and freight. This method, which most other nations use, adds $1 billion to the value of imports each month, compared to the more familiar F.A.S., or free alongside ship.

3. This is based on an OECD list of the fifty-six standard international trade classifications, OECD, *Trade by Commodities,* Series B.

4. Ibid.

5. In the first months of 1980, automobile imports into the United State reached $1.4 billion a month.

6. *The International Economic Policy Assn. Report* (1972), p. 24–28.

7. It is ironic that Richard Nixon should have borrowed the term NEP from Lenin, a term used by the Bolsheviks after the Russian Revolution.

8. Report of *Bank of International Settlements* (June 1978), pp. 61–65.

9. *Wall Street Journal,* March 2, 1981.

10. The cost of automobiles and parts in 1979 surpassed $14 billion.

11. Weekly *Ekonomickeskaya Gazette,* quoted by the *New York Times,* March 16, 1980.

12. The revised figures, published in the *Wall Street Journal, 1981,* show the United States trade deficit in 1978, 1979 and 1980 were $42.36, $40.37, and $36.36 billion respectively. The oil imports to the United States in 1980 declined 17.6% in volume, but the total cost was $70 billion.

13. *Wall Street Journal,* September 20, 1979, p. 1.

14. Report by Federal Reserve Bank of Cleveland, August 7, 1979.

15. Department of Commerce, *Survey of Current Business* (July 1978).

16. World trade dollar value in 1978 rose 14% over 1977 to $1.28 trillion.

17. The substitution effect causing people to save more of their incomes in response to higher interest rates is offset to some extent by the income effect. According to the income effect, higher interest rates allow people to earn the same amount of money on a smaller amount of savings, and those people save less as a result.

18. Statement by President Carter on September 26, 1978, Department of State publication *(Current Policy,* No. 34), September 1978.

19. Even the Geneva Agreement does not provide reciprocity for American exporters.

20. *Time,* November 13, 1978.

21. Otto Ekstein, of Data Resources, Inc., quoted in ibid.

22. *Wall Street Journal,* November 14, 1978.

23. See James C. Abeggen and T. Hout, "Facing Up to Trade Gap with Japan," *Foreign Affairs* (Fall 1978).

4
What Price Government Interventions and Shackles?

It is certain that since 1900 the road to freedom has become increasingly dangerous for those who prefer to mark their own path and safer for those fearful of highwaymen. In the past eighty years hardly an individual prerogative has not succumbed to public restraint through the machinations of government. Individuals have tossed their private freedoms into a common pot and given government the responsibility of redistributing them as it sees fit.

Peter Meyer,
"Eighty Years of Red Tape,"
Harper's (June 1980), p. 39.

A statesman may do much for commerce, most by leaving it alone. A river never flows so smoothly, as when it flows its own course, without either aid or check. Let it make its own bed, it will do better than you can.

Samuel Johnson

More pernicious nonsense was never devised by man than treaties regulating commerce.

Lord Beaconsfield

The purpose of this chapter is to examine some of the government regulations that are causing extra expenses, delays, and obstacles for the business and exporters in the United States.

American manufacturers complain that while other governments use every possible means to encourage exports, the U.S. government has put legal and administrative shackles on its exporters. They not only are subject to antitrust laws; antiboycott legislation, and antibribery laws but also to business constraints from pressure groups. In the following pages, we shall attempt to examine some of these complaints and to show the real reason for the comparative stagnation of exports and, conversely, for the tremendous increase of imports to the United States.

In 1978 and 1979, U.S. exports totaled about $142.8 and $182 billion, respectively, or about 6.2% of the gross national product. In terms of exports of manufactured goods, it would be helpful to compare export development in the United States with that of Germany and Japan between 1960 and 1978:

MERCHANDISE EXPORTS IN BILLIONS OF DOLLARS[1] (manufactured goods)

	U.S.	Germany	Japan
1960	$ 12.70	$ 5.10	$ 3.60
1971	$ 43.18	$ 37.27	$23.48
1975	$ 88.24	$ 72.86	$45.08
1976	$ 99.40	$ 86.02	$57.13
1977	$103.50	$ 97.73	$67.83
1978	$113.14	$110.19	$76.16

[1]SOURCE: United States Department of Commerce

These figures demonstrate the failure of U.S. exporters to keep pace with the nation's two biggest trade partners. It also shows the crucial relationship between exports and the health of the national economy. According to the U.S. Department of Commerce, every $1 billion in exports provides 40,000 jobs. It is clear that exports can and do provide a critical impetus to expansion of the U.S. economy and reduction of domestic unemployment. But the question must be asked if these contributions are optimal, or even if they are adequate. This is a particularly important question when we realize that exports of capital goods by Germany in 1977 exceeded U.S. exports of capital equipment, and the margin, in favor of Germany, has been growing very rapidly. In fact, between 1970 and 1976, German capital goods exports increased 280%, comprising 36.7% of total German exports. In Japan, meanwhile, the proportion of capital goods between 1970 and 1976 increased from 31% to 40% of its total exports.

Thus, if we wish to have a sound dollar and a strong economy, we must bear in mind the ever-narrowing gap between this nation and Japan in terms of capital-goods exports; and we must always remember that other countries such as the United Kingdom, France, Sweden, Italy, Belgium, the Netherlands, and Switzerland are also competing for more exports and bigger markets for their manufactured products. Japan and Germany have already proved that they can pay for higher oil prices by increased exports and also produce an unprecedented export surplus. Therefore the growth in our exports of manufactured goods is not only vital to the future of the dollar but also necessary to maintain employment in the United States.

In order to achieve these ends, U.S. exporters must be given every assistance in building a competitive edge in the world market. As the *International Economic Policy* special report stated: "Five elements are essential to the competitiveness of U.S. capital goods in the world marketplace: financing, quality, service, delivery date and price."[1] Unfortunately, it seems that the U.S. government's export policy has done everything possible to make those goals well-nigh unattainable.[2]

Lack of Sufficient Credit

Among the major industrial countries, the United States ranks last in assisting and extending credit to exporters. In 1976, 49% of Japanese exports, 40% of French exports, 38% of British exports, 10% of German exports, and only 8% of U.S. exports were financed by government banks and institutions.

In 1977 a survey of exporters' complaints was presented to the Senate Subcommittee on International Trade and Finance, which showed the following:

1. a lack of competitiveness of U.S. export-credit facilities relative to the nation's trade partners;

2. a lack of consistency in international export-credit practices;

3. a lack of consistency in international export-subsidy practices (i.e., the United States makes no attempt to offer its exporters the same advantages as other nations render their manufacturers);

4. a serious confusion of laws and regulations that actually hinders U.S. exporters from becoming truly competitive. In fact, there are almost as many laws and regulations related to U.S. world trade as there are varieties of export goods.

The survey represents a cross-section of U.S. manufacturers, with representation from every sector of industry. The main thrust of this survey is toward the competitiveness of the U.S. export credit system and how it matches up with the facilities of our trade partners. The issue of the great quantity of legislation and the many regulations that hinder U.S. exports is also discussed.

The survey indicates that between 1972 and 1976 annual loan authorization of the Export-Import Bank actually declined 8%. The clearest failure of the Export-Import Bank is shown in the fact that despite the increase in the international trade in the 1972–76 period, the United States lost a major market share to Japan and Germany, particularly in the capital goods areas.

In Japan and Germany the intervention of government in guiding and directing the economy is far more pronounced than in the United States. Japanese and German businessmen take it for granted that there will be a continuous dialogue between business leaders and government officials, and that neither will make major policy decisions or undertake major projects without consulting the other. Japanese and German businessmen, as a whole, do not object to their government's active involvement in business matters.

What Price Government Interventions and Shackles?

The U.S. administration contends that exporters are simplifying a very complicated situation. Export sales can be lost for a number of reasons, and thus it may be difficult to attribute loss of business to lack of credit alone. But exporters in a report to Congress included such information as delivery date, product, service involved, name of foreign competitors, and terms of U.S. and foreign financing.

The Export-Import Bank, in a survey of U.S. exporters with sales of $8.2 billion, found $900 million in lost sales because of lack of credit. However, a survey by the National Association of Manufacturers indicates that during 1975 a total of $3.2 billion was lost because of the lack of credit. Fifty-five percent of the U.S. exporters who responded to the survey reported lost sales on account of inadequate credit and financing.[3]

The following transactions represent a few of the cases cited in the survey that were presented to the Senate Subcommittee:

1. A heavy capital-goods manufacturer reported a potential sale of a cement plant to the Costa Rican government. The bid was awarded to a Spanish firm, which was able to offer credit terms of ten years with three years' grace on both principal and interest at the rate of 7½%. The Export-Import Bank's terms as to the total dollars and grace period were not sufficient.

2. An electrical power generator manufacturer won a bid on a two-power system to Venezuela valued at $55 million. The sale was eventually won by a Japanese manufacturer, who was able to provide a four-year grace period with repayment over ten years. Interest rates were fixed at 7½%. Financing of 100% of local cost was also made available.

The terms and conditions of the Export-Import Bank were: 10% cash payments and 90% in twenty semiannual installments, with the first installment due six months after completion of the plant. The Export-Import Bank would make a direct loan for 45% of the U.S. costs to be repaid from the last two installments. Interest rates were 8% fixed and the commitment fee was one-half of 1% per annum.

3. A major capital goods exporter won a $28 million order for the sale of a conveyor belt system to Pakistan. The Export-Import Bank refused to extend any loan or credit for the transaction. As a result the order was lost to France. The French exporter offered half of the loan for ten years at the rate of 1⅞% over London interbank offer rate and the balance over a period of twenty-five years.

4. A $31 million order from the Soviet Union was lost to a Japanese company. The U.S. Export-Import Bank, due to congressional regulations, showed no interest in the transaction. The Japanese Export-Import Bank's terms were five years in ten semiannual installments at an interest rate of

5½%. Furthermore, the down payment of 15% was financed by a Japanese bank.

5. An electrical-goods manufacturer reports that on several occasions substantial transactions were lost because of the lack of credit financing. "In one instance on a transport control system to Brazil with a total of $35 million of U.S. content, Eximbank offered credit terms of 10 percent cash down payment, 40 percent in direct credit and 30 percent with an Eximbank guarantee. Eximbank's interest rate was 9¼ percent per annum over nine and one-half years, coupled with a guarantee fee of one percent. Ultimately the sale was lost to a French consortium which was able to offer an 85 percent direct credit with a 15 percent cash down payment at 7½ percent per annum interest over ten years."[4]

6. On another occasion a $25 million telecommunication system sale in Iran was lost to a Belgian corporation. The Export-Import Bank's terms were 10% cash down payment and a 40% direct credit at 8½% over five years. The Export-Import Bank's terms were not competitive with either German or Belgian corporations. The German corporation offered a 90% direct credit at 8% interest over five years, while the Belgian firm's terms were a 90% direct credit at 7½% interest over eight years.

In the report to the Senate Subcommittee there are many instances when the customers were inclined to buy from the United States manufacturers but the terms presented by the Export-Import Bank were not acceptable, although there was no special commercial risk. Many transactions in Brazil, Mexico, and Venezuela were lost because the Export-Import Bank would not extend repayment beyond five years, which was Eximbank's maximum maturity for all transactions between $200,000 and $5 million.

The loss of these transactions represents the loss not only of sales, profits, and taxes in the United States but of thousands of jobs. If we use a Bureau of Labor Statistics estimate of 35,000 jobs related to each billion dollars' worth of exports in 1975, the total loss of jobs would surpass 112,000. A less conservative Treasury Department estimate of 58,000 jobs per billion dollars' worth of exports would bring the total loss of 187,000 jobs.

The American exporters prefer to export from the United States if possible. However, exactly 50% of the multinational corporations in the United States complained that because of inadequate financing they had been forced to supply goods from a foreign subsidiary in the past years. The major factors, according to a statement to the Senate Subcommittee, that causes these American corporations to use their subsidiaries outside the United States for sales to other countries can be summarized in six points:

> Eximbank financing for Eastern bloc purchase is unavailable to the American exporters.

What Price Government Interventions and Shackles? 125

Eximbank financing in many other countries is unpredictable or not available at all; for example, Turkey, South Africa, Algeria, Chile, Korea, Egypt, and several other countries.

Often the foreign interest rate is lower than the estimated blended Eximbank commercial rate.

Nearly always, Eximbank's requirements for a commitment are more stringent than their competitors' as to the information required.

Often, foreign competitors are able to cut short commitment time delays by using buyer credit lines, or "baskets" to support specific sales.

Repayment terms for medium-sized transactions ($500,000 to $5 million) are frequently of longer duration when shipping from a foreign source.

The growing tendency for U.S. exporters to utilize their subsidiaries overseas to supply finance from a foreign source as a "last-resort mechanism" to win a sale perhaps indicates the degree to which the administration in the past has failed to support American exports with credit financing.

Evidence of how the multinational corporations had to go through this difficult route was provided to the Senate Subcommittee by a paper-machinery manufacturer who described several sales that had to be channeled overseas because of lack of support of the Export-Import Bank:

> In 1975, a paper company concluded a deal to sell a newspaper mill to Argentina for $38 million. It applied to Export-Import Bank for financing and was advised that in view of the present conditions in Argentina they could not provide financing assistance. As a result of this refusal the manufacturer used its British subsidiary for financing and provided Argentina with the newspaper mill.

The question of competitiveness of the American exports is central to any future planning for expansion. U.S. exporters believe that under present GATT rules and the Export-Import Bank regulations this extension is very difficult. The Export-Import Bank Act, which goes back to 1945, is out of date. It requires that that bank should

> provide guarantees, insurance and extension of credits at rates and on terms and other conditions which are competitive with the government supported rates and terms and with other conditions available for the financing of exports from the principal countries whose exporters compete with the United States exporters.

Export-Import Bank's mandate is complicated by the lack of enough capital, by the policy, tradition, congressional interference, State Department's favoritism and the Bank's concern for profit. The end result of these conflicting mandates has been a credit facility whose priorities vacillate between providing U.S. exporters with competitive credit terms and other fiscal policy on budgetary objectives, including paying an adequate dividend to the U.S. Treasury.

From 1972 to 1976, according to U.S. exporters, "the major thrust of our experience is that the Bank is insufficiently competitive for reasons of slow response, the limited nature of its commitment to support any national export policy, its lack of programs comparable to those of counterpart institutions and its generally higher interest rates and charges."[6]

Many attempts have been made over the years to set up international guidelines governing the various aspects of the official export credit support program. Finally, in 1974, a preliminary "gentleman's agreement" was signed by major industrialized trading nations to establish a floor for officially supported export credit interest rates. Further efforts by the Berne Union and the OECD to establish various agreements binding the participants to limit in various ways their official credit support have been of no avail.

Because of the difficulties in reaching international agreement to broaden the scope of the 1974 "gentleman's agreement," several unilateral declarations were made by the United States and several other industrialized nations in June of 1976. The general terms of these declarations were:

1. Cash payment will be a minimum of 15% of the export contract value.

2. Interest rates will not be less than 8% for credits over five years to developed countries, 7¾% for credits over five years to intermediate countries, and 7½% for credits over five years to less developed countries.

3. Repayment terms will not be more than ten years to less developed countries and eight and one-half years to all others.

The consensus agreed upon by the United States, Germany, Japan, Britain, France, Italy, and Canada in 1976 and extended through December of 1978 solved few problems. It proved, however, that the trade partners can consult, discuss, and narrow their trade differences through agreements.

The trouble, so far, with declarations and harmonious schemes has been lack of adequate controls to assure adherence by all participants. Without the inclusion of some mechanism to assure compliance by all participants, no real progress could be achieved.

Despite all these declarations, the U.S. exporters contend that they are confronted with many problems that their counterparts have never experienced:

1. Various ceilings on loans to socialist nations, including the Soviet Union, penalize manufacturers as compared with other foreign competition. The result is that many times American companies are not even sent copies of

the tenders and a larger market is lost by U.S. exporters to Eastern Europe and the Soviet Union.[7]

2. The requirement that officially financed American exports should be shipped on U.S. carriers is very often a hindrance to sales.

3. The most damaging problem is political meddling and interference, which is often based on prejudice, impulse, and political opportunism. The review period requirement by Congress for any proposed export-import credit, or guarantee of $60 million or more, and for any nuclear-related technology, fuel, material, or goods and services, is time-consuming and highly detrimental to the American export trade.

This review requirement often is a hindrance to the conclusion of a contract when other business conditions have been resolved. Such procedures indicate the unreliability of dealing with a U.S. source of supply. Experience shows that politically oriented interest groups can block or delay approval of commercially sound transactions through Congress. The Jackson Amendment concerning Soviet and Eastern European nations and the restrictions of trade with Libya, South Africa, Chile, Saudi Arabia, Syria, Uganda, and other nations are examples cited by exporters.[8]

Furthermore, the United States has an unbelievable array of restrictions on any kind of arms shipments, as well as on anything with the potential of becoming a weapon, such as nuclear technology. It has a whole range of limitations on goods that the government deems to be in short supply or that are considered potentially hazardous. And the list of restrictions that exporters must take into account seems endless.

Military-Export Controls

The government, among other things, controls the export of arms and munitions to virtually all destinations. In addition, under such laws as the Foreign Assistance Act of 1961, it restricts the export of civilian items that might contribute to the military potential of countries engaged in, or threatening to engage in, regional conflicts.

Under the Mutual Defense Assistance Control Act of 1951 (the so-called Battle Act), strategic items are embargoed to nations threatening U.S. security, including the Soviet Union and nations under its domination. Control mechanisms to implement this embargo, however, are contained in the Arms Export Control Act and the Export Administration Act of 1974.

The Export Administration Act, for instance, authorizes the denial of exports of any kind to "any nation or combination of nations threatening the national security of the United States if the President determines that their export would prove detrimental to the national security of the United

States." The Commerce Department administers this particular act, under which the vast majority of U.S. exports are controlled, consulting extensively in its decisions with the Departments of State, Defense, Energy, and Treasury, as well as other concerned agencies.

Under the Arms Export Control Act, Congress prohibits foreign military sales that could have a significant adverse effect on the combat readiness of U.S. armed forces, unless the president determines that the sale is important to U.S. security.

Congress requires thirty days' advance notice of any proposed foreign military sale of major defense equipment for $7 million or more, or of any defense article or services for $25 million or more. It also requires thirty days' notice of a proposed export license for any commercially sold major defense shipment valued at $7 million or more, or for any munitions-list item valued at $25 million or more.

In addition, Congress requires thirty days' notice of the proposed approval of a commercial technical assistance or manufacturing license agreement involving the manufacturing abroad of significant combat equipment for a non-NATO country. And it prohibits any export license for major defense equipment sold commercially for $25 million or more, except to NATO countries, Japan, Australia, or New Zealand, or in furtherance of intergovernmental production arrangements.

Congress prohibits direct or indirect assistance of any kind for military operations in Zaire. It also prohibits military assistance, training, security-supporting assistance, military credits, or export licenses for commercially sold munitions-list items to Chile.[9]

Nuclear Technology and Materials

The amended Atomic Energy Act of 1954, the Nuclear Nonproliferation Act of 1978, and the amended Export-Import Bank Act of 1945 all provide controls on the export to virtually all destinations of materials that contribute to nuclear weaponry. In addition, the supplier nations of nuclear power have agreed to require safeguard for exporting to nonnuclear countries specific items that are judged to contribute to nuclear weapons capabilities.

The United States goes beyond even these multilateral controls in requiring safeguards for the export of such items to nuclear weapon countries as well as nonnuclear ones. It also requires the review of such exports not on the multilateral list as advanced computers, high-speed cameras, flash X-ray equipment, and certain laser systems. The rationale is that these items could be used for military purposes.

Until the early 1970s, U.S. manufacturers dominated the world marketplace in sales of nuclear-power reactors. Since then, the U.S. share of the export reactor market has dropped steadily each year from 100% in 1972

What Price Government Interventions and Shackles?

to 17% in 1977. And the reason for this severe decline can be found in the stringent regulations, indecisions, and changes of policy that govern nuclear-export controls in Washington.

Germany, France, Britain, Sweden, Canada, the Soviet Union—and, in the near future, Japan—all produce reactors for both domestic and foreign markets. In each of these countries the industries are supported and subsidized by their respective governments. In the United States the story is very different. Instead of being offered highly favorable financing arrangements and other political assistance, as nuclear industries have been elsewhere, U.S. vendors have often lost overseas reactor sales because they could not get export licenses and bank credit, or even the government's cooperation.

Other nations offer nuclear-fuel-cycle services that the United States will not, as a matter of policy, supply. France, for instance, guarantees the buyers of French reactors their uranium supplies, enrichment services, and the reprocessing of spent fuel. These are all very important services that no American corporation is able to provide.

Over the years the U.S. policy concerning reactor exports has vacillated. As a result, many potential buyers have turned to other nations to assist them with their nuclear programs. Grave doubts have arisen as to whether the United States can be considered a reliable supplier of nuclear-reactor fuel.

American reactor manufacturers have already lost out on such potentially large export markets as Pakistan, Brazil, and India because of continued delays in concluding contracts and credit assistance from the Export-Import Bank, and the lack of any kind of support from the U.S. government. As Dwight J. Porter, director of international government affairs for Westinghouse Electric Company, told the Senate Subcommittee on International Trade and Finance: "Nuclear power plants are much in demand around the world. They provide multibillion-dollar opportunities for U.S. exports, if only such exports are not jeopardized by Congress or the negative impact of other U.S. government policies."[10]

Foreign competition for nuclear exports is aggressive and formidable, as it is for any goods with defensive potential. Not only have other countries developed the productive capacity and sales organization to match U.S. marketing efforts; they have also, with the help of their governments, met American competition in advanced technology, traditionally an area dominated by U.S. companies.

Goods in Short Supply

The Export Administration Act of 1969, the Trans-Alaskan Pipeline Authorization Act of 1973, and the Energy Act of 1975 all prohibit the export of short-supply commodities. Crude oil and petroleum commodities are the only products at this time subject to short-supply limitations. Products included in these export quotas are aviation and motor gasoline, kerosene, jet fuel distillate, and residential fuel oils, butane, natural gas liquids, and certain general-purpose naphthas.

General Limitations on Trade

The U.S. government also imposes restrictions on which countries exporters may sell their goods to, and the list of embargoed nations increases daily. Nations of late have been added for alleged human-rights violations, for adhering to anti-Israeli and/or anti-Jewish boycotts, for harboring terrorists, or because they are part of the Soviet bloc of Communist countries or are ruled by a regime that Washington considers anathema to U.S. democratic ideals.

Human-Rights Violations

According to the Human Rights Act of Congress, "no security assistance may be provided to any country the government of which engages in a consistent pattern of gross violations of internationally recognized human rights. Security assistance may not be provided to the police, domestic intelligence, or similar law enforcement services of a country, and licenses may not be issued under the Export Administration Act of 1969 for the export of crime control and detection instruments and equipment to a country, the government of which engages in a consistent pattern of gross violations of internationally recognized human rights unless the President certifies in writing to the speaker of the House of Representatives and the chairman of the Senate Foreign Relations Committee that extraordinary circumstances warrant provision of such assistance and issuance of such licenses."

Antiboycott Controls

There exist three inconsistent antiboycott programs administered by three different departments under three different laws: the 1977 amendment to the Export Administration Act of 1969, which is administered by the Commerce and the Treasury Departments; the Tax Reform Act of 1976, which is administered by the Treasury Department; and the Sherman Antitrust Act, which is administered by the Department of Justice.

Under the Tax Reform Act, for instance, the so-called Ribicoff Amendment denies certain tax benefits to companies found participating in or cooperating with foreign boycotts. Furthermore, the Justice Department has said that, in certain circumstances, a U.S. company that complies with or assists in the Arab League boycott of Israel can be charged under Section 1 of the Sherman Act with implementing a conspiracy to boycott persons in the United States.

These three programs, passed under the insistence of pressure groups without enough consideration for the national interests of the United States, are implemented with confusion, vagueness, and difficulties by the Commerce, Treasury, and Justice Departments. This regulatory maze has caused serious delays and uncertainties in the business community, has complicated the activity of exporters, and has hindered potential exporters from marketing their goods and services to foreign buyers.

Terrorist Controls

The Foreign Assistance Act of 1961, Export Administration Act of 1969, and an amendment to the Export-Import Bank Act of 1945 all impose restrictions on the export of selected items to countries judged to be giving aid or haven to terrorists.

So far, these limitations have been used for domestic political reasons against Libya, South Yemen, and Iraq, among other nations. Thus, while the United States buys close to $5 billion worth of oil from Libya and Iraq, under domestic pressure, the administration and Congress prevent the sale of American products to these nations.

In 1978, for instance, the Commerce Department approved the sale of three Boeing 747s to Libya. The contract was signed, Libya paid for the planes, and Commerce officials issued the export license. On May 24, 1979, because of Libya's opposition to the Israeli-Egyptian peace agreement and its support of Ugandan president Idi Amin's action against Tanzania, Secretary of State Cyrus R. Vance asked Commerce Secretary Juanita M. Kreps to stop the previously approved sale "in light of events in Uganda."

The State Department also asked Commerce to disapprove the sale of other planes, such as the Lockheed L 100 Cargo Transport, which was to be sold to Libya in 1979. This time Secretary Vance's reversal came after Senator Richard Stone of Florida, a staunch supporter of Israel, protested against the proposed sale.

How can any government trust the decisions or the promises of the United States and the contracts of American corporations under such circumstances? The Libyan orders, if accepted, would have brought close to $2 billion annually. Unfortunately, the orders will now go to France, the Soviet Union, Germany, and England, where politics and business seldom mix.

Sanctions against Communist Nations

Section 402 of the Trade Act of 1974 (the so-called Jackson-Vanick Amendment) applies to those new market-economy countries that did not enjoy most-favored-nation treatment on January 3, 1975 (all nations but Yugoslavia and Poland). The president must either report that such a country permits free emigration or must obtain assurances of practices that will lead to freer emigration before permitting it to participate in any U.S. government program that extends direct or indirect credit, credit guarantees, or investment guarantees.

Section 409 of the same act (the so-called Helms Amendment) imposes essentially the same restrictions, but deals with the freedom of emigration of citizens in other nations to join a close relative in the United States.

The amended Export-Import Bank Act of 1945 and Section 613 of the Trade Act of 1974 put a ceiling of $300 million on Ex-Im credits for Soviet fossil-fuel research or exploration, and a $25 million ceiling on Ex-Im loans for Soviet credit purchases in the United States.

No wonder that U.S. trade with the Soviet Union dropped 25% in 1978, or that Germany's exports to the Soviet Union are twice as large as U.S. exports to that country.

Embargoes against Cuba and Southeast Asia

A virtually complete embargo exists on trade with Cuba and the Southeast Asian countries of North Korea, Vietnam, and Cambodia (Kampuchea). This prohibits all exports of U.S.-origin goods and technical data, or the products of U.S. technical data, and of goods and technical data from U.S. subsidiaries located abroad, although a few transactions have been licensed to Vietnam—mainly food supplies and medicine on humanitarian grounds. Items not on the strategic list of embargoed goods may be exported under special license to Cuba; and items manufactured abroad by a U.S. company not exceeding 20% of that company's output may be sold to that country.

Embargoes against African Nations

A virtually complete embargo exists on trade with Rhodesia and Uganda, and a selective embargo exists on trade with South Africa and Libya. In addition, the Export-Import Bank is restricted from financing exports to these nations.[1]

Limitations on Doing Business

Increasingly, the U.S. government has been imposing restrictions on the way in which corporations can do business. With more and more laws controlling illicit payments to foreign officials and imposing environmental and other constraints on products, the net result has been to reduce the

Controls on Corrupt Practices

The Foreign Corrupt Practices Act of 1977 is designed to eliminate illicit payments by U.S. companies to foreign government officials and political figures in order to do business or achieve a particular business goal in a foreign country.

Uncertainty about the meaning of certain provisions of the act, coupled with the almost total absence of any enforcement history, affects the ability and willingness of American corporations to operate in certain countries where local business customs and traditions may include significant payments to agents and brokers to complete business arrangements. Also, such normal and desirable dealings as reliance on a foreign joint-venture partner, sales agent, or subcontractor to handle local aspects of a business relationship are made more difficult. Thus, some U.S. companies, in the face of these impediments created by the Congress and the media, are losing their business to foreign corporations that are not bound by such vague and uncertain hindrances.

Faced with the withdrawal of many U.S. companies from overseas markets, President Carter in September 1978 directed the Justice Department to clarify the ambiguous antibribery law. Yet after years of study the uncertainties of the Foreign Corrupt Practices Act still persist, and the Commerce Department contends that the requested "guidance" seems many more months away, if it ever comes at all.

The reason for the delay is that the Justice Department, supported by key officials of the Securities and Exchange Commission, believes that the law is not enforceable and that the government would never be able to prosecute the violators. Therefore it would be better to keep the law ambiguous. To many prosecutors and SEC enforcers, clarification would amount to publishing what would be equivalent to a road map showing how companies are evading the antibribery law.

Says Assistant Commerce Secretary Weil: "The smaller companies, the ones that the Carter Administration is urging to boost exports to a greater extent, are the most severely hampered." And, he adds, "the more uncertainties that exist, the tougher it is on the little guy, the small or medium-sized firms. The big fellows can take care of themselves."[12]

One section of the statute requires little clarification. Company officers, directors, or employers convicted of paying bribes abroad to government officials, political personalities, or parties for the purpose of gaining or retaining business could be jailed for up to five years, and corporations could be fined up to $1 million.

"These penalties, plus provoking enforcement action by the SEC, clearly foreclose certain foreign markets in which payoffs grease the wheels of commerce. The field is wide open to Western European and Japanese exporters who are not bound by any laws or regulations. But the harsh anti-bribery law goes beyond just plain prohibitions and penalties. It also can be enforced against the executives of a corporation if their agents abroad are offering bribes. This provision is the source of great concern."[13]

According to a Commerce spokesman, "the uncertainties associated with visiting the sins of an agent upon an innocent principal back home is the core of the problem. They are frightening a number of legitimate businessmen from doing a great deal of legitimate business through commission agents."[14]

Unfortunately, the Justice Department prefers broad statutory language that gives its agents maximum flexibility. "If a company," states Richard Beckler, chief of the Justice Department's Fraud Section, "hires an agent under an arms'-length contract, if they pay him a commission generally consistent with going rates, if all the paperwork is handled properly, and if transactions with him are approved in the ordinary course of business, then you probably don't have the elements of a criminal case."

Under these circumstances, how can we expect any improvement in foreign trade and the increased export of U.S. goods?

How much business is being lost by American corporations as a result of this law is impossible to determine, but the figures used by some companies are close to several billion dollars. The hardest-hit firms are large international construction companies. These corporations state that in certain countries it is even impossible to receive a copy of the bidding lists without paying an "entry fee" to a local agent who has good connections with the government in power. In 1976 the United States ranked first in its share of the overseas construction market. Then came the Foreign Practice Act of 1977, which in the course of two years pushed the United States to fifth place—trailing Japan, Korea, West Germany, and Italy.[15]

In 1978, according to the *Wall Street Journal,* U.S. companies lost a $1.2 billion hospital construction program in Saudi Arabia to Eurosystem Hospitalice, a Belgian firm. In July 1979 the lid was lifted a bit on how the Americans lost the deal to a company allegedly unqualified for such a big project, and as a result the firm plunged into bankruptcy. The crash was attributed to "excessive" secret commissions estimated at $282 million that were paid to obtain the Saudi contract. The Belgian royal family was reportedly involved because Prince Albert, brother of King Baudouin, was the leading member of the Belgian business mission to Saudi Arabia that obtained the contract.[16]

Then there is the case of Swindell-Bressler Co., a large Pittsburgh-based engineering and construction firm that contends it was "cheated" out of a number of big overseas construction jobs because of payoffs to foreign government officials by European competitors. One of the projects was a $40 million brick plant in Iraq.

"We thought we had the thing all wrapped up," Harvey Trilli, corporation president, told the *Wall Street Journal*. "We had a team of people there for five or six weeks. All the terms were agreed to, including the pricing, and we were told the contract would be signed in a month. Then out of the clear blue sky, a German firm got the contract."

Trilli said he believed the Germans got the contract because they made a big payment to a high official in Iraq. (Bribery by West German companies to obtain foreign contracts is not illegal in West Germany, and the companies may even deduct such costs as a business expense for tax purposes.)[17]

Meanwhile, the Chicago Bridge and Iron Company complains that it has lost "in excess of $100 million of sales over the last three years due to the bribery of the other corporations." Midland-Ross Corporation in Cleveland cites two instances of subjected payoffs this year in overseas contract negotiations. Both involve paper mill equipment for two West African nations. The company says it lost the deals to Italian corporations that paid 10% of the contract's value to the president of one of the countries.

Cincinnati's Milacrom Inc., one of the nation's largest producers of machine tools and other industrial products, says it has lost most of its business because of "restrictions on where we can pay legitimate sales commission. But the other nations of the world do not play by our rules."[18]

One place where the table has turned most dramatically against U.S. companies is in the aerospace industry, where U.S. producers once held 90% of the market. For many years these aerospace companies were active participants in paying out millions of dollars in "commissions and fees" to some of the most highly placed "sales agents" in the world, reportedly including the leader of government in Iran at the time, Japanese politicians, and the husband of the queen of the Netherlands. Now, under the provisions of a 1977 law, they are required to sit on the sidelines watching Airbus Industries, a European consortium,[19] selling Airliner A 300 to many governments. "The Aerospatiales," according to American plane producers, are completely at liberty to take on anybody they wish as a consultant for a retainer or a commission. From 1978 to 1979 the consortium successfully sold the A 300 to Singapore, Indonesia, Thailand, Malaysia, and the Philippines. In Indonesia, for example, the agent of Airbus was reportedly a member of the cabinet.

Businessmen and government officials abroad, meanwhile, are responding with attitudes ranging from commiseration to amusement at the controls now imposed on their U.S. competitors. An informal poll of more than a dozen British and European businessmen indicated a unanimous opinion that the United States has lost business because of the restrictions of the 1977 law.

Frederick Catherwood, a former chairman of the British overseas trade, says that in many parts of the world companies cannot do business unless they pay the entry fee. And he raises the question of the extent to which a nation can impose its laws and regulations overseas. "Can you make illegal in your own country something which is only nominally illegal—but not enforced—in another country? The U.S. has said more or less, 'yes we can' and other countries have said 'no, we cannot.' Legislation against illegal foreign payments has minimal public support in the United Kingdom."[20]

When a subsidiary of British Petroleum, partly owned by the British government, was shown through SEC findings to have made payoffs totaling up to £5 million to win a Saudi computer contract, the British government refused even to discuss the case. Similarly, when the papers revealed that British Leyland had used bribes in many of its transactions, the British authorities refused to investigate.

It is alleged that business payoffs are a way of life in West Germany and Japan. Neither country has shown any concern regarding this allegation, and often the government officials help corporations succeed in their negotiations. Both countries take the attitude that business bribes are an established way of transacting business. Even after former prime minister Kakuei Tanaka was arrested and jailed on charges of receiving a $1.7 million bribe from a Japanese agent of Lockheed Aircraft Corporation, he was reelected as a member of the lower house of Parliament, receiving one of the largest votes cast in the election.

In 1978 the U.S. invited other nations to join this country in an anticommercial-bribery treaty. So far, there has been no response, and the U.S. draft treaty is languishing in an inactive committee of the United Nations Economic and Social Council with little prospect for any kind of agreement.

"Meanwhile," according to an article in the *Wall Street Journal,* "the unilateral American effort to upgrade the ethical standards of international business, is blocking off large chunks of the globe as unsafe areas for U.S. companies to solicit business. These 'sensitive areas,'" businessmen say, "include not only many developing nations in Africa, the Far East, and Central and South America, but also the oil rich nations of the Middle East."[21]

No one is against a logical and reasonable international antibribery law, but the current Foreign Corrupt Practices Act, combined with the Anti-Boycott Act and various other legislation, has tied the hands of American businessmen and totally disarmed them in the face of competitors who are armed not only with "commissions, fees, and bribes, but the blessing and support of their governments."[22]

A Lack of Cargo Preference

Commercial-cargo preference does not exist under U.S. law. Importers and exporters of commercial cargoes are free to use the most convenient or the least expensive carrier available, regardless of flag of origin. Some operators and unions within the U.S. maritime community want the government to establish a system of commercial-cargo preference that would bring U.S.-flag carriers a guaranteed share of commercial cargo. But other shippers consider this expensive and detrimental to the export of U.S. products. So far, the government has never defined the purpose of the preference cargo. Occasionally the administration has supported the idea and has been pressured by exporters to use American ships.

There is, however, a well-developed cargo-preference requirement on government-owned-and-financed cargoes. This category includes such items as agricultural commodities sold under P.L. 480, Export-Import Bank financed exports, defense-related materials, and foreign military sales on credit. The P.L. 480 program requires that U.S.-flag vessels carry at least 50% of these cargoes. One hundred percent of Export-Import Bank–financed cargoes must be carried on U.S.-flag vessels, although the Maritime Administration frequently grants waivers allowing 50% to be carried by foreign flagships. One hundred percent of all military cargoes must also be carried on U.S.-flag vessels.

Where the United States Has Gone Wrong

Under the Export Administration Act of 1969, exports of goods and technology of U.S. origin can be controlled for national security, foreign policy, and short-supply purposes. Implementing regulations to the act has established an elaborate export-licensing system, although the great bulk of U.S. exports leaves the country under a general license (a broad authorization permitting certain exports under specified conditions). Neither the filing of an application by exporters nor the issuance of a license document by the Commerce Department is required. And only 10% of U.S. exports requires a validated license, a formal document that is issued to an exporter after his signed application is approved.

Nonetheless, there are restrictions on many goods and virtual embargoes on a myriad of countries. The net result is that the export license process can include delays of up to several months, and that means trouble for U.S. exporters.

According to a report issued by Jonathan B. Bingham, chairman of the House Subcommittee on International Economic Policy and Trade, U.S. license impositions have caused delays and the loss of trade to American exporters. He writes:

Alarmists in Congress and the Executive branch have seized upon the national uneasiness over Soviet actions in Africa, and the national revulsion over the treatment of Soviet dissidents, to subject the entire concept of East-West trade to the most serious attack it has faced in the last 15 years at least.

In this emotional atmosphere, it will be extremely difficult to maintain a focus on the tough but crucial questions of export control policy as it applies to the Communist countries.[23]

Unfortunately, these export regulations are subject to the interference of lobbyists, pressure groups, Cold War advocates, and politicians. The original Export Administration Act was designed to further U.S. foreign-trade policy. Today, under the pressure of different interest groups, its scope is steadily expanding, both through the denial of export licenses for individual items and through broader embargoes. Thus, the current export licensing process is plagued by many problems:

1. the inefficiency of the process;

2. the presumption of license denial that is built into the process;

3. the interference of members of Congress;

4. the pressure from different vested-interest groups;

5. the existence of an entrenched bureaucracy—making export-licensing decisions—that is not accountable to those most affected.

The current process is so unwieldly that one wonders that it produces any decisions at all. The Commerce Department's office in Washington receives 70,000 applications a year. In 1979 it was close to 85,000. That works out to nearly 350 per working day. Backlogs are increasing as licensing officials slowly lose the paperwork battle. Too many products are subject to control, right down to microprocessors, that are generally available throughout the Western world and that a Soviet Embassy official could purchase for $15 from Radio Shack and carry it out of the country in his pocket. Too many agencies must sign off on too many licensing decisions, and there are no effective limits on how much time they can take to reach a determination.

In addition, the system, when closely examined, is structured so that there is a built-in incentive for those who oppose exports to Communist countries or to Arab states or who dislike big corporations, to use delay as a tactic. The result is that many applications simply disappear or languish in the bureaucratic maze until the customer finally cancels the order.[24]

It seems strange that in a free-enterprise society there should exist so many legal and administrative obstacles for the export of civilian goods. "A businessman should have the right to export a particular type of civilian product to a particular destination unless the government intervenes and determines that for some overriding reason of public policy that type of export should be controlled."[25]

To complicate the situation even more, this complicated and frustrating system is at the mercy of a cumbersome and obsolete bureaucracy that is the legacy of the old days, when export's role was so insignificant. "This bureaucracy," according to the chairman of the Subcommittee on International Trade, "has become accustomed to functioning in near-total secrecy without having to account for its decisions." He adds: "Rarely is a meaningful explanation for a denial or a delay provided to the exporter unless he happens to be well-connected in Washington. A prospective exporter seldom has an opportunity to sit down with licensing officials, present his case, rebut their arguments, and make sure they understand the equipment in question. A great deal of secrecy prevails; it is difficult even for committees of Congress, let alone the exporters, to find out the status of an application or, if it was denied, the reason for the denial."[26]

The broad power bestowed on the administration by the Export Administration Act of 1969 has been subject to pressure from many groups inside and outside Congress, even from foreign governments. Thus Taiwan was denied an export license because Communist China does not like Taiwan. The Mainland Chinese contended that the proposed machinery exports to China could be used to fabricate missiles. The administration denied the license because it feared that any other action would harm its delicate relations with Communist China in the midst of normalization negotiations.

In 1978, following the trials of two Russian dissenters by the Soviet authorities, President Carter canceled the sale of a Sperry Univac computer to the Soviet Union. Six months later, changing his policy, he approved the issuance of a license for the same computer. Alas, it was too late; the Russians had already purchased a French computer.

The main problem with this type of foreign-policy control is its instability and unpredictability. Business cannot thrive, or even survive, in a world of indecision, instability, and changing policies.

If the United States hopes once again to lead the world politically and economically, it must put its own economic house in order. It must realize that a large trade deficit and a weak currency only cause world chaos. A nation cannot increase its exports by speeches, congressional hearings, or press conferences. Instead, it must remove restraints and restrictions on trade and provide business with confidence, stability, and incentives.

What the Government Can Do

The above examples of misdirection show that the time has come for the administration and Congress to change their present policy of hindrance and adopt the following policy, suggested by the chairman of the House Subcommittee on International Economic Policy:

1. The assumption should always be that a company has the right to export, and that the U.S. government will intervene in that effort only for carefully formulated and important reasons of public policy.

2. The government policy should be predictable. The system of controls for national security must be simple, clear, and prompt. Trade interests must not be sacrificed to the vicissitudes of domestic politics and foreign pressures. Rules must not be changed in midstream, because the result is to create uncertainty in the minds of exporters and distrust in foreign markets as to the dependability of U.S. promises, contracts, and performance.

In the words of Subcommittee Chairman Bingham: "The American public, as well as policymakers, must keep in mind certain principles: that trade is in itself good for this nation; that there are limits to our influence; that export controls, like all aspects of foreign policy, must be open and as accountable as possible; that we have to be clear about our objectives, and, in trying to shape a policy, must avoid simple answers; and our trade policy should be an expression of what is good and not what is vindictive in us. With these guidelines, the Congress, the Executive Branch, and the American people should be able to evolve an export policy that supports and contributes to a constructive American foreign policy."[27]

The truth of the matter is that these roadblocks have created an atmosphere of uncertainty among businessmen and foreign customers. The *Government Executive*, in its September 1974 issue, expressed the feeling of the business community when it said: "While the U.S. Government takes little part in international commerce, other nations such as France, England, the Federal Republic of Germany, and Japan are encouraging further monopolistic practices as well as subsidizing major efforts in international competition."

Unfortunately, although these statements were made four years ago, they are just as true today. In August 1978 the Senate passed an amendment to the Military Assistance Authorization Bill that would have required an export license for shipping products "with a direct military application" to non-Communist countries "engaged in activities detrimental to U.S. interests."

According to the Congressional staff, the amendment would have exempted products sold to NATO countries, Japan, Australia, and New Zealand. It was aimed at products bought by many developing nations. It would have included helicopters ordered by Uganda and heavy-duty trucks ordered by Algeria, Libya, Syria, Iraq, and other countries.

If our purpose was to penalize these countries, we have utterly failed. In 1977 the United States purchased $5 billion worth of oil from Libya and then restricted sales of American products to that country.

It is all too clear that if we do not sell helicopters and trucks to Libya, Algeria, South Africa, or Iraq, then the Russians, the Germans, the French, the British, and even the Israelis will clinch those deals. In the end, American manufacturers will lose contracts, American workers will lose jobs, and the dollar will decline even further.

The Senate amendment created great concern among electronics manufacturers in particular, and as a result of their opposition the Senate-House Conference Committee eliminated the amendment.

But one defeated amendment does not change the fact that the United States can no longer claim to be the leader of the industrial world. The country now ranks third in machine-tool production, behind the Soviet Union and West Germany. And the Japanese have virtually taken over our markets for televisions, cameras, motorcycles, and small cars.

Says *Business Week:* "Where the U.S. government consistently harasses IBM, the Japanese Government consistently supports, encourages, and even subsidizes its computer industry. Where the U.S. government is hung up on antitrust, the Japanese government encourages joint efforts to create fewer but stronger computer markets."

Thus Japan's Ministry of International Trade and Industry created the Japan Electronic Computer Company, now capitalized at $200 million. JEC uses both government subsidies and low-cost government loans to finance the rental of Japanese-produced computers.[28]

Unfortunately, all the talk and efforts have so far produced few satisfactory results. For two decades different administrations have ignored the seriousness of the trade problem, the large military expenditures in Germany and Japan, and expanding foreign aid that has produced the present decline and devaluation of the dollar throughout the world.

Whether the current administration, without cutting foreign aid and military expenditures, increasing exports, or restricting imports, can correct the trade and balance-of-payments deficits is still in doubt. The coming year of retrenchment is likely to be of some help, by restraining imports and encouraging greater efforts to export American products.

But the fundamental question is whether there will be a radical change in public and private spending. This country has been running a massive deficit in its balance-of-payments for some twenty-five years. It is high time to give immediate and serious consideration to the following suggestions:

1. An immediate termination of unnecessary military expenditures abroad by giving such prosperous countries as Germany and Japan a choice between reducing U.S. military personnel to a token force, or relieving the United States from local expenditures in the host country. If neither of

these two suggestions is acceptable, the United States should issue scrip dollars to be used only for the purchase of American goods.

2. Since we cannot persuade Japan and Western Europe to change their systems of indirect subsidies, the United States must develop a system of taxes and subsidies tailored to curb imports and encourage exports of American products. Many U.S. businessmen suggest that one way to reduce the trade deficit is to shift from the corporate income tax to a value-added tax—a kind of sales tax that would be rebated to exporters.

3. A new state of mind based on a global-oriented industrial policy must be developed by the administration and the business community. This policy should involve persistent pressure by the government to eliminate tariff and nontariff barriers to U.S. exports. U.S. negotiators in the past have shown little ability or competence to protect our trade interests.

4. A more effective partnership between the U.S. business community and the government must be established. Greater effort at export promotion by business is of the utmost importance. Government and business should also develop a major program in the field of research and development aimed at helping this nation regain its international leadership in technological innovation.

5. A study of productivity and investment in capital equipment is essential to the success of this new economic policy.

6. Our national priorities must be reexamined in the light of the declining dollar and the weakened U.S. economic position in a more competitive world.

7. Such measures are absolutely necessary, because the United States cannot stand another decade of trade negligence and military expenditure abroad, foreign-aid giveaways, indecision, and lethargy. Otherwise, persistent disequilibrium in the U.S. balance-of-trade payments will create chronic unemployment, slow growth, recession, a declining dollar, a loss of confidence in U.S. leadership, and, eventually, the disintegration of the American economic system.

Notes

1. *International Economic Policy,* Special Report (NAM Export Credit Survey Report, December 28, 1977).
2. Ibid.
3. The Export-Import Bank survey covers a period of nine months in 1976. Thus, on an annual basis, total lost sales conceded by Eximbank would amount to $1.2 billion from the companies that responded.
4. National Association of Manufacturers Report to Senate Subcommittee on International Finance, April 14, 1978.

5. Ibid.
6. Report to the Senate Subcommittee, April 7 and 13, 1978. In 1980 the Bank's capital was increased to $40 billion.
7. In 1977 West Germany was the Soviet Union's biggest trading partner. The two countries exchanged about $5 billion worth of goods, while U.S.-Soviet trade declined by 28% to about $1.7 billion. A.E.G. Telefanker received $500 million of orders for the Soviet market. (Part of the business the company is doing involves selling American technology under license to German companies.) A.E.G. also won a $732 million contract for gas turbine pumps in 1976, using license from General Electric. American businessmen explain the Soviet withdrawal of business from the United States on political grounds. West German businessmen can get government guarantees and subsidies from Bonn for trade with Russia; but American businessmen get the Jackson Amendment, harassment from members of Congress, and hindrance from the bureaucracy in Washington.
8. In a recent debate on the Export-Import Bank Bill, Senator Towers of Texas submitted an amendment that, if accepted, would exclude 75 nations from using Export-Import Bank's credit.
9. Section 33, Arms Export Control Act: Sections 36(b), 36(c), 36(d), and 38(b); Arms Export Control Act: Sections 620(F) and 620(T); Foreign Assistance Act of 1961.
10. Testimony presented to the Senate Subcommittee on International Trade & Finance, April 13, 1978.
11. With the fall of Idi Amin in Uganda and the independence of Rhodesia, embargoes against these two nations have been removed.
12. Department of Commerce press release, May 29, 1979.
13. *Wall Street Journal,* May 30, 1979.
14. Quoted in ibid.
15. See the study by the National Constructors Association, Washington, D.C., 1979.
16. *Wall Street Journal,* August 2, 1979.
17. Ibid.
18. Statement by James A. D. Geier, President of Milacrom Inc.
19. Airbus Industries is owned mainly by French and West German aircraft makers, including Société Nationale Industrielle Aerospatiale, the French state-owned aerospace company.
20. Statement made to the *Wall Street Journal,* August 2, 1979.
21. *Wall Street Journal,* August 2, 1979.
22. Ibid.
23. Jonathan B. Bingham, *Foreign Affairs* (Spring 1979).
24. See *Foreign Affairs* (Spring 1979).
25. Ibid.
26. Congressman Jonathan B. Bingham's report in ibid.
27. See Marina N. Whitman, "A Year of Trial: The United States and the International Economy," *Foreign Affairs* (Fall 1978); Report of J. Bingham, chairman of the House Subcommittee on International Economic Policy and Trade, 1979.
28. *Business Week,* May 15, 1978.

5
The Impact of Taxation on International Trade

Kings ought to shear, not skin their sheep.

Robert Herrick

Overtaxation cost England her colonies of North America.

Edmund Burke

The general rule always holds good. In constitutional states liberty is a compensation for the heaviness of taxation. In despotic states the equivalent for liberty is the lightness of taxation.

Montesquieu

Taxing is an easy business. Any projector can contrive new impositions, any bungler can add to the old, but it is altogether wise to have no other bounds to your impositions than the patience of those who are to bear them.

Edmund Burke

As was noted in the previous chapters, three opposite trends have had a substantial impact on U.S. international trade relations over the past two decades: (1) the "Kennedy Round" of trade negotiations during the 1960s resulted in reducing tariffs by stages; (2) certain import duties in the United States and a few other nations were gradually lowered; and (3) as a result, Japan and many Western European countries adopted policies to encourage export subsidies and other nontariff barrier incentives.

The distortions to trade caused by these nontariff barriers, export subsidies, and tax burdens have had serious consequences for the economic well-being of the United States. Trade has become an increasingly important component of the U.S. economy. At the same time, the U.S. share of world exports has fallen sharply, and technology is no longer an American preserve. This means that the U.S. competitive position in world trade has declined just at the time that trade has become more significant to our economic health.

The escalation of export subsidies and tax incentives since 1960 reflects the importance of exports to countries like Japan, the Republic of South Korea, Taiwan, Hong Kong, and Western Europe. Exports from Western

Europe represent 27% of the region's gross products. Similarly, the ratio of exports to goods production in Japan is currently greater than 30%.[1]

To increase their exports, the United States' trading partners have developed broad national programs to (1) encourage manufacturers to produce better and cheaper goods for export; (2) provide businessmen with credits, subsidies, and all kinds of tax incentives. As a report by Nathan Associates states, these broad national export programs can be classed into two groups: nontax export incentives and tax-related export incentives. Nontax incentives include such programs as official credit assistance, insurance guarantees, cash grants, and rebates.

In recent years tax-related export incentives have been added, and as a result they have become the most pressing issues in the trade area. The debate within the Council of the General Agreement on Tariffs and Trade (GATT) over the income-tax practices of Belgium, France, and the Netherlands, and litigation in the U.S. courts over the imposition of countervailing duties on imports have focused world attention on the unfair practices of some of our trade partners.

Although tax-related export incentives are in theory forbidden under international agreements and GATT regulations, massive export incentives and subsidies have been developed by foreign governments. These practices, as is explained in this chapter, permit substantial export price reduction as well as significant increases in export profits and in the deductions that are applied to the nonprice determinants of export competitiveness, or both.[2]

What makes this situation more difficult is the mysterious interlocking system present in Japan and numerous government-owned corporations. Since these are subsidized by their respective governments, the already massive tax benefits oulined below are strengthened by the fact that they can manipulate profits and losses to gain additional advantages.

Although the United States has lately established a very weak tax-related export incentive system (DISC), foreign countries use many strong tax-related export incentives, such as the following:[3]

1. nontaxation of export income;

2. safe-haven rules that permit preferential treatment (or even nontreatment) of foreign-travel income, and allow foreign subsidies and dividends from export operations;

3. special deductions, credits, or reserves for export-related expenses and industrial development;

4. administrative practices that permit special tax treatment;

5. border tax adjustments, including the remission or rebate of indirect taxes.[4]

In a few countries income from direct export sales is completely exempted from taxation. Ireland, Brazil, and to a lesser extent Japan grant total or partial tax exemptions to profits made on exports.

But the most controversial tax practice is the use of safe-haven rules for the taxation of foreign-source income.

Safe-Haven Rules

The income of a foreign branch of a U.S. parent corporation is fully subject to U.S. taxation, less allowances for any foreign income tax actually paid. But in most of the major industrialized nations the same income is not subject to taxation. Those few countries that do tax such income do so at a very low rate.

In order to preserve the tax advantages—and thus the export stimulus—resulting from this failure to tax the income of offshore selling branches or subsidiaries, most foreign governments also give special tax treatment to dividends paid by such offshore entities to their parent firms. In the United States, of course, dividends received from an offshore subsidiary are fully taxed at the ordinary corporate-income-tax rates. In most foreign countries, such dividends are totally (or almost totally) exempt from taxation.

The advantages that can be derived from these foreign rules are obvious: by channeling all their exports through foreign-based sales offices, or subsidiaries located in tax-haven countries, exporting companies can escape from home taxation on substantial portions of their income. This occurs because the corporation's home government does not tax the income allocated to the offshore company, and then fails once again to tax the income that is repatriated by the parent firm.

France, Belgium, the Netherlands, Brazil, and Spain provide clear examples of how safe-haven rules are used for export subsidization. France totally exempts foreign-source income from taxes. In addition, to help industry, foreign-source income is defined in a very broad way so that it includes any income derived from a permanent establishment abroad, from operations abroad of dependent agents, and from operations constituting a so-called complete commercial cycle outside France. Under the complete commerical theory, a French company may derive nontaxable income without a permanent establishment abroad by simply conducting activities outside France. Moreover, the French parent may exclude from its taxable income 95% of all dividends received from an offshore subsidiary.

In Belgium, the income of an offshore branch is taxed at one-quarter of the ordinary corporate-income-tax rate, provided that the income arises from the activities conducted abroad and is taxed by the foreign government. In the Netherlands, a Dutch company is never taxed on income derived from a foreign branch. Foreign-source income is taxable only if it has not borne a foreign corporate tax. And in Brazil corporations pay taxes only for income earned inside the country. Income earned outside of Brazil by a foreign branch, or affiliate, is thus free from Brazilian taxes.

Another important aspect of foreign taxation that increases the value of the safe-haven rules is the fact that foreign losses are deductible from domestic profits, even though the foreign profits were not subject to tax. Thus there is a great incentive to establish new sales operations abroad, thereby substantially reducing the cost of potential losses and the risks of exporting.

United States Tax System

Since the introduction of the federal income tax in 1913, the United States has used a "classical" system of taxing corporations and their shareholders. Under a classical system, corporations and their shareholders are separately taxed. This is labeled by some people as double taxation.

A corporation's tax liability is not affected by the amount of dividends it distributes to its shareholders, and, conversely, a shareholder's tax liability depends on dividends received and is not affected by either the amount of tax paid by the corporation or the corporation's retained earnings and profits.

These principles also are applied to an American shareholder in a foreign corporation. No U.S. tax is imposed on the U.S. shareholder until the shareholder receives dividends from the foreign corporation. This arrangement is called "deferral," because the U.S. tax on the income of a foreign corporation is deferred until dividends are paid.

The bulk of American investment in foreign corporations is undertaken not by individual shareholders but by U.S.-based multinational corporations. So long as the earnings are retained abroad by the subsidiaries of the multinationals, the parent corporation pays no tax on the foreign income. Whenever a foreign subsidiary pays dividends, interest, royalties, and management fees to its parent corporation, the income is subject to U.S. corporate taxes.

The foreign-tax-credit provision allows the U.S. company to take a credit against its U.S. tax liability for income and withholding taxes paid to a host country on its earnings. This credit is applied to its U.S. taxes when the profits earned abroad are repatriated to the United States.

In the early 1950s the U.S. Treasury proposed eliminating the deferral of U.S. taxes in order to discourage the flow of direct investment capital abroad and to hasten the repatriation of direct investment income. Congress was unwilling, but in 1962 the Tax Reform Act did require dividend income from developed countries to be "grossed up."[5]

What this did was limit the tax haven by introducing "Subpart F," which was enacted to tax U.S. shareholders on a current basis on the income of a controlled foreign corporation (CFC) when the nature of the corporation and its sources of income combined to exhibit tax-haven characteristics.

President Nixon in 1971 sought to improve the balance of payments by including a tax preference for export income through the establishment of DISC (Domestic International Sales Corporation). The argument presented was that export income should enjoy a deferral comparable to foreign-investment income.

In 1973 the union-backed Burke-Hartke Bill to repeal deferral and foreign tax credits was voted down, but that same year the Senate tried to enact its version of the Tax Reduction Act, which also would have eliminated deferral. The House refused to go along. Meanwhile, Subpart F was extended and reinforced to cover more "tax loopholes." In opposing all of these changes, the MNCs have argued that higher taxes would undermine their competitiveness in the world markets without helping U.S. exports or employment. The host countries argue, why should profits made in their countries be subject to U.S. taxation?

The study of the impact of tax policies on MNCs would not be complete without understanding the tax systems of both the home and the host countries (see tables at end of chapter). It can be seen that the methods of taxing corporate direct investment income and remittances by home countries fall between current taxation at the home tax rate with full credit for host taxes to the complete exemption from the home tax, as in the case of France and the Netherlands. The host country generally taxes the affiliate's profits at the same rate as any other corporation established within its borders.

The table also lists the tax rates on corporate direct investment and remittance in selected host countries in 1976.[6] Canada and France have the highest statutory corporate tax rates, and, interestingly, Canada is where the United States has its heaviest investment. These figures would tend to dispute the contention of some that U.S. multinational corporations (MNCs) invest abroad in order to find tax "loopholes."

Also, it can be seen that realized corporate tax rates do not vary greatly; in most cases they range from 32% to 45%. The system of taxation thus varies from country to country mainly because of withholding rates and the treatment of distributed profits. It also varies because of the deductibility or nondeductibility, or the timing, of various costs, expenses, and reserve amounts.

Deferral

Under current U.S. tax policy, foreign-investment income from controlled foreign corporations is subject to corporate income tax but not until that income is repatriated to the United States. It has been argued that since payment of the U.S. tax liability may be deferred indefinitely without penalty, the MNC has access, in effect, to an interest-free loan of open-ended duration at the expense of the U.S. government. Further, businessmen argue that eliminating the deferral would—

1. remove incentives for foreign investment over domestic investment, thereby leading to an increase in domestic investment and consequent growth of the U.S. economy;

2. Increase U.S. revenues substantially;

3. Improve equity and fairness in the tax laws.

The 1972 revenue consequences of the present tax law are as follows: corporate pretax foreign earnings were about $24.4 billion, foreign taxes took about $12.2 billion (49.1% of earnings), and the U.S. tax took about $1.2 billion (5% of earnings). As these figures indicate, U.S. corporations pay substantial taxes on their income, but nearly all the revenue flows to foreign governments. U.S. tax collections are particularly small on foreign corporate dividends and on petroleum earnings.

Whether the $1.2 billion collected in 1972 by the Treasury is "too high" or "too low" depends on the vantage point of the viewer. Measured against the tax receipts under a standard of pure capital-export neutrality, current U.S. revenue collections are much too high. Capital-export neutrality would require the Treasury to pay tax refunds on foreign investment. If the law were changed to end deferral—to provide a deduction rather than a credit for that portion of foreign taxes which corresponds to U.S. state and local taxes, and to eliminate certain minor nonneutralities—there would be revenue gains. But these gains would be more than offset if the law were also changed to extend the investment tax credit and the asset depreciation range to investment abroad, and to allow foreign tax credits in excess of the tentative U.S. tax. In 1972 the revenue loss from a system of pure capital-export neutrality would have been almost $1.8 billion.

Measured against the tax receipts under a standard of pure capital-import neutrality, current U.S. revenue collections are also high. Capital import neutrality would require zero U.S. tax collections.

Finally, measured against the tax receipts under a standard of national neutrality, U.S. tax collections are woefully low. Under that standard, all foreign income would be taxed currently and only a deduction, not a credit, would be allowed for foreign taxes. U.S. tax collections would rise to nearly $6 billion. A tax burden of this magnitude might call into question both the investment of equity capital abroad and the utility of present corporate structures for doing business in foreign lands.[7]

Without the deferral of foreign-investment income, the total assets of foreign manufacturing affiliates would be reduced by $3.2 billion, which is 2.3% of their estimated total value. The total domestic assets of the multinationals might rise by $2.4 billion, which is only 0.7% of these firms' domestic assets. More important, new supplies of capital vary with the interest rate, stability, and the potential for expansion and profit. The primary reason that eliminating deferral would have so small an impact on foreign and domestic investment is that foreign governments now collect income and withholding taxes amounting to 45% of foreign-investment income. If deferral were repealed, the total taxes imposed on foreign-investment income would not exceed 48%, the statutory U.S. tax rate. If repealing deferral added only 3% to the total taxes on foreign investment income, the impact on the location of investment would likely be small.

But this is not to say that the United States has little to gain by eliminating deferral. The termination of deferral might produce only short-run revenue gains, and that is an isolated step. The revenue estimate for the complete total taxes paid by American investors to the U.S. Treasury (including taxes on domestic income) would rise by $1.2 billion, a 4.2% increase. Eliminating deferral thus has a comparatively larger impact on U.S. taxable income and tax payments than on domestic investment (a 4.2% gain versus a 0.7% gain). This striking difference reflects the presumption that eliminating deferral would encourage American investors to finance more of their overseas investment with locally borrowed funds than they now do.

If the subsidiaries borrow in local capital markets, the interest is deductible from their taxable income and not from their American parents' domestic income. The gains from encouraging American investors to refinance their foreign operations would thus constitute a major incentive to repeal deferral. But the difficulty is that many subsidiaries at the present time have borrowed as much as they can. In addition, some countries limit the amount of borrowing to invested capital.

Table 5.6 *assumes* that foreign and domestic investments are partial substitutes, and then proceeds to calculate the extent of substitution. If the assumption is wrong, the estimates of additional investment in the United States and larger U.S. tax revenue are also wrong.

Thus the primary benefits are quite different from those stressed by opponents to deferral taxes. The principal gain derives from the tax benefit of encouraging American investors to alter the capital structure of their overseas affiliates and to increase the portion of taxable income allocated to the U.S. parent. The more familiar gains—the more efficient pattern of international investment and the additional U.S. taxes collected on subsidiaries' retained earnings—may pale by comparison.[8]

The termination of deferral also could lead to a cumulative decline in the profitability and investment of both foreign affiliates and their U.S. parent corporations.[9] The U.S. multinational firms would have fewer funds available for reinvestment, and in order to maintain the same aftertax rate of return, they would surely concede some business to competing foreign firms. With slower growth and smaller sales, they might be less able to improve techniques of production, and they would have a smaller base for spreading research, administrative, and other fixed costs. The cumulative effect could be lower profits and a decline in investment, both in the United States and abroad. The final result would be that with lower taxes, foreign firms could buy existing U.S. facilities.

Apart from investment changes resulting from corporate decisions, foreign governments might alter their own tax rules in response to the termination of deferral. The changes could be designed not only to offset U.S. revenue gains but also to counter any shift of investment toward the United States. For example, foreign governments might provide special investment incentives for non-American firms. Through bank financing and other avenues, these incentives could indirectly attract capital from the United States.

This model assumes that higher U.S. taxes on controlled foreign corporations (CFCs) will, after a period of time, cause a cumulative contraction in their market share, profitability, and the remittance of interest, royalties, and management fees to their U.S. parent corporations. Moreover, CFCs would find it advantageous to distribute a larger share of their earnings and rely more heavily on debt finance. The predicted result would be a cumulative reduction in U.S. taxes, not only on the foreign earnings of CFCs but also on the associated types of foreign income paid to U.S. parent firms. In 1981, five years after the termination of deferral, the model estimates that U.S. taxes on all foreign-source income would be $400 million less than under present laws. In succeeding years, the adverse revenue impact would be even larger.[10]

A thorough study by the Department of the Treasury comes to the following conclusions. (1) The termination of deferral might produce only short-run revenue gains, and that as an isolated step. It would move the United States farther away from a system of capital-export neutrality. Moreover, adverse foreign competition could be intense, especially from Japan, Germany, France, and England, which are now moving fast to fill the vacuum created by U.S. corporations. (2) The revenue estimate for the complete termination of deferral ranges from $365 million to $630 million, depending on whether an overall or per-country limitation is used for the foreign tax credit. If allowance is made for behavioral changes, the revenue gains would be less and there might even be a revenue loss of up to $375 million from the termination of deferral.

The question of fairness, stated briefly, is that tax deferral creates a tax incentive to invest abroad—by denying tax reductions to those who do not go abroad. However, to argue that U.S. taxes should apply uniformly to the income of U.S. corporations, irrespective of where the income is generated, can lead to inequities of double taxation on the other side.

In conclusion, it can be seen that there are many variables to consider when evaluating the impact on foreign investments and tax revenues of the elimination of deferral.

Some observers believe that investment would be partly shifted back to the United States, thereby increasing economic activity in the United States as well as domestic corporate earnings. These observers contend that foreign and domestic investment are at least partial substitutes, and they say that when markets and investment opportunities are lost in one area, multinational firms will reallocate their sources to another part of the globe.

Other observers contend that little or no investment would be shifted back to the United States. They argue that profitable investment and production opportunities are highly specific to both time and place, and that the loss of foreign markets abroad does little to create new investment opportunities in the United States. Indeed, the loss of foreign markets might impair the access of American producers to new foreign technology and might impede the realization of economies inherent in large-scale production and international specialization, with a consequent attenuation of domestic investment opportunities.

We have seen that the offsetting increase in revenues may be of a short-range nature, and that in the long run the secondary and tertiary effects would begin to come into play and the income that the United States could tax might dwindle away. Furthermore, the consequences of the loss of foreign markets and the attenuation of domestic investment opportunities would result in a decrease in U.S. exports and U.S. employment.

In order to help U.S. exporters in 1971, Congress created the Domestic International Sales Corporation. According to the law, DISC acts as a commission agent for the buying and selling of goods for export and export sales promotion. DISC itself can be either an independent company (export management company, sales agent, or distributor) or a related subsidiary established solely to sell and promote the products of its parent corporation. The Revenue Act of 1971 required, however, that DISC be a separately incorporated entity in order to qualify for special DISC intercompany pricing rules and a partial deferral of certain export income. The incentive benefits that the DISC corporations offer American exporters are the following:

1. It offers an exporter a simple and objective way to determine international pricing and profit allocation, rather than burdensome compliance with the complicated and uncertain rules of Section 482 of the Internal Revenue Code.

2. One-half of DISC income in excess of 67% during a four-year base period is deferred from taxation as long as the deferred tax is reinvested in export operations. Small DISC corporations with income between $100,000 and $150,000 are entitled to partial tax relief.

3. At least 95% of both the DISC's income and its assets must be export-related.

So far, the experience with DISC has been very profitable and close to 10,000 corporations have taken advantage of the situation.

The increased profit and cash flow generated by DISC acts as a stimulant to exports in three ways: first, American corporations are encouraged to start or to expand export operations, and they are encouraged to spend more time and effort on exports; second, DISC provides the economic tools—productive capital and cash flow—to expand existing export business; third, DISC encourages companies to service international markets by manufacturing in the United States rather than abroad or through licensing agreements.

The heart of the DISC plan is its provision that a portion of taxes is deferred as long as it is reinvested in the export business. DISC results in the building of a capital fund that grows and is continuously reinvested in specified export activities and assets.

Among the most common export-related assets in which DISC-deferred taxes have been reinvested over the first five years of its existence are: "(1) Export receivables, where DISC funds are used to extend and finance credit to foreign buyers and to reduce the risk of higher costs of carrying accounts receivable on export shipments (that normally require a longer pay-back period than domestic sales); (2) funds for initiating, expanding, and improving export marketing and promotion programs; and (3) producer's loans, whereby DISC funds are made available to the DISC's parent for investments in new facilities, or the expansion and modernization of existing facilities for export, production, and the development of products adapted to export markets."[11]

The report of the Special Committee for U.S. Exports to the Subcommittee on International Finance of the Senate recommends that the DISC incentive be improved and expanded, to induce more firms to export and to stimulate those who are exporting now to export more. It further suggests that the Commerce and Treasury Departments conduct an intensive campaign to familiarize potential small business exporters with DISC and with other aspects of export opportunities.[12]

Foreign Tax Credit

Critics of U.S. tax policy have proposed repealing the U.S. foreign tax credit as well as deferral. It is argued that foreign tax credits subsidize foreign governments at American expense because the major part of the tax payments accrue to the host country, and the U.S. tax collections are correspondingly reduced. These critics propose that taxable income in the United States would include all foreign-investment income net of foreign income and withholding tax. Thus, instead of a tax credit, there would be a tax deduction.

The foreign tax credit developed out of a congressional recognition of the unfairness and discrimination involved in the double taxation of income. The scope of the credit has been limited, and the tax credit cannot exceed the total U.S. tax on all of the taxpayer's foreign income. In addition, when foreign taxes exceed the U.S. tax, the excess cannot be applied against the firm's liability on U.S. source income, nor can MNCs take an investment credit on foreign investments.

It has been estimated that if foreign taxes were treated as a business deduction rather than as a credit, corporate attitudes toward overseas business would have to be radically revised. The multinational that remits $700,000 in earnings would then pay $350,000 in U.S. taxes rather than $200,000. Since it must still pay $300,000 to its overseas host, the company's effective tax rate would total 65%.

The elimination of the foreign tax credit would seriously hurt the multinational, but the damage to the United States as a whole might be even greater. Edwin Mansfield, an economist at the University of Pennsylvania and a noted authority on technology, recently studied a group of innovations made by two groups of U.S. multinationals, one of which included chemical companies. Nearly 30% of the earnings the chemical companies derived from their new products came from overseas. And foreign earnings accounted for 34% of the total return of the other multinationals.

Mansfield asked the companies what would have happened to their domestic R&D budgets if they had been unable to pass their innovations on to their foreign subsidiaries. The chemical companies as a group would have reduced their U.S. budgets by 12%, while the other multinationals reported that R&D expenditures would have been slashed by 15%. Obviously, there is a close relationship between foreign profits and the amount of money companies are willing to commit to domestic research.[13]

The estimates presented in Table 5.3 show the serious impact of repealing deferral and the foreign tax credit and allowing only a deduction for taxes. In Case 1 the firm continues its traditional mix of debt and equity in financing foreign expansion; in Case 2, it uses only debt in financing new foreign investment and charges interest equal to the subsidiary's marginal cost of borrowing. The substitution of domestic for foreign investment is far greater in Case 1 than in Case 2. There would be gradual, substantial decrease in corporate earnings, new investment, and U.S. taxes. If the ability to compensate for lost liquidity by increased borrowing was small, the substitution effect might have been more than offset by the lost liquidity and domestic investment would fall also. Thus repealing the foreign tax credit would have a profound impact on an MNC's profitability, and in all cases on its rate of global investments and U.S. taxes.[14]

It has been stated by MNCs that the reduced profitability demonstrated above would force them into an unfavorable competitive position abroad in comparison both with local companies and with international companies based in countries other than the United States. With taxation at about double the rates existing elsewhere, the source of the income—and the income itself—would dwindle away. The foreign base credit is thus necessary to secure U.S. tax neutrality between domestic and foreign investment. To the extent that foreign investment is in addition to, rather than an alternative to, domestic investment, the comparison with taxes paid by other corporate investors in other countries seems more significant than the comparison with taxes on domestic investment.

U.S. subsidiaries abroad are in competition with local companies and local subsidiaries of non-U.S. parent corporations. Double taxation by the United States would discriminate against U.S. foreign subsidiaries in favor of their competitors. Thus it could be concluded that tax or other restrictions on foreign investment by U.S. companies would not reduce the amount of such investment but merely change the nationality of the investing companies. No matter what the nationality of the foreign investing company, the impact on U.S. domestic production and employment is the same.[15]

Perhaps the major issue should be that the effect of any change in home or host tax policy on government revenue must be estimated and must also take into account the resulting behavior of the firm as well as the reactions of other countries. (The tax impact on the firm's decisions is felt in the home and host countries' balance of payments, employment, and price levels.) Thus, the formulation of tax policy entails more than just weighing revenue consequences.

Tax Incentives of Other Nations

Most industrial nations of Western Europe and Japan either do not tax this same income at all or they charge a very small tax. Germany and Canada are the only two countries that have adopted Subpart F equivalents to discourage the establishment of subsidiaries in tax-haven countries.

Most of our trade partners also give special tax treatment to dividends paid by such offshore entities to their parent corporations. In the U.S. alone dividends received from an offshore subsidiary are fully taxed at the ordinary corporate tax rates. In most foreign countries all dividends received from subsidiaries are exempt from taxation.

The advantages that these corporations have over their American counterparts are very obvious: by charging most of their exports through foreign-based sales offices or subsidiaries located in tax-haven countries, they can escape home-country taxation on a large portion of their income. This result is possible because the parent corporation's government does not tax the income allocated to the offshore company, and then fails once again to tax the income that is repatriated by the parent corporation. France, Belgium, the Netherlands, Brazil, and Spain are good examples of how safe-haven regulations are used for export subsidization. As mentioned earlier, France totally exempts foreign-source income from taxation. In addition, foreign-source income is defined in so general and broad a way that it includes any income derived from permanent establishments abroad and from operations constituting a so-called complete commercial cycle outside France. Under this theory of complete commercial cycle, a French company may derive nontaxable income without a permanent establishment abroad by simply conducting activities outside France. Moreover, the French parent may exclude from its taxable income 95% of all dividends received from an offshore subsidiary.

Belgian Tax Situation

In Belgium the income of an offshore branch is taxed at 25% of the ordinary corporate-income-tax rate, provided that the income arises from activities conducted abroad and is taxed by a foreign government, regardless of how low that government's tax rate may be. The amount of tax paid in the foreign country is deductible by the parent corporation. Moreover, Belgium does not tax the income of a foreign subsidiary, and 95% of the dividends received from the subsidiary can be excluded on the tax returns. Under most Belgian tax treaties, income from foreign sources is exempt from tax in Belgium. Foreign-branch losses are fully deductible by the domestic parent, even though the income of the branch would be exempt from tax in Belgium under a tax treaty.

Not only is income from a foreign subsidiary not taxable in Belgium, but there is no provision comparable to Subpart F of the U.S. Internal Revenue Code. Therefore a Belgian company can freely take advantage of the establishment of a foreign sales subsidiary located in a tax-haven country.

Also, favorable intercompany pricing has been permitted by the Belgian government, especially in the late 1950s and early 1960s, as a way of encouraging the establishment of export industries.

The government may grant an exemption from real estate taxes on fixed assets for a maximum period of five years. Profits realized from the sale of fixed assets and shares may be subject to a reduced income-tax rate when the proceeds are invested in a development area within a period beginning six months before the tax period during which the profits are realized and expiring twelve months after the end of that tax period.

No import tax or custom duties are imposed on merchandise imported to Belgium as long as it is reexported within a short period of time and not used or transformed in Belgium.

Belgian corporations may discount commercial paper received in an export transaction at a rate usually more favorable than that applied to commercial paper. Also, a special government agency called the *Office National du Ducroire* insures long-term export credits against general commercial and political risks as well as any losses that might arise from currency fluctuations. The *Office Belge du Commerce Extérieur* provides the following government-subsidized services: market studies and planning; practical information regarding commercial regulations and techniques; publications; documentation (diplomatic reports, statistics); legal help; advertising assistance; participation in commercial and industrial fairs; and the organization of business conferences. Also, the Belgian government grants an interest subsidy, under which a portion of interest payable on the loan of the investor is paid directly by the government. Non-interest-bearing loans of up to 50% of the proposed investment may be granted to finance research and development of new products and new production techniques to be employed in Belgium. Finally, the government gives financial assistance to meet the cost of training workers.

Tax Incentives in Japan

Japanese corporations are taxed on a worldwide basis under rules similar to those in effect in the United States. But Japanese law has no provision similar to Subpart F of the U.S. Internal Revenue Code. The allowable foreign tax credit is computed on an overall basis.

Japan imposes an excise tax (commodity tax) on manufacturers and importers selling seventeen types of commodities. Foods and other essential commodities are not subject to this tax. Beverages, motor vehicles, and all luxury items are taxed up to 30%. Commodities exported are exempt from the excise tax. If any product is exported after being taxed, the tax is returned.

Japan has many direct tax benefits for exporters. Corporations deriving income from overseas transactions are entitled to deduct limited amounts credited to a reserve for overseas market development. The transactions include the export of goods, the sale of goods to an exporter, and the processing of goods to be exported, provided the payment is in a foreign currency. The deductions may start from 1% to 1.7% of the export value of goods purchased from others. Twenty percent of the amount credited to the reserve must be returned to income each year in the five years immediately following the creditation.

Corporations holding 10% or more of the shares of a "specified overseas enterprise juridical person," or 1% or more of particular shares of a "specified investment juridical person," can deduct amounts credited to a reserve for losses from such investments up to a specified ratio of the acquisition cost of the shares.

A Japanese corporation can establish a deductible reserve for foreign-exchange losses on its net long-term receivables. Amounts deducted must be added back to taxable income in the next accounting period.

Entertainment expenses related to export activities up to $14,000 plus one-quarter of 1% of capital per corporation are allowed to be deducted from taxable income. The deduction for entertainment expenses in excess of the above sum is limited to 25% of expenditures.

Japanese exporters can receive medium- and long-term credits from the Export-Import Bank of Japan, a government-related agency. Generally, medium-term sales are supported by means of direct loans at preferential rates of interest. Medium-term credits are not supported in Japan. Long-term credits that exceed five years are available from the Export-Import Bank to both buyers and suppliers. The bank usually supports 48% to 64% of the contract value. The rate charged as of December 1978 ranged from 7.75% to 8.75%. These rates include all types of financing charges but not insurance costs.

Domestic corporations are allowed substantial special deductions for certain overseas transactions in an accounting period beginning on or before March 31, 1976. These transactions are as follows:

1. Sales or licensing of industrial property rights and furnishing of technological knowledge are deductible at up to 70% of the proceeds from the transaction.

2. Thirty percent of any item received from the sale of copyrights is deductible.

3. Twenty percent of the proceeds from consulting or the rendering of technical services related to the manufacturing or construction of production facilities, or technical guidance regarding agriculture and fishing, is deductible.[16]

Tax Incentives in France[17]

France is the most aggressive nation in encouraging exports, closely following Japan and West Germany. France basically offers direct tax incentives and a tax structure that has a decisive impact on export expansion.

Foreign-source income in France is exempt from any income tax. Domestic-source income is "all profits realized by enterprises exploited in France." As interpreted by the French government, the following categories of income are considered to be foreign-source income:

1. income derived from an establishment abroad;

2. income derived from the operations of dependent agents abroad, or from operations that constitute a "complete commercial cycle."

In other words, the tax exemption in France applies to all income derived from the direct and active conduct of a business abroad either by a French company or by a foreign company. Similarly, any income derived by a French company's agent from strictly foreign activities is not taxable in France.

Income of a foreign subsidiary of a French corporation is exempt from income tax. There is no provision in the French Internal Revenue Code comparable to Subpart F of the U.S. Internal Revenue Code. "There is no credit for foreign taxes paid unless a tax treaty so provides, but a French parent corporation is entitled to exclude 95% of the dividends received from a foreign subsidiary." This exemption is possible only if the French corporation owns at least 10% of the outstanding stock of the foreign corporation. On subsequent distribution to its stockholders, the French company might be liable for 33⅓% of the gross amount of tax-exempt dividends received from foreign subsidiaries. But the corporation is free to determine whether the distribution is made out of previously taxed or untaxed earnings, and as long as taxed earnings exceed the amount of distribution to stockholders, the corporation may escape the supplementary tax. Moreover, the shareholders are entitled to tax credits equal to 50% of the cash dividend.

A French company is allowed the use of intercompany pricing rules in order to attain the maximum development of exports and to establish enterprises intended to sell French products. Furthermore, a company that possesses an exporter's card may sell to foreign affiliates at prices approaching the cost, provided "the transaction is motivated by commercial necessity other than the desire to transfer profits abroad." This policy has raised protests in the United States because of the belief that it converts the French basic policy on foreign-source income into direct export incentives.[1]

The French corporations also have a choice of being taxed either on a worldwide or consolidated basis. Under each system credit is given for foreign taxes with per-country limits of the French tax rate. The advantage of choosing either method is that losses of foreign operations can be used to reduce the taxable income from domestic operations. This provision was enacted to help French companies compete with American and British corporations.

The French corporations are also allowed special reserves for losses of foreign business and for investments in developing countries. In addition, when a French company sets up a joint export program, it can enjoy the following advantages:

1. Medium- and long-term loan funds are available from public sources.

2. It can avail itself of rediscount facilities for drafts drawn by the shareholders upon the company.

3. The shareholder's investment in the stock of the company is deductible in the year made. The company, however, may depreciate its assets in the usual manner.

4. Capital gains on the sale of shares in the company may be reinvested without taxation within one year in shares of a similar company.

Banks and finance companies that grant loans to finance exports or foreign trade are allowed deductions to cover the risks attached to these credits.

Exporting companies that sell on medium-term credit are entitled to create a special deductible reserve to cover the risks inherent in the extension of credit abroad. Credit terms must be between two and five years. Since 1948 French exporters have also had the advantage of extensive risk insurance via a government corporation. The credit guarantees covered by this corporation can be classified in nine categories:

1. production risk: guarantees against sudden interruptions of sales and the resulting losses to manufacturers or exporters prior to export;

2. credit risk: guarantees against the risk of nonpayment by the foreign purchaser once the goods have been exported;

3. accident risk: guarantees against damage to exported goods prior to their delivery;

4. commercial risk: guarantees against the insolvency of the foreign purchaser;

5. exchange risk: guarantees against currency fluctuation, devaluation, and revaluation;

6. inflation risk: guarantees against cost increases of executing the contract. The coverage is not available for goods exported to EEC countries;

7. market-development risk: guarantees against expenses related to initial foreign operations, including administrative and the building up of inventory abroad;

8. exhibition expenses: guarantees the company's participation in industrial fairs (excluding fairs held in EEC countries) by covering expenses incurred, including publicity costs, living and travel expenses of agents, and the cost of returning the goods exhibited to France;

9. political risk: guarantees against acts of foreign public authorities.

Corporations moving their production facilities outside Paris are granted indemnities to cover moving expenses. The grant may cover up to 60% of the total expenditures for their transportation and reinstallation expenses.[19]

Germany's Tax Incentives

German companies are taxed on their worldwide income. The law provides for a tax credit on taxes paid to the host governments, but only to the extent of the German rate on the same income. However, most tax treaties exempt profits of foreign branches from German taxes. In this case, the German corporation may, on application, still deduct its foreign establishment's losses from its income in Germany.

The losses are first deducted from any profits made in the foreign countries and then from income in Germany. The remaining unabsorbed loss can be carried forward over a five-year period. When sufficient profits are made in the host countries, the amount of the losses deducted in Germany must be restored.

Income of a foreign subsidiary is not taxable in Germany. However, if a subsidiary is domiciled in a country with low taxation and is not active itself, the income of this subsidiary may be deemed to be income of the German parent company. Taxes paid by the subsidiary on its income may, on application, be used as a tax credit in Germany. This provision is somewhat equivalent to Subpart F provisions under the U.S. Internal Revenue Code, although much less stringent.

Dividends received from a foreign subsidiary are taxable to the parent company unless a tax treaty provides otherwise. Under most German tax treaties, Germany does not include income dividends received from subsidiaries where the German parent company owns 25%, or more, of the stock of the subsidiary.

In areas where no tax treaties exist, foreign-source income may still receive very favorable treatment. First, a German corporation is taxed at the rate of 51% but on its undistributed profits only. Profits that are intended for distribution to shareholders are taxed at the reduced rate of 15%.

Under certain conditions, the federal minister of finance can grant complete or partial tax forgiveness, provided that the relief serves the interests of the German economy as a whole.

Taxation at a flat rate of 25% applies to income from foreign unincorporated entities, or from an investment in a foreign commerical entity located in non-tax-treaty countries. In some cases, a foreign subsidiary's losses may lead to a deferral of taxes on the parent's income. On acquiring or establishing a corporation abroad, the German parent company may get a deductible reserve for the loss of the subsidiary to be allocated to the percentage of shares owned. This reserve must be restored to income after five years, or as soon as profits have made up the losses. The subsidiary must be 50% owned. If a corporation is located in a developing country, the limit is 25% of the ownership. The foreign subsidiary must be either a manufacturer or a distributor, or must be an agency or perform trade services.

This provision is supplemented by tax-deferral devices to encourage the export of capital goods in exchange for an interest in a foreign company. The German parent is allowed to defer German corporate income tax on the profits realized on the transaction by creating a deductible reserve equal to the profit. The reserve is gradually dissolved after five years at a minimum rate of 20% over a period of five years.

There are other incentives provided through government-sponsored insurance companies, whose function is to guarantee exports by assuming part of the obligation for uncollectible receivables or for the manufacturing cost of equipment, if the goods ordered are not taken over by the foreign customer.

In the case of export receivables, financing is possible either with private banks or with a government-owned institution at preferential rates. Private banks purchase only receivables that have not been guaranteed by the government-sponsored insurance company. The financing of export transactions by a government-owned institution is available for exports to developing countries and exports of ships. In these cases, long-term credits may be extended on both a supplier and a buyer basis. Like France and England, Germany provides "mixed credits."

The German government provides assistance to exporters by making available information on the import requirements of individual foreign countries, import procedures, legal questions, customs duty rates, and available financing. In addition, all German government agencies provide assistance to German businessmen all over the world.

Germany also gives direct cash grants ranging from 5% to 30% to corporations that are prepared to invest for economic development in selected countries. These subsidies have a direct effect on the sales of German machinery and capital goods.[20]

Since 1975 the credit on investment income of individuals has been limited to 15%, with the excess above 15% being deductible. In the case of business income, a carry-over of any excess credit is provided.[21]

In Brazil corporate income tax is applied only to corporate profits earned within Brazil. Income earned outside of Brazil by a foreign branch or subsidiary is thus free from any kind of Brazilian tax. Furthermore, the dividends paid by a foreign subsidiary to the parent company are also exempt from taxation in Brazil, even when the offshore subsidiary pays no income tax in the host country.

In Italy, Law 639 grants an Italian exporter remission of a variety of taxes not directly related to the exported merchandise. The nature and amount of this rebate vary from case to case.

West Germany's comprehensive program to reshape its economy and expand exports includes long-term investments to develop new technological processes and restrain unemployment. "To be sure, West Germany remains unquestionably well-off. We are certainly not passing through a mid-life crisis in Germany," states Count Otto Landsdorff, the economic minister, "but we must make every effort to keep fit."[22] A healthy, expanding economy, with $200 billion worth of exports in the next twenty years is the goal of German planners.

The Dresden Bank forecasts a 3% growth in the economy and a 5% to 10% increase in exports in the next five years. Growth averaged 8% in the 1950s, 4.7% in the 1960s, and 3% in the 70s.

Because of rising energy costs, German imports are likely to grow faster than exports over the next five years, and German businessmen are recommending more exports as well as greater consumer spending.

Acknowledging pressure and competition from outside, the government has pushed hard to increase help to high-technology industries. Despite the weak spots, the German government and industry believe that the country can achieve a restructuring of its economy so that it will be able to meet the competition of tomorrow.[23]

"Our future lies in the production of high technological goods and organizational know-how," states M. Rodenstock, an executive of the industrial association. "Research development, and innovation are the key to our technical, economic, and social progress."[24]

The Netherlands

In the Netherlands corporations are subject to income tax on their worldwide income. However, the employees of foreign permanent establishments and the owners of foreign real property are exempt from Dutch tax if there is a treaty providing an exemption, or if the income is subject to tax in the foreign country. In the case of income taxed in a foreign country, relief is given in the form of a tax reduction equal to the percentage that the foreign-source income bears to the worldwide income. In addition, losses of the foreign branch may be deducted from domestic taxable income, but with a corresponding adjustment in the compensation of the domestic tax liability for foreign-branch profits for subsequent years. This adjustment prevents a double deduction of the loss.

Dividends received by a Dutch shareholder from a foreign subsidiary are free of Dutch income tax, if the Dutch company controls as little as 5% of the stock of the foreign company, and if the investment is related to the business activity of the parent company. This exemption applies not only to dividends but also to such items as capital gains and interest.

Patents, royalties, dividends, and interest received from abroad are subject to the company income tax after deducting foreign taxes, for which a credit is given. If these accounts are derived through a foreign permanent establishment, they are exempt, provided the permanent establishments are subject to an income tax in the country of service.

Norway

Taxation of foreign source of income. Corporations centered in Norway are taxable on their worldwide income. However, one-half of the income from foreign real property and income from permanent establishments abroad is exempt from tax.

A nonresident corporation is not taxable on its income, other than the income attributable to a Norwegian permanent establishment after it has been distributed to its Norwegian shareholders. If a Norwegian company either alone or with not more than nine other Norwegian residents owns at least 95% of the shares in the foreign corporation, and that corporation owns real property or business establishments outside of Norway, then Norwegian taxes are levied on only-half of the dividends distributed by the foreign company.

Patents, royalties, dividends, and interest received from abroad are fully taxed in Norway after deducting foreign taxes. If the royalties, dividends, and interest are derived through a permanent establishment in a foreign country, taxes are levied on only one-half of the income. Dividends received from a foreign subsidiary are likewise partially tax-exempt if the requirements discussed above are met. Foreign taxes paid are deductible expenses. There is no credit allowed.

United Kingdom

Resident companies are subject to tax on their worldwide income. Generally, a company's residence is located at the site of its central management and control. Relief from double taxation is given bilaterally by way of a treaty, or unilaterally through a credit.

Nonresident corporations are taxed on income derived from trading within the United Kingdom through a branch or agency established in that country. There is no current taxation on other income of nonresident corporations. A credit is given for taxes paid by the foreign subsidiary on its profits, if the resident parent holds not less than 10% of the voting power in the distributing company.

Foreign income, including dividends, patent fees, and interest received from foreign sources, must be grossed up with the appropriate amount of foreign tax and then included in the income of the resident company. A credit is then granted. The same rule applies to patent royalties, dividends, and interest obtained through a permanent establishment in a foreign country.

A credit is given for foreign taxes paid, which may not exceed the amount of United Kingdom tax corresponding to the gross foreign income. In addition, a credit is given to taxes paid by a distributing subsidiary.

Canada

In Canada resident corporations are subject to tax on their worldwide income. Relief from double taxation on foreign-source income is given via a credit for the foreign taxes paid or by an exemption through tax treaties.

Nonresident corporations are taxed on income from the conduct of a business in Canada. If a foreign corporation is a foreign affiliate of a Canadian taxpayer, special rules apply.

The income of a foreign affiliate is generally not taxed currently. An exception is provided for a Canadian shareholder of a foreign affiliate, who is required to include in his income his proportionate share of the affiliate's investment income and capital gains, whether or not distributed. Dividends received by a Canadian corporation from a foreign affiliate are exempt from taxes to the extent that they are paid out of pre-1976 profits. Dividends paid out of post-1975 profits are exempt if earned in a country with which Canada has a comprehensive treaty. If dividends are earned in a nontreaty country, they are partially taxable in Canada. The exemption depends on the amount of foreign tax paid by the affiliate and the amount of any withholding tax to which the dividend may have been subjected.

Interest, dividends, and royalties must be included in the gross income of a Canadian recipient subject to a credit. A foreign tax credit is allowed to prevent double taxation. Where income is not exempt under treaties, the credit is allowed up to the effective Canadian rate on the foreign income.

The GATT Controversy over the Taxes

For over two decades the United States' efforts to introduce a real system of free trade and to obtain a revision of the international rules on export subsidies have proved totally useless owing to the consistent refusal of other nations to enter into serious discussions on the subject. The frustration of the United States in not reforming the GATT rules was, in fact, a major reason for the adoption of the DISC legislation in 1971. The United States Congress came to the conclusion that if the rules could not be made more fair to the United States' exporters, then the creation of some system that could help American exporters and yet not violate the GATT rules was justified and reasonable. In keeping with this principal goal, DISC was carefully designed to offer export benefits to the United States firms in a way that would not violate GATT principles. To avoid infringing the GATT restrictions on "exemptions" and "remissions" of direct taxes, DISC was limited to a partial deferral of tax on income earned from exports.[25]

Where DISC grants only a deferral of a portion of taxes on income from exports, most foreign exporters enjoy so many advantages that they can avoid payment of taxes on substantially all export income. As we have seen in the previous pages, this tax exemption is achieved in Western Europe and Japan by many ruses, including:

1. outright exemption of export-derived income;

2. failure to tax the income or dividends from sales, subsidiaries, or divisions in offshore tax-haven countries;

3. various tax credits for export-related investments and expenses;

4. large rebates or revisions of indirect taxes;

In Japan the commodities taxes imposed on manufacturers, importers, and retailers run as high as 30%, and the maximum value-added tax rates in Western European countries in some cases are as high as 40%. The exports in both Japan and Western Europe are exempt from both taxes.

Some trade partners of the United States use their indirect tax systems to grant additional subsidies, with exporters receiving so-called tax rebates, which are in fact wholly unrelated to the exporter's liability for domestic indirect taxes.[26]

Despite the fact that DISC provides only a fraction of the benefits received by Japanese and Western European exporters, its adoption was greeted by many complaints on the part of other trading nations. In 1972 the Western European community filed a complaint under GATT regulations alleging that the DISC program violated Article XVI:B4 of the GATT charter, which forbids the granting of any subsidy on the exports of their products. "The result of this subsidy will be selling American products at a price lower than the comparable price charged for the like product to buyers of the domestic market."

The United States has denied that DISC in any way violated the GATT provisions, and at the same time filed its own complaints against certain income tax practices of France, Japan, Belgium, and the Netherlands. In each case, the complaint stated that the exporting countries had not taxed the income of offshore sales of branches and the subsidiaries, had failed to tax the dividends paid to the domestic parent company, and had allowed companies great flexibility in allocating income between the domestic parent and tax-haven affiliates. The resulting exemption of export income from domestic taxation is, in virtually every instance, a far greater subsidy than the deferral provided by DISC.

A special GATT panel was appointed to study all the charges. In November 1976 the panel reached preliminary decisions on all four complaints. In each case the panel concluded that the export incentive "in some cases had effects which were not in accordance with obligations under GATT and that there was a prima facie case of nullification or impairment of benefits which other parties were entitled to expect under the General Agreement" of the different cases before the panel. The DISC decision posed the greatest difficulties for the panel for the following reasons:

1. Previous GATT considerations of the issue had never classified the mere deferral of taxes as an export subsidy. Indeed, one GATT panel that dealt with this issue concluded "that such deferral was in gray areas" where there was no international consensus as to whether it was a subsidy or not.

2. Subsidies violate GATT regulations only when they result in a reduction of export prices below prices charged in comparable domestic transactions. The complaining parties presented no evidence whatsoever that DISC causes such "bi-level pricing."

3. Despite the above evidence, the panel found a prima facie case that DISC "in some cases infringes GATT principles." Why? Because of the failure to charge interest on taxes deferred under DISC, classifying that ambiguous facet of DISC "as a tax exemption." The United States representatives argued against this wishy-washy conclusion of the panel and asked for a clear decision. When this request was turned down, they asked that the panel's reports be taken up by the GATT council.

In contrast the U.S. position, the European Community refuses adamantly to permit any GATT Council consideration of the panel reports concerning Belgium, France, and the Netherlands. Instead, it urged the Council to consider only the DISC report, and to order the United States either to abandon DISC or to give compensation to other countries, and to ignore entirely the companion panel reports relating to the much greater European subsidies.

The major reason for the European Community's intransigent position is its belief that the U.S. Congress, in its opposition to big business, will abolish DISC. The Europeans and Japanese hope that by creating a deadlock in GATT until the U.S. Congress takes unilateral action to rescind DISC, they can keep their cake and eat it at the same time.

A similarly hard line has characterized the positions of the major trading nations in Europe and Japan with respect to the use of indirect tax rebates or remissions to subsidize exports. For more than a decade the government of the United States has argued that the GATT distinction between direct and indirect taxes discriminates unfairly against the United States. There is no economic basis for that distinction. Nevertheless, representatives of Japan and the European nations have refused to give serious consideration to any change in the present GATT rules.

Since the United States attempts have produced little tangible result, American corporations resorted to court actions. In several cases major U.S. industries are asking that countervailing duties be imposed on imports that benefit from remission of the Japanese commodities tax and the European value-added tax. In the Japanese case the Zenith Radio Corporation is challenging imports of consumer electronic products that receive commodities tax rebates ranging from 5% to 20%.

In another case the U.S. Steel Corporation is asking that duties be imposed on the twenty million tons of steel imported into this country to offset VAT remissions ranging from 8% to 20% on steel exports from the seven Common Market countries and Japan. The other cases deal with rebates paid to Sears, Roebuck and other retailers for sales of Japanese radios.

The value of radios, steel, and electronic-product imports involved in these cases runs into billions of dollars, but the significance of the cases goes far beyond these specific imports. Almost all consumer products exported from Japan benefit from commodities tax rebates—automobiles, for example, receive rebates of 30%. In the Common Market substantially *all* exports of any nature whatsoever benefit from VAT rebates or remission.

The issues raised by the *Zenith* and *U.S. Steel* cases will be taken to the United States Supreme Court. On April 23, 1978, a three-judge Customs Court panel unanimously ruled in the *Zenith* case that countervailing duties should be imposed to offset the rebate of the Japanese commodities tax, but on July 28, 1978, the Court of Customs and Patent Appeals reversed by a vote of 3 to 2. Zenith has announced its intention to appeal to the Supreme Court. U.S. Steel has also confirmed that it will take its case to the highest appellate tribunal, if necessary.

Despite the protests, suits, and even threats of reprisal, neither Japan nor the European Community has yet shown any willingness to compromise or even to discuss a revision of the GATT rules. Soon after the initial *Zenith* decision, the Japanese government submitted an official protest to the United States. Later a GATT special panel issued a report contending that the *Zenith* decision violated the GATT rules and that the action taken by the United States, under the countervailing-duties law, would invite retaliation by affected GATT members. That report was immediately endorsed in strong terms by the GATT Council. The policy of Japan and Western European countries has been to put maximum pressure on the U.S. government to prevent any reprisal or countervailing duties, while

The Impact of Taxation on International Trade

continuing at the same time to argue that the GATT rules on indirect-tax export subsidies are nonnegotiable.

The question is asked why the United States government in each case does not resort to retaliation by imposing the same indirect tax on export subsides, imports value-added tax, or commodities tax exactly in the same manner that the Japanese and the Europeans apply them.

The controversy with GATT and trading partners has brought home the message that U.S. exporters are placed in a disadvantageous position vis-à-vis foreign exporters. On the one hand the latter receive a tremendous advantage from their governments in the form of indirect rebates, and on the other hand the United States government, for political reasons, resists imposing any countervailing measures.

The continued increase in automobile and steel imports to the United States (over $20 billion in 1979), the huge trade deficit, and the increase in unemployment have created increasing U.S. public and congressional pressure for some immediate and decisive action. Meanwhile Japan and Europe should realize that the United States' resources and patience are not inexhaustible and that their intransigence could eventually bring about countervailing duties on substantially all imports from Western Europe and Japan.

The controversy over export-subsidy rules may appear at first glance to be esoteric, with highly technical arguments on each side of the issue. The stakes, however, are very high, and the significance to American trade policy is very substantial. As this study shows, the present international subsidy rules place U.S. exporters at an intolerable disadvantage in competing with heavily subsidized foreign firms in world markets. The direct-tax benefits received by such foreign companies are very great indeed, and they permit those corporations either to increase their profits on export sales or to reduce export price significantly, as has been the case with foreign textiles, steel, automobiles, radios, and televisions in the United States. Rebates and remissions paid to foreign firms have helped them to sell their products in the United States at prices 20% lower than the prices paid by their domestic customer.

Since 1970 the United States has suffered a trade deficit of more than $140 billion and has sought to negotiate for the reform of the GATT rules to no avail. The United States position is that existing international rules place American exporters at a serious disadvantage by allowing other nations to grant massive export incentives.

The United States' complaint has two major aspects:

1. Despite the fact that, at least in principle, the GATT places strict limitations on the use of direct-tax systems to promote exports, the ambiguity and nonenforcement of the rules has resulted in the prolifera-

tion of the substantial direct-tax export promotion system outlined above. Almost the only exception is the United States, which carefully tailored DISC to conform to the GATT rules.

2. The GATT rules give carte blanche to the remission or rebate of indirect taxes on export transactions. This places the United States at a major disadvantage, because it has made a policy choice to rely principally on its revenue on progressive income taxes rather than regressive indirect taxes. The United States position is that any policy choice made for legitimate domestic reasons should not place a nation's exporters at a disadvantage in international trade.[27]

The success of the United States in future trade and negotiations will depend in a large part upon the United States' willingness to ask for reciprocity. From this standpoint, the trade issue and the GATT's attitude are of major importance. There should be no change in the DISC position, and Congress has to come out with new laws providing protection for United States industry and exports.

Conclusion

As this chapter illustrates, our trade partners are striving hard to expand exports through both nontax and tax incentives. Unfortunately, American exports in many cases are at a disadvantage. It is essential that Congress take a very serious look at the tax and other laws that are impediments to production and exports. Any tax shackles on corporations have far-reaching consequences on both the home and the host country's trade, investment, balance of payments, employment, and price levels. Congress should know that the formation of a tax policy entails more than just weighing revenue consequences.

Because of the sensitivity of all countries to the taxation of corporations, there must be increased cooperation and communication among countries to bring about greater stability in international trade. A policy of the international harmonization of corporate income taxation is one proposal currently being considered. In an exploratory investigation, it was calculated that full harmonization among the nine members of the European Economic Community and the United States would have resulted in a welfare gain of several billion dollars from the ensuing direct-investment flows.

In lieu of the above, a tax policy for multinational firms might be dictated by intracountry equity considerations. This involves allocating the firm's tax base among the countries where it operates on the basis of value judgments as to each country's fair share. Implementation of this would require a broad international consensus.

It can be seen that in the 1980s, "There is no such thing as a closed national economy. Government policies that ignore this or try to contravene it for national advantage will almost always have adverse consequences. To tax unrepatriated foreign income of U.S.-based companies ignores the fact that those companies, through their investments and technology, are a major source of world economic development, and that this benefits the United States as well as other nations. There is no way that the U.S. government can set a sound economic policy, even a domestic policy, without understanding that economic activity in the United States is inseparable from that in the rest of the world."[28]

TABLE 5.1

STATUTORY AND REALIZED CORPORATE INCOME TAX RATES ON MANUFACTURING FIRMS, 1975–76

Country	Corporate Tax Rate	Statutory Tax Rates — Distributed profits tax rate, if different	Local Income Taxes	Realized Corporate tax rate	Withholding tax rates on dividends distributed to U.S. — Statutory or Treaty Rate	Realized Rate on grossed-up dividends	Total realized tax rate on grossed-up dividends
Canada	48.0		13.0	41.1	15.0	8.8	49.9
Europe:							
Austria	55.0	27.5	15.0	53.4	5.0	2.3	55.7
Belgium	42.0	0		37.5	15.0	9.4	46.9
Denmark	36.0			32.5	5.0	3.4	35.9
France	50.0	25.0		48.0	5.0	2.6	50.6
Germany	51.0	15.0	13.0	43.0	15.0	8.5	51.5
Greece	38.2	0		11.9	30.0	26.4	38.3
Ireland	50.0	27.0		12.7	5.0	4.4	17.1
Italy	43.8			41.9	5.0	2.9	44.8
Luxembourg	40.0		14.0	17.1	5.0	4.1	21.2
Netherlands	48.0			36.0	10.0	6.4	42.4
Norway	26.5		21.3	40.5	15.0	8.9	49.4
Spain	32.8	0		30.3	15.0	10.5	40.8
Sweden	40.0		25.0	43.1	5.0	2.8	45.9
Switzerland	8.8		28.0	27.1	5.0	3.6	30.7
United Kingdom	52.0	26.2		44.6	15.0	8.3	52.9
Oceania:							
Australia	47.5			42.9	15.0	8.6	51.5
New Zealand	45.0			51.7	5.0	2.4	54.1

TABLE 5.2

TAXATION OF CORPORATE DIRECT INVESTMENT INCOME AND
REMITTANCES IN MAJOR HOME COUNTRIES,[1] 1967

Home Country	Tax Relief on Foreign Branch Income	Tax Relief on Foreign Subsidiary Dividends and Other Remittances	Foreign Direct Investment, End 1967 (billion U.S. dollars)
Belgium	Partial exemption and deduction[1, 2]	Partial exemption and deduction[3]	2.0
Canada	Credit	Exemption	3.7
France	Exemption	Partial exemption[4]	6.0
Germany, Fed. Rep.	Credit[2]	Credit[2]	3.0
Italy	Partial exemption and deduction[5]	Partial exemption and deduction[5]	2.1
Japan	Credit	Credit	1.4
Netherlands	Exemption[6]	Exemption[6]	2.2
Sweden	Credit[2]	Credit	1.5
Switzerland	Partial exemption[7]	Partial exemption[7]	4.2
United Kingdom	Credit	Credit	17.5
United States	Credit	Credit[8]	59.5

SOURCES: United Nations (1973 b), Chown (1974), and various official and unofficial sources.
[1] After deducting foreign taxes, 75% is exempt from corporate tax.
[2] Exemption is sometimes accorded by treaty.
[3] Subsidiary dividends, after deducting foreign taxes, are subject to 10% *précompte mobilier;* 90% to 95% of the remaining income is exempt from corporate tax.
[4] Of grossed-up dividends, 95% is exempt from corporate tax.
[5] Entire income is exempt from business profits tax, but corporate tax applies to income, after deducting foreign income tax (withholding tax is credited).
[6] In principle, foreign-source income is subject to taxation; in practice, exemption with progression is granted on foreign income that has been taxed abroad.
[7] In practice, foreign-source income is subject to taxation; in practice, only net worth tax is applied.
[8] Dividends from less developed host countries are taxed after deducting and crediting the foreign income tax. Constructive dividends from certain tax-haven income are subject to tax.

TABLE 5.3

ESTIMATED IMPACT OF REPEALING DEFERRAL AND THE FOREIGN TAX CREDIT AND ALLOWING
ONLY A DEDUCTION FOR FOREIGN TAXES PAID: ON NEW DOMESTIC AND FOREIGN INVESTMENT,
NEW FUNDS ADVANCED TO SUBSIDIARIES, CONSOLIDATED AFTERTAX INCOME, AND DOMESTIC
AND FOREIGN TAXES PAID BY U.S. MANUFACTURERS, 1974

		Case 1 (Initial Parameters)		Case 2 (Reliance on Debt)	
	Initial Value	Absolute Change	Percentage Change	Absolute Change	Percentage Change
Domestic Investment	36,400	9,291	25.5	3,970	10.9
Foreign Investment	18,300	−10,283	−56.2	−4,997	−27.3
New Funds for Subsidiary	2,710	−15,725	−580.3	−8,060	−297.4
Consolidated After-Tax Income	15,149	−2,974	−19.6	−3,107	−20.5
U.S. Taxes Paid	6,005	3,028	50.4	2,953	49.2
Foreign Taxes Paid	5,001	−504	−10.1	−144	−2.9

NOTE: Initial Values and Absolute Changes expressed in millions of dollars. Estimates include the repeal of deferral.
SOURCE: Thoma Horst, "American Taxation of Multinational Firms," *American Economic Review* (May 1976).

TABLE 5.4

Termination of Deferral with Assumed Adverse Impact on Competitive Position of U.S. CFCs
(in millions of dollars)

	Calendar Year Tax Liabilities	
	1976	1981
Estimated U.S. revenue from corporate taxation of all foreign source income with termination of deferral[1]	2,610	3,200
Estimated U.S. revenue from corporate taxation of all foreign source income under current law[2]	2,245	3,600
Estimated change in U.S. revenue with termination of deferral	365	−400

Office of the Secretary of the Treasury   April 6, 1976
Office of Tax Analysis

[1] The 1976 figure is based on estimated 1976 revenues plus the potential revenue from complete termination of deferral. The 1981 figure is adapted from a model developed by Robert B. Stobaugh, "The U.S. Economy and the Proposed U.S. Income Tax on Unremitted Foreign Earnings of U.S. Controlled Foreign Manufacturing Operations Abroad," Harvard Business School, 1975.

[2] The 1976 figure reflects the Tax Reduction Act of 1975. The 1981 figure assumes an annual growth rate of 10% in the foreign source of U.S. corporations.

TABLE 5.5

Estimated Impact on Eliminating Deferral for Manufacturing Firms, 1974
(in millions of dollars)

Variable Affected	Impact Assuming No Change in Intra-Firm Financial Practices	Estimated 1974 Value	Percentage Change
Total Domestic Assets	2,436	338,400	.7%
Total Foreign Assets	−3,216	140,400	−2.2%
Intra-firm Financial Transfer	−11,046	28,080	−39.3%
Consolidated After-Tax Earnings	−755	43,123	−1.8%
U.S. Income Taxes*	1,233	28,815	4.2%
Foreign Income & Withholding Taxes	−433	9,569	−4.5%

*U.S. income taxes include taxes paid on parents' domestic income.

SOURCE: Thomas Horst, "American Taxation on Multinational Firms," *American Economic Review* (May 1976).

TABLE 5.6

Termination of Deferral with Assumed Changes in Investment Location and Means of Finance
(in millions of dollars)

	1976 Calendar Year Tax Liability	
	Current Dividend Distribution Rate	100% Dividend Distribution Rate
Total actual and potential U.S. revenue from current taxation of CFC earnings, with specified investment and financing changes[1]	1,000	260
Actual revenue from Subpart F, total	250	250
Potential revenue from termination of deferral with no investment nor financing changes	365	−375
Potential revenue from possible changes in investment and financing:[2]	385	385
(1) Effects on foreign source income—		
(a) Decrease in CFC earnings	−15	−15
(b) Decrease in royalties, fees, and interest repatriated to the United States	−10	−10
(2) Effects on domestic source income—		
(a) Increase in domestic investment	90	90
(b) Increase in use of equity capital in the United States and increase in use of external debt abroad	320	320
Addenda: Change in foreign revenue from corporate income and dividend withholding taxes[3]	−210	630
(1) Effect of 100% dividend distribution rate on dividend withholding taxes	—	840
(2) Effect of reduced size and increased use of external debt by CFCs on corporate income tax and withholding tax	−210	−210

Office of the Secretary of the Treasury   February 4, 1976
Office of Tax Analysis

[1]The estimates assume: (i) dividends from less developed countries are "grossed up" for purposes of calculating the tentative U.S. tax and the foreign tax credit; (ii) worldwide pooling of CFC profits and losses, and an overall limitation on the foreign tax credit; (iii) specified behavioral changes in dividend distribution rates, investment, and financing.
[2]The estimates represent the revenue impact after full adjustments to the current taxation of CFC earnings, including adjustments to the Tax Reduction Act of 1975. The adjustments would, in fact, take several years. The estimates are adapted from a model developed by Thomas Horst, "American Multinational and the U.S. Economy," *American Economic Review* (May 1976), cf. pp. 356 & 359.
[3]The estimates assume no change in foreign tax laws.

TABLE 5.7

Estimated Revenue Consequences of Alternative Standards of Tax Neutrality, 1972
(in millions of dollars)

	Capital-Export Neutrality	Capital-Import Neutrality	National Neutrality
Estimated U.S. revenue under existing law	$1,230	$1,230	$1,230
Elimination of deferral and recognition of foreign corporate losses	410		
Deduction rather than credit for foreign taxes comparable to state taxes	170		
Elimination of Western Hemisphere trade corporation	50		
Inclusion of less developed country dividends in gross-up requirement	40		
Extension of 7 percent investment tax credit to equipment expenditures abroad	−500		
Extension of asset depreciation range to foreign investment	−180		
Allowance of foreign tax credit for taxes paid abroad in excess of the present limitation formulae (mainly petroleum taxes)	−3,000		
Adoption of a territorial system of taxing foreign income		−1,230	
Tax all foreign income currently and allow a deduction but not a credit for foreign taxes			4,730
Estimated U.S. revenue after changes	−$1,780	$ 0	$5,960

Note: These estimates make no allowance for the possible response of firms and foreign governments to changes in the U.S. tax law. For a more detailed description, see G. C. Hufbauer and J. R. Nunns, "Tax Payments and Tax Expenditures on International Investment and Employment," *Columbia Journal of World Business*.

Notes

1. *Business Economics* (January 1978).
2. For a study of tax-related exports, see U.S. Treasury Department, 1976, Special Committee for U.S. Exports, 1977, and Senate Subcommittee on International Finance, March 9, 1978.
3. Domestic International Sales Corporations (DISC) legislation was passed in 1971. Corporations that qualify under this law are not subject to the same U.S. taxation on their earnings and profits as are others. DISC may defer taxes on half of their income. They are also taxed at 24% rate rather than 48%.
4. Ibid.
5. This means basing the tentative U.S. tax (before deducting the tax credit) on subsidiaries' dividends inclusive of foreign income tax allocated to those credits.
6. The most comprehensive data available at the host country level on direct investment are those for 1976, and on tax rates those for 1978.
7. Gary Hufbauer, "A Guide to Law and Policy," in *U.S. Taxation of American Business Abroad* (Washington, D.C.: American Enterprise Institute, 1975), pp. 4–6.
8. Thomas Horst, "American Multinationals and the U.S. Economy," *American Economic Review* (May 1976), pp. 149–52.
9. Ibid.
10. Gary Hufbauer, and David Foster, *U.S. Taxation of the Undistributed Income of Controlled Foreign Corporations*, Department of the Treasury (Washington, D.C., 1976), p. 34.
11. Robert R. Nathan Associates, "U.S. Foreign Trade and Employment" (May 1977), unpublished manuscript used in a hearing before the Subcommittee on International Finance of the Committee of Banking and Housing of the U.S. Senate, April 5, 1978.
12. See Export Policy, Subcommittee on International Finance, U.S. Senate, Part 6, April 5, 1978.
13. *Fortune* (August 1975), p. 120.
14. T. Horst, "Taxation of Multinational Firms," *American Economic Review* (June 1977).
15. George Kopits, *Taxation and Multinational Firm Behavior: A Critical Survey*, International Monetary Fund Staff Papers, 23 (November 1976): 651.
16. For further information, see the Library of Congress, Congressional Research Service, Export Stimulation Programs of Canada, France, Germany, Italy, Japan, Switzerland, and United Kingdom, 1977.
17. Ibid.
18. Richard Hammer, Price Waterhouse and Company, A Report to the Senate Committee on Banking, Housing, and Urban Affairs, March 9, 1978.
19. See United Nations, GATT studies in International Trade, Trade Liberalization, Protectionism and Interdependence, by Blackhurst & Co., Geneva, 1976.
20. Ibid.
21. Source of tax information: The Council of International Policy, Washington, D.C.
22. German Information Bulletin, March 1980.
23. Reports of Dresden Bank and Commerzbank, May 1979.
24. Ibid.
25. Export Policy, Senate Subcommittee on International Finance, Part 3, March 9, 1978.
26. Ibid.
27. See the Report of the House Committee on Ways and Means, 93rd Congress, 1st Session, and House Report No. 93–571.
28. See chapter 8, Nasrollah S. Fatemi, Gail Williams, and Thibaut de Saint-Phalle, *Multinational Corporations* (Cranbury, N.J.: A. S. Barnes and Co., 1976), pp. 278–79.

6
U.S. Economic Growth and Its Problems

> Corporations have been burdened with regulatory excess to the point of stifling normal improvement in efficiencies.
>
> Glen McLaughlin
> Four Phase System Corporation

> The United States is losing its competitive edge in technology because American industry is spending less on research and because the federal government withdrew much of its support for industrial research at the end of the Apollo Space Program and the Vietnam War.
>
> The American Association for
> the Advancement of Science, 1978

Since 1900 increases in productivity have been responsible for 50% of the growth in U.S. gross domestic product. In fact, for half a century, from 1916 to 1966, increases in total productivity were responsible for most of the huge growth in the business sector. When one considers that the other 50% of GNP growth during that period was the result of increases in inputs of human and natural resources—and that those inputs lagged behind the rise in population—then all of the increases in the standard of living in the U.S., "defined as real income or product per capita, have been due to productivity increases."

By historic standard the growth of American productivity was rapid during most of the postwar period. But since 1966 the growth rate has been declining at an alarming pace and now stands 40% below what it was before that date. If the United States hopes ever to regain its trade domination, it is essential that it first identify the causes of this productivity decline and then do something to reverse the process.

Needless to say, the lack of productivity gains and the surge in unit labor costs have become major issues among the nation's economic planners. They consider them "the most troublesome underlying cause of inflation."[1]

In his January 1979 message to Congress, then President Carter stated that reduced productivity in the United States means that the nation's economic power and potential have diminished. The president's report blamed declining productivity for both inflation and the slow growth in

American exports, and warned that the continued sluggishness of productivity growth was hampering the country's ability to create new jobs and provide a higher standard of living. Increasing productivity, President Carter declared, will help "combat inflation, reduce labor costs, produce more goods for export in competitive markets, and lead to a higher standard of living."

Actually, until 1974 the decline in U.S. productivity was not particularly disturbing from the standpoint of long-term growth, because it was partly the result of short-term fluctuations in some factors that typically display irregular movements, chiefly a drop in the uses of labor and capital from their 1965–66 peak.[2] Then in 1974 the productivity decline became both disturbing and puzzling, and the short-term shifts responsible for the slowdown prior to that year were no longer sufficient to explain the shortfall. Says Edward Denison, one of the nation's leading experts on productivity: "The major productivity series—output per person employed, output per hour, and output per unit of input—all show much the same pattern of retardation."[3]

Productivity in the United States increased by an average of 2.4% a year during the quarter century from 1948–73—a total of 82% for the period. It then dropped a total of 5.6% from 1973 to 1975. Even after recovering in 1976, productivity remained lower than the three years before; its 1973–76 growth rate was -0.5% a year.

Developments in manufacturing productivity and unit labor costs in the United States and most of the other industrial market countries were much less favorable in 1977, 1978, and the first part of 1979 than in 1976, because output growth either slowed substantially or declined in each of the eleven countries. In 1976 most of the countries recovering from recession had shown productivity gains from the low 1973–75 levels, but this was shortlived.

In the second quarter of 1979 productivity fell at the fastest rate in nearly five years. The 3.3% drop in output per hour from first-quarter 1979 was the largest since the 6.3% decline in third-quarter 1974.[4]

For 1977–78 Japan had the largest gain in manufacturing productivity and the smallest increase in unit labor costs. Canada, Belgium, France, Germany, and the Netherlands had gains that all exceeded the U.S. manufacturing productivity increase of 2.6%. Productivity rose only slightly in Italy and declined in the United Kingdom in 1977 but rose again in 1978. Increases in unit labor costs in Canada, Germany, and the Netherlands, however, were less than the 6.3% rise recorded in the United States, with Italy recording the largest increase by far, 17%.

Measured in terms of U.S. dollars, unit labor costs in all countries except Canada showed substantial increases. (Canadian unit labor cost fell only because of the decline in the relative value of the Canadian dollar.) Japan, Germany, and the Netherlands had the smallest increases in unit labor costs when measured in their own currencies, but the largest increase when measured in U.S. dollars, because their respective currencies showed strong gains against the American dollar. Except for Canada, only France had a smaller 1977 increase than the United States.[5]

In 1976 Canada and Sweden were the only two countries to have larger gains in labor cost than those of the United States; unit labor costs measured in dollars remained virtually unchanged in Japan and fell in all of the other countries.

Increases in hourly compensation during 1977 and 1978 ranged between 9% and 15% in all of the countries but Italy, where a high inflationary rate of 18% was recorded. In Sweden and England the rates of increase in compensation were moderate; in Japan and Germany the 1977 and 1978 increases were significantly above the 1976 rates. In all cases though, the 1977 and 1978 rates of gain continued to be less than the very high rates that prevailed between 1973 and 1975.

During 1977–78 the U.S. produced the highest gain in manufacturing employment. Unemployment compared with 1975 declined sharply. At the same time, employment also rose in Denmark, Britain, and the other Common Market countries in 1977 and 1978. Britain also reversed a three-year trend of decline by increasing working hours, but the United States had the largest 1977 and 1978 gains in total hours. Unfortunately, the United States and most foreign countries failed to continue the productivity improvement that began in 1976.

Japan, the traditional leader in productivity—8.8% per year since 1960— was again ahead of every nation with a 5.9% gain in 1977 and 8.8% in 1978. Meanwhile, Japanese manufacturing output per hour advanced 10% in 1960–73.

Similar gains of about 2% to 5% in Belgium, Denmark, France, Germany, and the Netherlands in 1977 and 1978 were substantially less than the 1960–70 rates of productivity improvement in those countries. In Italy productivity rose very little in 1977, while Britain registered a decline, and its level of output per hour stood only a fraction above the 1973 level. However, manufacturing productivity increased in 1978 to 4.4%.

Although the United States showed a strong rise in output in 1977 because of increases in the labor force and hours worked, its productivity was behind that of Japan, Belgium, France, Germany, Canada, Italy, and the Netherlands. While other nations increased their productivity in 1977 and 1978, the U.S. increased only its workweek and the size of its labor force (see table at end of chapter).

As of 1978 neither Japan nor any of the European countries had attained their pre-1974 levels of manufacturing employment, and only Italy had increased its total hours to the approximate prerecession level. The timing of the recession and its effects on employment varied from country to country, but in general total manufacturing hours declined in

U.S. Economic Growth and Its Problems

most countries in 1974, and in every country in 1975. Also, in 1975 employment in every industrial nation except Sweden declined. However, the United States, recovering from recession, showed solid gains in both manufacturing employment and total hours of work in 1976 and 1978. In contrast, employment and hours of work continued to decline in Japan and all the European nations except Sweden in one or both years.

Increases in unit labor costs reflect the extent to which increases in hourly compensation have outstripped productivity gains. In 1975 unit labor costs increased in all countries, rising 6.3% in the United States and 3% in Japan and Germany. But in 1976 unit labor costs fell in Germany, remained unchanged in Japan and Belgium, and rose in the United States. In comparison, from 1975 to 1978 unit labor costs rose substantially in the United States, Canada, and four of the European countries. Only Japan and Germany registered small gains in unit labor costs between 1975 and 1978. Meanwhile, productivity in the United States during the 1970s grew at a slower rate than in any other industrial country except the United Kingdom.[6]

Of course, aggregate economic growth can be improved by increasing the supply of natural resources or labor and capital goods, as well as by increasing productivity, but it is the latter that is so important to domestic and foreign competition. "That is, as factor inputs are increased, so too is factor income at prevailing prices." Thus increases in productivity decrease unit costs and the total price of production. That is why the decline in U.S. productivity after 1966 was partly related to the increases in the cost of production and the decreases in the competitiveness of American manufactured goods.

"According to the production theory, rates of change in productivity may be calculated as the difference between rates of change in the real gross product and in a weighted average of human and non-human factor inputs."

Real capital inputs are assumed to be used proportionately to real stocks of capital (including natural resources and land), gross of capital consumption allowances. Labor inputs are measured in terms of all persons engaged in production. The relative weights of the factor inputs are their shares in gross national income, which average about two-thirds for labor and one-third for capital.[7]

The tables at the end of the chapter show that real gross product in the United States rose by an average of 4% between 1948 and 1966, but then declined to 3% at an annual rate for 1966–78. "Total factor input, on the other hand, accelerated from a 1.2% average annual growth rate in the first period to 1.7% in the second. This was due entirely to an acceleration in the growth of the labor force, employment, and total hours worked, since capital grew at approximately the same rate in both periods. If the growth rates of total factor inputs are subtracted from those of real products, the result shows that the growth rates of total productivity fell sharply from 2.7% for 1948–66 to 1.3% for 1966–77.

"At the same time, output per labor hour dropped from the 3.2% average annual growth rate for 1948–66 to 1.9% for 1966–77. During this period the rate of capital substitution for labor (through research and capital investment) declined from 0.8% a year on the average for 1948–66, to 0.6% for 1966–77."[8]

With respect to labor-force participation ratios, the most striking downward trend has been among males 55 years of age and older. Apart from increased income and the ability to retire at an earlier age (this trend is the result of such other factors as increases in private pensions, the improvement of Social Security, and the availability of disability benefits under both private and public systems), some economists maintain that the decline in labor productivity is related to payroll and high salary-income taxes, which drive a wedge between the wages paid by employers and those received by the employee, and which reduce the aftertax remuneration of the self-employed. Further, the progressiveness of the personal-income-tax system tends to decrease the hours worked by people in the upper-income brackets.

Factors Influencing Productivity

Economists have suggested several theories for why productivity has slowed so significantly since 1966. Edward Denison contends that almost one-third of the 0.55 percentage-point slowdown between 1964 and 1969 was the result of changes in the age-sex composition of the American work force. As Denison explains: "The bulge in labor force growth in the latter 1960s increased the proportion of youth. Also, the increase in the proportion of women accelerated. Since both groups receive below-average compensation, this relative growth was a factor retarding the productivity advance as measured."

Voluntary early retirement and the mandatory retirement of those who reach the age of 65 (now 70) contributed to the sharp increase of young people relative to all other age components of the labor force. And because these new entrants have experience well below the average of the men and women they replace, the negative result on productivity has been very telling, particularly during the past five years.[9]

Economist George Perry, who studied the productivity shortfall between 1965 and 1970, concludes that 28% was the result of accelerated changes in the percentage of youths and women in the labor force.[10] But while Denison feels that the rest of the productivity slowdown he measured was "the result of a decline in the intensity of demand relative to capacity," Perry comes to almost the opposite conclusion, claiming that 36% of the slowdown he observed was related to a decline in the rate of capacity utilization. In other words, business was underestimating the potential demand in the economy.

The intensity of demand is an extremely important component of productivity. John Kendrick expresses it thus: "As the ratio of actual to potential real products changes, productivity changes, but to lesser extent. Capital stock and input estimates have not been adjusted for changes in rates of utilization, so capital productivity is obviously affected. Although employment and hours do fluctuate cyclically with output, a certain overhead component in labor input also causes labor productivity to reflect cyclical movements in aggregate demand. Intensity in demand was somewhat higher in 1966 than in 1948." But the Council of Economic Advisers estimates that the ratio of acutal to potential real product in 1977 was about 7% lower than in 1966. This change was responsible for lowering 0.3 percentage points from the productivity growth rate during this eleven-year period.[11]

The Causes of Decline of Productivity

There are many theories expressed by different groups concerning the decline in productivity, but economists in general believe that the following twelve problems deserve particular attention:

1. *The decline in the quality of labor.* There is no question that, despite the changes in age-sex composition, there has been a significant decline in the actual labor efficiency. The ratio of hours "at work" to hours paid for, for instance, has declined at an average annual rate of about 0.1% since 1971. Furthermore, according to a survey by the University of Michigan, unproductive time at work—such as coffee breaks and attending to personal business—has increased by an average of at least 0.2 percentage points since 1966. Besides this, the study contends, the efficiency of hours actually worked has declined. (There are also speculations that labor efficiency has been adversely affected since 1968 by negative social trends, but this will be discussed separately.)

Economists have called particular attention to the general lack of motivation to perform that seems prevalent in the labor force. Much of this, they say, is the result of a lack of interest in the job or concern for the success of the enterprise, particularly when remuneration is not tied to performance and productivity.

Says Kendrick: "It is here that the quality of working, life programs, job designs, labor-management productivity teams or broader company productivity programs, incentive pay, or profit-sharing schemes, and other methods to elicit worker cooperation in improving efficiency and cutting unit costs can play an important role."[12]

Since 1970 the National Commission on Productivity, created by Executive Order and reorganized by Congress in 1975, has attempted to encourage productivity through labor-management committees. At present there are about 300 of these joint committees operating in the United States, the most important of them being the labor-management team of the United Steelworkers of America, which has concentrated on increasing the international competitiveness of the steel industry.

Even some nonunion companies have established productivity improvement programs involving labor-management committees in plants and offices. And these efforts have been strengthened by the research of the American Productivity Center, a private nonprofit institution established in 1977. The suggestions made by all the committees and other private and public institutions include work simplification, job redesign, flexible work schedules, the expansion of part-time jobs, autonomous work teams, incentive pay systems, and the joint planning of training programs.

Unfortunately, despite all the plans and efforts, little change has taken place. In fact, recent union negotiations seem far more concerned with employment, job security, insurance systems, retraining, and relocation than with "productivity bargaining." Thus many economists and businessmen are suggesting that the president, through his secretary of labor, mount a nationwide campaign to promote joint labor-management programs to improve productivity and thereby improve the international competitiveness of American production.

2. *Declining opportunities for major new advances.* Throughout most of the postwar period, advances in knowledge, and thus in productivity growth, have been exceptionally large. In fact, the whole period was once regarded as the beginning of a golden era that would provide the world with a higher living standard, cheaper and better goods, and the scientific means to cure all disease and social ills.

The postwar jump in productivity can, in fact, be traced to a wave of new advances in knowledge that made possible seemingly unlimited cheap energy sources and a surge in science-based technology. But it is now argued that the law of diminishing returns has caught up with the industrial world, and the "technical revolution" is past.

Orio Giarini, secretary-general of the International Association for Risk and Insurance Economics Research, believes that we are rapidly reaching the point where current science-based technology has exploited all the major possibilities uncovered by the scientific advances of the past century. He contends that the world must now wait decades for the reservoir "to be replenished."[13]

F. M. Scherer, former director of the Federal Trade Commission's Bureau of Economics, also believes that innovations come in waves that gradually diminish. To illustrate the decline in the rate of innovation, Scherer points to the fact that the number of patents issued to domestic corporations peaked in 1971 and had declined by 20% in 1976.[14]

3. *The deterioration of American technology.* For the past three years there

has been a major debate in the United States over faltering American ingenuity and the deterioration of technology in this country. While the participants all agree that U.S. technology has slackened, they differ enormously in the extent to which they think technology has declined and the causes for this slowdown. Some argue that there has been no decline in ingenuity but only in the way in which our productive resources are being used.

Denison, for one, believes that the nation's economists must "disentangle changes in the speed with which Yankee ingenuity solves problems of production and distribution from a possible lengthening of the lags between the solution and implementation of new government regulations and other institutional changes." In fact, he adds, "the main reason for suspecting a decline in Yankee ingenuity seems to be the retardation of productivity growth, a development for which there are many alternative suggestions."[15]

Denison and other economists also lament the fact that technology receives no guidance from the U.S. government or the public, particularly in manufacturing and construction.

However, Delbert Tessar of the University of Florida believes that the deterioration in U.S. technology has been so intense that American companies have been forced to hire European technicians to compensate for American inactivity in machine technology.[16] He contends that the National Science Foundation has supported little basic research in mechanical engineering and mechanics and that this weakness can be found particularly in the field of high-quality consumer products and in light industry. He cites the automobile, television, steel, and textile industries as examples of this weakness.

4. *Declining capital investment.* Fixed-capital formation in the United States has declined for at least the past ten years, and this has affected the average age of American plants and equipment. According to the Council of Economic Advisers, this drop in the rate of capital investment may be responsible for the loss of half a percentage point of productivity growth a year.

Between 1948 and 1973 the ratio of capital to labor grew to 3% a year. Since 1973, however, the rate of increase has been only 1.75% annually. The problem has been acute in certain industries, such as steel (see the last part of this chapter).

5. *Tax policy and the effects of government regulations.* The most direct way that government interference affects productivity is by heavy taxation and measures that divert labor, capital, and land from more productive uses.

Funds also are diverted by programs involving pollution abatement, workers' safety and health, food and drug regulations, as well as by the Consumer Product Safety Commission, the Environmental Protection Agency, the Equal Employment Opportunity Commission, the Federal

Trade Commission, and many other agencies. The negative impact of health, environmental, and safety regulations alone has subtracted 0.2 percentage points from the average annual growth rate of industry between 1966 and 1975. By 1976 the negative impact had risen to 0.4 percentage points.

Filing reports, making and preserving records, and completing data in order to meet government requirements also absorb resources that could otherwise be used to produce measured output.

The Commission on Federal Paperwork estimated that meeting the requirements of the federal government cost American business $25 billion to $32 billion in 1976.[17] This is 2.4% to 3.1% of 1976 nonresidential business income in the United States. If one takes the requirements of state and local governments into consideration, this loss could add up to 4.6%

An Office of Management and Budget study suggests that the total hours required to meet federal reporting requirements in 1977 exceeded 350 million hours a year. In fact, this burgeoning of government regulations during the past decade has had such an impact on American industry that Senator Lloyd Bentsen, chairman of the Joint Economic Committee, calls it "America's No. 1 growth industry."

Businessmen throughout the country mirror the complaint of Glen McLaughlin, that, "as each new tax and each new regulation is imposed, another layer of incentive to perform is removed and otherwise creative efforts are diverted to unproductive, but lucrative, jobs of avoiding taxes and doing battle with bureaucrats. This is a tremendous waste of national resources. However, it is occurring at an accelerating rate."[18]

6. *The delay and postponement of projects.* Government rules for obtaining new project permits in many industries cause delays of many months between the first consideration of a project and its completion. These delays not only postpone the introduction of new ideas and new technology but also reduce the flexibility of firms, vis-à-vis changes in production, marketing, and competition.

7. *The negative social trends.* The trends of the mid-1960s, which resulted in student unrest, increased drug abuse, crime, and anti-business and anti-profit sentiments associated with the Vietnam War, had an unfavorable impact on productivity advance.

8. *Equal opportunity regulations and antiefficiency laws.* Productivity depends on the efficiency and ability of the men and women who are responsible for production. Because of new legislation that denies confidentiality to appraisals of students, government employees, and other applicants, prospective employers find references of less value that are often vague and unobjective. Equal-opportunity regulations have also added new criteria for the hiring, promotion, and release of workers that may affect resource allocation adversely in the short run and add to the costs of training and personnel management.

Businessmen emphasize that the one thing that most adversely affects their ability to allocate their resources efficiently is the increased uncertainty caused by Washington. Government intervention in personnel and resource allocation and changes in tax laws have placed nearly all business in the category of regulated industry.

9. *The effects of higher tax rates.* "The reason for the poor performance of our economy (that is, significantly deteriorating productivity trends in the past dozen years, accompanied by accelerating inflation) has been the growing burden of government."[19]

The tax burden at all levels of government in 1978 was 41% of national income, compared with 34% in fiscal 1966.

Australian economist Colin Clark states that when government expenditures exceed 25% of national income, it has a disastrous effect on productivity and inflation.[20]

A government with too much money to spend on defense and other projects that do not help consumer-goods research and investment absorbs the capital resources of a nation. It also absorbs more and more of the labor force into public employment, where productivity is low. Altogether, big government spending dries up capital, restrains the growth of total output, and hurts exports.

10. *The lessening of competitive pressures and the deterioration of management leadership.* A study of Burton H. Klein of the California Institute of Technology claims that the early postwar "golden age" of U.S. productivity growth was the result of a highly competitive economy that generated a wide diversity of ideas. But after 1965, the study contends, both the nature of competition and the quality of management changed.

Since then there have been few new firms, primarily because of the unavailability of risk capital. The closeness of existing firms and the oligopolistic nature of most industries have caused large firms to become more bureaucratic and less able to deal with innovation and risk. Imaginative, eager, and innovative scientists and engineers are being replaced with lawyers and business school graduates, who perform the same function in modern societies as did genetic inbreeding in feudalistic societies.

Erick Lundberg, a Swedish economist, contends that business has a tendency to entrust executive positions to lawyers who can work with government agencies to obtain subsidies on loans, or to businessmen whose job is to deal with unions and to silence pressure groups. He contends that these soft political appointments produce short-term results and influence management to neglect investment in research and capital equipment. They also encourage the sacrifice of long-term productivity, expansion, and business soundness for short-term accounting profits, which eventually hurts the firm and its stockholders.[21]

11. *The role of energy in productivity.* Some economists and government

experts believe that productivity per worker in the United States will never again increase as in the past. Once the oil and natural gas reserves of the United States and other countries are exhausted, and prices rise even further, it may be very difficult for the industrial nations to preserve an affluent way of life based on the cheap energy and natural resources of the developing countries.

Most of the industrialized nations of the world are now more than 75% dependent for their energy on imports of oil and uranium. The price and costs of these energy sources can reasonably be expected to appreciate 20% a year. So far, productivity in the U.S. oil and gas industry has been kept at a high level by drawing down fuel reserves that were discovered in the past. But as the United States tries to be more self-sufficient in basic energy productivity, more conservation in energy becomes most essential and, as a result, more productivity and expansion becomes very difficult.

Productivity until recently depended on labor, technology, and natural resources, especially cheap energy. Because the price of energy has risen ten times since 1973, and because we near the limits of technological progress, it will not be possible to increase one kind of productivity without sacrificing another kind.

Denison, however, challenges this idea. "First, the increase in the price of imported oil was the main component of a deterioration in the terms of trade that reduced the nation's command over goods and services by about 1%, but this did not directly change national income (or other output measures, such as GNP) or productivity.

"Second, the government did intervene, with controls over fuel consumption and choice of fuels, to try to reduce present and future imports.

"Third, the high price of energy resulting from the higher price of imported oil probably caused non-residential business to use less energy per unit of labor."[22]

In addition, he says, the Western European nations and Japan have always depended more on expensive foreign oil than the United States. Why has this decline affected a country that produces more than 60% of its energy—a larger portion than any other industrial nation?

Says Edward F. Renshae: "Our knowledge with regard to how to promote improvements in productivity is rather meager, and, in terms of certainty, about on a par with our knowledge of how to control inflation. The large amount of unemployed resources that now exists in the United States and the high degree of positive association that has existed over time between changes in productivity and changes in total output would suggest, however, that the most effective way to increase productivity in the next year or two will be to adopt those fiscal, monetary, price, and wage measures that are likely to be the most effective at reducing inflation."[23]

Achieving a continued reasonable expansion of our economy and our productivity in the near future will not be so easy as in the past, because energy is no longer so cheap, labor is no longer so motivated, and government regulations are far greater in number.

12. *The decline in industrial research and development.* The bulk of technological advance stems from public and private research programs. After rising for two decades between 1946 and 1966, to 2.91% of the gross national product, advance in technology declined in 1977 to 2.1%. Nearly half of this amount was spent by the government on military and space technology. As a result, "the slack of knowledge resulting from R&D obtained by cumulating outlays over the lifetime of the resulting new products and processes decelerated considerably after 1966. It seems likely that informal inventive and innovative activity, largely representing the myriad small improvements devised by plant managers and workers to the major technological advance, also decelerated."[24]

Between 1960 and 1968, the annual growth rate of research in the United States was 6.5%, and by the 1969–78 period it had declined to 2%. This change brought a warning from the American Association for the Advancement of Science: "The United States is losing its competitive edge in technology because American industry is spending less on research and because the Federal Government withdrew much of its support for industrial research at the end of the Apollo space program and the Vietnam War."[25]

Research and Development in the United States

Research and development is really the only way to generate the knowledge and flexibility required for a business or, indeed, a national economy to progress and stay competitive. This important fact has been only superficially recognized in the past by U.S. business and government, but the recent decline in productivity, the need for larger foreign markets, and the decrease in U.S. competitiveness both at home and abroad have led to a new awareness about the role of R&D spending.

Economists give three reasons to explain why R&D has been neglected over the past decade:

1. It is almost impossible to measure any aspect of research and development activities beyond current-year expenditures. In contrast, one can add up current investment in fixed capital stock, obtain a reasonable estimate of its depreciation, and then approximate the value of the capital stock accumulated during the period. The result can be partly checked with engineering and physical retirement data. Yet it is another matter entirely to locate the stock of knowledge, measure how much is forgotten or transplanted to other industries, and reliably determine the profitable

lifetime of even the successful research efforts of a given firm. Economists not only have failed to measure R&D, but also are unable to appreciate its broad significance in total economic performance.

2. Even if they do suspect its impact, they are too willing to assume that market factors will ensure that the proper volume of research efforts is forthcoming from the private sector.

3. Since it is assumed that it would be difficult to measure R&D results, either immediately or at the end of each year, the obvious question is how can we convince businessmen that higher spending on research and development will produce better results?

According to Dr. Roger E. Brinner, an analysis of output, employment productivity, and price behavior in manufacturing industries over the past three decades indicated that high-technology industries have surpassed low-technology ones. The former expanded at a 6.7% compound rate from 1950 to 1974, compared with a 2.3% for the latter. Output per employee in high-technology industries, meanwhile, increased 4% compared with only 2% or less in the low-technology companies. Not only did productivity increase in the advanced industries, but the gains in output per worker were also responsible for more jobs. In fact, the gains in employment of the more advanced industries surpassed their conservative counterparts by a large margin of 2.6% to 3%. "The enhanced domestic and international competitive posture generated more than enough demand to expand employment at a rapid pace," observes Edward Denison.[26]

How do we distinguish between industries with a high-technology base and those with a low-technology component? One method that economists use is to examine the average ratio of research and development expenditures to the portion of gross national product produced. It is estimated that industries with a research effort index of 0.07, or better, are "high-technology" and those with a research effort index below 0.02 are "low technology."

The National Science Foundation data also suggest a breakdown into high, low, and mixed technologies. "The line between high and mixed technology is defined as 0.07, the average ratio of research and development expenditures to output for all manufacturing. Similarly, the division between mixed and low technology was defined as 0.02, the average ratio of total expenditures for research and development to the gross national product."

The traditional theory that monetary and fiscal policies should be able to keep the economy at a full-employment level and prosperous has proved inaccurate. If such a theory were accurate, the creation and adoption of high technology would have had no impact on aggregate job creation. To the contrary, R&D not only has enhanced the standard of living but, by

U.S. Economic Growth and Its Problems

generating innovative products, has created growth markets at home and abroad and more jobs for American workers. These new products and the demand generated by their creation provide work for many unemployed workers and new job seekers.

If the economy is near full employment, high technology increases productivity and performs the function of reallocating labor to more effective uses. If the economy is in a recession, the high-technology and growth industries can be expected to increase domestic employment. Furthermore, the price record of industries with a strong research and development effort is clearly superior to those with weak research records.

Many economists, government planners, and businessmen have tried to quantify the rate of return to R&D expenditures but without much success. The reason, of course, is the lack of sufficient data and the absence of an observable capital stock of accumulated knowledge. But there is a consensus on the fact the R&D does boost employment growth, protect against business cycles, and curb inflation.

"During the 1950s, the output prices of advanced industries rose at only 1.6% a year, compared with the 3% average for low- and mixed-technology industries." The 1960s presented an even sharper differential—0.8% (high) compared with 1.4% (mixed) and 2% (low). The margin of superiority rose again during the early 1970s. High-technology industries generated inflation averaging only 1.3% a year, while prices in the mixed sector acclerated to a 7.5% pace, and those in the low sector increased to a 5.3% pace. This favorable price behavior in the high-technology industries is the direct result of research and development planning.

In addition, the private rate of profit derived from R&D expenditures is substantially above the return on traditional investments. Although there are no accurate data, an approximate figure of 15% to 20% emerges from several studies, compared with a 10% to 15% return on fixed capital investment.

This relatively high return implies that the sharply declining share of GNP devoted to R&D since the mid-1960s has had, and will continue to have, a serious negative impact on aggregate productivity growth and inflation. "During the past two decades, R&D has contributed 0.3% a year to full-employment capacity growth. Unfortunately, a 0.2% deterioration has been apparent in each successive five-year interval, that the contribution has fallen from 0.63% in the 1955–60 interval to 0.05% in the 1970–75 interval."[1]

Total industrial research spending in the United States has barely kept up with the need of the nation and inflation. Measured in constant 1972 dollars, R&D spending has hovered within a $19 billion to $21 billion annual range during the last ten years. Federally funded research and development, meanwhile, has declined in every year but one between 1966 and 1976, averaging a 5.5% yearly drop.

However, industry's own R&D funding has increased in real terms in every year except two since 1966, averaging a 3.8% annual real gain over that period. As far as exports are concerned, private R&D spending exerts more impact than federally funded industrial research. Federal spending is mostly associated with the defense industry, which has some effect on the private economy—such as the development of narrow and wide-bodied jets and advances in integrated circuit technology.

The deterioration of U.S. research and development is shown by comparing it with GNP. Industrial R&D spending in the U.S., as a percentage of GNP, has declined gradually in the last decade, from 2% in 1967 to 1.5% in 1978.

However, many economists believe that since the nation's GNP growth is concentrated primarily in the service sector, where relatively little research is undertaken, measuring the growth and decline of research and development with GNP is distorted and quite inaccurate.

Therefore a comparison of U.S. R&D performance with the performance of other industrial nations is more appropriate. The comparison reveals that the United States' lead in this area is being slowly eroded, most notably by Japan and Germany.

The most alarming aspect of this comparison is that in Western Europe and Japan government R&D efforts are considerably less devoted to space and defense programs and focus far more on industrial programs, university programs, and private nonprofit research institutions. Japan, for example, allots fully 78% of its federal R&D budget to those activities—which amounts to one-fifth of all research and development instituted in Japan.

The experience with Japan in the areas of television, radios, cameras, and transceiver equipment shows the strengths of that country's research and trade facilities, and our comparative weaknesses. In 1977 the U.S. trade deficit with Japan in high-technology goods was $3.6 billion. About 70% of this shortfall was accounted for by imports of consumer electronic goods. Most important, Japan's production of high-technology goods has increased five times in the last ten years, from $2 billion in 1967 to $10 billion in 1977.[28]

A comprehensive study by Jack Bronson[29] shows that research and development in the high-technology industries are a way to maintain world market position and global corporate earnings. "The U.S. trade balance is more favorable in those product groups which were research-development intensive," Bronson reported. "But in areas which were neglected, this country lost both foreign and domestic markets to other countries. Not only have Japanese manufacturers taken over a substantial segment of U.S. color televison trade (about 25%), but they have also taken the lead in developing new generations of consumer electronic products."

For instance, the videotape recorder, originally invented and marketed in the United States, has been completely taken over by Japanese firms that now manufacture this sophisticated equipment in Japan and license such U.S. firms as RCA and Zenith to market these products in the United States under their own brand name.

The above example describes trends that are taking place in two contrasting economic environments that are slowly but surely contributing to the widening competition gap. In Japan there is a sustained rate of growth, a burgeoning trade surplus, and an economic environment that is conducive to expanding industrial investment in R&D and plant facilities. In the United States the trade deficit, the weak dollar, high rates of unemployment, and an inflation-inhibiting growth and expansion of the economy have had a reverse effect.

Another good example of these differences is the tire industry. In the year immediately after World War II, U.S. tire companies enjoyed immense advantages over their European competitors. But as the European auto industry revived, tire requirements changed. European motorists drove smaller European cars faster and harder over more winding and rougher roads than their American counterparts.

For instance, Michelin, the family-owned French company, started a research plan that eventually led to the invention of the 1940s of the radically different radial tire. Michelin also had the advantage of being integrated into the European automobile industry. With a 53% interest in France's Citroën, it could see that an enormous sum should be spent on R&D—which resulted in 1960 in the invention of the steel-belted tire.

"In the 1960s, Goodyear and Michelin were following diametrically opposed strategies—both closely linked to the broader geopolitical designs of their home nations." Says Dan Morgan, *Washington Post,* "As France dismantled its colonial empire, President Charles de Gaulle exhorted French industry to strive for greatness through technology."

At the same time, U.S. multinationals were starting to establish plants that utilized less than the latest in advanced technology in Africa, Asia, and Latin America. And the billions of dollars that they invested in setting up tire-manufacturing operations around the world began draining surplus capital away from research and development.

As the U.S. companies created a worldwide network, Michelin poured hundreds of millions of dollars into radial-tire development and into building new radial-tire plants in its home territory of Europe. Thus, when radial tires began to sweep Europe in the 1960s, U.S. manufacturers found themselves stuck with conventional tires and lost markets to Michelin.

In 1966 Michelin started selling some of its "X" series radials in the United States under a Sears label. Yet not until 1969 did General Motors alter the suspension system of some of its models to accommodate radials. Ford quickly followed, using steel-belted radials on its luxury Lincoln Continental.

As demands increased, Michelin built a new tire plant in Greenville, S.C. Unfortunately, none of the U.S. tire companies had predicted or planned for the age of the radial. In 1973 only Uniroyal had a U.S. radial-tire plant in operation.

Today, largely as a result of this negligence, the United States is the world's leading tire importer. Americans spend $1 billion a year on foreign tires. One passenger-car tire out of two sold in the United States is a radial, compared with one out of twenty-five in 1970.

Michelin, as a result of its progressive research plan, has moved into fourth position in its sales in the United States, while Firestone's volume has waned. It has lost millions of dollars, damaged its popular name, and been forced into a merger with another company. Since 1970 more than 91,000 American workers in the tire industry have lost their jobs.[30]

The negligence of the automobile industry in the areas of research and development and energy saving is a tragedy. In 1978 $14 billion worth of automobiles were imported into the United States. This situation and the energy crisis forced President Carter to persuade the auto industry to develop new scientific knowledge to improve the performance of American-made cars. In fact, in an unprecedented meeting with automobile executives, Carter suggested a joint research program of government and industry.[31]

The automobile industry for some time has argued that the mandated fuel-economy standard of an average 27 miles a gallon by 1985 would be too costly in view of the gasoline savings that would be achieved. In response, Congress and most economists argue that if the Japanese and European corporations that started production after the war have been able to solve this problem, then surely the U.S. auto industry ought to be able to catch up.

President Carter applauded the new attempt of the automobile industry in the areas of research and development, and commended the "research program in which the industry and government would split the bill as a major new innovation in basic research in automotive technology."

Although no final figures have been agreed upon between the government and industry, the plan may call for government spending of up to $100 million over a three-year period—only about twenty years overdue.

The purpose of the research will be to develop new scientific knowledge in such areas as friction and wear, combustion, new lightweight and stronger materials, processing materials, fluid dynamics, noise, and vibration. Research on engine and transmission is apparently excluded.

This decision of the U.S. government to go along with a joint industry effort reflected the concern of the Carter administration about the backwardness of automobile technology resulting from the underinvestment in basic research.

What has happened to Chrysler is another example of the lack of planning and the negligence of research and development. Instead of producing cars for today's market, the company has continued to produce "gas-guzzling" big cars, which has resulted in the loss of hundreds of millions of dollars. Chrysler became the first large automobile corporation to appeal to the federal government for assistance. The Carter administration responded with a special federal loan guarantee for the ailing company but rejected its request for a $1 billion advance against its taxes.

Chrysler is suffering from two serious problems: (1) a lack of sufficient research and planning to prepare a car suitable for a market that is more concerned with gas mileage than with size and exterior beauty; and (2) a lack of research to enable it to comply with government requirements for emissions, fuel, and safety standards.

Another shocking example of R&D shortfall is what is happening to the U.S. atomic power industry. Many U.S. scientists and businessmen are concerned that France is quickly supplanting the United States as the world leader in the civilian nuclear industry. They warn that the United States could find itself unable to continue taking commercial advantage of worldwide nuclear development

A few years ago, when then President Carter realized that he could not persuade other powers to go along with his nuclear policies, he suggested the International Nuclear Fuel Cycle Evaluation Conference in Vienna. Then he decided that Washington would not permit the commercial reprocessing of spent nuclear fuel in the United States. That technique not only recovers reactor fuel but also produces plutonium, the chief ingredient of nuclear weapons. The administration argued that uranium reserves were too abundant and the proliferation risks too high to justify the process. It also decided not to plunge ahead in the development of breeder reactors, at least those based on plutonium, because of the risk of proliferation. And it asked other nuclear powers to stop selling reprocessing technology to Third World countries and to reexamine their own needs for the process.

The European countries thought the U.S. policy a naive strategy to defend the interests of the U.S. nuclear industry. The French, with no oil, little coal reserves, and a finite supply of uranium, saw the absolute necessity of moving ahead quickly toward nuclear energy. "To Paris, breeder reactors and reprocessing of spent fuel looked like the legendary perpetual-motion machine to energy independence. Furthermore, to defray the enormous, if undisclosed, cost of a full-cycle nuclear power development program, the French wanted to contract with other countries to reprocess their fuel. Britain and Germany also have bent back the idea of the complete fuel cycle."[32]

France is already building a commercial breeder and hopes to make later models. In fact, the French are so far advanced that Paris is able to flex its muscles for a virtual renegotiation of the Eurotam Treaty that was to have made nuclear development a Common Market undertaking. If the French system proves correct, the United States could end up importing breeders from France.

These developments are good examples of how negligence, or lack of enough R&D planning in today's competitive business world, can adversely affect nations and people around the world. They also show that whenever private investment in U.S. R&D declines, it has serious implications for both productivity and employment.

Furthermore, the industries are cited in which the United States is ahead of other nations because of high technology and high R&D—aerospace, computers, chemicals, and pharmaceuticals. The lead in aerospace and electronics is the result of the significant amount of money funneled through government agencies. In the other two industries (chemicals and pharmaceuticals), the bulk of the R&D funding comes from internal corporate cash and the stock market. This provides some indication that when the government and the private sector funnel R&D money to industry, it prospers—creating more exports and more jobs.

Patricia Logan writes:

> Both technology and technology-based products are of major significance to the United States in terms of international trade as well as generating jobs and products for domestic consumption. The export of technology, as distinct from the export of products, brings revenues to U.S. companies, and thus to the U.S. economy in the form of license fees and royalties. In 1977 the gross income from such sources was $2.95 billion, compared to $660 million in 1965.[33]

However, the total contribution of R&D and high technology to U.S. economic welfare cannot be measured solely in terms of the trade balance. The tremendous increase in U.S. industrial productivity since the end of World War II can be attributed primarily to the enormous amount invested in research and development between 1947 and 1965. At the same time, the average annual increase in output per man-hour in private industry ranged from 2% to 6%, with the greatest increase occurring in the communications and utility sectors, where the growth in real output reached 7.5% per year by 1970.

Thus advances in productivity are responsible for a large part of this nation's economic progress, and these upward trends are expected to continue through 1990.[34] "One of the most important weapons in our arsenal against inflation is increased productivity, which can be achieved through technology and innovation."[35]

However, since 1970 the direct economic gains on international trade resulting from the sale of technology-intensive products have been declining rapidly. It is the consensus of both economists and business leaders that our leadership in both R&D and advanced technology is eroding.

Unfortunately, there is no standard way to determine current U.S. achievements in applying technology to improve either the national well-being or the U.S. position in international markets. However, we can get some insight by studying the data on per capita income as well as the amount spent on research and development.

A study of nineteen OECD member countries shows a significant correlation between per capita income and expenditures on research and development as a percentage of GNP. It also indicates that a high level of R&D leads to increased productivity and higher exports. In particular, comparison between the U.S. and Germany shows that while German expenditures increased from 1.4% in 1963 to 2.7% in 1976, U.S. expenditures dropped from 3.3% of GNP to 2.2% during the same period. (The U.S. expenditures also included about 50% for defense-related R&D, which has limited impact on the commercial sector.)

In fact, more than one-fourth of the funds spent in the United States for scientific research and development goes to military technology—three times the amount devoted to energy. Altogether, 47% of R&D spending in the United States is consumed by three items: military technology, basic research, and space. Only 15% goes to health, agriculture, and business; and 8% goes to energy.

Consequently, research on fossil fuels, such as oil and coal, has been neglected. Even after the energy crunch of 1973, research funds for such energy sources as solar power have remained scarce, reflecting the lack of vision of the post–World War II mentality.

Countries such as Japan and West Germany, meanwhile, have committed a very small portion of their research funds to military purposes (2% and 1%, respectively). Instead of developing their own national security equipment, they buy it from the United States.

Thus in the U.S. any funding for military, space, and basic research comes mainly from the government, while in other countries governments spend a large sum of money on private industrial research.

By 1975 France's revenues in the aerospace industry (compared with 1970) had grown by 35%, while U.S. sales grew by 31.1% and the EEC nations by 27%.

In addition to transport aircraft, the U.S. aerospace industry exports an array of other products, such as general aviation aircraft, helicopters, engines, parts, spares, accessories, and military aircraft. In 1970 the total world military export market amounted to $6 billion, of which the U.S. share was 53% and the Soviet Union's share was 26%. In 1977 U.S. military agency sales exceeded $7.1 billion. By 1979 they had reached $12 billion. Deliveries of high-technology military weapons to the Middle East countries in 1972 totaled only $400 million, but by 1978 they had jumped to $5 billion, or more than two-thirds of the total. Since 1972, France, England, and West Germany also have joined the market in high-technology military weapons.[40]

Although high-technology products still make a positive contribution to the U.S. balance of trade in all categories, a new trend of declining R&D support by both the U.S. government and industry is now apparent. Total spending for R&D dropped from 3% of gross national product in 1964 to 2.2% in 1977. The ratio is expected to decline to 2% by 1985. Meanwhile, total R&D dollars spent, when adjusted for inflation, have been declining annually.

Consequently, the United States is gradually slipping from its technological position. Patent activity by non-U.S. inventors is also rising. For example, 37% of all U.S. patents went to foreign inventors in 1976, compared with 17% in 1961. This increase in "foreign patents," according to Edgar Weinberg of the U.S. Department of Labor, is disquieting not because it is a reflection of a loss of creativity of U.S. scientists or the quality of their inventions (which is not the case) but rather because R&D outlays tend to have a "positive correlation with productivity growth, and a decline in the U.S. proportion of patents could foreshadow a slowdown in the flow of new products and processes."[41]

There is no consensus or even a good explanation for this slowdown. Some economists studying the future of U.S. productivity contend that "the bottleneck is not science and technology, per se, but lies instead in the arrangement-making process among government, private enterprise, and science and technology."[42]

Thus the problem of productivity and technology is interwoven with many other factors, including the state of the national and international economy, the profitability of capital investment, the patent situation, inflation, taxes, antitrust laws and other government regulations, domestic politics, labor cooperation, plant efficiency, the skill and knowledge of management, the mood of pressure groups, and the politics of the administration and Congress.

Resolving the crisis of production, trade, monetary problems, and productivity involves first a sound and practical long-range plan, then cooperation among the administration, management, scientists, labor, inventors, distributors, and, above all, Congress. While in other countries business and government are united in their efforts to promote exports, production, and trade, in the United States different groups pursue different and sometimes conflicting goals. The result is that, because of these differences and conflicts, the following barriers that slow the diffusion of technology and productivity growth are created:

1. lack of producer information about the specific needs of customers;

2. neglect of innovation in managerial skills;

3. neglect of the education of labor in new and modern technology;

4. opposition of labor to new technology;

5. lack of sufficient information about business among legislators;

6. lack of enough dialogue between the administration, business, labor, and Congress;

7. uneasy relations between many universities and big corporations.

Capital Expenditures

Besides research and development, a second major element in productivity is capital formation. A steady investment of new capital is needed to produce new machinery and new technology for the improvement of productivity. "Expenditures for new plants and equipment, whether for expansion or replacement, allow the stock capital to be modernized and more efficient automated technology to be introduced."[43]

The National Center for Productivity and the Quality of Working Life, in a report on productivity, highlights a number of unfavorable trends in American business and productivity growth:

1. The rate of growth in the capital-labor ratio since 1967 has slowed down significantly. This decline in capital investment is closely related to the poor growth of productivity. "The capital-labor ratio (the ratio of the net stock of fixed and non-firm business capital to total employee hours) increased at an annual rate of 3.3% for the 1947–67 period. The rate for the 1967–73 period declined to 1.9% a year, and to 1.2% for the 1973–77 period. These figures exclude investment to meet environmental standards. Economic adjustments to take cyclical fluctuations into account in the capital-labor ratio show about the same degree of slowdown."[44]

2. Real fixed investment in productive facilities in the United States is below the 10% annual rate of increase needed to improve American technology, create full employment, and generate the productivity required for 1980.

3. The use of capital investment in the United States has changed. Of the total dollars invested, large sums are spent on meeting environmental goals and new governmental regulations, which in 1978 exceeded 9% of total capital investment. If these mandated capital expenditures are excluded, investment has actually declined in the manufacturing sector since 1966.

A study done for the Transportation Department by Harbridge House, Inc., in Boston last November estimated that the big three auto makers will have to spend nearly $44 billion between 1979 and 1983 specifically to meet government-mandated improvements in their cars. "It is likely," according to this study, "that all but General Motors in the auto industry will find themselves very capital-constrained. In this high-roller game, even Ford is a small company."

Federally mandated features for cars have already added about $666— 10% of the average sticker price—to vehicles sold today. What is happening to Chrysler and the auto industry is just a symptom, according to the Center for American Business at Washington University in Saint Louis. "The disease is excessive regulation of American industries."[45]

4. Lagging investment seems to be the result of a deterioration in profitability. "There are many ways to measure profitability, but all tend to show similar trends," says the report of the Department of Commerce. "In 1977 after-tax rates of return on capital averaged 5% to 9%, compared with an average of 8% during the mid-60s." These rates are considered particularly low in view of the greater risks and uncertainties of investment today. The low rate of return combined with the decline in research and innovation has produced the present depressed productivity and has discouraged capital investment.

Scientists and engineers have expressed different points of view. They believe that in order to increase productivity we have to concentrate on innovation and capital investment. Too often they disregard the management-worker interface. Recent studies have shown that there is an increasing recognition that managing today's work force better is vital to any productivity improvement. Efforts to meet the expectations of workers for better working conditions and to make more effective use of their creativity have resulted not only in labor peace but also in increased productivity.

"To achieve the twin objectives of greater productivity and worker satisfaction, a variety of human resource programs are being tested," says the Joint Economic Committee. "New techniques, such as group incentive systems, flexible work schedules, autonomous work teams, job design, and goal-setting approaches, have had varying degrees of success."

Capital expenditures in the United States are about 9% of GNP, compared with 35% in Japan and 22% in the United Kingdom.[46] The situation has its roots in early 1970, when competition intensified in the world economy, and Japanese and West European firms began redesigning industries for more efficient production and automated plants to further increase export volume and reduce unit product costs.

Thus the enormous capital credits these governments gave investment and the impressive productivity gains achieved permitted the Japanese and West European firms to absorb most of the increase in export costs resulting from the high price of energy and currency appreciations.

U.S. Economic Growth and Its Problems

In contrast to the progressive efficiency of foreign firms, U.S. firms, especially in medium- and low-technology industries, retrenched by moving offshore to reduce their labor costs and to overcome foreign import restraints while neglecting their basic research and development.

It is this lack of efficiency and this lack of improvement in medium and low technology that have led to the enormous trade deficit with Japan, Germany, and even Taiwan. In 1978 the U.S. trade deficit with Taiwan was $2.6 billion. (Under pressure, Taiwan recently agreed to buy a turbo-generator plant in order to reduce its surplus with the United States. But the Taiwanese prime minister grudgingly stated, "If the bidding had been open, the Japanese would have offered us a deal for 35% less on the generators. I do not want to be critical of America, but your productivity is so low you cannot compete with the Japanese, and not just in T.V. sets.")[47]

The significance of the above statement is that the competitiveness of the U.S. economy is not only being threatened by the low-wage economies of East Asia but also by a modernized and automated Japan in a wide range of industrial products, including textiles, generators, motor vehicles, televisions, and consumer electronics. And this competition may eventually spread to the most sophisticated components of the computer and aerospace industries.

U.S. plant and equipment expenditures in 1978 were $153.1 billion, 13.3% more than in 1977. After adjusting for the reported change in prices, spending increased only 4.5% in 1978. Business plans for new plant and equipment expenditures in 1979 totaled $170.2 billion, or less than 9% of GNP.

The share of manufacturing spending for 1979 was $77.5 billion. The largest increases were by the aircraft industry, 31%; paper, 30%; electrical machinery, 25%; nonelectrical machinery, 25%; and other nondurables, 25%. Motor vehicle and chemical plants increased by between 14% and 20%; petroleum, rubber, and beverages by about 5%. Petroleum companies are now planning large increases in spending for transportation facilities and nonpetroleum activities.

Meanwhile, other manufacturing industries, excluding rubber, planned small increases, while in the rubber industry a 1.5% decline was anticipated. Although the year-to-year changes in investment of iron and steel, nonelectrical machinery, paper, and chemicals showed more strength in 1979 than the year before, the food and beverage industry, textiles, motor vehicles, nonferrous metals, and stone-clay-glass showed far less strength.

"Non-manufacturing industries plan spending of $93.2 billion, 9% more than in 1978; last year, spending increased 13%," says John T. Woodward in *Survey of Current Business*. "The largest increases are planned by railroads, 19%, and gas utilities, 15%. Airlines plan a 13% increase, and the 'other' transportation groups, electric utilities, and mining firms plan increases between 9.5% and 11.5%. The 'Communications and Commercial' group plans a 6% increase. The year-to-year changes in investment programs of gas utilities and 'other transportation' show more strength this year than last; changes in the programs of airlines and 'Communications and Commercial' show less strength."[48]

Capital Spending in the United States 1970 to 1979[49]

1970	5.7%	growth
1971	1.8%	"
1972	8.5%	"
1973	12.5%	"
1974	12.4%	"
1975	0.2%	"
1976	6.8%	"
1977	12.7%	"
1978	13.3%	"
1979	11.2%	"
1980	8.8%	"
1981	10.8%	projected

Majority-owned foreign affiliates of U.S. corporations planned a 15% increase in capital expenditures, to $35.2 billion, in 1979, following an 11% increase in 1978.[50]

For 1979 the latest plans were also revised downward. However, the percentage increase from 1978 remained about the same because the 1978 base was lower. The 1979 downward revision centered on petroleum and primarily reflected the fact that in the OPEC nations most of the petroleum industries had been nationalized and the producers and owners were now responsible for capital investments.

The petroleum investment of $10 billion was about the same as in 1978. The sharpest increase, of $800 million, was planned in Norway—primarily for North Sea exploration and development, as well as for pipelines and associated facilities to bring North Sea petroleum onshore.

In most of the other developed countries, affiliates planned small increases or actual declines. Foreign affiliates of U.S. companies in the United Kingdom planned an increase of $3 billion. This was actually lower than the investment in 1978, partly because most of the exploration oil projects had been completed.

In Japan a decline in spending was planned, following a large increase in 1978. Total investment in all industries was expected to be $1.2 billion. Most of the investment was to be used for liquefied petroleum gas facilities, pollution controls, and storage facilities.

In the developing countries, increases in investment in the petroleum industries were planned in Egypt, Cameroon, Nigeria, and many areas of offshore Africa. In Saudi Arabia, Kuwait, and the other OPEC areas, spending plans for American corporations were down, reflecting the slowing of some large projects in Iran and the government's takeover of

U.S. Economic Growth and Its Problems

the exploration of the natural-gas-collection network, additional post facilities, and saltwater injection systems to assist in the more complete extraction of petroleum.

In Indonesia spending in petroleum industries for 1979 also was down, reflecting the huge spending in 1978 after the conclusion of a new agreement on production-sharing and tax arrangements.

Meanwhile, "international and unallocated" affiliates planned a 38% increase, or $500 million, following a sharp decrease in 1978. (The recovery of tanker rates, after several years of decline, led to the acquisition of new and used tankers.)[51]

Foreign investment in U.S. firms is now increasing. At present it is not a significant factor in helping American industry. But if such investment is monitored and, if necessary, controlled by a central authority, it could be extremely advantageous.

The fact that some high-technology industries are looking for capital outside the United States shows that present levels of domestic capital investment and research and development are not sufficient. Aerospace firms are for the first time forming joint ventures with foreign countries. Thus Boeing will join Japan on a $600 million venture to build a small, wide-bodied, low-noise, short-takeoff airbus for use on domestic Japanese routes. The General Electric Company has joined forces with Snecma, owned by the French government, to produce the CEM 56 aircraft engine for use in STOL aircraft. Pratt and Whitney will join forces with a German consortium. Their new engines will be used to produce the next generation of commercial aircraft, replacing the American near-monopoly in this area. Other companies, such as Britain's Rolls-Royce, are trying to put together an engine consortium with French, German, Swedish, Italian, and Belgian manufacturers.

Similarly, California's Northrop Corporation is joining with other aerospace companies in obtaining the capital investment needed to be competitive. Behind this great surge is the fear that high technology in aerospace is slipping and that a boom in commercial airplane orders and hefty defense spending is imminent.

The deterioration in mass communications technology in the United States is a fiasco. At a time when there is a shortage of energy, there are not enough railroad facilities in the country to handle the surge in traffic. the Missouri Pacific Railroad alone is looking for $1.7 billion in new capital investment. This is an increase of more than $247 million above 1978 capital spending.

The steel industry, after several years of negligence, now realizes that it has to compete with 20 million tons of imported steel. Thus. U.S. Steel and a number of other steel makers were planning to spend some $3 billion in 1980 and $3.2 billion in 1981 to replace or modernize existing facilities.

To meet all of its requirements, the steel industry will have to spend a minimum of $5 billion annually between now and 1983, applied as follows: about $1.5 billion to install additional capacity that is tied to an annual 2.5% growth rate, about $2 billion annually to maintain existing capacity, about $1 billion annually to meet pollution control requirements, and about $500 million a year for other nonsteel activities.

Realizing the problems of the market and the great increase in imports, the steel industry's $3 billion capital spending in 1979 was considerably short of the minimum $5 billion capital investment needed.

Planned expansion programs over the next decade also fall short of the projected need. If profitability and capital availability do not improve, the result will be increased imports at premium prices, fewer new jobs created, fewer existing jobs maintained, slower economic growth, and a larger trade deficit.

The steel industry complains that many of its problems are the result of government policies and say that the solution lies there as well. In fact, to overcome the current economic problems, the country needs a change in the government's basic economic policies to encourage the generation of capital sufficiently large to provide adequate supplies of vital materials, energy, and employment.

There is a close relationship between plant and equipment investment and jobs. Rising investment means that jobs are created immediately to produce the plant and equipment to operate and maintain them, and to supply them with necessary materials and services.

A wide variety of public policies to meet the required expansion have been suggested, including "stop dumping foreign steel, permit faster capital recovery under the tax laws through shorter depreciation periods for production facilities, and [allow the] first-year write-off of pollution abatement equipment and extension of investment tax credits."[52]

For many years Japan and Western Europe have tended to maintain employment in their steel industry by increasing exports to the United States at prices reflecting less than the full costs of production. The effects of such policies on the domestic industry are to aggravate the already cyclical nature of U.S. business. Unfortunately, according to steel industry executives, the safeguard against these practices that was approved by Congress has not been seriously enforced.

Many American corporations are accelerating capital spending at this late hour because they realize that their competitiveness both at home and abroad is diminishing. According to W. Paul Cooper, president of Acme-Cleveland Corporation, "there are more and more real-capacity expansions and large modernization programs. Lord knows, the country needs it."[53]

The United States has played the role of technological and marketing bellwether for Europe and the world throughout the postwar era. True, the United States has no monopoly on invention or on the discovery of new products and processes. However, of 110 significant postwar innovations, 74 were first marketed and commercialized by U.S. firms.

Whatever the relative economic disadvantages of the past negligence, the consensus is that the United States should strive to retain its leadership in areas of high technology and try to stop the erosion in medium and low technology. The government's concern is evidenced by several congressional investigations, studies by the Office of Science and Technology, the International Trade Commission, the National Science Foundation, and the Departments of State, Defense, Treasury, Labor and Commerce.

"Industrial representatives are also very much aware that a review of our policies and practices regarding the creation and transfer of high technology is an urgent requirement. Foreign products incorporating technology acquired from the U.S. are beating out American productions in markets around the world, including the U.S. itself," says J. Fred Bucy, Jr., in the Report of the Defense Science Board on Export.[54]

In view of all these findings, concerned groups recommend a national policy based on:

1. understanding the nature of technology and the various factors that govern its creation, dissemination, commercialization, and contributions to the national welfare;

2. encouraging a continuing stream of creative technological innovation within the United States;

3. developing and instituting a coordinated system of controls and incentives that will assist in the optimization of national benefits from technological innovation and application.[55]

A congressional committee should examine the current laws and regulations that hamper the progress of technology and exports and consider revoking or modifying these laws. The competitive status of the nation as a whole could benefit from removing the red tape and shackles that increase the cost of production, hinder progress, and hamper trade.

Congress should explore ways of allowing innovative corporations a rapid write-off for capital investments that are required for research and development and increased productivity.

Congress must review the tax system and explore ways to help corporations that are innovative and spend enough on R&D.

Methods of encouraging and facilitating government-industry cooperation should be examined. A new department similar to what other nations call the Ministry of International Trade, Industry, and Technology could help coordinate both private and public plans and programs. This department would be responsible for helping industries maintain and increase their superior technological base, for offering suggestions for long-term competitive financing, for encouraging a free and open world trade environment with equality of market opportunity, and for making recommendations to the administration and to Congress on eliminating laws and regulations that hamper trade and increase production costs.

Urgent attention is needed to increase the funds available for investment changes in the tax law to provide investment tax credits and more favorable capital-gains provisions.

The present inefficient and confusing regulatory process must be either improved or abandoned. There are too many regulatory delays and uncertainties for both producers and exporters. "In order to maximize the social benefit from our innovation process, a requirement to consider reasonable alternative approaches to and costs of achieving proposed regulatory objectives could help counteract the present single-minded focus on a narrow specific approach and objective. Better coordination of regulatory activities could help facilitate a more timely and effective process."[56]

Unfortunately, the total policy (if it can be called a policy) of the administration and Congress concerning business is both feeble and contradictory. A recent survey presented to the Senate Subcommittee on Finance shows many different examples of laws, executive actions, and court rulings that impede production and exports. The clear and unavoidable conclusion is that unless a more favorable, well-organized, and stable national policy is created in the areas of research and development, capital investment, taxation, and international trade, the nation will continue to lose its share in the world market to foreign rivals.

TABLE 6.1

Larger industrial countries: Changes in real gross national product and its components.

Countries	Years	Real gross national product	Consumption private	Consumption public	Gross fixed investment private non-residential	Gross fixed investment private residential	Gross fixed investment public	Exports	Imports	Changes in stocks[1]
					annual changes, in percentages					
United States	1976	5.9	1.3	4.8	23.2	−6.6	6.8	19.1	0.5	
	1977	5.3	5.0	3.2	8.7	20.7	−6.5	2.4	9.7	1.0
	1978	4.4	4.5	1.1	8.4	4.2	6.9	10.7	11.0	1.1
	1979	2.3	2.6	1.3	6.2	−5.7	−6.2	10.1	4.5	0.7
	1979 IV	1.0	1.6	0.8	3.4	−7.0	−2.8	9.2	3.1	0.1
Japan	1976	6.5	4.5	3.6	1.4	8.6	2.8	20.0	8.0	0.8
	1977	5.4	3.8	4.0	3.1	1.5	12.3	11.2	3.5	0.6
	1978	6.0	5.5	5.9	7.0	6.1	18.3	1.9	8.2	0.6
	1979	6.0	5.9	4.6	16.5	−2.4	3.2	6.6	18.1	1.1
	1979 IV	6.4	4.1	2.5	11.3	−5.0	0.5	18.5	9.4	1.1
Germany	1976	5.3	3.4	2.0	6.7	6.2	−3.0	11.5	11.1	1.4
	1977	2.6	3.1	0.6	7.1	3.0	−4.3	4.3	4.7	1.1
	1978	3.5	3.5	3.9	6.8	4.2	7.7	4.4	5.9	0.8
	1979	4.4	2.8	2.8	9.5	8.6	5.0	5.0	10.2	2.4
	1979 IV	4.4	2.6	2.8		9.9		3.6	8.8	1.9
France	1976	5.1	5.6	6.1	6.1	−1.3	[2]	10.7	20.7	1.3
	1977	2.9	3.1	0.4	0.1	−2.7	[2]	8.4	2.0	1.2
	1978	3.7	4.5	7.8	2.6	−1.6	[2]	6.4	6.3	0.7
	1979	3.4	3.4	5.0	3.6	1.2	.	7.6	11.9	1.7
	1979 IV	3.9	3.0	1.3		4.9		8.2	8.4	2.6
United Kingdom	1976	3.6	0.2	1.9	3.0	−0.2	−2.3[3]	9.1	4.2	0.4
	1977	0.8	−1.3	−1.0	9.4	−6.8	−13.6[3]	6.6	1.0	1.1
	1978	3.1	5.5	2.0	7.4	13.9	−8.9[3]	1.9	3.7	0.7
	1979	0.6	4.5	1.1	−0.2	−15.2	−2.5[3]	2.0	11.0	1.7
	1979 IV	1.0	2.8	0.2	−0.8	−1.1	1.0[3]	3.5	14.0	0.9
Italy	1976	5.9	3.5	2.6	4.4	−3.4	[2]	13.2	15.4	2.6
	1977	1.9	2.3	2.3	−0.9	1.2	[2]	6.7	−0.2	1.2
	1978	2.6	2.9	1.8	−0.6	1.2	[2]	10.1	8.1	0.9
	1979	5.0	5.1	2.7	5.7	1.2	[2]	8.9	14.0	2.0
	1979 IV	5.1	6.4			4.0		0.9	4.2	.
Canada	1976	5.4	6.3	1.6	−0.4	19.3	−6.5	9.3	8.3	0.8
	1977	2.4	2.9	2.9	1.2	−5.1	−0.3	7.0	2.2	0.2
	1978	3.4	3.0	1.3	1.0	−4.6	2.2	9.3	4.1	0.4
	1979	2.9	2.3	−0.9	10.4	−7.4	−0.2	3.0	5.6	1.6
	1979 IV	2.1	1.5	−1.8	12.8	−6.0	−1.1	−0.5	0.0	1.4

[1] As a percentage of previous year's gross national product.   [2] Included in the private sector.   [3] Includes public corporations.
Source: Bank for International Settlements, *Fiftieth Annual Report 1 April 1979–31 March 1980*, p. 35.

TABLE 6.2

EMPLOYMENT AND LABOR PRODUCTIVITY

Countries		Employment					Labor productivity*				
		1963–73 average	1976	1977	1978	1979	1963–73 average	1976	1977	1978	1979
		annual averages, percentage changes									
United States	Total economy	2.1	3.1	3.4	4.1	2.2	1.6	2.5	1.7	0.1	-0.4
	Manufacturing	1.7	3.7	3.6	4.0	2.5	2.8	4.4	3.1	0.6	2.4
Canada	Total economy	3.1	2.1	1.8	3.3	4.0	2.4	3.3	0.6	0.1	-1.0
	Manufacturing	2.2	1.0	0.0	1.6	3.9	4.2	4.3	2.7	5.7	-0.4
Japan	Total economy	1.4	0.9	1.4	1.2	1.3	8.7	5.5	4.0	4.7	4.6
	Manufacturing	2.7	0.0	-0.4	-1.0	0.5	11.7	12.3	5.1	8.0	12.1
United Kingdom	Total economy	0.1	-0.5	0.2	0.4	0.6	2.9	2.6	2.2	2.6	1.0
	Manufacturing	-0.6	-3.1	0.3	-0.5	-1.3	4.2	4.9	0.6	1.6	.
France	Total economy	0.8	0.5	1.0	0.0	.	5.5	4.6	3.2	3.5	.
	Manufacturing	1.0	-1.1	-0.8	-2.1	-1.4	.	9.2	5.1	4.6	6.0
Germany	Total economy	0.0	-1.1	-0.2	0.7	1.3	4.8	6.2	2.8	2.7	3.1
	Manufacturing	0.5	-2.4	-0.8	-0.6	0.4	5.8	8.9	4.5	3.2	5.0
Italy	Total economy	-0.8	0.8	1.1	0.4	0.1	5.1	5.1	0.8	2.1	4.8
	Manufacturing	0.4	-1.4	1.0	-0.8	0.3	5.7	9.0	-0.9	3.0	8.9

*In the case of manufacturing industry, adjusted for the number of hours worked.
SOURCE: Bank for International Settlements, *Fiftieth Annual Report 1 April 1979–31 March 1980*, p. 3.

TABLE 6.3

OUTPUT AND PRODUCTIVITY GROWTH

	Productivity[1]			Gross national product		
	1960–73	1973–79	1975–79[2]	1960–73	1973–79	1975–79[2]
Countries	annual average changes, in percentages					
United States	2.1	0.2	1.0	4.1	2.5	4.5
Japan	8.8	3.4	4.7	10.2	4.1	6.0
Germany	4.4	3.2	3.8	4.5	2.4	3.9
France	4.9	2.8	2.1	5.7	3.0	3.6
United Kingdom	3.1	0.7	2.0	3.2	0.8	2.1
Italy	5.6	1.6	3.0	5.1	2.8	3.8
Canada	2.5	0.3	0.7	5.6	3.1	3.5

[1] Based on civilian employment.
[2] This sub-period corresponds to the period of recovery from the 1974–75 recession.
SOURCE: Bank for International Settlements, *Fiftieth Annual Report 1 April 1979–31 March 1980*, p. 53.

TABLE 6.4

HOUSEHOLD INCOME AND SAVING IN THE UNITED STATES

	1960–69	1970–74	1975	1976	1977	1978	1979	1st quarter	2nd quarter	1979 3rd quarter	4th quarter
	in percentages										
Saving ratio[1]	5.9	7.3	7.7	5.8	5.0	4.9	4.5	5.0	5.4	4.3	3.5
Financial saving ratio[2]	3.7	5.8	7.1	4.5	3.0	2.8	2.8	2.8	3.8	2.6	2.0
Real disposable income[3]	4.1	3.4	2.1	3.7	4.2	4.6	2.3	4.2	2.8	1.8	0.5

[1] Ratios of personal saving to disposable income on a national accounts basis.
[2] Gross saving minus physical investment (mainly consumer durable goods and residential construction) on a flow-of-funds basis.
[3] Annual rates of change in real personal disposable income.
SOURCE: Bank for International Settlements, *Fiftieth Annual Report 1 April 1979 31 March 1980*, p. 40.

TABLE 6.5

ESTIMATED CAPITAL EXPENDITURES OF EIGHT OIL COMPANIES FOR 1980 AND 1979
(in billions of dollars)

	1980	1979	% Chg.	1980	1979	% Chg.	1980	1979	% Chg.	1980	1979	% Chg.
		Exxon			Gulf			Arco			U.S. Shell	
Total Expenditures*	7.50	6.90	+8.7	3.00	2.39	+25.5	3.00	1.90	+57.9	2.70	2.40	+12.5
Oil & Gas E&P**	4.60	4.70	−2.1	1.80	1.61	+11.8	1.00	0.65	+53.8	1.90	1.66	+14.5
United States	1.80	2.30	−21.7	0.93	1.05	−11.4	0.90	0.61	+47.5	1.66	1.44	+15.3
Foreign	2.80	2.40	+16.7	0.87	0.56	+55.4	0.10	0.04	+150.0	0.24	0.22	+9.1
Refining-Marketing	1.50	1.10	+36.4	0.55	0.40	+37.5	0.30	0.20	+50.0	0.70	0.66	+6.1
United States	0.30	0.30	...	0.38	0.21	+81.0	0.24	0.19	+26.3	0.70	0.66	+6.1
Foreign	1.20	0.80	+50.0	0.17	0.19	−10.5	0.06	0.01	+500.0	0.00	0.00	...
		Socal			Conoco			Phillips			Getty	
Total Expenditures*	2.60	2.26	+15.0	2.00	1.70	+17.6	1.50	1.40	+7.1	1.37	0.96	+42.7
Oil & Gas E&P**	1.70	1.60	+6.3	1.28	1.10	+16.4	0.74	0.75	−1.3	0.98	0.65	+50.8
United States	1.10	1.09	+0.9	0.59	0.47	+25.5	0.31	0.42	−26.2	0.77	0.52	+48.1
Foreign	0.60	0.51	+17.6	0.69	0.63	+9.5	0.43	0.33	+30.3	0.21	0.13	+61.5
Refining Marketing	0.60	0.39	+53.8	0.26	0.18	+44.4	0.33	0.35	−5.7	0.32	0.19	+68.4
United States	0.20	0.16	+25.0	0.21	0.13	+61.5	0.33	0.35	−5.7	0.24	0.15	+60.0
Foreign	0.40	0.22	+81.8	0.05	0.05	...	0.00	0.00	...	0.07	0.04	+75.0

*Acquisition costs excluded from total company capital expenditures: Exxon's $1.2 billion in 1979 for Reliance Electric; Gulf's $121 million in 1979 for Amalgamated Bonanza; U.S. Shell's $3.6 billion 1979 for Belridge Oil; Getty's $628 million in 1980 for Reserve Oil & Gas and $281 million in 1979 for Ashland properties.
**Exploration and Production.
SOURCE: *Petroleum Intelligence Weekly*, March 17, 1980.

TABLE 6.6

U.S. Market Share for R&D-Intensive Industry Sectors (96)

	1968	1976
Chemicals	22	17
Electric Machinery	22	19
Nonelectric Machinery	27	24
Total Manufacturing	20	16

U.S. Enterprise-Funded R&D

	Constant 1972 Dollars ($ billions)	Percent of GNP
1970	11.4	1.06
1975	12.1	0.98
1978	12.7 (est.)	0.91

TABLE 6.7

Ratio of Personal Saving to Disposable Income

Countries	1975	1976	1977	1978	1979
	\multicolumn{5}{c}{in percentages}				
United States	7.7	5.8	5.0	4.9	4.5
Canada	10.9	10.2	10.0	10.4	10.3
Japan	22.5	22.4	21.1	20.1	19.5
France	18.6	16.4	16.9	17.8	16.7
Germany	16.4	14.7	13.7	13.8	14.6
Italy	25.4	23.7	25.8	26.4	26.7
United Kingdom	14.0	13.4	13.3	14.2	15.8

Source: Bank for International Settlements, *Fiftieth Annual Report 1 April 1979–31 March 1980*, p. 39.

TABLE 6.8

	Investment Ratio		Output Growth Rate		Productivity Growth	
	Percent of GNP	*Rank*	*Percent*	*Rank*	*Percent*	*Rank*
Japan	29.0	1	10.8	1	10.5	1
West Germany	20.0	2	5.5	3	5.8	3
France	18.2	3	5.9	2	6.0	2
U.K.	15.2	4	2.9	5	4.0	4
U.S.	13.6	5	4.1	4	3.3	5

EXPORTS OF MANUFACTURERS

	1968		1976			
	$B	*96 Market Share*	*$B*	*96 Market Share*	*Growth Ratio*	*Rank*
Japan	12.2	10.1	64.6	13.5	5.30	1
FRG	22.3	18.5	90.7	18.9	4.07	3
France	9.4	7.8	43.0	9.0	4.57	2
U.K.	12.7	10.5	38.3	8.0	3.02	5
U.S.	23.8	20.0	77.2	16.1	3.27	4

Notes

1. Studies of the Joint Economic Committee of Congress, October 1979.
2. Edward Denison, *Survey of Current Business,* Department of Commerce, August 1979.
3. Ibid.
4. *Wall Street Journal,* August 28, 1979.
5. U.S. Department of Labor, Bureau of Labor Statistics, November 29, 1978. Also see Department of Commerce, *Survey of Current Business,* August 1979.
6. Keith Daly and Arthur Neef, pamphlet prepared and published by the U.S. Department of Labor, Office of Productivity & Technology, November 19, 1978; see also Department of Commerce, *Survey of Current Business* (August 1974).
7. John W. Kendrick, *Proceedings of the Academy of Political Science* 33, no. 3 (1979).
8. Ibid.
9. The National Bureau of Economic Research estimates that the real results of research and development, education and training, health, and mobility represent over 40% of the productivity. But Denison estimates the increase in labor quality as input of 0.5 percentage point of growth rate, or about 22% of the rate of productivity advance.
10. Department of Commerce, *Survey of Current Business,* August 1979.
11. John W. Kendrick, "Increasing Productivity," paper presented to the American Council of Life Insurance, 1979.
12. Ibid.
13. The Geneva Papers on Risk Insurance, No. 6.
14. F. Mathes Scherer, "Technological Maturity & Waning Economic Growth, Arts & Science," Northwestern University (Fall 1978).
15. Edward Denison, *Survey of Current Business* (August 1979).
16. Delbert Tessar, "Mission Oriented Research for Light Machinery," *Science* (September 1978).
17. Senate Subcommittee on Government Operations, 94th Congress, 1st Session, 1976.
18. Quoted in *Survey of Current Business* 59 (August 1979), pt. 2.
19. House Committee on Ways and Means, 95th Congress, 2nd Session, 1978.
20. Colin Clark, "Public Finances and Changes in Values of Money," *Economic Journal* 45 (December 1974).
21. "Executive Incentives versus Corporate Growth," *Harvard Business Review* (July-August, 1978).
22. Department of Commerce, *Survey of Current Business* (August 1979).
23. Edward F. Renshae, "The Substitution of Inhuman Energy for Animal Power," *The Journal of Political Economy* (June 1963).
24. "Proceedings of the Academy of Political Science—1979."
25. Statement by the American Association for the Advancement of Science, quoted in *Washington Post,* June 21, 1978.
26. In Department of Commerce, *Survey of Current Business* (August 1979).
27. Roger E. Brinner, "The Anti-Inflation Leverage of Investment," *Academy of Political Science* 33 (1979).
28. Gary Hufbauer, Deputy Assistant Secretary of the Dept. of the Treasury, "A Statement before Senate Subcommittee on International Finance," May 16, 1978.
29. Dr. Jack Bronson's Report for the Office of Foreign Economic Research Bureau of International Labor Affairs, U.S. Department of Labor, December 1976.
30. See "French Radial Tires," by Dan Morgan in the *Washington Post,* March 9, 1979.
31. In 1980, 28% of cars sold in the United States were foreign-made. The United States' total loss was close to $20 billion.
32. *Business Week,* August 27, 1979.
33. Patricia Logan, "Those Worrisome Technology Exports," *Fortune* magazine, May 22, 1978. (Based on the reports of the Department of Commerce.)
34. The Conference Board, "The U.S. Economy in 1990," 1972.
35. Ibid.
36. Report by World Watch Institute, published by Newhouse News Service, August 1979.
37. Tariff Commission figures cited in hearing before the Senate Subcommittee.
38. "Japan's New Electronics Goodies," Business Brief, *The Economist,* April 22, 1978.

39. Nasrollah S. Fatemi, Gail Williams, and Thibaut de Saint-Phalle, *Multinational Corporations* (Cranbury, N.J.: A. S. Barnes and Co., 1976), p. 84.

40. *Survey of Current Business* 58, no. 5 (May 1978).

41. *Spectrum* (October 1978).

42. Simon Ramo, quoted in ibid.

43. Edgar Weinberg, U.S. Department of Labor, in *Spectrum* (October 1978).

44. Ibid.

45. *Business Week*, August 20, 1979.

46. The Joint Economic Committee recently suggested that real business fixed investment in the United States must be raised to more than 15% in order to keep the country's economy competitive with Japan and Germany.

47. *New York Times*, May 12, 1979.

48. John T. Woodward, *Survey of Current Business* (January 1981).

49. Ibid.

50. A majority-owned foreign affiliate is a foreign business enterprise in which a U.S. company owns, directly or indirectly, at least 50% of the vesting rights. The latest survey shows that there are 5,000 majority-owned foreign affiliates (*Survey of Current Business* [March 1979]).

51. Department of Commerce, *Survey of Current Business* (April 1979).

52. See *Report of Joint Economic Committee*, Congress of the United States (94th Congress), June 9, 1976.

53. *Business Week*, May 21, 1979.

54. J. Fred Bucy, Jr., Report of the Defense Science Board on Export, February 4, 1976.

55. Senate Subcommittee on International Finance, May 16, 1978.

56. Dr. Lowell W. Steel, Director of Research and Development Planning, statement before Senate Subcommittee on International Finance, May 16, 1978.

7
The Transfer of Technology

> Industrial society is the application of technical knowledge to social affairs.
>
> Saint-Simon

> My visit to Asia helped to convince me that a major concept of our time is that of technological society. Europe as seen from Asia does not consist of two fundamentally different worlds—the Soviet world and the Western world. It is one single reality: industrial civilization.
>
> Raymond Aron

> The technological society is based on order, certainty, and precision; it would be organized by "new men," engineers, industrialists, planners, and it would be based on knowledge.
>
> Daniel Bell

The relationship between the transfer of U.S. technology abroad and the nation's position vis-à-vis trade, production, and employment has become a very significant question in recent years. At issue is whether the relatively unimpeded flow of "advanced" U.S. technology overseas is helpful or harmful to American exports and employment. The pattern and timing of the impacts of technology transfers are also of interest to policymakers, management, and labor. Which industries are most affected by these transfers? What is the timing and what is the extent of the effect of transferring knowledge to potential competitors abroad?

For example, a particular technology transfer may have a net beneficial impact on U.S. exports and business in the long run, but it may levy substantial adjustment costs on a particular industry in the short run. Hence both the net impacts and their pattern and timing are of crucial interest to policymakers. Transfers of technology can benefit as well as harm the American economy. Presumably, the benefits and costs should be measured in terms of the alternatives, namely, what would have occurred in the absence of the transfer? In this chapter some of the assumptions and problems concerning the transfer of technology to both developed and developing nations will be discussed.

Definition of Technology[1]

Technology is knowledge or information that permits some task to be accomplished, some service to be rendered, or some product to be produced. Conceptually, technology can be distinguished from science, which organizes and explains data and observations by means of theoretical relationships. Technology is thus applied science, for it translates scientific relationships into practical use.[2]

Admittedly, this definition is a very general one and provides very little guidance as to how technology might be measured. Edwin Mansfield has examined the broader question of technology change, the progress by which more output is produced from the same amount of input, or less inputs are required for the same amount of output. What he explores is "the advance of technology, such advances often taking the form of new methods of producing existing products, new designs which enable the production of products and important new characteristics, and new techniques of organization, marketing and management."[3]

This definition of technological change, which is associated with changes in factor productivity, is probably too restrictive in a world where new products are constantly being introduced and tastes are changing, often in response to the availability of new products. Technological change associated with new or improved products should also be considered. But it is important to remember the difference between product and process. A new process implies a changed technological relationship among the inputs used to produce an output. Process innovation has been much more intensively researched than product innovation.[4]

To summarize these different definitions: technology is a way of combining inputs—capital and intermediate goods, the human skills, including managerial abilities, and unskilled labor, and natural resources—in a specific appropriate form to produce an output. All manufactured goods thus embody technology, some to a greater extent than others. Advanced technology is complex, expensive, time-saving, and labor-saving. It is the result of research and development or the application of science to improving the methods of production. It is therefore not surprising to find that most high technology is centered in the developed countries, where scientific knowledge and facilities for research are readily available.

Therefore high technology is an expensive asset that is not easily available. It is bought and sold in an imperfect market. Its owners exercise monopolistic control through patents, licensing agreements, and other legal restrictions.

The mere act of transfering technology is of less significance than the dynamic effects that follow when the technological input takes root in the host country and starts a self-sustaining process.

Technology is generally transferred according to the following means:

1. through multinational corporations;

2. through international organizations and public agencies;

3. through multilateral, intergovernmental agreements.

So far the most effective way to transfer technology has been through private commercial firms, but in many developing countries mixed systems prevail. The size, the politico-economic system of the country, and the pattern of industry also influence the choice of means.

Many nations believe that industrial technology is the key to the solution of a number of social economic problems such as poverty, hunger, unemployment, and underemployment.

In a detailed survey of industrial development of the world, a United Nations report states that most technological changes have emanated almost entirely from the developed countries, and the developing countries have tended to import and adopt these often highly labor-saving technologies without regard to price or whether they are appropriate to the conditions in their countries. In many cases the developing countries have had no choice but to adopt capital-intensive technologies because there were no other options left.

The United Nations report advises, therefore, that developing countries trying to industrialize must widen their range of choice of appropriate technologies available to them. The U.N. study points out that the adaptation of the appropriate technology, as in the proper selection of production mix, may bring both income and employment gains. In assessing the appropriateness of technologies, nations ought to consider the indirect as well as the direct implications.

In addition to employment concerns, the application of technology must take into consideration the linkage between industrial and agricultural sectors. "At the heart of the problem of underdevelopment is the dualistic nature of these sectors; one is technologically modern and dynamic, the other is traditional and static. The agricultural sector provides a pool of unskilled labor as industrial inputs into urban industries, and a supply of wage goods as well as raw materials."[5] Furthermore, until recently, direct and indirect taxes from the agricultural sectors supported both government and industrial developments. This policy of neglecting and milking the agricultural sector to help industry created many problems in both the socialist and the developing countries. The situation is now changing, as exemplified by the green revolutions in Taiwan, India, and Japan. New agricultural technologies are now being experimented with, and the increased availability of fertilizers, tractors, and industrial products is helping the situation.

The developing nations must now place more emphasis on transferring technology to expand rural industrialization, which not only helps a country to become self-sufficient in food and fiber but also helps its exports and foreign-exchange supply.

Methods of transferring technology from one country to another take different forms:

1. private foreign investments, mostly through multinationals;

2. turnkey arrangements;

3. the supply of equipment, know-how, and expertise, usually through service arrangements;

4. individual exports;

5. licensing agreements;

6. joint-venture agreements

Historically, multinationals have been responsible for the transfer of technology to both developed and developing nations. In cases where the host country has been able to assimilate and control the flow of private capital and technology consistent with national development objectives, such investment has proved highly beneficial. In cases where the developing governments have no programs, plans, or skilled labor, the use of private investments as a means of transferring technology has produced problems. As a result, the opponents of the multinationals allege that:

1. The advanced, capital-extensive technologies that private foreign investors tend to bring with them are often unsuitable for developing countries where capital and skilled labor are rare.

2. The technologies preferred by the multinationals are based either on extractive minerals or the use of inputs of intermediate goods imported from the developed countries. These inputs are often highly specialized and also embody extensive technology.

3. Multinational corporations are oligopolistic, and in some cases that puts them in a position to exercise economic and political control in order to stay in power and to repatriate their high profits.

Multinationals, of course, refute these allegations and point to the success of their technology in Western Europe, Japan, Iran, Kuwait, Saudi Arabia, Taiwan, South Korea, Venezuela, and other developing nations. Furthermore, they emphasize that wherever the governments had plans and programs, they have cooperated wholeheartedly in carrying out these plans. In every area, the multinational corporations warn, an effective technology policy requires first a national awareness, an institutional structure, a formal development plan, and a system of education with a central institution directing research and development.

The United Nations Advisory Committee agrees with this assessment and adds that an effective program for industrialization in the developing countries should include the complete control of decision making regarding the selection of technologies and their methods and conditions of transfer; the maintenance of an inventory of industrial and technological research potential; the analysis and processing of all information accumulated; the examination and refinement of proposals for using existing industrial and technological research potential; and finally the formulation of recommendations—with the aid of the multinationals involved—of methods for establishing industrial and technological research programs. Every plan should have a budget and evaluation of the economic and financial position of the country, national development priorities, and a final goal. It also should avoid unnecessary duplication. The emphasis at this stage should be placed on the development of industrial manpower, educational planning, and a training program for those who will be managing and administering the new projects.

The Choice of Proper Technology

The first question for a country planning industrialization to ask is how the technology will be used. Some countries purchase technology for prestige, others for military strength, many for the capacity to generate employment, but all agree that the purpose of industrialization is to produce the greatest good for the greatest number of people.

If we accept the above assumptions, then we have to agree that the appropriate technology for any country should produce the kind of goods and services suitable first for local needs and then for export markets. In planning, every nation has to take into consideration its human and material resources, its financial capabilities, and its competence to cope with the socioeconomic changes brought about by new industries. The technology chosen should be dynamic and useful in tackling the old concerns as well as the new problems.

Consideration should be given to all aspects—technical, social, political, financial, commercial, and administrative. Research should be based on the strengthening of industry and on solving potential problems resulting from the changes. No country can achieve real development if the machinery and the majority of the workers needed have to come from outside. Polluting the air, clogging the streets with imported cars, creating a runaway inflation, crowding the cities with unskilled peasants, neglecting agriculture, and importing thousands of foreign scientists, teachers, and technicians to administer the new technology and manage industry all indicate a lack of planning and a weak economic system. It would be impossible to make an optimal choice without a well-balanced program based on the needs of the country. Profitability should be understood in the broadest sense of the long-term economic and social benefits for the common good and not in the narrow sense of the short-term advantages for a particular firm.

Employment is an important factor in the selection of an appropriate technology; but developing nations, like the industrial countries, gradually are discovering that far more is required in their choice of technology than simple quantitative industrial output or total gross national product. Standard indicators of employment and industrial growth or GNP cannot measure qualitative changes in growth such as technological advances, the well-being of the people, national solidarity, or the extent to which large groups may share in the gains from the blessings of industrialization. The developed nations are well aware that as the quality of growth has taken on new importance, so have increased employment opportunities, a better distribution of income, a universal educational system, the attainment of social objectives, and an improved political and economic environment for the indigenous labor force of the country.

The eloquent General Assembly Resolution 2626 states:

> As the ultimate purpose of development is to provide increasing opportunities to all people for a better life, it is essential to bring about a more equitable distribution of income and wealth for promoting both social justice and efficiency of production, to raise substantially the level of employment, to achieve a greater degree of income security, to expand and improve facilities for education, health, nutrition, housing, and social welfare, and to safeguard the environment. Thus qualitative and structural changes in the society must go hand in hand with rapid economic growth, and existing disparities—regional, sectoral, and social—should be substantially reduced. The objectives are both determining factors and end-results of development.[6]

In order to comply with the above goal, every developing nation should consider the following points before making its final decision:

1. Regardless of the level of technological development of a country, the technology used should be adapted to the conditions prevailing in that country. Natural, technical, and socioeconomic factors should be taken into account. For instance, the adaptation of both hardware and software is necessary for profitability and reliability. Furthermore, the process of development should lead to the creation of indigenous technologies.

2. Before a foreign corporation is invited to introduce a particular product into the domestic market, the host government should evaluate its usefulness and suitability for meeting local needs.

3. The country should assess the appropriateness of the technology and its capacity to complete the plan, and decide where possible information and sound advice from international institutions can be obtained.

The Transfer of Technology 221

4. The multinationals should be encouraged to make contributions toward research and development of the kind most suited to national or regional needs.

5. The developing nations have shown a growing concern about the high cost of technology. Right now the cost of using the patents, licenses, trademarks, and technical services needed at all levels will be close to $5 billion a year. The developing countries contend that they cannot afford to spend a sum as vast as $5 billion, especially in light of the fact that the technology provided by the multinationals has already been used and overused. They argue that these corporations have already derived ample compensation from its use in the developed countries for which it was primarily intended. Hence the transfer to the developing countries does not entail any significant extra cost.[7]

6. The multinationals vehemently disagree and contend that the cost of research and development is very high and must be paid for out of profits made on the sales of these and other products. Furthermore, research tends to be centralized because of the cost factor and because researchers need to work near centers for testing, education, and information exchange. This means that research tends increasingly to be done in industrialized countries. In a free enterprise system, technology belongs to the corporation or individuals. It is a very valuable asset developed at substantial cost and with tremendous effort.

Finally, patents only serve to give the owner temporary lead time in establishing a market for the products. Of far greater importance is the know-how associated with the research, the manufacture, testing, and marketing of the products. The licensing of technology is useful only where there are already educational facilities as well as trained and experienced scientists within the country who have the ability to produce items of the quality desired for the country.

What good does it do to have sophisticated technology in a country where the telephone does not work, where 90% of the machines, parts, and operators are imported, where most of the teachers, scientists, and physicians have left the country, and where the government has to spend hundreds of millions of dollars in order to replace the indigenous talent? How can a country establish steel mills, electronic industries, and petrochemical factories where there are not enough trained engineers, few laboratories, and no scientific-research establishments? Before flooding the country with foreign machinery and technicians, there must be a plan for educational institutions, laboratories, vocational schools, and business and managerial establishments geared to the training of the men and women who would manage and administer the new industrial complex.

7. Machiavelli, in *The Prince,* warned that if a country needs help from

outside it should always look for alternatives and never place itself at the mercy of one power.

This is absolutely true about the transfer of technology. The developing nations should always explore ways of importing technology from other than one source. They should acquire the capacity to determine which technology best suits their needs. In order to preserve their sovereignty and also attain their goal of industrialization, the developing nations should attract private investments as well as aid from the international organizations. Technology becomes obsolete very rapidly. To protect competition, a constant supply of fresh ideas and new research is essential.

Another major area that both governments and multinationals have to take into consideration is the relationship between technological resources and environment. Resources and environment are intimately related to industrial technology. All too often both the developed and the developing nations ignore the environmental problems associated with using non-renewable natural resources that are vital to modern industry, such as the pollution of air, water, and land that occurs as an undesirable side effect of industrialization. The problems, in essence, are that present industrial technologies have in some cases resulted in a disruption in the ecological chain, thus requiring the recycling of resources. As recent studies indicate, the developing nations in their enthusiasm for rapid change have spent billions of dollars on new airports, highways, buildings, and the importation of cars and industrial machinery without concern for secondary effects. The result is that while the plans for industrialization have not been completed, agricultural production has declined and cities have become polluted, overcrowded, clogged with cars, and plagued with a lack of housing in addition to shortages in vital goods, while costs rise for everything. Thus developing nations now require massive investments in new technologies that will solve both aspects (input and output) of the environmental problem in coming decades.

And because the environmental problem is worldwide in scope, it can be solved only through a comprehensive, cooperative, international action program of technological change involving, where necessary, short-term national sacrifices in order to achieve long-term worldwide gains.

As stated earlier, the technology used should be adapted to the conditions prevailing in that country, regardless of the level of technological development. Thus resources as well as socioeconomic factors, national traditions, and natural factors should be taken into account. For instance, countries rich in capital and oil and short in labor—like Iran, Kuwait, and Saudi Arabia—could very easily develop capital-intensive technologies such as petrochemical and electronic industries. In countries like India and Egypt, where capital is short and employment is an important factor, labor-intensive technologies should be employed in most industries. Capital-intensive technology should be used in sectors where available production factors make this technology economically profitable.

The reasons for such adaptations are many. Industrial production in many developing nations is a fraction of the size of the kind found in the industrial countries. Resource endowments, skilled labor, and capital are also different. Modification and adaptability are necessary as a result of the rapidly changing relative prices of machinery, materials, energy, and other industrial inputs. Moreover, different physical considerations are involved.

Changes in processes and equipment are often required to meet local climatic conditions and to ensure up-to-standard product quality to make it possible to treat raw materials with particular characteristics, to carry out special operations, and to improve productivity.

Socioeconomic factors largely determine the size of the enterprise, the characteristics of products, manufacturing processes, and the design of the place of work. Way of life, family size, manual dexterity, average population size, and other factors largely determine the type and quality of consumer products manufactured and the organization of production.

In some cases the research undertaken to solve problems facing the developed countries has led to solutions that are valid for both developed and developing countries. This area of research and development is so vital that developing nations must undertake the necessary research or entrust part of their research programs to multinational corporations. High-cost industrial and technological research may be carried out by regional groups in multidisciplinary or specialized institutions.[8] The program of research should include the following projects:

1. the systematic survey, assessment, development, and utilization of local natural resources and raw materials, including the adaptation of these raw materials to nonconventional or new industrial uses;

2. the improvement or adaptation of production techniques and technical development of processes for local conditions;

3. the establishment of pilot plants;

4. the provision of various services for industry, such as testing, quality control, and selection of machinery, as well as specifications and general technical assistance;

5. assistance in standardization activities, either by assuming direct responsibility or by actively participating in the work of a separate standards institute;

6. industrial economic studies, such as market surveys, comparisons of the economics of different processes, investigations connected with preinvestment studies, surveys and statistics of various industrial sectors, and, generally, all matters concerned with the establishment of new industries;

7. management and productivity studies aimed at strengthening production and improving management.[9]

It is generally accepted that development is not synonymous with mere growth but encompasses many other considerations concerned with human welfare: cultural, spiritual, and material. The process of growth through technology, whether carried out by governments or by private corporations, must be made to benefit the masses of the people and not a few privileged sectors. Particular attention must be paid to raising productivity through the attraction of new capital and technology from outside. Employment in new industries should be not only productive in the economic sense but also satisfactory and stimulating to the individuals. Development policies that do not have employment objectives are liable to lead to further inequalities and social frustration.

An important aspect of development is to find a solution to the increasing inequalities of economic growth and welfare among nations as well as to the sharp disparities in their respective scientific and technological levels. There is urgent need to assist the multinationals in the developing world. They have shown in their work in the developed countries that they can increase production, reduce economic gaps, increase employment, and create affluence through national efforts and international cooperation in line with the principles of the new international interdependence and partnership.

The multinationals in their work in Europe, Japan, and the other developed nations have proved that development is concerned not only with profits but also with the quality of life, as well as the full realization of the potential of man. The postwar cooperation introduced an enlarged view of development in Canada, Western Europe, and Japan, as well as enhanced self-reliance and interdependence. The time has come when developing nations and multinational corporations should establish such a partnership based on mutual interests. Development is more than a rhetorical appeal to mankind. It is an essential need, a basic process, and a sincere way to achieve the objectives of man's welfare and contribute to peace.

There is no doubt that the multinationals have a vast store of knowledge available. Their power of production is close to $1.9 trillion; their sales in 1976 were $1.7 trillion. Their achievements in the United States and other developed nations have improved man's welfare. It is high time that the developing nations within their sovereign rights take increasing account of their science and technology and their application as an integral part of their development policies. All this knowledge and technology are of little use if there is no political will or if there is a lack of the means and capacity to use it. This implies, basically, that there is a need for policy design and implementation by the governments of the developed and developing

The Transfer of Technology 225

countries and the multinational corportions regarding production and transfer of technology.

International cooperation is essential at various levels of transfer of technology. As has already been pointed out, it may take place through both the governments and the multinationals, or directly through a combined international machinery. The latter may be part of the United Nations system or regional organizations, or may function by means of bilateral agreements and mechanism. Such cooperation may assist in the identification and evaluation of priorities and may also take the form of financial and expert assistance, training, and information. Cooperation among developing nations themselves is of special importance, in view of their experience in the adaptation of technology to specific development projects and of their scientific discoveries geared to the needs of developing economies.[10]

What Is the Prospect for the Developing Nations?

1. A major problem confronting the developing nations is the need to achieve balance between the inflow of capital and technology from outside and the industrial activities within their borders.

The process of technology transfer necessitates tremendous changes in developing countries, particularly if the Lima target of 25% of industrial production by the end of the century is fulfilled. While capital transfers can flow both bilaterally and multinationally, technology comes only from multinational corporations (except in the case of the socialist countries).

2. Traditionally, direct investment and technology have come mostly from the subsidiaries and branches of multinational corporations. Until a few years ago most of these investments were concentrated in extractive industries. The total multinational investment in the developing world was $66 billion in 1975 out of a total foreign investment of more than $250 billion. About 60% of these investments came from the United States, followed by multinationals from England, France, West Germany, the Netherlands, Switzerland, Belgium, Italy, and Japan. Over the last four years the share of Japanese corporations in the developing countries has risen significantly.

With the nationalization of most utilities and mass transportation systems in recent years, there has been a very important change in foreign investment in the developing nations. For instance, the pattern of petroleum-industry ownership in the OPEC countries has been radically modified so that the government has gained partial or complete control of oil production, starting with Iran in 1952; Argentina in 1963; Algeria, Bolivia, and Peru in 1969–71; Kuwait, Saudi Arabia, and the other Mideast nations in 1969–75; and Indonesia and Venezuela in 1975–76. In the mining and plantation sectors, also, there has been a growing nationalization of foreign investments in Zaire (Unione Minier); the same pattern has occurred in the copper industry in Chile and Zambia, with bauxite in Jamaica, tea plantations in India and Sri Lanka, iron ore in Venezuela, and various extractive industries in the United Republic of Tanzania. Foreign banking and insurance industries have either been taken over or brought under strict regulations in many developing nations.

These successive nationalizations have not reduced the close relationships between developing countries and the multinationals. Still, the nationalized industry does have to depend on the technology, service, managerial skills, transportation, and marketing expertise of the big corporations. Fortunately, both sides have realized their interdependence. The multinationals have improved the efficiency of their services and accepted most of the new regulations, and the developing countries have offered new arrangements such as joint ventures, turnkey projects, service contracts, and technology licensing.

In the past the supply of technology through wholly owned subsidiaries and multinational affiliates was surrounded by a veil of secrecy. This secrecy permitted the parent company to decide the nature of the technology, remuneration, information, and production.

Now, with the new arrangements in the developing nations, the issue of licensing and its confidentiality should be considered from every point of view, including the licensee enterprise and the larger interests of the developing country itself. In certain matters the interests of the licensee enterprise and those of the country may not necessarily coincide, especially if the licensee is a foreign-owned, private entity. In this case the question of confidentiality arises initially before contract negotiations start. The licensor at this point insists upon the draft of a prenegotiation secrecy agreement that specifies the time, amount, and manner of disclosure as well as the two parties' respective rights and obligations.

In several agreements for licensing technology to developing countries, some of the following provisions have been inserted:

1. Licensed technology continues to be the property of the licensor and shall not be used or exploited by the licensee once the agreement expires or is terminated.

2. No secrets of the licensed technology shall be disclosed to a third party without the permission of the licensor.

3. The technology that has been rented shall be used solely for the purposes expressed in the contract.

4. The licensee guarantees the confidentiality of the license and is responsible for any violation of this contract by its employees.

The most important issue in the new arrangements is the use of licensed technology after the expiration of the contract and further research and development during the life of the agreement. The licensors in many instances insist that after the expiration all the drawings, blueprints, documentation, and information conveyed to the licensee should be returned to the licensor, but the developing nations argue that at the termination of the contract all machineries, technology, trademarks, and know-how should be transferred to the licensee. Mexico, Argentina, Brazil, and the Andean group, as well as Iran and India, do not accept any registration that prohibits the free use of data and information transferred once the relevant patent has expired. In some cases the negotiations relating to the initial technology agreement result in the arrangement on the part of the patent holder to forgo its patent rights beyond the period of the technology contract.

But the issue that may cause concern is the disclosure of information to a third party. In most developing countries efforts are made to increase the local content to manufactured products through linkage with local manufacturers of parts, components, subassemblies, or processed industrial materials. A provision in the agreements restricting disclosure of information to a third party without the licensor's permission can, if strictly interpreted, considerably circumscribe and confine the licensee's choice in the procurement of intermediate products, parts, and components. This provision can be, and on occasions has been, used to bring about a higher degree of vertical integration in the licensee enterprise on the grounds that disclosure to third parties, who could otherwise be used as subcontractors or suppliers, would not be permissible from the viewpoint of the licensor.

Some developing countries, in order to avoid the problems of obtaining technology from private corporations, have suggested acquiring foreign technology through centralized acquisition agencies, such as the ones that exist in the socialist countries. No significant action has been taken in this field so far because technology acquisition has hitherto been viewed only from a national perspective. Furthermore, each nation has different resources, manpower, and capital, as well as distinct objectives and plans.

The best that one could expect is that developing countries will share information and experience on technology contracts. This policy of information would also extend the area of technological choice and greatly improve the bargaining power of developing countries.

The issue of technology transfer thus covers a wide range, extending from the implications of licenses with specific contractual provisions to the question of the joint acquisition of technology and the establishment of regional pools of information sharing among several countries.

Finally, it must be reiterated that the conditions of and prospects for technology transfer to developing countries are rapidly changing. These changes call for a greater understanding and appreciation on the part of transnational corporations. At the same time it is essential that the developing nations realize that the moment has come to put an end to confrontation and to face the challenge of partnership, cooperation, and interdependence. The future of the developed and developing nations depends on a mutual sharing of knowledge and technology and the adaptation of a collective approach toward solving the common social, economic, and political problems of the world.

The Transfer of Technology to Developed Countries

The transfer of technology to other industrialized nations by American multinationals has attracted considerable attention both in the United States and abroad. During 1960 widespread concern grew in Europe over U.S. technological domination. It was feared that the European countries were too small to support the large outlays on research and development that were needed by emerging technology-intensive industries. But recent studies show that throughout the 1960s Europe and Japan steadily improved their position in high-technology products. By 1967 (with the exception of the aerospace industry, which was heavily aided by U.S. government expenditures) industry-financed research and development and nuclear energy research were undertaken in European countries and Japan on a par with those of the United States.

In the 1970s the tables were turned, so that today concern is growing in the United States over the narrowing of the "technological gap" and the European and Japanese challenge. The erosion of the United States' competitive advantage in industries that require high technology has motivated critics to take a protectionist stance. Policies are being advocated that would protect high-technology industries from foreign competition and give government subsidies to certain industries. However, it may be argued that just as European reactions to U.S. technological domination in the 1960s were often exaggerated, so the U.S. reaction to the closing of the technological gap may often be exaggerated, and the protective challenge to the multinationals counterproductive.

It is almost impossible to monopolize any invention or to define exactly what technology is, and, correspondingly, it is difficult to measure. The U.S. Bureau of Economic Analysis narrows down technology transfers by using data on U.S. receipts and payments of fees and royalties, since most royalties and fees are payments for the use of technology. However, there are values in technological transfers not included in these payments. Existing data on fees and royalties from abroad provide only a very crude indication of the amounts of technology being transferred.

The problem is that we do not really know how to measure units of technology, and thus can not be sure whether changes in the dollar amounts of receipts and payments of fees and royalties represent changes in the amount of technology being transferred, changes in the prices being paid for technology, or changes in both quantities and prices. For example, in economic downturns, the prices paid in new technology transactions may fall along with the prices paid for many other production inputs. Shifts in the economic bargaining position between the seller and buyer of technology may also influence its price.

Also, the royalty and fee data may not accurately reflect the value of private-sector technology transfers because they do not include all the payments made for these transfers and because they may reflect such things as tax considerations rather than just payments for technology. For example, some technology is sold in exchange for equity in the receiving enterprise, just as some technology is traded to foreign affiliates of companies without charging explicit fees or royalties. These factors would thus cause technology payments to understate the value of the transfers.

On the other hand, fees and royalties often include payments by subsidiaries for headquarters managerial staff, payments for film rentals, and payments for the use of trademarks and copyrights. Also, multinational corporations may have an incentive to overcharge for fees and royalties in order to avoid foreign taxes and dividends.[11]

The existing data on U.S. payments and receipts of fees and royalties are also inaccurate for evaluating the present trends in high technology. Most of the receipts and payments belong to technologies that were transferred years ago, and they do not represent current inflows and outflows. Since the U.S. government does not collect information right now on technology sales or purchases, little information is available concerning the magnitude of the current transfer of technology from the United States. Data from an earlier OECD study show that during the 1960s the United States was the major supplier of technology as measured by fees and royalties within the OECD. America's receipts for patents, licenses, and fees accounted for between 50% to 60% of total receipts.[12]

One possible way to measure technology transferred from multinationals to their foreign affiliates would be to track research and development expenditures allocated to foreign operations. Another approach for measuring the value of any technology transferred to a foreign country would be to set up a "resource cost system." This means identifying two groups of factors that influence transfer costs: (1) those associated with the degree to which the transferrer understands the technology; and (2) those identifying the technical and managerial competence of the transferee. It should be noted that the cost of transferring technology may also be affected by factors that are not related to technology differences among countries, such as the costs of translating documents and of transporting goods, or consultant fees; but these costs can be separated out to some extent. However, it is possible that the total costs of transferring technology may be quite different from the total value of the technology transferred.[13] For example, if a U.S. multinational builds a plant in India to produce steel for the first time, it appears that there has been a technological transfer, since steel being produced in India until now was much less sophisticated. The fact that a U.S. firm may be the first to produce steel in that country does not necessarily represent a technology transfer, however. It could be that the technology already existed in India but was not being incorporated because of capital shortages. Thus, what at first appears to be a technological transfer may actually be a transfer of sorely needed capital.

To summarize, technology is a two-way street and is in many cases universal. Three principal problems in measuring international transfers of technology must therefore be considered:

1. We must identify those transactions, such as trade, foreign investment, and managerial skills, which actually contain a technology transfer.

2. We must separate and measure the payments made for the technology component of export and investment transactions.

3. We must identify the real flows of technology. In most cases we have seen that proxy measures of technology transfers are subject to large and unknown errors. In some cases, better data are needed to improve our ability to measure the real value of technology transferred to other countries.

Fees and royalties received by U.S. corporations in 1976 and 1977 were $4.3 billion and $4.6 billion, respectively. Half of that came from Western Europe and 12% from Japan. Canada was responsible for 16% of the receipts. The total payments of the United States for fees and royalties were $471 million and $451 million, respectively (Table 7.1).

The growth in importance of industry-financed technology has led to greatly increased competition in research and development in Western Europe, Japan, and the United States. However, the multinational corporations have been most successful in the management and transference of technology.

In the past the United States has contributed most of the significant technological advances in many fields. Although it is claimed that 20% of the ideas for technological advances were originated in Europe, less than 5% were first implemented in Europe. The United States, in many cases, has been very efficient at taking innovative ideas and successfully producing them for commercial use.

Research and development in American industry increased in real terms by 5% annually between 1966 and 1971. Since then it has dropped from 1% of GDP in 1971 and 0.96% in 1976. In Germany and Japan, at the same

The Transfer of Technology

time, it has increased from 1.13% and 1.09% of GDP to 1.16% and 1.18%, respectively.

Advocates of the multinational corporations believe that their success has been the result of their ability to manage technology. After having invested large sums of money in the development of a new product or process, corporations have a definite interest in maximizing their returns on these investments by transferring the new technology into production in as many locations as possible. The "higher" the technology, the bigger the investment needed and hence the greater the incentive to establish production subsidiaries abroad.

To multinationals, transfer of technology and capital is as beneficial to the home country as it is to the host nation. It raises the standards of living and improves the allocation and use of world resources. Without the application of technology and the development of energy resources, neither the United States, Western Europe, Japan, nor the OPEC nations would have been able to increase their GNP and national incomes more than tenfold in less than thirty years.

Critics in the United States argue that we are losing our competitive advantage in trade through the diffusion of technology, and losing jobs in the process. They ask for a national technology strategy to keep American technology at home and thus prevent competition with American products. The question repeatedly asked without getting a clear answer is, how are we going to achieve this end? Is it possible for a nation to monopolize any kind of technology or new invention?

Seldom in history do all of the advantages in technological progress lie with one side. In a thorough and profound study, the *Institut für Weltwirtschaft* in Kiel states:

> Technological progress continuously creates new products. It is universal. Its leads and lags are a steady source of international trade. A country which is able to generate a higher rate of innovations than other countries will be able for a time to produce a greater proportion of new goods. For countries which are less capable, it will take longer to specialize in the production of new goods.

The most advanced countries possess a comparative advantage in the production of new technologies. On the one hand, these countries are relatively abundantly endowed with skilled manpower that is intensively used in research and development. On the other hand, a high per capita income provides domestic markets capable of absorbing new products—e.g., new consumer goods, labor-saving household devices, and new labor-saving investment goods. When products become more sophisticated, highly qualified manpower becomes less critical and the other factors of production gain influence in determining comparative advantage. In the course of increasing sophistication of products, or processes of production, the comparative advantage shifts to less advanced industrial countries that can already handle the technology in question and are able to compete successfully with the innovating country because they enjoy the advantage of lower wages.[14]

Research and technology, like other forms of ideas, cannot be imprisoned. The U.S. experience with government secrecy in atomic energy and in missile and space technology shows that in the most sensitive areas a delay factor, at most, can be introduced. The state of basic scientific information now appears to be such that any advanced industrial nation can reproduce innovation.[15]

Moreover, efforts to control licensing and the transfer of technology may well lead to a further increase in research and development on the part of foreign firms eager to compete with U.S. products. Canada, Western Europe, and Japan are well aware of the benefits to be gained by stepping up their own research in high technology and are spending a larger part of their GNP on research. They also resent the fact that almost all the research and development of American multinationals is done in the United States.

Since no nation has a monopoly on innovation and inventiveness, any limitations by one country would invite retaliation by others. During the last ten years the economic and political relations of nations all over the world have been dramatically changed by events beyond the control of any power. Among these events have been the energy crisis, the growing power of the OPEC nations, the expansion of trade, the huge transfer of dollars, the expanding operations of the multinational corporations, and the heightened economic importance of ever-increasing technological advance. While the United States has lowered its research and development for nonmilitary technology, Western Europe and Japan have increased their R&D in this area. The conjuncture of these dynamic forces has created many important issues and problems for business, labor, and national policymakers.

It is a source of great concern for a country whose technology and capital resurrected Western Europe and Japan thirty years ago from the ashes of war to face today an annual trade deficit of $30 billion.

Because of inadequate capital investment and research and development, the U.S. auto industry must be salvaged by congressional consideration and French capital. U.S. shipbuilders have abandoned their old and inefficient shipyards, U.S. tire companies are surrendering their markets to Europeans, and the U.S. steel industry is producing at only 65% of capacity—all this while imports from Europe and Japan have passed 20 million tons annually. Former President Carter, among others, has thus called for "the revitalization of America's industries and government aid to steel corporations."

As in the 1950s and 1960s, the multinational corporations are clearly an important channel for revitalizing industry and for transmitting American know-how abroad. The same spirit that gave rise in the 1950s to IBM, Exxon, General Electric, Xerox, Boeing, Texas Instruments, Rockwell International, and Polaroid offers hope for a new burst of American productivity. There should be less government interference, more free exchange of scientific information, and tax benefits for industries that expedite R&D.

The National Commission on Technology, Automation, and Economic Progress, in its report to the president and Congress, stated:

> The vast majority of people quite rightly have accepted technological change as beneficial. They recognize that it has led to better working conditions by eliminating many—perhaps most—dirty, menial, and servile jobs; that it has made possible the shortening of working hours and the increase in leisure; that it has provided a growing abundance of goods and continuous flow of improved and new experience for people and thus added to the zest for life.[16]

Similarly, the view that international technology exchange is both necessary and beneficial is supported by another U.S.-government-sponsored panel on the international transfer of technology. In its report to a Senate subcommittee it stated:

> If we are going to solve the major problems facing humanity—overpopulation, air pollution, water pollution, and many others—we need a vast generation and exchange of technology. Practically all economists agree that a free flow of technology contributes in important ways to a rising standard of living both in this country and elsewhere.... The exchange of technology among economically developed nations and its application to research, production, and management are increasingly seen as vital elements in the development and maintenance of buoyant national economies.[17]

However, the optimistic view of economists concerning the benefits of technology transfer is not shared by everyone. There are many who dispute the surveys and believe that the United States should strive to retain technological leadership. They express concern that the United States is unduly eroding its position by exporting technology without adequate safeguards. They also argue that the export of American technology has reduced the potential for expanding U.S. trade, has contributed to intensified import competition in the U.S. domestic market, and has caused the loss of many job opportunities in this country.

In order to get an impartial, clear answer to the questions raised by both sides, it is important to analyze the relationship between technology and trade in order to evaluate the effects of technology transfers on the American labor market and on trade flows.

Before the Second World War most economists and governments tended to focus their analysis of international trade questions on "factor endowments, factor mobility, and the theory of comparative advantage." It is only during the last twenty years that concerted efforts have been made to integrate technological considerations into the theory of international trade in the industrial world.

On the quantitative side, only limited information is available. The well-known Danish economist Erik Hoffmeyer, in thorough study of trade patterns in the United States, discovered that some corporations in this country tended to specialize in research-intensive goods, and, as a result, the exports of these corporations increased twenty-three times in the period between the end of the war and the mid-sixties, while exports of traditional goods merely trebled.[18]

According to a study by the U.S. International Trade Commission, the trade flows that resulted from the transfer of technology affect U.S. trade and production patterns, and, consequently, they should have price and income effects in those industries concerned by these changes. For example, technology transferred by the United States to Mexico should have a price (and production) effect in the industry impacted by the technological change. The products thus affected will probably be repriced by both the United States and Mexico to reflect relevant adjustments.[19] Price changes in the host country's trading goods should thus lead to price and volume changes in U.S. exports and imports competing with the host country's products affected by the technology transfer. To analyze the impact of these changes in the United States, one should focus on the effects on U.S. trade patterns and the degree to which such effects are the result of technology transfer.

The U.S. Tariff Commission, in its exhaustive study of multinationals, found that corporations in the high-technology industries (based on R&D intensity) continue to generate a better ratio of new exports to imports than do other firms in the high-technology class. The direct erosion of U.S. comparative advantage in trading high-technology goods is concentrated in the performance of nonmultinational firms.[20]

The commission study further found that U.S. multinationals, while they are clearly the leaders in the large net outflow of technology to foreign countries in recent years, have not caused the expected erosion of the U.S. trade advantage in high-technology products. Where trade has been eroded, it was the result of the shackles and obstacles created by the administration and Congress.

High-technology manufactured goods and agricultural products (which are also technology-intensive in the United States) have had very positive effects on the trade accounts for many years, while low-technology manufactured goods have registered slow progress.

Income Distribution Effects of Transfer Technology

The other aspect of technology is its impact on income distribution. In the U.S. economy those sectors which sell technology are likely to see their incomes increased, while those sectors which are adversely affected by the new foreign competition resulting from the technology transfer are likely to find their incomes falling. "Theoretically, if there has been a net positive income change for the economy as a whole, those sectors that experienced income increases can compensate those sectors that experienced income losses until every sector is at least as well off as before the technology transfer occurred. However, an efficient income-transfer mechanism is required to assure the result."[21]

Thus far, the home-country technology transfer has had two benefits: (1) the creation of new markets for technology-intensive U.S. products and techniques, which include sophisticated tools and equipment, machineries, data processing, computers, chemicals, petroleum equipment, aircraft parts, experts, and technicans; and (2) the rapid expansion of many U.S. companies, which, with their strong R&D bases and production throughout the world, have direct access to overseas technology.

For example, a company such as IBM has cross-licensing arrangements with dozens of European companies, including Phillips in the Netherlands, ICI in England, Siemens in Germany, and some fifteen Japanese companies.

IBM's magnetic-tape manufacturing facilities in Boulder, Colorado, was set up under a cross-licensing agreement with the Sony Corporation of Japan. It uses Sony patents and a great deal of the technical know-how of the Japanese company. In addition, an important part of the development work on IBM's computer systems, specifically IBM System 360 and IBM System 370, was done in the company's eight overseas development laboratories.[22]

Labor union officials, however, disagree with these surveys and allege that the export of technology from the United States has reduced our leadership in many industries and product lines. American multinationals, according to these spokesmen, have transferred American technology and know-how to their foreign subsidiary plants. And there have been additional technology transfers through patent agreements and licensing arrangements of U.S. firms with foreign companies.

As a result, labor spokesmen conclude that foreign plants, created and operated efficiently with American technology, with lower wages and costs, and with higher productivity and tax advantages, can undersell American products and take away jobs from American labor.

Floyd Smith, president of the International Machinists, answered advocates of free trade and the free transfer of technology with the following statement: "Perhaps protectionism is a dead end, but it is just as likely that free trade, without any safeguard, is economic suicide."

The U.S. International Trade Commission, in a report to the Senate subcommittee, contends that the direction of employment changes will be the same as that of the net income effect. With other influences remaining constant, a negative income effect results in decreases in total employment, and the reverse occurs for a positive income effect. However, distributional effects may occur that can reinforce or offset the net income effects. Labor will thus be affected to the extent that relative labor-intensive industries are affected by the technology transfer.

> It should be noted that there also exists for labor an additional effect, regardless of the impact of net income and distributional effects. Any change induced by technology transfers—that which affects industry production patterns—probably leads to labor market adjustments which are associated with some costs. Adjustment costs for labor arise because of the impact of negative income effects and because of any distributional effects. That adjustment costs always arise in the latter case is due to the lack of complete geographical mobility in labor markets.[23]

Furthermore, any immediate loss of jobs that might result from exports of technology would be substantially mitigated by exports of component parts to the subsidiary and by the return of royalties, fees, and profits to the parent firm. The subsidiary, as the first firm with the innovation, can thereby increase its production and its demand for more machines and components from the United States.

The subsidiary will also have advantages in building up an efficient industry to the extent that no local firm will be able to equal it for a considerable time after obtaining the actual technology. All exports of machinery and components from the United States during this period thus mean more profits and jobs.

The multinational corporation taking technology abroad tends to create a market for its products by introducing foreign consumers to items that the subsidiaries are not able to produce in sufficient quantities. The result is additional demand not only for the goods themselves but also for more high-technology U.S. products.[24]

Caution should be exercised so as not to place too much emphasis on the U.S. as a generator of technology. It is the leading innovator, but the United States is not the only owner of technology. If a transfer of technology from the United States does not occur, there may be a loss of income to the seller, but this does not necessarily imply that the country desiring the technology does not obtain a competitive technology elsewhere, or develop a domestic alternative. Hence the net long-term effect if the United States does not transfer the technology in question may be a loss of income and influence to the United States. In the words of Robert B. Stobaugh:

> A plausible hypothesis is that the possibility of a firm's exporting, making foreign investments, or selling licenses would induce it to engage in certain R&D programs that would not be economical if the U.S. market were the only one considered; thus, U.S. technological innovation would be increased and in turn U.S. economic growth would increase.[25]

Technology transfer abroad should therefore be viewed as a dynamic process that may affect the U.S. economy in different ways, and an analysis that views only a particular aspect of its impact can at best give only a partial and incomplete view of the consequences for the American economy.

To summarize this discussion, any review of policy toward technology transfer to developed countries should recognize that the effects on U.S. trade, production, and employment may vary greatly by industry. Since different transfers may have different effects, they should probably be evaluated on an industry basis. However, even on an industry level, there are serious questions about whether the economic effects of technology transfer can be extracted from existing, or even improved, data on U.S. trade, licensing, and investments. First, there is no common agreement on what we mean by technology, the technology transfer process, or advanced technology industries. Second, existing data-gathering efforts do not focus on measuring the value, volume, or direction of U.S. technology transfers abroad. Hence it becomes extremely difficult to identify what loosely may be termed as a technology component of U.S. transactions in international trade, investment, and licensing. Third, the effects of U.S. technology transfer from available data show that it has been beneficial to economy, to the development of high technology, and to the labor force of the country. In 1978 U.S. multinational income from abroad—dividends, profits, patents, and licenses—was close to $37 billion.

As far as the effects on labor are concerned, according to the Department of Commerce, while there have been some job displacements as a result of multinational investments, in the long run multinationals have produced more jobs in the United States than an industry that produces only for domestic consumption.

Conclusion

As already noted in this study, considerable concern has been expressed about the possible loss of U.S. technological leadership through exports of technology-intensive products, licenses, cooperative agreements, and performances of R&D abroad by foreign subsidiaries or joint ventures. Very few data have been presented that would ascertain the actual reverse impact of technology transfer on the U.S. economy. It is important, however, to maintain historical perspective and to understand market realities. Technological transfer is not a new phenomenon. For example, the company from which General Electric was created one hundred years ago was deeply involved in international technology transfer. The Thomson-Houston Company that took the route to joint ventures, and vestiges of those operations, can still be identified in France and Great Britain. Edison also took the route of cross-licensing.

We must remember that U.S. companies cannot act unilaterally in technology transfer. Not only must they respond to the wishes of their customers regarding technological self-sufficiency, but they also must recognize that other countries—such as West Germany, Japan, France, Britain, and the socialist countries—compete on a technological basis.

In some cases, joint technological ventures may be the only mode of gaining entry to foreign markets. The joint venture of General Electric and Snecma in jet engine development is a good example of this cooperation. Similarly, the joint production of engines for Airbus A 300 was made possible by the cooperation between General Electric and several French companies.

Universal technological supremacy for a single nation is neither attainable nor economically desirable. Industries and technology in every country must go through a process of growth and maturation.

In considering policy alternatives affecting technology transfer, we must keep in mind the dynamics of the resource-allocation process as well as shifts in emphasis that occur in different segments of an economy with the passage of time. A key feature of Japan's announced strategy for future growth is to identify and nurture those industrial segments which are younger and more likely to enjoy rapid growth in the future. In contrast, one policy option being seriously considered in Great Britain is to take advantage of the windfall from North Sea oil reserves to build the nation's traditional industries.

Any proposal to change the present system of international technology transfer should be viewed in the light of its likely effect on resource allocation, markets, research and development, and trade both within the United States and elsewhere and on the long-term viability of any comparative advantage that the country plans to protect.

TABLE 7.1

Fees and Royalties: Payments and Receipts in 1976 and 1977
(in millions of dollars)

	1976	1977
Total Receipts	4,302	4,590
From Affiliated Foreigners	3,472	3,678
From All Others	830	912
Total Payments	471	451
To Affiliated Foreigners	276	250
To All Others	195	201
Western Europe:		
Total Receipts	2,083	2,263
From Affiliated Foreigners	1,700	1,848
From All Others	383	415
Total Payments	319	328
To Affiliated Foreigners	150	154
To All Others	169	174
Eastern Europe:		
Total Receipts	20	22
From Affiliated Foreigners	—	—
From All Others	20	22
Total Payments	1	1
To Affiliated Foreigners	—	—
To All Others	1	1
Canada:		
Total Receipts	673	711
From Affiliated Foreigners	633	668
From All Others	40	43
Total Payments	142	131
To Affiliated Foreigners	135	124
To All Others	7	7
Latin American Republics and Other Western Hemisphere:		
Total Receipts	360	399
From Affiliated Foreigners	299	331
From All Others	61	68
Total Payments	31	9
To Affiliated Foreigners	26	4
To All Others	5	5
Japan:		
Total Receipts	498	540
From Affiliated Foreigners	257	283
From All Others	241	257
Total Payments	−24	−26
To Affiliated Foreigners	−36	−38
To All Others	2	12

Australia, New Zealand, and South Africa:

Total Receipts	248	255
From Affiliated Foreigners	202	206
From All Others	46	49
Total Payments	0	−1
To Affiliated Foreigners	−1	−2
To All Others	1	−1

Other Countries in Asia and Africa:

Total Receipts	434	400
From Affiliated Foreigners	381	342
From All Others	53	58
Total Payments	1	
To Affiliated Foreigners	1	8
To All Others	—	1

Notes

1. Harvey Brooks defines technology as "the use of scientific knowledge to specify ways of doing things in a reproducible manner." In this sense, the organization of a hospital or an international trade system is a social technology, as the automobile or a numerically controlled tool is a machine technology. An intellectual technology is the substitution of algorithms (problem-solving rules) for intuitive judgments. Harvey Brooks, "Technology and the Ecological Crisis," quoted in Daniel Bell, *The Coming of Post-Industrial Society* (New York: Basic Books, 1976), p. 29.
2. National Bureau of Economic Research, New York, 1970.
3. Edward Mansfield, *The Economics of Technological Change* (New York, 1968).
4. *Technology Transfer*, U.S. International Commission, U.S. Departments of Commerce and Labor, 1977.
5. United Nations, Special Issue for the Second General Conference of UNIDO, 1974.
6. General Assembly Resolution 2626, "The Goal of the Second Development Decade."
7. United Nations, "The Impact of Multinational Corporations on Development," New York, 1974.
8. See Industrial Research Institutes, Sales No. 71 (U.N. publication).
9. Ibid., Sales No. 69.11 B39, vol. 10.
10. Report of the Committee for the United Nations Conference on Science and Technology for Development, United Nations, 1977.
11. See *Technology Transfer, a Review of Economic Issues* by the U.S. International Trade Commission, U.S. Department of Commerce, June 1978.
12. OECD, *Gaps in Technology* (Paris, 1980).
13. See Kenneth J. Arrows, "Classificatory Notes on the Production and Transmission of Technological Knowledge," *American Economic Review* 52 (May 1969).
14. Karl A. Stroetman, ed., *Innovation, Economic Change and Technology Policies* (Bonn, Germany, 1976).
15. Center for Multinational Studies, *The Benefits and Problems of Multinational Corporations* (mimeographed copy).
16. International Economic Subcommittee of the Emergency Committee for American Trade, February 1972.
17. Senate Subcommittee on Finance, February 1973.
18. See Nasrollah S. Fatemi, Gail Williams, and Thibaut de Saint-Phalle, *Multinational Corporations*, 2nd ed. (South Brunswick, N.J. & New York: A. S. Barnes and Company, 1976), p. 107.

19. Senate Subcommittee on International Finance, May 10, 1978.
20. U.S. Tariff Commission, *Implications of Multinational Firms for World Trade and Investment and for U.S. Trade & Labor,* 1973.
21. Hearings of Subcommittee on International Finance of the U.S. Senate, 95th Congress, Second Session, May 16, 1978.
22. Fatemi and Williams, *Multinational Corporations,* 1st ed., p. 68.
23. U.S. International Trade Commission, *Technology Transfer,* June 1978.
24. Organization for Economic Cooperation and Development, *Gaps in Technology,* General Report, Paris, 1973.
25. Robert B. Stobaugh, "A Summary and Assessment of Research Findings on U.S. International Transactions Involving Technology Transfers." Papers and Proceedings of Colloquies, National Science Foundation, Washington, D.C., July 1974.
26. See Joint Hearings of the Subcommittee on International Finance of the Committee on Banking, Housing & Urban Affairs and Subcommittee of Science, Technology & Space, May 18, 1978.

8
The Future of the Developing Nations

A lasting peace cannot become reality when people of many nations of the world suffer mass starvation.

>Jimmy Carter, former
>president of the United States

I call on world leaders to take the initiative in finding a new approach to closing the gap between rich and poor nations.

>Willy Brandt, former chancellor
>of West Germany

1

The developing nations for a long time were the forgotten part of the world. For all their potential wealth and miserable predicaments, they attracted neither the attention of the developed world nor its imagination except when the developed world needed their cheap resources and their markets. Until the formation of the nonaligned association in the 1960s and the energy crisis of the 1970s, the world was content to have the developing world remain in relative oblivion.

In the decade of the 1950s and 1960s, the developed world's attention was focused on Western Europe and Japan. It was the oil crisis of 1973 that gave a shock to the complacent developed nations. For the first time they realized that the developing nations—with 75% of the population of the world having close to $400 billion of exports, with 80% of the potential petroleum of the world and many other resources—were asking for a higher standard of living, a better price for their raw materials, and technical assistance to develop their resources and their industries for the benefits of their people. It also became very clear that these billions of people in the developing countries having total imports of more than $350 billion could become consumers of the agricultural and industrial products of the United States and other developed nations. Despite all difficulties, red tape, and obstacles, the present trade of the developing nations with the United States is much larger than their total trade with Western Europe and Japan.

The one-hundred-plus nations of the developing world, whose strengths and weaknesses, whose importance to the prosperity, trade, and industry of the United States, and whose hopes and illusions are briefly discussed in this chapter, are the central concern of U.S. economic policy as well as a heavily influential factor in all other areas of foreign relations. No political or economic problems of the 1980s can be solved without first comprehending the feelings and aspirations of developing countries; and second, a way must be found to assure these countries that the age of exploitation of one group by another group is over and that future trade and international relations must be based on mutual respect, mutual interest, and a true partnership. The cost of years of indifference—followed by confrontation—has been heavy for both sides. The dark days of colonialism and confrontation should be put behind and the dawn of cooperation and true partnership be welcomed.

2

Underdeveloped (or *developing*) *nation* is a term that defies precise definition. This is due largely to the nature of economic development, which is an open-ended process. There is no viable human community on earth that has not achieved some degree of economic development; and there is no community, no matter how advanced, that has reached its apex.

In view of the nature of economic changes, it is clear that the terms *developing* or *underdeveloped* are purely relative descriptions. They derive their meaning solely from some basis of comparison. Thus it may be said that the United States is a highly developed nation today compared with its economic status on the eve of the First World War. But fifty years from now a new generation of Americans looking back from the vantage point of a much more advanced level of technology and perhaps a more welfare-oriented society may view the United States in the second half of the twentieth century as a developing nation. Indeed, there are aspects of the economies of the developed nations that even today point to serious underdevelopment. These include the high volume of unemployment, persistent inflation, economic stagnation, the continuance of poverty in the midst of plenty, inadequate health care and educational systems, the sordid urban and rural slums, wasteful and inefficient commuter transportation, polluted air, contaminated rivers and lakes, and the failure to utilize constructively vast amounts of industrial and human resources.

In common usage, *underdevelopment* is defined as the failure to attain an adequate level of living for a large majority of a country's population as measured by the standards already achieved in other countries. Usually, per capita national income is used as the measure of development.

However, the use of such data to determine the level of development creates problems. Japan, Germany, and Britain, for instance, stand considerably below several of the oil-producing nations when viewed from the perspective of per capita statistics, even though they are in actuality far more advanced.

Despite all these shortcomings, the per capita national income estimates constitute the best available indicators of relative position along the ladder of economic development. Thus, while the data for the developing countries may be underestimated by 50% or more, and the data for the industrial countries inflated by as much as 15% or 20%, they do serve to highlight the great disparity in living standards that exists between the developed and developing nations. Using per capita national income as a crude measure of economic development, we find that the nations of the world array themselves in a continuum from very poor to very rich, with numerous intermediate ranges characterized by varying degrees of poverty and affluence, which in turn reflect great variation in the degree of economic development attained so far.

According to the United Nations' reports, approximately three-quarters of the world's population resides in the developing countries—including the People's Republic of China. This puts the rest in the category of developed market economies and developed centrally planned economies.

The developing countries circle the globe in a broad belt that includes, in particular, all of the tropical and subtropical lands and two extensive areas beyond: (1) the dry world, which encompasses all of Northern Africa and the Arabian peninsula, and extends northeastward across the Anatolian and Iranian plateaus, through much of central Asia to the great Khingan mountains of northeastern China; and (2) the monsoon area of Asia, which extends northward from the subtropics to include all of Pakistan, India, and the small states along its mountainous northern boundary, Mainland China east of its massive mountain and desert areas, Korea, and Japan.

To understand the developing nations and the problems they face in striving to improve their economic position, it is essential to consider them in relation to their resources, their land, their need for capital, their trade, and the environmental factors that have shaped their social and cultural heritages.

The developing nations of the world may be divided into four major geographical regions: monsoonal Asia, the dry world, sub-Sahara Africa, and Latin America. Each of these regions shares a complex of characteristics and underlying conditions that sets it apart from the developed nations.

What all the nations agree on is that the majority of the developing

The Future of the Developing Nations

nations live in abject poverty. However, opinion as to why the developing nations are plagued by the present situation is less harmonious.

But whether it is Western democracy, democratic centralism, or the Islamic economic system, socialism, Euro-Communism, or African socialism, the basic question is how to improve the economic life of these peoples. This goal and purpose present a challenging future to leaders of both the developed and the developing nations.

The idea of how to develop and use the resources of the developing nations for the good of their people has increasingly become the central theme of the world's most important forums inside and outside the United Nations. Developed nations depend on trade with, and the resources of, the developing nations. Developing nations also are well aware that without effective cooperation from the developed countries and the use of their technology, their capital, and their markets, all their efforts to provide even basic necessities of life to their people will not yield any fruit.

This cooperation, they all agree, must take the form of restructuring the international trade, international investment, international monetary, and international political regimes. But this new order of international cooperation must have the genuine support of the developed nations, with an understanding of the historical, economic, and political problems of underdevelopment that affect three-quarters of the population of the world.

Furthermore, these new plans for development must lead to opening various countries for extensive trade and major economic changes.

"The whole international economic system," says James Grant, president of the Overseas Development Council of the OECD, "needs restructuring, not so much as a favor to the developing countries but more so because of the future needs of the developed world." As Grant sees it, the industrialized countries face the 1980s and 1990s with the dour prospect of continued inflation, higher-priced raw materials, and slower growth. In order to combat the inflationary and recessionary trends, the two camps must cooperate with one another. If this does not happen, it is unlikely that either the developed or the developing nations will experience lower inflation and higher growth rates before the end of the century.

It must be remembered that the developing nations have long acted as the suppliers of cheap energy and other raw materials and have been customers for highly priced industrial and essential consumer products from the developed world—most pointedly from the developed market economies.

A look at the population of the world and the gross national product of its people shows that in 1978 1.6 billion of the total population of 4.86 billion lived in the developed countries and 3.2 billion resided in the developing areas of the world. Of this total Africa accounted for 455 million and Asia for 2.35 billion, with the remainder living in Central and South America and Oceania.

It is important also to note that the total population of the world will be growing at a rate of 2% during the rest of the century (as predicted by the United Nations). The irony of the situation is that the population of the developed world will, in turn, be expanding at a low rate of 0.8% compared with the 2.4% predicted for the less-developed world.[1] Under these circumstances, the developing countries will, in the aggregate, have a population of 5.14 billion by the year 2000. It is gratifying to contemplate what a sizable market for consumer products would be available if technology could help them to develop their resources.

In 1978 the developing nations accounted for only a quarter of the world's gross national product. This left approximately three-quarters of the world's wealth in the hands of the developed nations, which have only a quarter of the world's population (35% in the United States).

Because of population differences, income differences, production levels, and resource availability, developing countries present strong internal differences in the levels of their per capita income and their standard of living.

Among the developing countries, thirty-four are classified by the World Bank as low-income countries because of low per capita income—$250 per person per year or less. Countries included in this group are copper- and cobalt-rich Zaire, oil-rich Indonesia, and technologically advanced but population-haunted China and India.

Fifty-eight developing countries are classified in the middle-income category, with an average per capita income of $750. This average does not give a true picture of the extensive differences in the income levels of the individual countries grouped in this category. For instance, incomes range from $300 to as high as $4,000 in such an assortment of countries as Egypt, Nigeria, the Philippines, Algeria, Mexico, Iraq, Iran, Trinidad, Israel, Portugal, Greece, Spain, Brazil, Argentina, Chile, Syria, Taiwan, South Korea, and the Ivory Coast.

Aside from the United Arab Emirates, Qatar, Kuwait, Libya, Venezuela, and Saudi Arabia, the developing countries cannot match the developed market economies' average per capita income of $6,500 and the nearly $3,100 in the centrally planned economies.

Disparities in levels of gross national product or gross domestic product and in per capita income are accentuated by the rates by which they have grown in the past and are likely to grow in the future. Between 1960 and 1976 the average rate of growth in the developed countries was approximately 3% per year, while the countries in the middle-income group registered an average 2.8% annual increase and the low-income group only a 0.3% increase.

It is this shared perception of global inequity that unites more than 120 developing countries with per capita incomes ranging from $250 to $15,000. This perception gave birth to the idea of a New International Economic Order (NIECO) at the Sixth Special Session to the United Nations General Assembly in 1974. It has been also the most significant driving force behind the activities of both the Group of Seventy-seven and the nonalignment movement since the inception of these groups two decades ago.

The most important goal of the developing countries, presented by the Group of Seventy-seven at the meetings of the United Nations Conference on Trade and Development (UNCTAD), is the structural reform of world trade, aid, and investment. The group's demands include "raising and stabilizing the price of raw materials; lowering of tariff barriers; international monetary reforms; expanding international financial reserves; a new international set of rules on debt scheduling; and a code of conduct on the transfer of technology."

These demands are accompanied by a list of grievances that blame the developed nations and their multinational corporations for the current economic predicament of the developing countries and for their not being able to trickle down the benefits of economic growth to the lower substrata of the nations. The industrial nations' response is that as a result of their cooperation in investment and technology, many of them have made great economic strides in the last thirty years as measured by the gross national product of such oil-producing nations as Saudi Arabia, the United Arab Emirates, Kuwait, Iran, Iraq, Venezuela, Libya, and Algeria; and such non-oil-producing nations as Taiwan, South Korea, Brazil, the Ivory Coast, Argentina, India, Hong Kong, and Singapore.

The complete lack of understanding and the absence of any reevaluation throughout the 1970s have helped increase the conflict between the developed and the developing nations. The developed nations have tended to blame the lack of progress in some of the Third World countries on the absence of domestic order, responsibility, and stability. To alleviate poverty they have also said that the developing nations must first provide wise planning—including a system of education that could produce professionals, managers, and technocrats—and also provide direct access for the lowest strata of society to the indigenous infrastructure of science and technology. It is unfair, the developed nations have complained, to blame them for the age-old social and economic maladies of the developing nations. While the developed nations have admitted that they must make some accommodations and take some new approaches, they have disagreed considerably over the degree of concessions they would be willing to consider.

The issues confronting both the developed and the developing nations may be divided into three groups: (1) the pricing of raw materials, (2) trade, and (3) investments and the transfer of capital.

The developing countries possess in abundance almost all the natural resources essential for the development of industry in the developed nations. While countries such as the United States, the USSR, and Canada have access to all but a few very scarce commodities, Europe has become increasingly dependent on the developing world for its raw materials. And because of the waste of the past, the United States since the 1970s has had to depend more and more on obtaining energy and other strategic materials outside its borders. In many cases the nation has had to turn to the Middle East, Asia, Latin America, and Africa for these resources.

The developing nations not only have asked as much as the traffic will bear but have also used their resources as a political tool. In Iran the overthrow of the shah and the attitude of a hostile revolutionary government doubled the price of oil and created panic all over the world. The invasion of Zaire by a group of rebels forced the big powers to rush all the military assistance available to Mobutu, despite the notoriety for corruption, torture, and mismanagement. No nation was worried about the demise of Mobutu, but all were extremely concerned about the loss of Zaire's resources.

The bickering over the price of raw materials from the developing nations and of the industrial goods of the developed nations has been going on for almost twenty years. The oil-producing nations have chosen the route of the cartel and unilateral price increases, but other developing nations are still waiting for a response to their demands for massive financial transfusions to their stricken economies. The developed nations, meanwhile, still cling to the outmoded policies of the past. Despite many meetings and discussions inside and outside the United Nations, the dialogue between the two groups has been mixed in contentious rhetoric.

This deadlock has proved too expensive for both sides. In February 1980, after studying the problem for two years, a blue-ribbon international commission headed by former West German chancellor Willy Brandt issued a major warning to both the developed and the developing nations.[2] If mankind is to survive, the report says, the gap between the rich and poor must be bridged very quickly in the following ways:

1. The international negotiations on developing nations must deal not only with assistance on the price of raw materials "but with new structures." This new order must produce a comprehensive and innovative approach to the problem of development.

2. To finance industrial and agricultural development and stave off mass starvation in the neediest countries, the commission urges the distribution of $60 billion in annual development funds by 1985. (In 1979 the aid fund was close to $20 billion.) The commission's first concern is to boost food production and distribution. It is recommended that attention should be devoted to emergency shortage problems, major price-fluctuation prob-

lems, and, the longer-term problem of increasing the capacity of the developing countries to feed themselves through expanded domestic production. The developing world, the commission adds, needs a minimum $8 billion a year in new food aid to increase local food production and ensure regular supplies to the hungriest regions.

3. Energy is one of the most essential resources for both developed and developing nations. Besides price-stabilizing agreements with producer nations, the world has to come forth with a plan for energy conservation and for increased investment in alternative energy sources.

4. The world's current economic system is no longer adequate to meet the needs of the developing nations. It is imperative that a new system—more responsive to the developing nations, and based on improved terms of trade for Third World goods—be devised.

Over the longer term, the commission presents the world with a number of more ambitious challenges, ranging from the eradication of disease and poverty to the elimination of hunger, the termination of the arms race, and the realization of the fact that aid to developing nations is "simply enlightened self-interest."

The report also emphasizes that whatever sum is spent on raw materials in the developing nations is eventually funneled back to the industrial countries through the purchase of much-needed industrial products.

To implement all or part of the report, the commission calls for a summit meeting of perhaps twenty-five international leaders "as rapidly as possible." Such a meeting, according to the commission, could provide "a new impetus for future negotiations" and "could launch new ideas for a world economic recovery program."

According to the report, there must be a comprehensive reordering of international priorities and a massive transfer of wealth to the developing nations—not from charity but from the urgent necessity to head off world economic collapse in the 1980s or 1990s. "The development issue," concludes the commission report, "is one of the two crucial issues of this century, the other being the armament problem. Since there is now a risk of mankind destroying itself, this risk must be met by new methods."

It is no wonder that two-thirds of the Declaration of the Venice Economic Summit meeting, held on June 24, 1980, deals with the problems of energy and relations with the developing countries:

> We are deeply concerned about the impact of the oil price increases on the developing countries that have to import oil. . . .
> We approach in positive spirit the prospect of global negotiations in the framework of the United Nations and the formulation of a new international development strategy. In particular, our object is to cooperate with the developing countries in energy conservation and

development, expansion of exports, enhancement of human skills, and the tackling of underlying food and population problems.

A major international effort to help these countries increase their energy production is required. . . .

We ask the World Bank to examine the adequacy of the resources and the mechanisms now in place for the exploration, and development, and production of energy sources. . . .

We are deeply conscious that extreme poverty and chronic malnutrition afflict hundreds of millions of people of developing countries. The first requirement in these countries is to improve their ability to feed themselves and reduce their dependence on food imports. . . .

We underline the importance of wider membership of the new aid convention and of an equitable replenishment of the International Fund for Agricultural Development. . . .

We strongly support the general capital increase of the World Bank, increases in the funding of the regional development banks, and the sixth replenishment of the International Development Association. We would welcome increases in the rate of lending of these institutions within the limits of their present replenishments, as needed to fulfill the program described above. It is essential that all members, especially the major donors, provide their full contributions on the agreed schedule.[3]

The truth of the matter is that many people in the administration of the developed countries are concerned about the "possible formation of cartels like the Organization of Petroleum Exporting Countries with monopolistic control over prices and allocation of supply. . . . In addition, the Soviet Union, in many cases, is the only major alternative to supply from Africa, Latin America, and Asia in the matter of such metals as platinum, gold, and chromium."[4]

Some see the situation far more optimistically. They argue that after years of benign negligence the developed nations are actually expressing considerable hope when they seek accommodation and a fair deal, and the developing nations are facing up to the realities of cooperation. As the National Commission on Raw Materials in the United States explains: "Leaving energy aside, any significant material shortage that the U.S. will experience will result from short-run shocks that produce shifts in demand and supply large enough to exceed immediate adjustment capabilities of material-producing and material-using industries."[5]

To understand the importance of the developing nations' resources to the industry of the developed nations, we have to examine the available data for world production of some important raw materials used by the industrial countries, among them oil, iron ore, bauxite, chromite, cobalt, tin, manganese, copper, industrial diamonds, lead, silver, gold, and coal.

Major producers of these raw materials are Rhodesia, Liberia, Venezuela, Turkey, Iran, the Philippines, India, Cuba, Pakistan, Yugoslavia, South Africa, Nigeria, Brazil, Libya, Saudi Arabia, Kuwait, Zambia, the United Arab Emirates, Iraq, New Caledonia, Zaire, Bolivia, Malaysia, Indonesia, China, Thailand, Gabon, Mexico, Ghana, Algeria, Monaco,

The Future of the Developing Nations   251

Zimbabwe, New Guinea, and many other countries in Africa, Asia, and Latin America.

Western Europe, Japan, the United States, and the other developed nations depend on some if not all of these strategic materials; without these materials, the whole industrial complex of the developed world would plunge into total chaos.

There are wide differences of opinion on the impact that private foreign investment has had in the past in developing these raw materials, and on the part it may play in the future. But one thing is clear: the formation of the multinational corporations and their investments in the developing countries has had a decisive positive impact on trade and living standards for those nations which now enjoy stability and a firm development plan.

One of the most vital contributions of the multinationals has been the transfer of technology. In fact, industries in the developing countries can readily be grouped into "complex technology," "medium technology," and "simple technology" categories.

Complex technology includes the production of machinery, chemicals, electrical goods, pharmaceutical goods, and autos, oil exploration and refining, and the extraction of mineral resources. Medium technology includes the production of iron, steel, and metal products, the sugar industry, vehicle assembly, and textiles. Simple technology consists of agricultural-based industries.

In countries such as Brazil, Pakistan, South Korea, and Taiwan, 64% of the multinational investment is related to complex technology, 14% to medium technology, and 22% to simple technology.[5] Not only have these nations been able to raise their overall employment figures, they have also been able to boost levels of skills and training. In some cases, training has been conducted by the multinationals in cooperation with their host government; in others, certain enterprises have training centers in their home country or in another developing country.

Generally speaking, according to a report by the United Nations, MNCs in developing countries have contributed not only to the development of mineral and agricultural development but also to the upgrading of the labor force. Particulary in countries at a low level of industrialization, the more sophisticated work and training conditions provided by the multinationals can also have a strong direct effect on overall living standards and industrial relations.

The governments of the developing countries have attempted to persuade the multinationals to comply with local labor and welfare regulations and not to conflict with the governments' social development strategies. The aim is to avoid forming an "enclave" manpower that would be isolated from the rest of the country's industrial workers, or on the other extreme, exploiting the abundantly available manpower by offering much lower salaries.

Developing-Nation Trade

In the past the importance of the developing nations in the world economy has been based on their capability to supply vast amounts of vital energy resources, as well as strategic raw materials. Up until 1970 the share of developing countries in the world trade of manufactured goods was very limited. The value of their manufactured exports to the developed countries in 1970 was about $7 billion.

The industrialization strategy of the 1960s consisted primarily of import substitution. To encourage and protect the development of their own manufacturing industries, the big industrialized nations resorted to tariff or other restrictions on imports. The developing nations, therefore, were faced with a twofold problem: how to reduce their own imports and how to produce cheap goods for export to the developed countries.

In 1970 the Group of Seventy-seven protested that such international institutions as GATT and the International Monetary Fund were biased against the developing countries in their global distribution of trade and investment.

This charge may have been true in the 1960s; however, since the first energy crisis of 1973, the major trends in international political and economic relationships have in fact favored the developing countries, increasing their relative strength and enhancing their bargaining powers in international conferences.

Meanwhile, a United Nations study on multinationals and Latin American trade claimed that subsidies of foreign corporations in Latin America were purposely not exporting, "to avoid competition with their own affiliates on the world market." At the same time, the study charged, these corporations were monopolizing local Latin American markets through their own commercial networks.

The study, which covers 634 enterprises responsible for 80% of total Latin American exports (within the region and to the outside world), further states that subsidiaries of the multinationals do not on the whole export more than local enterprises.

Of course, the situation differs according to the country involved. Whereas local enterprises in Latin America are dominated by export of food products, textiles, and steel, multinationals are major exporters of chemical products, vehicles, and other high-technology goods.

The impact of multinationals on trade is, in fact, twofold: they contribute to the exchange of goods that takes place between countries and the exchange of goods (raw materials and semifinished and finished goods) among the multinationals.

Up until 1970 the bulk of the world's export and import trade was controlled by the developed nations, leaving the developing countries with a limited share. An examination of the trade in commodities and manufactured goods before 1970 shows both the insignificance of the level of trade and the exploitation of natural resources at a low price. There also were, in the areas of commodity trade, large imbalances for the developing nations. The overall economic result was a disruption of the world market in raw materials, characterized by a disparity between the developed nations and the developing nations. In many areas, because of monopolistic controls, the price of some commodities in 1970 was the same, or cheaper, than it had been in 1950, while the price of manufactured goods quadrupled. A good example is the price of crude oil, which was lower in 1970 than in 1950.

Beginning with the first decade of the development orchestrated by the Group of Seventy-seven at the United Nations, a new challenge was presented to the developing nations. They realized that their success would depend on their domestic stability as well as on new programs and policies. Meanwhile their task was greatly aided by industrialization, improved access to markets in the developed nations, and a more generous flow of technology and investments.

As a result of a decade of planning and an increase in the price of commodities, several of the developing nations propelled themselves into world markets on an even-trading basis with many of the developed nations. Exports from developing countries increased at a faster rate than world exports, or than exports from the developed nations. Thus since 1972 exports have grown more than 3.4 times, compared with 3.16 for the world, and 2.94 for the industrial countries. Developing-nation trade with the industrial countries has increased 3.3 times, while trade among the developing countries has grown 3.5 times.

In some cases, such as textiles, shoes, and steel, exports from developing countries are outcompeting the products of the industrial nations, particularly because of lower wages and higher productivity.

This new force in international trade has been the focus of considerable attention in the developed countries, as they grope for a way to respond to the increased competition from some of the developing nations (see tables at the end of chapter).

What is the cause of this rapid expansion in trade by certain developing countries? Fifteen years ago trade in both manufactured goods and strategic raw materials was dominated by the industrial nations. As soon as some developing nations were able to assert political and economic power, they concentrated on fostering development through the industrialization and expansion of their exports. Fortunately, they were able to get support and cooperation from the multinational corporations. As a result, they are today able to compete aggressively in the areas of textiles, shoes, and even some chemical products and steel.

In this chapter we shall examine several newly advanced developing countries whose exports have doubled and tripled in a short time: Brazil,

Mexico, Argentina, South Korea, Taiwan, Hong Kong, Singapore, Nigeria, Egypt, the Ivory Coast, and Burma. It is important to recognize that there are other countries such as India, Kuwait, Saudi Arabia, the United Arab Emirates, Libya, Iran, Venezuela, Pakistan, Iraq, and Thailand that have made great strides in industrialization, although they are not yet big exporters of manufactured goods.

On the other hand, the overwhelming majority of developing or less-developed countries do not approach the more advanced developing nations in terms of economic growth. Rather, they continue to face stark poverty and population problems coupled with economic stagnation and very few resources to call upon for any sort of development. These countries are unaffected by multilateral trade negotiation tariff reductions, commodity stabilization plans, or other assistance from the multinational corporations. These nations, the majority of the developing world, are becoming increasingly vociferous about their grievances and are asking for a new order in the world economy.

The ingredients and nutrients needed for the development of the less-developed countries go beyond the purpose and confines of this chapter, and as such will not be discussed. Rather, the factors, policies, programs, and actions that have helped propel some of the developing countries into the "takeoff" stage, where they play a significant role in international trade, will come under consideration.

One factor continually emerges as a key to successful economic development: the appropriate government plans and policies taken to foster development. A government may easily frustrate development by pushing too hard and too quickly toward certain goals—often embodied in five-year development plan—thus upsetting many deeply held traditional values of ideas. (One need only look at the events in Iran.)

Since most of the developing countries are strapped with inadequate resources for financing economic development, strategic planning is necessary to identify those projects which will most efficiently and effectively meet the short-term goals of development. Many countries do not go through this process, and as a result their planning is fragmented, irrelevant to the needs of the nation, costly, and often ineffective. The results are most often seen in the political arena, where diverse groups within the society express the feeling that they have not benefited from, but rather have been abandoned by, their government's policies and plans. The resulting instability and conflict have been witnessed numerous times.

In the late 1950s some of the developing nations, witnessing the U.S.-assisted industrial miracles of Western Europe and Japan, started to plan for industrialization by inviting American multinationals to help them with technology and capital. Their first step was to concentrate on the growth of import-substitution industries, then to use industrialization as a way to boost exports to the more populated countries. Hong Kong, Singapore,

The Future of the Developing Nations

South Korea, and Taiwan—because of the small size of their domestic markets and their need for foreign capital—had the greatest success in capturing world markets. However, it soon became clear that this strategy was not having the desired positive effect on economic development for several reasons:

1. It led to incomplete industrialization because it promoted manufacturing development only in relation to domestic demand and promoted the growth of manufacturing employment with respect only to a small proportion of total surplus labor.

2. These import-substitution policies encouraged inefficiency of production, a general rise in the price level, a distortion of cost structures, and consequently a decline in external competitiveness due to the degree of protectionism mandated by such policies.

As a result of the situation described above, many of these developing countries instituted far-reaching reforms aimed at reducing the negative effects of their import-substitution policies and thus commenced a new outward-oriented policy of industrialization based on export promotion. This enabled them to benefit from their rapidly growing external markets and to overcome demand problems in their domestic markets. Additionally, as foreign exchange earnings were needed to pay for their increased imports and the higher debt servicing associated with economic development programs, strong export earnings became essential.

Among the reforms that accompanied these new outward-oriented policies were (1) formal exchange-rate devaluations and realignments; (2) comprehensive monetary and fiscal stabilization measures and reforms; and (3) the easing of industrial licensing requirements, import tariffs, and duties, and the introduction of foreign direct-investment laws and other protectionist devices. Generally, the governments of these more successful developing countries began to take a much more active role in promoting exports, through direct financial assistance as well as through the changes in their economic policies.

Hong Kong and Singapore

It has been claimed that hard conditions and a lack of natural resources forced the two city-states Hong Kong and Singapore to orient their economic planning and manufacturing policies toward export markets. Unlike most other nations of the world, the two cities do not have any agricultural lands or mineral resources, and their domestic markets are not large enough to serve as an initial base for industrialization.

Thus Hong Kong has had to rely on the export of manufactured goods in order to participate in foreign exchange. And with a population of two million in the late 1950s and a relatively high per capita income derived from its trading activities, the city-state had a larger domestic market for manufactured goods than the majority of the developing countries.

Like other countries with small home markets, Hong Kong could have chosen a policy of complementing the income from its trading activity with the export of a few manufactured goods while relying on its domestic market to sustain a wide range of government-protected industries. Instead, Hong Kong policymakers decided to make the city not only an industrial but also a free market, buying and selling from Japan and the other market economies as well as from Mainland China and the Soviet Union. The policy led to huge export and income growth rates.

Industrialization was achieved in two stages in Hong Kong. First, an infrastructure was developed in which transportation systems to China and the outside world were set up. Technological innovations were advanced, and modern communication systems and financial institutions were introduced. A skilled labor force was encouraged, and more than 1.5 million workers from China were welcomed and trained for new industries. Next, the capital-goods sector financed the development of textile and steel industries—and the emphasis was not so much on producing consumer goods for the island as on creating a system to mass-produce goods for export.

Following this stage, the city-state began erecting hotels, shopping centers, dockyards, and office buildings. Simultaneously, a period of mass production and mass consumption in Japan, Western Europe, and the United States helped the burgeoning island economy. By 1979 Hong Kong was exporting $12.8 billion worth of goods and services, compared with $2.8 billion in 1971. In those same eight years its exports to the United States alone almost quadrupled, from less than $1 billion in 1971 to more than $4 billion in 1979, and its exports to the EEC countries grew to nearly $3 billion in 1978 from $600 million in 1971.

Hong Kong has inundated the markets of the developed nations with its products—ranging from textiles to chemicals, machinery, cement, and steel, among others. The United States has been the largest market for Hong Kong (30%), followed by the United Kingdom (10%), West Germany (8%), Japan (7%), Singapore (5%), and Australia (5%).

Meanwhile, Japan has led the other nations in supplying 21% of the region's imports, followed by China (17%), the United States (13%), Britain (6%), Singapore (5%), and Taiwan (5%).

Singapore's Development

Singapore also went through an import-substitution phase aimed at establishing domestic industries to serve its local market. Contrary to the practice of most of the other developing countries, however, Singapore used protectionism only as a temporary measure, quickly superseding quotas with tariffs that, in turn, were to be lowered and eventually eliminated. In fact, the number of commodities subject to quotas and tariffs was reduced to a considerable extent following a short import-substitution phase, which came to an end in the late 1960s. By 1972 only three items were subject to quotas, while tariffs were eliminated on a number of commodities and reduced on others. Also, even during the import-substitution phase, custom duties were much lower in Singapore than in othe developing countries.

Much of Singapore's success today can be traced to the industrialization policy. It began in the early 1960s, a policy that was based on three premises. First, the direct effect on employment of a rapid expansion of the existing export sector would be minimal because trade is not very labor-intensive. Second, in the early 1960s Singapore was heavily dependent on income from trade and from the British bases on the island—together, these produced one-third of the gross national income. Yet these two sources of income were unstable and insecure, and the nation had relatively no indigenous natural resources to exploit. Intensive industrialization and diversification of economy seemed to be the only means of survival. Third, if the process of industrialization were properly managed, Singapore would be in a good position to become a successful manufacturing center, given its advantages—a traditionally hard-working and adaptable labor force, a strategic geographical position, and a previously developed sociopolitical, financial, and physical infrastructure.

Given these factors, industrialization appeared to be both feasible and necessary. The size of Singapore's domestic market, however, ruled out a total dependence on import-substitution. Any long-run growth of the manufacturing sector would have to depend on export trade.

The most important force behind Singapore's industrialization was the coordination of its tax and tariff policies, industrial training and recruitment, and other policies to help the domestic manufacturing sector. Furthermore, an Economic Development Board was set up to plan for an industrial revolution. The board's first step was to create an environment of stability and profitability so that multinationals would establish plants in Singapore.

The policy of the board, in the long run, was "to ensure that both the physical and mental resources employed in Singapore's industrial sector be turned to a high level of technical refinement from the start, and also that goods produced would either have assured markets in the parent company's country, or be of sufficient quality to sell competitively anywhere in the world."[7]

The EBD was the main institutional source of long- and medium-term industrial and commercial financing until 1968, when the Development Bank of Singapore assumed this function.

Other factors contributing to Singapore's industrial growth during the 1960s and 1970s were the availability of skilled labor, relatively low wage rates, efficient and effective financial and commercial services, government stability, and good communication and transportation facilities.

Between 1961 and 1968 the value of the output of Singapore's manufacturing sector quadrupled, as did the value of its manufactured exports. The composition of manufactured output and the direction of manufactured exports also shifted dramatically during this period.

At the beginning, the emphasis was on relatively unsophisticated goods, mostly for domestic or neighboring countries. By 1970, however, the growth industries were chemical and petroleum products, machinery, electrical products, shipbuilding and ship repairing, and vehicles. At the same time, Singapore's exports were expanding in the United States, Japan, and Western Europe. Whereas in 1960 38% of its exports went to developed countries and 55% to developing areas, in 1977 these respective figures were 47% and 48%.

It appears that the successful developing nations of Asia, such as South Korea, Taiwan, Singapore, and Hong Kong, have concentrated far more on the developed countries as markets for their exports than have the other developing nations:

	Developed countries		Developing countries	
	1960	1977	1960	1977
Taiwan	56	70	43	26
Hong Kong	54	70	43	26
Rep. Korea	89	73	11	17
Malaysia	58	62	36	32
Singapore	38	47	55	48
Thailand	47	54	48	41
Brazil	81	61	13	30

SOURCE: *World Development Indicators*, the World Bank, 1979.

In 1978 Singapore exports totaled more than $10.1 billion. The U.S. share of Singapore's exports was 15.6%, Malaysia's 15%, Japan's 10%, and Hong Kong's 8%. In 1971 trade with the OPEC nations accounted for only 6% of Singapore's total exports. By 1978 this percentage had increased to 14.5%. Singapore's trade with Latin America also increased from $47.2 million in 1971 to $320 million in 1977. Meanwhile, its imports reached $13 billion in 1978, with Japan contributing 16%, Saudi Arabia 16%, Malaysia 14%, and the United States 13%.

In 1965 Singapore's top trading partners were Malaysia, the United Kingdom, Japan, the United States, and Australia. Today, the order is different, reflecting Singapore's quest for higher technology as well as its newly found status as the world's third largest oil-refining center. Singapore's increased trade with the United States is the result both of the increased competitiveness of its products and of the massive influx of technology and capital equipment from American multinational corporations.

However, not everything that has taken place in Hong Kong and Singapore is "rosy." In the near future both may face some problems that are peculiar to countries that have reached a certain level of economic, social, and political development.

Along with their economic success, these nations also must cope with the rising expectations of both workers and poor people. There is great pressure for higher wages, social benefits, job security, and job preferences.

In addition, there is the possibility that such factors as shorter hours, lower productivity, market saturation, competition by other developing nations, and labor disturbances could erode much of their comparative advantages.

Taiwan and the Republic of Korea

Taiwan and South Korea completed the first "easy" stage of import-substitution during the early 1960s, which meant replacing the imports of nondurable consumer goods and their principal direct inputs. At that time the two nations adopted outward-looking policies oriented toward the exportation of labor-intensive products. This was done with a view to accelerating economic growth in a situation where continued import substitution in the framework of national markets would have been increasingly costly.

In both Taiwan and Korea, a free-trade regime was applied to investments and exports, supplemented by some additional incentives. Taiwan faced the challenge of potential economic strains by creating stability and by winning the confidence of investors. From 1952 to 1977 production in Taiwan increased at an average rate of 5% for agriculture and 10% for industry.[8]

In its initial stage of development, Taiwan depended heavily on U.S. aid, which totaled about $1.5 billion.[9] The United States also accepted responsibility for Taiwan's defense and the training of its army, which saved the country many millions of dollars. Beginning in 1965, net domestic savings increased sharply. National savings and foreign investments replaced foreign aid as the primary source of capital. In recent years, again, foreign investment has become very essential to industrial growth in general, as the carrier of high technology, and as a source of capital for the expansion of export-oriented industries.

Early on, Taiwan revised its code of laws and produced a clearly defined legal system to protect the property rights of investors. It also clarified its tax system and assured investors a return flow of profits and capital.

The nation created a rapid communications system, food transport facilities, and enough power to support the new industrial projects. It also worked to improve the efficiency of existing factories by reducing the consumption of raw materials, conserving energy, improving the quality of products, and training managers in modern management techniques. In addition, Taiwan was aided by the fact that it had a large number of skilled laborers who were willing to help build up the new industrial base.

Alongside this industrial expansion, several other measures were adapted to augment the supply of foreign exchange, such as the development of tourist trade, the building of food-processing plants, and participation in construction and other industrial projects in the Middle East. In the early stage of its development, Taiwan had to rely heavily on agricultural exports. Between 1952 and 1976 agricultural production grew by 5% per year—more than twice as high as the 2% growth rate in Mainland China and many other developing nations.

Another source of success was Taiwan's ability to restructure its industrial and exportable products to adapt to constantly changing world demand. This was evidenced by the shift from sugar and rice as the principal exports in the 1950s to processed agricultural products and textiles in the 1960s, and to electronics and machinery in the 1970s. The reason for this flexibility and dynamism was the existence of entrepreneurs and a highly motivated and skilled labor force.

One lesson that developing countries must learn is that a modern economy is necessarily a dynamic economy that can absorb and utilize new production techniques and adjust itself to changing market conditions. It is a lesson that the American automobile industry forgot and is now paying a heavy price to relearn. The driving force behind this dynamism are the workers, technicians, and managers who can plan, predict, and implement, and who are highly motivated to produce, innovate, and exploit economic opportunities.

Taiwan's response to these challenges was, first, to emphasize the importance of rising consumption standards and education, and second, to allow the free enterprise system to work by rewarding hard-working and enterprising people. At the same time, the government took steps, through fiscal policies and such other measures as an antipoverty program and repricing agricultural products and public utilities, to reduce any inequalities in income distribution. As a result, per capita real consumption increased by more than 4% a year during 1952–76.[10] In education, the government-financed nine-year free education system raised the enrollment rate for males in secondary education from 18% in 1952 to more than 70% in 1977.

In both Taiwan and Korea, a free trade regime was applied to exports and was supplemented by many government incentives. Exporters had the freedom to choose between domestic and imported inputs, they were exempted from indirect taxes on their outputs and inputs, and they paid no duty on imports of raw materials. The same privileges were extended to the producers of domestic products that were used in export production.

In Taiwan reduced direct taxes, preferential credits, facilities for the rapid collection of export proceeds, and direct subsidies to the exporters of several commodities provided a slight advantage to manufactured exports over import substitution in 1968, and there was little discrimination against primary activities.

Taiwan's main industries include textiles, clothing, electrical and electronic equipment, processed foods, chemicals, glass, and machinery. The country is also rich in resources: rice, bananas, pineapple, sugar cane, soybeans, coal, gold, copper sulphate, and some crude oil.

Between 1971 and 1978 Taiwan's exports increased more than six times from $1.9 billion to $12.6 billion, and its biggest customer was the United States. About 39% of its total exports found their way to this country. Imports to Taiwan, meanwhile, were $11 billion in 1978, 33.4% from Japan, 21.6% from the United States, 7% from Kuwait, and 5% from Saudi Arabia.

South Korea

After World War II, the division of the Korean peninsula left the Republic of Korea separated from power, chemical fertilizers, and various raw material supplies in the north. Damage from the Korean conflict, which amounted to an estimated $2 billion, further entrenched the failing economy.

During the following decade, mainly with the assistance of the United States, the economy began to recover. By the early 1960s industrialization was beginning.

In 1961 the government introduced the first Five-Year Economic Development Plan for 1962–66, based on the objective of developing the country's infrastructure and light industry. Subsequent plans, introduced for consecutive five-year periods, stressed development of heavy industry, the improvement of income and living conditions for the rural masses, and increasing exports of both heavy and light industrial and chemical products.

During the years constituting the first Five-Year Plan, Korea's real GNP increased by an annual average of 8.3%—the rate of increase ranging from 3.5% in 1962 to 13.4% in 1966.

Until the early 1960s Korea, like many other developing countries, followed an industrialization strategy based primarily on a policy of import substitution. In the early 1960s, however, after the completion of import substitution in nondurable consumer goods and their inputs, the Korean industrialization strategy changed to one of export promotion. This strategy shift was first adopted by the military government that came into power in 1961.

Perhaps the most important policy reform was the adoption of a realistic exchange rate in May 1964. Before this, Korean exports were stifled by the overvaluation of the won, even though other measures—such as an export-import linking system, multiple exchange rates, inexpensive credits, and preferential tax treatment—helped compensate. Comprising part of a larger, more comprehensive financial stabilization program, the exchange rate depreciation amounted to approximatey 50%. This reform was reinforced in March 1965 with the adoption of a unitary, fluctuating, exchange-rate system that could reflect realistic demand-and-supply conditions.

Government policies to actively promote exports included general anti-inflationary monetary and fiscal measures, as well as traditional financial measures to provide incentives. These included reductions in or exemptions from various taxes and customs duties, export credits provided at preferential rates, accelerated depreciation on facilities used for the production of exports, and discounts on power and transportation rates. All export industries were entitled to total exemption from the business tax and a reduction of 50% on income and corporate taxes. Imported raw materials incorporated in export products were exempted from import duties and the commodity tax.[11]

Additionally, bank credits were available to exporters at an annual rate of 6%. This provided a strong incentive for exporting, since it normally cost 26% a year for bank credit for domestic transactions. Other indirect subsidies included a 30% reduction in the cost of transporting exports by rail, and a reduction in the charges for electricity used in producing exports.

This array of incentives was complemented by various other measures, including new export products or opening new foreign markets, a spoilage and waste allowance on imports, and automatic approval for raw materials imports used in the production of exports. The government also provided marketing assistance through the Korea Trade Promotion Corporation (KOTRA), established in 1962. In addition, the government assumed a supervisory planning function—it formulated annual export targets and a geographic export-marketing strategy, recommended quantities of certain products to be directed into various markets, and suggested the appropriate marketing techniques to be used. The government also enacted an Export Products Inspection Law to ensure product quality.

Korea's impressive economic growth began with the shift in its industrialization policy to active export promotion. Before 1960 exports hovered around the $20 million level, accounting for approximately 1% of GNP. In 1960 Korean exports totaled $33 million.

After 1962 Korea's exports began to take off. Export expansion during the years from 1962 to 1976 averaged more than 40% annually, rising in nominal value from approximately $55 million and 2% of GNP in 1962 to approximately $14.97 billion and 32% of GNP in 1978. The real value of exports, meanwhile, increased at an average annual rate of 37% during these same years. Export growth declined during 1974–75 because of the adverse effects of the worldwide recession, but recovered in 1976 with an increase in nominal value of more than 50%.

In the 1950s and early 1960s most Korean exports were primary products—tungsten, iron ore, fish, raw silk, etc.—while manufactured exports constituted only a small fraction of the total. After 1962, however, exports of the latter increased much more rapidly. In 1966 exports of manufactured products accounted for 52% of total exports; in 1969 this percentage increased to 77% of total exports. By 1976 exports of such manufactured goods as clothing, electrical machinery, textile fabrics, iron and steel sheets, plywood, and footwear and wigs comprised nearly 90% of total exports.

Thus industrialization through export promotion entailed a significant change in the orientation and structure of Korean industry. While the primary sector grew at approximately 5% per year during 1962–78, the share of GNP accounted for by this sector declined from approximately 40% in 1962 to 20% in 1976. Manufacturing, on the other hand, increased the value it added to GNP from approximately 10% in 1962 to 36% in 1978.

The growth of Korean exports was concentrated in the United States and Japanese markets; exports to these two countries comprised 72% of Korea's exports in 1969, approximately the same share as in 1960. In 1977 this share declined to 53%, with the Common Market countries taking up the slack.

Korea showed its ability to offset the higher cost of energy inputs after 1973; between 1973 and 1977 its exports to the Middle East increased elevenfold, primarily by supplying workers to Saudi Arabia and Kuwait. At the end of 1974 there were 395 Korean workers in the Middle East; by the end of 1976 this figure had risen to 23,490. Korean contracts in the Middle East rose from $110 million in 1973 to more than $2.5 billion in 1976, and these figures are likely to continue expanding in the future.

The availability of large amounts of foreign aid from the United States during the 1950s, the restoration of normal diplomatic relations between Korea and Japan in 1965, and the influx of foreign credit and direct investments in the export industries from these two countries had some rather beneficial effects. On one hand, they provided Korea access to foreign technologies that could yield productivity increases, and on the other hand, they gave the country foreign markets. In addition, the heavy reliance of Korea's exporters on the two major markets reduced the urgent need for market diversification and thus for investment in building up marketing organizations and trade connections. These developments made it possible for Korea to build relatively large export industries specializing in one or a few articles, such as plywood, wigs, and sweaters, and to avoid marketing problems by placing these outputs in a few national markets.

Today, Korea faces problems similar to those mentioned in the analysis of Singapore. In recent years wages have gone up rapidly, along with increases in the prices of imported raw materials and inputs. Also, the relatively high interest rates and high cost of infrastructure development are likely to increase the prices of Korean exports in the future—unless productivity and quality improvements offset these cost increases. The degree of concentration in several export commodities and markets that Korea has developed may meet stiffer competition in the near future from other exporters, most notably Taiwan.

Essentially, this means that in order to continue its excellent rate of economic growth through exports, new commodities will need to be produced and new markets penetrated.

Burma

This is a case of failure—the result of poor and wrong planning, a lack of technology, an incompetent managerial staff, insufficient foreign investment, and a lack of confidence.

Burma is a good example of a "developing" country that tried too quickly to achieve a certain state of development. Its development program was based on a very insecure financial base—receipts from exported rice and, to a lesser extent, petroleum. As many nations have painfully discovered, relying on a food crop to finance economic development presents three acute problems: first, the foreign demand for the crop may change without notice; second, the price of the crop may vary according to world supply and demand; and third, natural conditions may totally destroy a year's crop, yielding no receipts with which to finance already committed projects.

In pre–World War II Burma there was a predominance of rice and oil among exports, controlled largely by foreigners, and the economy was highly dependent on foreign trade for its growth and vitality, with the majority of exports being primary commodities subject to erratic price fluctuations. The war destroyed more than half of Burma's man-made wealth, plus its oil wells, silver and tungsten mines, and harbor installations. In 1946–47, the second full year after the war, total output in Burma plunged approximately 40% below its 1938–39 level. Thus it is perhaps unfair to expect great results from Burma's development plans, given the destruction caused during World War II. Nonetheless, government policy ought to be examined for its flaws.

Foreign consultants were called into Burma in the early 1950s to assist in drawing up an extensive and seemingly all-encompassing development plan. One of the chief recommendations made by the consultants was in line with what Burma officials desired most: an intensive program of industrialization would be the only productive way of absorbing the annual increase of some 50,000 to 60,000 working-age men into the labor force.[12] The size of the industrial and related investments needed to do this absorption job, based on the capital-intensive industries recommended, was estimated at approximatey $84 million to $105 million per year.[13]

In August 1952 the government held a major economic meeting known as the Pyidawtha Conference, at which it endorsed immediate action to invest some $227 million in the basic sectors of the economy. The conference also adopted major programs for agriculture, land nationalization, transportation and communications, housing, education and health, as well as programs for locally developed improvement projects and a plan for more democratic local administration. In fact, it seems that the government has a plan for everything. The critical shortcoming of the Burmese program for economic development, however, was that it was to be financed in large part by the government, mostly through *anticipated* export surpluses, of which rice was the largest component.

Burma's crippling problems started in 1954, when rice export prices reached their peak the previous spring of 1953. The termination of the Korean conflict, bumper crops, and the U.S. disposal of surplus wheat and rice in Asia contributed to a sharp break in commodity prices. These problems, coupled with the weakening of Burma's hold on the Indian and Ceylonese markets for rice, its loss of the European market after World War II, its growing dependence on high rice prices, and its loss of sales to the importing countries of the Far East spelled trouble for the nation. Compounding all this, the State Agricultural Marketing Board (SAMB) overestimated its bargaining power and delayed much too long in its decision to lower its export prices for rice to the world level, in response to the increased world supply and reduced demand.

As a result, foreign-exchange receipts and reserves, used to finance the grandiose domestic development plans, began to decrease as rice export sales declined. Exacerbating the situation, proper statistics were not kept by Burmese economic and financial authorities, and as a result, they did not learn of the seriousness of the situation until it was much too late. On January 14, 1955, the Ministry of Finance and Revenue submitted a memorandum pointing to the government's dwindling cash and foreign-exchange balances, and called for drastic measures: a 25% cut in current government expenditures by wholesale "across-the-board" reductions in personnel; reductions by a similar percentage in expenditures for diplomatic and consular establishments; and the complete suspension of relatively unimportant departments and projects. This was the beginning of the end. Programs continued to be cut, and the shortages of foreign-exchange reserves, coupled with new import restrictions, fueled rampant domestic inflation.

Cleary, the nonessential programs should have been eliminated from the beginning. By 1957–58 there was a sharp decline in the size of the new rice paddy, and the crop was almost one million tons smaller than the previous year. This meant a more significant decline for rice exports, foreign-exchange earnings, budgetary revenues, and the government's capital investment and fiscal programs. A military government took over in 1958, contributing to the total demise of the economy as well as of the freedom of millions of poverty-stricken Burmese.

The purpose of exposing the problems faced by Burma is to find out what the nation did wrong, so that other countries may save themselves this costly error.

The responsibility for the problems of post–World War II Burma lies in the three main goals it set: nationalization, Burmanization, and industrialization. The threat of nationalization, for example, effectively deterred the nation's private rice millers from maintaining and modernizing their plants, with great loss to the economy. The same threat deterred other new investment, both domestic and foreign, that was critical to economic development.

The government firmly believed that planning was the road to welfare, that investment would automatically result in greater production and productivity, and that it had only to formulate plans and engage experts to carry them out. Officials believed that industrialization was the key to progress, and they pursued it blindly.

Instead of diverting all the profits from rice exports to the domestic industrialization program, more emphasis should have been placed on the development and diversification of the agricultural sector where millions of Burmese worked. Whereas Burma concentrated on the export of rice to pursue domestic industrialization, with the expectation of "development" in ten years, neighboring Thailand expanded its export crop to include maize, cassava, kenaf, oilseeds, beans, shrimp, and other primary products. In contrast to Burma's performance, Thailand increased the sale of its diversified exports at an annual compound rate of 7.4% over the period 1955–64. Thus Burma painfully learned about the importance of export diversification for the purpose of obtaining more secure foreign-exchange receipts, which in turn finance the goods needed to foster economic development. It also learned the cost of pursuing a policy of "blind industrialization."

In addition, Burma found that government policy and regulation may also be an impediment to development. Whereas Burma heavily regulated the growth and sale of rice, Thailand in 1955 dissolved its rice monopoly. As a result, competition fostered lower prices and the greater world price competitiveness of Thai rice exports.

The Burmese also became overzealous in their use of and belief in planning. As one author points out, "one detects the feeling that if the Burmese do not possess a steel mill or an institute of technology, then a plan will be the next best thing."[14] Thus a peculiar sanctity seems to attach to reports, statistics, and, above all, to diagrams and scale models that give the desired future an illusion of immediacy.

Hence, after thirty years of such mistakes, Burma, with a population of more than 32 million in 1978, had a per capita income of $120, exports of only $242 million, and an international reserve of $140 million. Burma's main export customers were Indonesia (14%), Singapore (13%), Sri Lanka (11%), and Japan (10%).

On the other hand, Thailand, because of its policy of diversifying crops and developing its mineral wealth, was able to increase its exports of less than $500 million in 1960 to more than $4 billion in 1979, attaining an international reserve of $2.3 billion and a per capita income of close to $500.

Latin America

Export growth has enhanced the economic strength of Argentina, Brazil, and Mexico. It has increased their credit-worthiness for substantially higher external borrowing, which in turn has helped finance large investments in industry, mining, and general infrastructure development. Export growth has also improved the capacity of these countries to adjust to the adverse effects on their external financial position of the 1974–75 recession in the industrial countries.

After two years of unprecedented deterioration in their current accounts from 1974–76, and considerable fears that much of the export growth they had experienced for the past decade would be negated by this recession, most of the Latin American and Caribbean oil-importing countries have finally improved their current account balances. However, the dark shadow of past loans and the costly oil import bills they are now paying do not bode a bright future. A substantial portion of this recovery in their current account balances was related to a major improvement in their terms of trade, due in part to a general recovery in demand but also to widespread rises in commodity prices.

There are certain key factors that have enabled the above-mentioned Latin American countries to embark on an externally oriented policy of export expansion. It is to these factors that we now turn.

Argentina

> Argentina's problems are political rather than economic. If they could have political stability, they would have a real economic miracle, for the infrastructure is already well-developed and the country has substantial resources. The take-off would be terrific.[15]

This 1976 statement effectively foreshadowed what is increasingly the case in Argentina's renewed economic development today. Indeed, Argentina has come nearly full circle from its strong world position in the 1930s and 1940s, after a dreadful performance culminating in the 1976 coup d'état. It has placed more emphasis on the private sector, while discounting the "subsidiary function" of the state. Thus the government may intervene directly in the economy only in the event that there is no possibility of private capital interests doing so. With this in mind, the government has cautiously renewed its industrialization program—for example, contracts have been signed with major Japanese steel companies to improve and develop Argentina's steel industry.

The country's problems, culminating in the coup d'état by a three-man junta in March 1976, are finally receding. Inflation is down to 150% from 400% two years ago and 1500% in 1976. Foreign exchange reserves are now above $10 billion, relatively equal to the country's outstanding debt. Internally, the economic ministers are continuing to remove import tariffs and government subsidies to business, in order to decrease the deficit and to force domestic companies to be more productive and efficient. The currency is currently on a schedule that devalues at approximately one-half the rate of inflation. In addition, there has been pressure for greater productivity by Argentinian enterprises.

According to a senior Argentinian government official, the situation that came to a crisis in 1976 was caused by the political and economic policies followed by the country for the preceding thirty years.[16] This policy may be characterized as follows:

1. Increasing intervention of the state in the economy. The state, by developing activities that were previously reserved for the private sector, and by establishing strict regulations on other sectors, stifled the productive factors of the country. This increase in intervention led inevitably to higher state expenditures that were not accompanied by corresponding revenue increases. This created a budget deficit of massive proportions, which, financed mainly by the printing of money, became one of the main causes of the persistent inflation plaguing the country.

2. A closed economic system, derived from the economic autarchy imposed since the beginning of the postwar period. This isolated Argentina from the general world trend of extraordinary economic and

technological progress that took place after World War II. It also failed to provide encouragement to the productive activities of the country, causing a relative decrease in trade, and a decrease in the volume of imported capital and technology that could have modernized the economy.

3. These economic trends led to an overall lack of growth in the economy, causing severe domestic stagnation and the loss of Argentina's relative position in international markets.

Prior to 1976 the subsidies given to foster exports were not sufficient to affect the high cost of domestic inputs used in export production. Furthermore, high protection continued to be given to industries engaged in import substitution, and the resulting bias against exports was especially evident in the case of agricultural and primary products.

In 1976, after the coup, a series of drastic reform measures were initiated to bring the economy to where it is today. Perhaps in five more years we shall truly witness the tremendous impact these measures have had in turning the Argentine economy around. This new economic plan included the following measures: (1) a reduction in the fiscal deficit, to be achieved by reducing the number of personnel in the central administration and in public-sector enterprises, and by encouraging private investment in nonessential state enterprises and in companies that had been subject to public intervention to maintain employment; (2) tax reforms, including a wealth and capital-gains tax; (3) further issues of bonds to help finance the public debt, both within Argentina and abroad; (4) a gradual liberalization of the exchange market by transferring trade transactions to the free market, with a view to achieving a single free rate; (5) denationalization of bank deposits, in order to reactivate banking and financial activities; (6) promotion of exports and multilateral payments with other countries; (7) a new foreign-investments law with adequate guarantees to attract foreign companies to form subsidiaries in Argentina; (8) large-scale investment in the agricultural sector to increase production and productivity and to provide prices and lower duties for grain and meat exporters, and the abolition of slaughtering quotas for meat producers and the state monopoly on the marketing of grains and oilseeds; (9) expansion of the energy and mining sector, with participation from foreign companies in the exploration and development of petroleum and mineral deposits; and (10) a price policy ruled by market forces rather than by government controls (although excessive price increases could entail prosecution), accompanied by periodic wage increases when economic conditions permitted.

These reforms have contributed significantly to greater price stability, and they are creating appropriate conditions for investment and economic growth based to a greater degree on private initiative. Additionally,

Argentina is 90% energy/oil–sufficient and will become a net oil exporter in the near future when two major hydroelectric projects shared among Argentina, Paraguay, and Brazil are completed. The above scenario, coupled with the 95% literacy rate of the Argentine public, has put the nation on the top of the list of countries to watch closely in the 1980s.

Argentina's problem is mostly political, and if the leaders can bring order out of the present chaos many of the country's economic problems can be solved. The country has enough trained managers and administrators, technocrats, and skilled labor. Argentina is very rich in agricultural products, and its industry is advanced and produces textiles, chemical, metals, machinery, and automobile products. In 1978 the country's gross national product was close to $40 billion; per capita income reached $2,000; its exports were $6 billion—mostly to Brazil, the Netherlands, and the United States. Its trade showed a surplus of more than $1 billion and its international reserve in 1979 was $5.66 billion.

Brazil

By the early 1960s Brazil had concluded a decade of strong economic growth through industrialization, first by consumer-goods import substitution and later by increased capital goods production. Government intervention in such sectors as iron and steel, petroleum, transportation, and public utilities was integral to the rapid growth achieved. The government also invested heavily in infrastructure development.

Starting in 1964 the government initiated various reforms and measures that contributed to greater export expansion. In particular, the government took five major steps to modernize the country's financial markets, which previously were more of an impediment than a contribution to growth. First, it raised the yields on financial instruments enough to encourage new savings and to divert the money from real estate to foreign projects. Many developing countries do not maintain these kinds of realistic interest rates on domestic savings, and usually the rate in real terms is very negative. For example, a country with an inflation rate of 40% and an interest rate on savings of 10% is actually providing −30% interest. In such an environment, any sensible person would invest in other areas. Thus the importance of maintaining interest rates on savings at attractive levels should not be minimized.

Second, the government created medium- and long-term debt markets to finance the government, business, and housing sectors. Third, it provided access to new equity funds by corporations and to ownership of equity by the general public. Fourth, it insured that investment in socially desirable sectors and regions—i.e., the Northeast—would receive financial assistance. Finally, it made certain that business would not be constrained by inflation in internally generating funds for use in expansion.

Because these innovations in Brazil's financial markets added to the nation's capacity to mobilize savings through noninflationary means, they provided a strong base from which domestic business could more aggressively compete in world markets. This is crucial for a developing country.

Brazil took other, more explicit, steps to foster export expansion. From 1965 to 1967 it generalized indirect tax exemptions on exports of processed foods, minerals, and manufactured products and their inputs, and it instituted duty drawbacks on imported inputs used in export production. This action had the effect of increasing incentives for exporting, as opposed to import substitution, by reestablishing the equal tax treatment of production for both foreign and domestic markets.

Export subsidies were also granted in the late 1960s in the form of tax credits, reductions in income taxes, and preferential export financing. In 1971 the subsidy equivalent of tax benefits averaged 20% on Brazilian exports of processed goods. Generally, subsidies that were added to the value of exports varied considerably—from 6% on petroleum products to 38% on beverages. And while Brazil promoted some agricultural exports, it discriminated against many others. (This is a trend that appears often in developing countries that are following a policy of industrialization and product diversification. There seems to be an implicit, or even explicit, bias against the agricultural sector.)

Brazil is very rich in agriculture and has made tremendous progress in industry. Yet this progress is lopsided, and the majority of the people are deprived of a decent standard of living.

Its agricultural products include coffee (it is the largest grower), cotton, soybeans, sugar, rice, corn, and cocoa. Its industrial products include textiles, steel, autos, aluminum, chemicals, drugs, shoes, appliances, paper, glass, and machinery. Brazil holds one-third of the total iron reserves in the world, as well as supplies of mica, quartz crystal, chrome, diamonds, manganese, thallium, gold, nickel, coal, and gemstones.

Brazil's gross national product in 1978 was $190.8 billion, its per capita income was $1,500, and it had exports of $12.4 billion, imports of $13.5 billion (U.S. 23%), and international reserves in January 1979 of $11.4 billion.

But the dark shadow on Brazil's economic horizon is its enormous debt and an inability to service it. The situation has only deteriorated in recent years because the nation is the biggest user of imported oil among the world's developing nations—one million barrels a day in 1979. Brazil is also the biggest borrower in the international markets: it is currently in debt to the tune of $50 billion. And the government has only exacerbated the problems. In 1979 when the price of oil doubled—costing Brazil $30 million a day—the government machine ran wild. Add to this a debt service that may reach $12 billion in 1980, and you have a nation in deep trouble.

Although Brazil has become the world's eighth-largest market economy, of late there has been increasing concern by international bankers in general and American bankers in particular about the nation's solvency.

American interests are involved in Brazil in many ways:

1. The country is the largest single customer of U.S. banks; its more than $14 billion in loans to American bankers equals the combined equity capital of the eight largest banks; and it is the biggest borrower from German and Japanese banks.

2. Brazil was developed by some of the largest American multinationals and at present is host to many of their subsidiaries.

3. It is capable of finding massive substitutes for fossil fuels; it already has the world's largest hydroelectric construction program and is pressing forward with plans to replace petroleum products with plant-based fuels.

4. Since 1970 it has multiplied its GNP five times and has increased its per capita income to $1,500. Among the developing nations, only South Korea can match this record.

Despite all this economic progress, however, Brazil has failed to eliminate poverty, has opened only about two-thirds of the country to development, and has failed to reduce inflation—which in 1979 caused domestic food prices to rise by 80%.

On December 7, 1979, Brazil devalued the cruzeiro 30%. The purpose was to cut into a current account deficit of $10 billion by stimulating exports. This was the third devaluation for 1979, which brought the total devaluation for the year to 104%. The sharp devaluation, the doubling in the price of imported oil, and the high interest rates on its loans made Brazil's payment on its foreign debt a near impossibility and brought the country to the brink of default.

In 1980 Brazil was expected to borrow $18 billion to fulfill its foreign debt commitments (which already equal 25% of gross national product) and to meet its petroleum bills.

All this deficit financing has tarnished Brazil's former reputation as a safe place for investment. A decade ago Brazil launched a plan for economic development and export expansion with some very good successes. Now, because of overexpansion, the high price of energy, inflation, and super-bureaucratic shackles, the situation is running out of control.

The government is pinning its hopes on a 1981 bumper crop to recover from the drought losses in food production and export earnings of the past two years. But Brazil's economic crises reach far beyond a few good harvests. The real problem is that "Brazil has been using artificial means to sustain levels of consumption and activity that are far greater than the productive capacity of its economy," writes *Forbes* magazine, adding,

"Brazil is not alone in this, but it is unique in the degree to which it has used foreign loans and accelerated its money machine.

"So Brazil managed the energy crisis by tapping the great pools of capital built up in international money markets as a result of OPEC surpluses. But this game may soon end.

"Brazil has the resouces to provide for its people and to live in the world economy but, like the U.S. and other oil-hungry nations, it will have to apply new ingenuity and discipline to do so."[17]

Mexico

Beginning in the mid-1960s the country gave duty-free treatment to border industries that process imported materials for reexport, mainly to the United States. There were few subsidies to domestic export industries until 1971, when a tax rebate scheme was introduced, along with a system of preferential export credits. In 1973 tax rebates amounted to 8.5% of the value of manufactured exports. However, to a large extent, they represented rebates of indirect taxes paid at earlier stages of production.

In 1976 tourism and border trade (mainly Americans traveling across the border to shop) accounted for 35% of Mexico's total exports of goods and services. From 1971 to 76 receipts from tourism alone averaged 39% of total foreign-exchange receipts on the current account. In the first half of 1978, however, the relative importance of tourism declined to 20% of foreign-exchange receipts, mainly because of an increase in revenues from manufactured goods and oil exports.

Agriculture is an important segment of Mexico's economy and holds strong potential for the future. As of 1977 Mexican farmland was still divided into small, uneconomic units, many of them owned by the state. While the nation has a potential arable area of 179 million acres, only about a fourth (46 million acres) of the total acreage is harvested. Crops and farm prices are controlled by the government, just as imports and exports are. Large estates have been nationalized, and the government has distributed nearly 60 million acres of arable land and pastures to small farmers, but an additional four million farmers are still without land.

As for industry, Mexico is fast becoming a net exporter of steel, and with its vast reserves of oil, the country will be in excellent shape for the 1980s. The government is currently implementing a policy that will substantially reduce import barriers. Consequently, the share of Mexico's GNP accounted for by trade—which amounted to only 14% in 1977—will be much higher in the years to come.

Mexico produces, steel, chemicals, electric goods, textiles, rubber, paper, cement, shoes, glass, and handicrafts. Its chief crops are cotton, coffee, sugar cane, tomatoes, wheat, corn, rice, tobacco, beans, and cocoa. Its mineral wealth includes silver, gold, copper, lead, zinc, antimony, mercury, graphite, molybdenum, sulphur, coal, gold, opal, and bismuth (50% of the world supply). As of 1979 Mexico's reserve of crude oil was 16 billion barrels, but the country needs several billion dollars' worth of investment and high technology to develop it.

Mexico's GNP in 1978 was close to $80 billion, and per capita income reached $1,100. Imports in 1978 were $7.11 billion (63% from the United States), and its exports reached $5.89 billion (58% to the United States). Its trade deficit was made bearable by $2.19 billion in income from tourism. International reserves in 1979 dropped to $2.04 billion.

In Mexico, as in Brazil, the twin problems are (1) how to cope with a fast-growing population that mostly lives in poverty on land that produces very little, and (2) how to reduce foreign debt and save more for investment.

According to the data published by the *Journal of Commerce,* the Mexican foreign debt—which in 1976 totaled $18 billion—reached $29.6 billion in 1979. It is predicted that Mexico's debt will reach $40 billion by 1982. In 1979 Mexico renegotiated $10 billion of its existing debt for a longer term. Thus by 1979 only 4.7% of the nation's debt was to be repaid in less than one year. In contrast, 11.9% was short-term debt in 1977, compared with a hefty 18% in 1976.

Twenty-eight percent of Mexico's debts were financed by Japan, 15% by the United States, and 11% by Europe. However, only 4.7% came from the World Bank and Inter-American Development Bank. The remainder (about 83%) was supplied by private foreign banking consortiums.

The principal borrowing sector in 1979 was energy, which means that "petroleos Mexicanos" got the lion's share, with the Federal Electricity Commission receiving the rest.

In the area of debt servicing, 44¢ of every dollar paid out goes to interest payments—which is equivalent to 40% of the income from Mexico's total exports of goods and services

In the last few years the tendency has been toward a dollarization of debts, and there has also been a heavy leaning toward private banks rather than governments. The Americanization of Mexico's debts is seen "by some as providing the United States with a pressure source to extract more petroleum from Mexico."[18]

Africa South of the Sahara

The story of Africa south of the Sahara is not so promising. Nigeria has made some progress, but it is just at the beginning stage of its "takeoff." Nigeria's industry, apart from petroleum, is insignificant. It is composed of food-processing and automobile assemblies. It has a crude oil reserve of 18 billion barrels, but, unfortunately, all the income from oil has had little impact on industrialization. Its gross national product in 1978 was nearly $30 billion, its per capita income was $550, and its imports totaled $12.1

The Future of the Developing Nations

billion (23% from the United States, 15% from Germany, and 10% from Japan). Nigeria's exports in 1978 were $10.39 billion (29% to the United States, 14% to the United Kingdom, and 11½% to the Netherlands). Its international reserve in 1979 was $2.03 billion.

The story of Zaire is an example of how a rich country, because of corruption and poor planning, can plunge into chaos and abject poverty. Zaire is a nation with more than 900,000 square miles, a small population of only 25 million, and rich agricultural and mineral resouces; yet its per capita income is less than $200. Zaire's total exports in 1978 were $985 million, its imports were $608 million, and its national debt was close to $6 billion. Its international reserve in 1979 was $165 million—the lowest in the world.

Despite the development of its industry by Western countries and despite its pro-Western label, the Zairian regime has done very little for its people and bears little in common with the West. A government board controlled by Mobutu Sese Seku, the president of Zaire, sells all copper, cobalt, diamond, and other mineral resources to foreign corporations. For instance, the De Beers diamond syndicate has been granted the monopoly right to purchase all diamonds.

This kind of heavy government control tends to hamper agriculture production and encourage lawlessness. According to the *Wall Street Journal*, Zaire's unreasonable regulations have led to a great deal of bribery and smuggling—which costs the country hundreds of millions of dollars worth of foreign exchange and taxes. "The Zairian form of government is described by one Peace Corps volunteer as 'a kleptocracy,'"[19] says the *Journal* report, which claims that Zaire is plagued by the twin calamities of control and corruption. Most of Zaire's diamonds, the *Journal* contends, are smuggled out of the country by venal officials and sold in Congo, across the river. The smugglers "go either on the ferry that connects the capital of Brazzaville and Kinshasa or with barges and dug-out canoes in the remote jungles up-river. They carry not only diamonds but other items—even large loads of coffee—to the open market. The hard currency obtained from this trade is lost to the Zairian nation [and also to Western creditors, who are supposedly monitoring Zairian trade through the International Monetary Fund]. Because of monetary controls and lack of confidence at home, most Zairian smugglers keep their money in Brazzaville or in Europe. Smugglers have made Congo a leading diamond export nation. . . . The diamonds come from Zaire, which has one-quarter of the world's supply."[20]

The case of the Ivory Coast is different. It is a good example of what exploitation of a natural advantage (agriculture) and prudent planning can do for a developing economy.

In a continent of single-crop economies, the Ivory Coast has successfully diversified its agriculture since 1960, when it achieved independence. The northern part of the country, traditionally desolate and very dry, now produces sugar and other crops suited to a dry climate. The southern part of the country has become Africa's leading exporter of pineapples and bananas. The Ivory Coast also has become the world's leading exporter of coffee and cocoa, and it is a principal supplier of timber to Europe.

After France, the United States is the Ivory Coast's principal trading partner, with more than 60 U.S. firms operating in the country. The Ivory Coast maintains a favorable attitude toward foreign investment, which in turn contributes to the country's remarkable economic growth.

This country, the richest in West Africa, has an excellent trade balance and a highly developed infrastructure—consisting of paved roads, concrete houses, running water and a well-developed port. Yet, like most developing countries, it is not without its problems, especially political ones.

The French presence in the Ivory Coast economy is overwhelming. While the agricultural sector is owned mainly by natives, the major industries and a lot of commerce are in French hands. The number of French working in the country has been estimated at more than 60,000, six times as many as in the days when the Ivory Coast was a French colony. Frenchmen occupy the majority of upper-echelon positions, including those in management, education, and the government. The World Bank recently estimated that expatriates, mostly French, account for more than 80% of all jobs requiring upper-secondary training, and one-third of the jobs requiring lower-secondary background. This creates significant social pressures on expatriates, mainly the French.

The fragility of the present situation can be seen in government efforts to redistribute part of the national wealth. From 1970 to 1976 the government borrowed money in international markets to finance domestic programs—many of which could be labeled as attempts to "buy off" discontent on the part of the native population. But in the past several years, as the economy has been plagued by high inflation, declining coffee and cocoa prices, and poor export receipts in the face of shallow European demand, cutbacks in public works and construction spending have been increased. And this reduced spending can create problems for the future economic and political situation.

The government's public financing has played a major role in the country's economic development and has generated substantial investment on the part of the private sector. In many instances the government has shown no hesitation at stepping up its involvement in economic affairs when it found its objectives jeopardized by a reluctant or wary private sector.

One of the most powerful government incentives has been investment in supportive facilities and services. In the early 1960s public investment in infrastructure—which is basic to any successful development policy—amounted to 40% of total investment. With total investment advancing from 15% of GNP in the early 1960s to 21% in the first half of the 1970s—a rise deemed necessary by the government to meet its ambitious growth objectives and to put its impressive economic potential to work—the public investment share grew to 60% of total investment in the early 1970s.

Since independence was achieved in 1960, the educational system has experienced rapid expansion. Starting from a very low base at independence, when only 33% of the primary-age group was enrolled in school, the country now has approximately 55% of this group enrolled, and there are good prospects for achieving universal primary education by 1985.

During the same period of time, enrollment in secondary schools grew from about 15,000 to nearly 90,000, and enrollment in the university, which was established in 1959, was about 6,000 in the academic year 1975–76. This rapid numerical growth in the system of formal education is a very real accomplishment.

Public and semipublic enterprises have proliferated rapidly as a consequence of greater direct public sector participation in the country's development. The government operates twenty-six state enterprises, contributes through budgetary transfers to the operation of twelve public institutions, and holds a majority participation in nineteen mixed companies. Unfortunately, data on these undertakings are sparse and inadequate.

The Ivory Coast has enjoyed political stability uncommon in many developing countries. Its leader, President Houphouet-Boigny, has ruled since independence in 1960 and continues strong.

Since independence, the government's primary economic objective has been to maximize growth by exploiting the country's comparative agricultural advantages. The government has welcomed the participation of foreign venture capital, expertise, management skills, and even unskilled labor. While encouraging the development of a healthy private sector, the government has simultaneously established a large number of specialized agencies and parastate companies to manage development programs. The result is a mixed economy that stands out among Third World states in its degree of openness to foreign inputs.

In 1960 total industrial output in the Ivory Coast amounted to a mere $87 million. In an effort to expand this output, the government implemented appropriate programs to attract foreign investment. A liberal investment code was enacted into law, providing investors with exemptions from import duties on raw materials. Tax holidays and unrestricted repatriation of profits and earnings were also offered. As another incentive for foreign investment, the government developed its infrastructure to provide an excellent all-weather road system, a reliable power-supply grid, and strong domestic and international communications links.

The government also established a large network of specialized parastate corporations in order to develop key sectors of the economy that otherwise might have been neglected. Accordingly, while the small peasant farmers continued to produce the Ivory Coast's two main export crops—coffee and cocoa—the specialized state industries developed and expanded newer agro-industries such as palm oil, sugar, pineapple production and processing, and rubber production and transformation. Today investment spending by the public sector continues to exceed that of the private sector.

The Ivory Coast's development strategy appears to have had considerable success: since 1960, real gross national product has increased at an average annual rate of 7.5%.

The main stimulus to the economy has been from three main exports: coffee, cocoa, and timber. As it continues its diversification of primary exports, the country will maintain its strong economic performance, buoyed by export receipts.

Nonetheless, the Ivory Coast faces the plight of any country dependent on raw materials and agricultural commodities for export receipts—it is subject to erratic price fluctuations because of demand-and-supply conditions prevailing in world markets. Thus, when the Brazilian coffee crop is poor, or when it is ravaged by frosts, the economy benefits. The reverse is also true.

This is an excellent example of basic international trade dogma prevailing throughout the developed and developing countries. What is one country's gain must necessarily be another's loss. Consequently, it is evident that countries vie bitterly to expand, maintain, and develop markets for their exports. It is often the most aggressive that are the most successful—the Japanese are perhaps the best example of this.

The Ivory Coast economy faced some significant problems in the late 1970s that are common in many developing countries. In early 1978 the economic authorities believed that the economy was seriously overheated and that its foreign indebtedness was increasing at a much too rapid pace. Accordingly, they initiated corrective measures to dampen inflationary pressures and ease the spiraling debt.

In consultation with the World Bank and the International Monetary Fund, the Ivory Coast government instituted a program to improve the country's external debt profile and to reestablish control over growth in the monetary aggregates. Consequently, foreign borrowing for 1978 was significantly reduced, and government spending was pared. Many industrial and social spending programs were cut or delayed.

Relying on tools of monetary policy similar to those that the U.S. Federal Reserve uses, the central bank implemented policies to dampen inflation and to decrease the rate of investment in public spending programs. The central bank reduced inflation from 27% in 1977 to 13% in 1978, while not seriously affecting the economy's overall rate of growth. (Fortunately, the country's GNP is mainly a result of agricultural production rather than changes in investment flows.)

The above case studies show that countries such as Hong Kong, South

The Future of the Developing Nations

Korea, Taiwan, Singapore, Argentina, and Mexico, during the last ten years, have been able to create a new export industry that pays for their imports and a portion of future development programs. Countries like Egypt, Kuwait, the United Arab Emirates, Iraq, Iran, India, Libya, Algeria, Nigeria, the Ivory Coast, Ghana, Saudi Arabia, Greece, Spain, Portugal, and Venezuela are in the "takeoff" stage of attempting to develop their resources and create industries that will help raise their standards of living, reduce their imports of manufactured goods, and expand their exports of industrial products (see tables at the end of chapter).

For the nonoil developing countries, this state of development seriously depends on foreign investment. For all developing nations, it depends on the transfer of technology and an environment favorable to industrialization and outside cooperation.

The Oil-Producing Countries of the Middle East

All along the northern, western, and southern shores of the Persian Gulf, the oil-producing nations are industrializing in a big way. They are building steel mills, textile mills, aluminum smelters, cement factories, petrochemical industrial complexes, fertilizer plants, liquid petroleum gas facilities, vast modern office buildings, airport facilities, primary and secondary schools, technical colleges and universities. New nations and a new world are being created on the sands of the Middle East.

This new world of the oil-producing Middle East—Kuwait, the United Arab Emirates, Qatar, Saudi Arabia, Iraq, Iran, Algeria, and Libya—once past the "takeoff" stage, will be a challenge to both the developed and developing countries.

Assuming that events in Iran stabilize and that the Israelis and Palestinians find a constructive and just settlement to their present cruel and destructive conflict, the area around the Persian Gulf offers the following opportunities:

1. There is a potential market of close to $100 billion in goods and services to the developed nations. In 1980 the nations of the area will spend $55 billion on construction alone. Forty percent of the workers and contractors are from South Korea, Taiwan, Thailand, the Philippines, Palestine, Pakistan, and India.

2. For the next ten years a huge market for machineries, technology, and services.

3. The large monetary surpluses of these nations can stimulate new investments in developed countries and offer aid to developing nations. Some of these nations have already replaced the nineteenth-century banking houses of Europe.

4. In the decade of the 1990s these nations can provide the world with surplus manufactured goods and with healthy competition for the industrial world.

The various states have different reasons for industrialization. Iran has to build a strong infrastructure to provide manufactured goods for its population of 35 million. Iran and Iraq are the only two countries in the area with a large producer and consumer population and a great potential for industrial as well as agricultural development. Bahrain and the United Arab Emirates—which have served throughout history as the center of trade between the Middle East and India and China—are now trying to build an industry that will not only serve their own populations but also provide a big surplus for exports when the oil runs out, perhaps within two decades. Kuwait has enough oil and capital but is attempting to create an industry based on its vast oil industry so that by the 1990s 70% of its oil can be exported as refined products. Kuwait also is becoming very active as the center of international finance and investment.

In Kuwait, the United Arab Emirates, and Qatar we find Palestinians, Iranians, Middle Easterners, Pakistanis, and Indians outnumbering the native-born citizens and working with great enthusiasm and harmony for the creation of modern industrial nations. The success in the fight against poverty, disease, and illiteracy has been beyond all expectations. People in these three countries enjoy free education, free medicine, and full employment. The standard of living is high, and wages are very reasonable.

The vast industrial projects of the Gulf area are the result of ten years of planning and the realization that there was little chance either to develop agricultural projects or to build prosperity on the income from oil alone. Therefore the plan in most of the countries has been to concentrate on industries related to oil and gas.

The Saudi industrialization plan, for instance, is based on developing refineries, petrochemical plants, and steel mills.

The new steel capacity in Iran, the Arab countries, Taiwan, South Korea, and the other developing nations poses real problems for Japan and Western Europe. In 1970 the developing nations imported close to 30 million tons of steel; by 1982 they will be producing close to 125 million tons. That means that they will have a surplus of 10 million tons of steel for export.

The Saudi GNP for 1981 could reach $150 billion, and its imports could be close to $50 billion. The nation's building of new cities, huge industrial complexes, refineries, schools, universities, and hospitals has progressed steadily.

Saudi Arabia's major industrial projects are centered at Jubail on the Persian Gulf and at Yanbu on the Red Sea. These two industrial centers are being built from scratch. The costs for harbors, schools, hospitals, roads, workers' housing, water systems, power plants, and other facilities are estimated at $35 billion. Saudi's steel mill at Jubail has the capacity to produce one million tons of steel. More than 500,000 people from the Arab countries, South Korea, Western Europe, and the United States are taking part in building a new and modern Saudi Arabia.

In March 1979 the nation reported an international reserve of $19.6 billion. Since then, with a 70% increase in the price of oil, this reserve has surpassed $60 billion.[21]

With a population of one million and a GNP close to $20 billion, the United Arab Emirates is today a new nation. Eighty percent of the population are literate, many of them recent emigrants during the last fifteen years. The country's new industry in Ruwais, Jubeil, and an aluminum company in Dubai are examples of how the oil money has changed the surface of a desert country. The Dubai industrial complex, which cost $1.4 billion, includes a 515-megawatt power station and a plant that desalts 25 million gallons of water a day.

In the petrochemical industry, the Middle East buildup may become a real source of trouble for European and Japanese producers by 1985. From Algeria to the United Arab Emirates, every government is planning and constructing petrochemical plants. By the mid-1980s, according to a report in the *Wall Street Journal,* "there could be a problem for producers in developed countries. The trouble would come in the area of chloride products used primarily in the making of plastics and fibers. The Saudis are concentrating in that area, and despite the tariffs they could provide tariff competition, particularly for European companies like Hoechst, Montedison, ICI, and Rhone-Poulenc. Besides, the Saudis and other oil producers could use their oil-supply weapons in attempts to force reductions in petro-chemical tariffs."[22]

Despite the economic progress mentioned, there are still many difficulties in the area of industrialization. Except for Iran, Algeria, and Iraq, the oil-exporting countries do not have enough trained people to manage the different institutions of the country.

In addition, manpower shortages result from the nature of the desert sand, the saline water (or little water at all in some places), the hot and humid weather during the summer, the occasional poor planning, the long distances to markets, and the sheer inexperience in business (except in the case of Kuwait and Dubai). Poor planning, especially in Iran, has produced fiascos in the industrialization drive. Also, most of the developing nations have been the victims of waste and wrong advice from thousands of foreign advisers. "We have been the victims of multinational consulting firms," says Saeed Ghobash, minister of planning of the U.A.E. "They have promoted projects merely so that they could profit from them."[23]

Developing Nations' Old Debts and New Investments

Unfortunately, even with the comparative stability in the price of oil in 1980, the combined current account deficit of the nonoil developing nations rose to $70 billion, up from $47 billion in 1979. How can this be financed? What are the long-term implications for the developing nations?

The immediate prospect is for the nonoil developing nations to borrow a total $45.4 billion from the private capital markets in 1980, raising their total debt load to $326.7 billion from $284 billion and their debt service ratio to 18.8% from 16.4%.

If we add to this sum the external debt made without official guarantees, the total medium- and long-term external debt of the developing countries would rise to $400 billion by the end of 1980 from $142.1 billion at the end of 1974.[24]

These figures show the serious possibility of deterioration by the mid-1980s, with a total current account deficit of $208 billion for the nonoil developing countries by 1986. This assumption is based on a 15% per year nominal rise in exports and imports. Over the same period, the trade account is projected to show a smaller deterioration—from a deficit of $70 billion in 1980 to $162 billion in 1986. This divergence between the current account and the trade account deficits is the result of the accumulating burden of debt service payments.

INDICES OF THE DEBT AND ITS SERVICES
(percentages)

	1974	1977	1978
Accumulated Debt/GNP			
Low-income countries	20.6	25.4	25.6
Middle-income countries	15.4	20.1	23.2
Accumulated Debt/Exports			
Low-income countries	147.1	156.1	168.3
Middle-income countries	59.0	81.8	94.1
Debt Service/Exports			
Low-income countries	10.9	13.2	15.2
Middle-income countries	10.5	13.0	17.1
Interest Payments/Exports			
Low-income countries	3.2	4.6	5.2
Middle-income countries	3.4	4.3	5.3

SOURCE: World Bank, World Debt Tables, vol. 1, December 28, 1979, p. 5.

The debt service ratio of this group of countries would climb to 34.6% by 1986. In real terms (1980 dollars) debt service will increase approximately three times over this period, implying a growth rate in real debt service of 16% per year—well beyond the historical and expected growth of exports.

The Future of the Developing Nations 283

The export volume of the developing nations has increased at an average 6% a year since 1977 and is unlikely to grow, in a world of slower growth, by more than 5% per year through 1985. "This increase in debt service commitments arises from the need of this group of countries to raise new finances to meet their current resource gaps, as well as servicing existing debt."[25]

According to recent figures from the World Bank, at the end of 1980 nearly seven developing countries owed 45% of the unpaid public and private external debt of the developing nations. The private debt reveals greater concentrations: ten countries owed 68% of the amount outstanding.

The increase in the developing countries' debt cannot be analyzed solely as a financial problem. Such an increase must be seen within the context of international economic relations taken as a whole—in particular, the structure and trends of international trade.[26]

Among the structural elements causing the growth of the external debt are: the tenfold increase in the price of petroleum in the last seven years, the insufficiency of internal resources, the serious deficit in the current balance of payments of the nonoil developing nations, the tightness of liquidity in international capital markets, the difficulties present in negotiating the outstanding debts, the problem of meeting debt interest and installments, and the slow pace of the internal process of capital formation.

Every year the developing countries must transfer to the developed countries a certain amount of their income in the form of royalties, interest, and direct payments for petroleum and imports of consumer goods, machinery, and plants. In many cases, the exports of these nations are not large enough to meet their needs, and as a result they have had to increase their external debts.

Foreign financing—if it is aimed at investment and development of resources and industry— serves the interest of these nations. But in many cases foreign financing is neither an absolute need nor a fiscal solution. On occasion it is squandered and leads to the evasion or postponement of important internal reforms.

Recent experiences in Zaire, Chile, and some other countries have shown that not all foreign financing can be considered a net increase in the capacity for internal accumulation. In quite a few countries external financing is often used to finance current budget deficits and useless arms purchases, and to line the politicians' pockets. This means that the massive use of foreign borrowing increases the cost of money and contributes to deterioration in the capacity for national capital accumulation and savings.

In fact, one of the most dramatic changes in the world economy in the seventies was the serious increase in the chronic current balance-of-payments deficits of the non-oil-exporting developing countries. Between

1975 and 1979 they accumulated a global trade deficit close to $150 billion dollars, which is greater than the most pessimistic forecasts at the beginning of the decade.

The mounting debt, according to developing nations, is to a great extent the result of inherent imbalances in the pattern of international trade—both in the trade structure and in the regional distribution of trade among these nations. Add to these grievances the high price of oil, and you get an external debt of over $400 billion by the end of 1980.

To a large extent, the financial difficulties of developing countries arise from the need to sustain positive rates of growth; from such negative factors as the slowdown in the export of commodities, fluctuations in the economic activities of industrialized countries, protectionist barriers imposed by the latter upon manufactured goods coming from developing countries; and from the persistent deterioration in their terms of trade as a group. Economic growth demands investment in infrastructure, and this makes for a substantial volume of imports. Given the income distribution and related consumption patterns in developing countries, new income generated by such investments results in new imports in the future. Consequently, economic growth gives rise to increased pressure for two kinds of imports, those which are basically necessary and those which may be considered superfluous but constitute a social and political gain.

In this situation, economic growth demands not only a faster process of internal capital formation and improvement in its use but also a growing generation of foreign currency. This can be achieved either by exports of goods and services or by foreign borrowing.

So far, developing nations have been fortunate in their external borrowing because of the sharp expansion of international monetary liquidity. Between December 1971 and November 1979, developed countries unilaterally expanded the international reserve of their currencies by a total 160 billion SDRS. At the same time, total international reserves of the oil-exporting countries, excluding gold, rose from $55 billion in 1975 to $65 billion in November 1979. Nevertheless, what is most impressive in the financial world of gloom and doom is the increase in reserves of some nonoil developing countries. These few nations, through their exports and savings, increased their reserves from $28 billion in 1975 to $73 billion in November 1979.

Also, exports of the developing nations as a group (exclusive of the oil-exporting countries) grew from $15.9 billion in 1952 to $177.2 billion in 1976. About 60% of the developing countries' manufactured goods are exported to developed countries and the oil-producing nations of the Middle East.

Unfortunately, the problems of the developing nations are many and complicated. While it took industrial nations two hundred years from the "takeoff" stage to reach one of "mass consumption," the developing nations are attempting to cover that period in a few decades. The process of development has resulted in a rising indebtedness, and the two recent oil crises only exacerbated the situation. As a result of huge amounts of debt and the need for even more borrowing, the developing countries are pressing for new concessions from the industrial nations.

While foreign investments could be a great help to the developing countries, it is essential for the nations that look for help beyond their borders to first put their economic house in order. This calls for a political commitment to match the official rhetoric with energetic political action to establish honest and efficient economic institutions that improve the living standards of the people. Without radical changes in social, economic, and political processes, no amount of external capital could help the developing countries.

Taking into consideration the enormous demand and the shortage of capital, future financing methods should be applied to economic activities on a priority basis, particularly in the following areas: food and agriculture, energy, raw materials, industrialization, technology, and transportation.

At present there are several ways of filling external financing needs:

1. foreign aid or capital transfers from official sources of developed countries;

2. multilateral financing of a global mechanism through common funds and institutions;

3. contributions by the World Bank groups for development;

4. contributions by the regional banks and funds;

5. international capital markets;

6. direct investments and other higher forms of cooperation in financing by multinational corporations;

7. financing of economic development through export credits;

8. borrowing from private banks.

Since external financing through private banks and foreign aid is getting more difficult, it is suggested that developing countries in the future resort to financing through multinational institutions. The International Bank, the IMF, the Latin American Bank for Development, the Arab Development Fund and Bank, the OPEC fund for aid to developing countries, the African Bank, the Asian Bank for Development, and the Common Market Fund for the financing of commodity stocks are among the many institutions that have been helping developing countries. (It is essential, by the way, that the developing countries and socialist states with surplus capital join in financing the development projects of the less fortunate nations.)

Already, several important assistance projects in the developing nations are high on the agenda of the developed nations: (1) elaborating on the strategy for the Third Development Decade (1980–90); (2) initiating global negotiations on the most important international economic issues within the UNO; (3) establishing a system of international economic cooperation between the developing countries, under the leadership of the "Group of Seventy-seven"; (4) establishing a global system of trade preferences among the developing countries; (5) establishing cooperation between state enterprises in the developing countries; and (6) setting up of multinational marketing companies composed of the developing countries.

The decade of the 1970s marked an intense period of North-South dialogue. A more constructive tone was set in 1975 with the Seventh Special Session of the United Nations, the Conference on International Economic Cooperation in Paris, and the UNCTAD Conference on Trade in Nairobi. In 1979 the North-South dialogue involved weighing a variety of politically, economically, and socially desirable goals—development, growth, efficiency, equity, and stability. Some progress was made in these discussions. Some measures were taken that have benefited both sides and have brought the developing nations closer to the point of view of developed countries. Under the leadership of the United States, the following decisions were adopted:

1. New agreements on rubber and sugar. Negotiations are well along on a Common Fund, with a final package hopefully to be concluded before the end of 1980. Also, the liberalization of the IMF's Compensatory Finance Facility, which was instituted in 1975 and expanded in 1979, has been a great help to raw material exporters.

2. In the Tokyo Round the industrial countries agreed to cut tariffs by about one-third and impose greater discipline on nontariff trade barriers. In addition, the United States has signed twenty-seven bilateral agreements with developing countries. Furthermore, all the industrial countries had previously implemented preferential tariff systems to help the less-developed nations.

3. New facilities established in the IMF and enlarged quotas will make funds available in greater quantities and on more flexible terms to meet a variety of developing-country adjustment problems.

4. In the past four years replenishments involving more than $100 billion have been negotiated for multilateral development banks and funds. This includes a $40 billion general capital increase from the World Bank, which will guarantee its ability to cooperate well into the 1980s. Meanwhile, the International Fund for Agricultural Development was established in Rome, and individual industrial and OPEC countries have expanded their generous assistance.

The Future of the Developing Nations

5. Special attention has been given to the poorest developing countries. Official development assistance to them has risen from a level equal to about 4% of their combined GNP in 1971 to approximately 10.3% in 1978.

6. At the meeting of UNCTAD in 1978, participants agreed to establish an interim fund for science and technology for development. Earlier, at the Tokyo summit, the developed countries agreed to double the resources of the international agricultural-research centers that focus on developing-country agricultural problems.

7. Since the sharp rise in OPEC oil prices, most of the non-OPEC developing nations have been hard pressed to pay for their petroleum imports. The effects upon these nations have been devastating.

Responding to the needs of oil-importing developing countries for new sources of energy, the World Bank and its affiliate, the International Development Association, approved $2.85 billion in energy loans during the fiscal year of 1979.

This included financing that involves oil exploration, geophysical surveys, evaluation of reserves, and drilling in sixteen countries. It also sponsors the completion of an energy-sector review that identifies needs and resources in fourteen countries.

Furthermore, the World Bank in its annual report to 135 member nations has suggested the creation of a new energy affiliate. The Bank believes that the needs of developing countries are so critical that no stone should be left unturned.

The Bank's "preproduction activities" of the exploration are actually divided into three phases. (1) The first phase involves geological and geophysical surveys. These are usually conducted by specialized contractors using aerial photography, bore holes, field examinations, and other means to determine the existence of oil. This phase of the exploration process can cost between $1 million and $5 million per project. (2) The second phase is exploratory drilling. This operation is very expensive and there is no assurance that oil will indeed be found. Costs run between $10 million and $50 million per 10,000 square kms. Capital is rarely available in most developing countries for this high-risk venture. The World Bank's plan involves financing of this stage of exploration. (3) If reserves are found during exploratory drilling a third phase, appraisal drilling, will proceed. This phase is less risky, and oil of commercial quality may be found.

Besides the financing of oil exploration and production projects, the World Bank is assisting in comprehensive energy planning. These projects could include revising energy plans, instituting legislative and administrative codes, reorganizing energy planning and exploration, and applying new and more efficient technology to the use of traditional energy sources.

In its role as a catalyst, the Bank can participate and assist in negotiations between developing nations and multinational oil companies.

The Bank report also indicates that loans to the poor countries "have lagged behind the needs of developing countries. Total World Bank and IDA lending in fiscal 1980 reached $11.5 billion compared with $10 billion in the previous year."

The largest share of the Bank's lending in 1979 went to agriculture and rural development concerning eighty-five projects designed to help nearly five million farm families. Most of these families live in the poorest countries; many of them are suffering from famine or chronic nutritional deficiencies.

Despite lagging international aid transfers, there has been during the 1970s "increasing concern with the condition of the poorest groups in the developing countries." The Bank has shifted its lending from a concentration on the basic facilities needed for development—such as highways and port projects, which absorbed 60% of the loans in the 1960s—to projects in agriculture, rural development, energy exploration, education, health, nutrition, and urbanization.

Although the International Bank is the largest international development lending institution, it does not supply more than 1% of total investment in the developing countries.[27] "But its function as a catalyst in shaping perceptions of economic problems and designing policy help the developing countries more than the money the bank lends."[28]

In every aspect of the success of the international organization in the developing countries, the United States and other industrial nations stand to gain. In a report to Congress the United States executive director at the World Bank stated that there was direct correlation between developing nations' higher income and increased exports from the developed nations.

> Higher economic growth in the developing countries brought about an increase in food consumption, production and imports. As the world's largest agricultural exporter, the United States has been in a unique position to capitalize on this situation. That is why U.S. agriculture exports to these countries grew from $2 billion to $10 billion in the past decade; and it explains why the developing countries are likely to be one of the fastest growing agricultural markets.[29]

The table on page 289 represents U.S. agricultural exports to the developing nations.

In 1960 the World Bank created the International Development Association (IDA) to aid developing nations by offering soft loans with low interest and easy terms. These soft loans are available to nations whose per

U.S. AGRICULTURAL EXPORTS TO DEVELOPING COUNTRIES
1968–78
(millions of U.S. $)

	Total	Soybeans	Soybean Oil	Grains
1968	2,212	48	89	1,204
1969	1,971	55	88	984
1970	2,335	97	161	1,125
1971	2,524	96	203	1,086
1972	2,800	110	134	1,447
1973	4,975	216	105	3,223
1974	7,609	269	242	4,732
1975	7,543	257	199	4,853
1976	6,836	291	209	3,785
1977	7,383	455	370	3,186
1978	9,710	632	500	4,770

SOURCE: Hearings before Subcommittee on International Development, Institutions and Finance, March 21, 1979.

capita gross national products were $520 in 1975 dollars. These countries have a population of over one billion people. (They do not include Mainland China, whose per capita income is below $500.) At present over 100 nations are assisted by the IDA

Unlike the International Bank, most of whose funds are secured by borrowing in international markets, the capital of IDA is totally dependent on contributions of donor governments. Thirty-three nations that donate to the Association agreed in January 1980 to donate $12 billion for the sixth "replenishment" of the Association to finance lending during the bank's fiscal years 1981, 1982, and 1983.

The agreement takes effect when 80% of the total is officially pledged. The U.S. share is 27%. The Senate authorized the U.S. share on June 21, 1980, but the House of Representatives has not yet made up its mind.

Examples of projects financed by the Association:

1. $40 million for rural nursing and parental care centers in Kenya, where the life expectancy is fifty-three years compared to seventy-three in the United States.

2. $25 million for animal husbandry and reforestation in Cameroon.

3. $30 million for pumping and irrigation along the Blue Nile in the Sudan. Other loans came from Latin America, Africa, and Asia. To fill the gap created by the delay of the U.S. contribution, Japan, West Germany, and other industrial and some OPEC nations—even nonmember Switzerland—have provided temporary funds to keep the Association going.

World Bank Cofinancing

In an effort to make more funds available for development, the World Bank has been trying to stretch its resources through cofinancing. Cofinancing arrangements are those in which resources from other banking institutions and a developing country are joined with the World Bank in order to finance a development project. The source of these outside resources may be other official aid agencies (national or multinational), export credit banks, or private commercial banks.

Cofinancing allows the World Bank to spread its funds to more projects. This is especially important, given their desire to directly improve the welfare of the poorest sectors of the Third World population. Cofinancing should make it possible for the World Bank to fund these "basic human needs" projects as well as continuing their traditional efforts in financing developing countries' infrastructure. It should be noted, however, that cofinancing is not likely to increase the absolute amount of external assistance available for development. It is supposed that the cofinancing provided by official co-lenders is money diverted from bilateral or other aid channels.

Cofinancing arrangements with the World Bank are flexible, allowing them to accommodate different conditions from one project to another. "The role which the Bank plays in cofinancing may vary considerably depending on factors such as the wishes of the borrower, the capacity and experience of the co-lender, and the type and source of cofinancing." These varying arrangements can, however, be broadly categorized as "joint financing" and "parallel financing." Under a joint financing scheme, there is a common list of goods and services required for the project. The World Bank and the co-lender share the financing of the items in agreed proportions. "Parallel financing" involves two separate lists of the goods and services required. The World Bank finances the items of one list and the co-lender finances the items of the other.

Most cofinancing has been with official sources of aid, either the aid agencies of member governments (e.g., USAID) or other MDBs (see the following table).

Cofinancing-Projects Financed, FY 1973–76
(Amounts in U.S. $ millions)

Fiscal Year	Total		Official Sources		Export Credits		Private Financing	
	No.	Amount	No.	Amount	No.	Amount	No.	Amount
1973	34	450.5	32	357.6	4	90.7	1	2.2
1974	41	1,380.4	36	674.5	12	621.2	2	84.7
1975	56	1,887.2	54	950.0	7	878.7	2	58.5
1976	66	2,246.6	58	1,247.2	12	753.4	5	246.0

These aid agencies benefit by stretching their aid and having greater impact on developing countries than if they were acting alone. Cofinancing also gives the co-lender the benefit of World Bank expertise in appraising a particular project in order to be assured of its benefits and viability. The World Bank will also provide project supervision and handle the administration of the loan, if need be. These services are particularly helpful to the newer, smaller, and less experienced official aid agencies. The development aid funds established by OPEC members have benefited by the expertise offered by the World Bank (see the following table).

COFINANCING-DISTRIBUTION BY OFFICIAL SOURCES, FY 1973–76
(Amounts in U.S. millions)

Fiscal Year	OPEC			Multilateral			Other bilateral	
	Percentage of total amount	Projects Amount	No.	Percentage of total amount	Projects Amount	No.	Percentage of total amount	Projects Amount
1973	7%	26.1	3	25%	87.7	10	68%	243.8
1974	6%	38.5	3	47%	317.7	19	47%	318.3
1975	54%	517.7	17	17%	160.0	17	29%	272.3
1976	36%	455.9	26	21%	267.6	24	43%	523.7

In the case of experienced co-lenders such as the USAID or IDB, the World Bank assumes less responsibility for the loan and project supervision.

Cofinancing with an export credit bank is commonly done under a parallel financing arrangement. The World Bank finances a portion of the project, usually the civil works component. For the balance of the financing, the borrowing country negotiates with different national export credit banks for acceptable terms. The borrower then accepts bids from manufacturers and consultants from nations whose export credit banks have given acceptable terms. Besides financing its portion of the project, the World Bank can also handle the appraisal and day-to-day supervision.

This new development in North-South dialogue is not based on altruism but on the mutual interests of both sides. A spokesman for the U.S. government explains this mutual interest in the following words:

> For the United States, the developing countries are increasingly important both economically and politically. They are major suppliers of raw materials, including, of course, oil and our most rapidly growing export markets. For example, from 1970 to 1978, U.S. exports of capital goods to developing countries quadrupled from under $5 billion to over $22 billion. In fact, taken as a group, developing countries now account for more U.S. exports than the European Common Market and Japan combined. During the recessionary period of 1974–76, while exports to industrial countries stagnated or declined, exports to developing (includ-

ing oil-exporting) countries continued to expand. Without that demand for U.S. goods, our unemployment and production would have been even worse. About 24% of our $170 billion in overseas direct investments is in developing countries, as well as around 31% of the $190 billion in U.S. bank claims on foreigners. Profits and interest from these investments and loans play an important role in helping to offset the merchandise and trade deficits we have run in recent years.

The cooperation of the developing countries is becoming increasingly essential if we are to use the world's resources efficiently. It is also in our strong security interest to see that most of these countries find that we and our allies are receptive to their desires for improved economic growth.

Thus, it is not only out of humanitarian concern but also for hardheaded economic and security reasons that the U.S. should listen carefully to the concerns enunciated by the developing countries in the North-South dialogue.[30]

To summarize the present situation, the developed nations are now ready to work with the developing nations, provided that the latter put their acts together and speak with one voice.

In 1979 at the meeting of UNCTAD in Manila, the developing countries produced a long list of demands with no particular focus. The conference produced very few positive results. The same thing happened at Havana in 1979. Not only did they present a long list of demands with little focus on or attention to the interests of industrial countries, but they also put forth a totally unrealistic proposal for a $300 billion fund to promote industrialization in developing countries. Once again no progress was made.

The reason for this confusion is that, so far, developing nations have not been able to articulate their real priority needs. The wide diversity of interests has divided them into several groups. The poorest countries need increased official development assistance and external funds to pay for their oil bills. The middle-income countries want balance-of-payments support and improved and stable conditions for their raw materials—which have been plagued by the cheap and unstable prices of commodities. The wealthier developing countries are most concerned about access to industrial markets, private capital markets, and technology. Oil-importing countries want stable oil prices and financial help to pay for the oil. Oil-exporting nations are worried about industrial-country inflation and the security of their financial assets. Policies that might help one group of developing countries are of limited value or even harmful to others.

The developed nations, at this time, understand and sympathize with the aspirations of the developing countries. They also have an enormous stake in the continuing smooth functioning of the international economic system. The United States is the world's largest exporter and importer of both raw materials and manufactured goods, and largest overseas investor, and the largest international debtor as well as the largest creditor. Therefore, as the leader of the developed countries, the United States

The Future of the Developing Nations

would like to help the developing nations without creating any major changes in the system. The real question is how to find a solution with a high probability of improving the system for everyone. Furthermore, the system must promote efficient use of the world's financial resources.

In a sense, then, the North-South dialogue involves weighing a variety of goals, and if the two sides wish to continue making progress, they have to examine the factors that have contributed to success in the past. Two points are worth emphasizing. First, the dialogue has been most productive when it has focused on specific issues and on realistic proposals. UNCTAD II dealt with trade preferences and UNCTAD IV on a commodity agreement and the Common Fund. The developing countries continued to press these themes at subsequent international meetings, and positive accomplishments were eventually forthcoming. Second, progress is most likely when there are some clearly mutual interests involved.

The developed nations have proposed that the global negotiations address four key topics: a worldwide trade pledge to resist protectionist pressures and to promote positive adjustment; assistance for exploration and development of energy resources in energy-deficient countries; improvement of world food security by fulfilling national targets of the food aid convention, backing these commitments with food aid reserves, and improving food storage and distribution in developing countries; and the taking of suitable steps to facilitate the recycling of payments surpluses.

It should be pointed out that global negotiation, even if successful, could not solve all of the problems of the developing nations. Genuine economic development depends on a complex variety of factors. The institutions and the rules of the international economic system are, of course, important, but at least as important are the policies of all the nations involved with respect to inflation, growth, and international trade, which together set the tone of the world economic environment.

It is also in the interests of the developing nations to focus serious attention on the problems of development rather than on the rhetoric of meetings and conferences. Among the priority development issues for 1980 that every nation ought to pay attention to are food, energy, population, and economic adjustment.

Assuming that the developing nations follow the above priorities, then the demands should revolve around three specific themes—how and where to obtain external capital for development; how to assure the availability of technology for development; and how to increase the decision-making power of developing countries in the economic system.

Developing countries should concentrate on increasing the productivity of their resources. To this end they must increase the amount of scientific and technological research that will be of benefit to them. The terms under which that technology is transferred to developing countries should be reexamined and improved. A way also should be found to increase the capacity of the more advanced developing countries, to select, adapt, and apply technology to their basic needs and specific requirements.

Finally, the developing countries are seeking a role in international economic decision making. Since they are both producers and consumers of the world's raw materials and manufactured goods, it is appropriate that they be included in international forums that deal with the questions of commodities, trade, investment, energy, price stability, and productivity.

It has been suggested by some pessimists that North-South relations could be headed for extremely hard and bitter times over the next five years. As evidence they cite the crippling effect of higher oil prices, coupled with the dual problems of inflation and recession in industrial countries. The point is well taken, but this and other important economic issues can be addressed constructively through existing international institutions that have served the global community well in the past.

A major development in international economic policy was the successful conclusion in 1980 of the multilateral trade negotiations. Though not quite satisfactory, these negotiations provide a framework for expansion of U.S. exports in the future; they establish binding commitments among all major trading nations; they provide much opportunity for the U.S. exports and transfer of technology and craftsmanship to the developing nations.

The primary task before both sides now is to consolidate and make full use of those international economic instruments that have been put in place or improved. Once the new agreements are implemented and given a chance to work, then it can be determined what further steps need to be taken. Vigilance and an active policy by all parties in support of fair practice must form an integral part of nations' economic activity.[31]

TABLE 8.1

GROSS BORROWING BY DEVELOPING COUNTRIES ON FINANCIAL MARKETS

U.S. $ million

Group of borrowing countries	1973	1974	1975	1976	1977	1978	1979
Oil-exporting countries							
Capital-surplus, oil-exporting	399.9	165.0	70.4	175.0	1,751.5	1,245.2	939.2
Developing	2,552.4	709.7	3,210.1	3,403.5	5,367.4	10,581.2	8,240.3
	2,952.3	874.7	3,280.5	3,578.5	7,118.9	11,826.4	9,179.5
Other developing countries							
High income	53.2	40.0	—	260.1	164.6	125.0	386.9
Upper middle income	1,685.1	3,004.3	3,120.1	5,083.3	5,301.0	9,995.9	12,640.3
(of which: Brazil)	(883.1)	(1,630.0)	(2,154.8)	(3,501.6)	(3,409.3)	(5,856.8)	(7,165.6)
Intermediate middle income	2,519.0	2,866.2	4,186.8	4,942.2	6,643.9	11,244.0	18,090.0
(of which: Mexico)	(1,355.2)	(1,528.4)	(2,436.2)	(2,402.1)	(4,005.2)	(6,368.9)	(10,846.6)
Lower middle income	504.8	1,273.1	895.9	1,995.5	1,981.0	3,208.2	3,459.5
Low income	311.3	301.3	34.5	—	396.0	262.2	785.3
	5,073.4	7,484.9	8,237.3	12,281.1	14,486.5	24,835.3	35,362.0
People's Republic of China	—	—	—	—	—	—	3,070.0
Total	8,025.7	8,359.6	11,517.8	15,859.6	21,605.4	36,661.7	47,611.5

TABLE 8.2

Best Loan Conditions Available to Selected Public-Sector Borrowers
(maturity and spread)

	Brazil		Mexico		France	
1974	12	5/8-3/4	10	1/2	10	3/8-5/8
			12	1/2-3/4		
1975	7	1 3/4	5	1 1/2	5	1 1/4
1976	7	1 7/8	5	1 1/2	7	1-1 1/8
			7	1 3/4		
1977	5	1 7/8	5	1 1/2	5	5/8
	8	2 1/8	10	1 1/4-1 3/4	8	7/8-1
1978	10	1	8	3/4	10	1/2
	12	1 1/4	10	7/8-1		
	15	1 1/2				
1979			6	1/2	15	3/8-1/2
	12	5/8-3/4	12	5/8		

TABLE 8.3

BORROWING IN INTERNATIONAL CAPITAL MARKETS* BY PURPOSE OF THE BORROWER 1974 TO JUNE 1979

(a) Amounts (US $ millions)

Purpose	1974	1975	1976	1977	1978	1979 1st half	1974 to June 1979
Bank & Finance	8001.8	9249.6	13530.1	15807.8	21665.9	12513.6	80768.8
Transport	3697.4	2911.9	2714.9	2748.0	4553.3	2832.9	19458.4
Public Utilities	4586.3	4186.2	9976.4	6389.1	12226.0	6673.7	44037.7
Petroleum & Natural Gas	2470.0	2881.4	4245.8	5917.2	9203.2	3488.8	28206.4
Natural Resources	516.9	790.2	1619.3	745.5	1262.5	652.5	5586.9
Industry	5164.8	8166.2	9325.1	10817.0	16233.3	8070.9	57777.3
Public & Community Services	721.8	171.7	1136.6	2073.2	1400.8	841.7	6345.8
International Organizations	5404.4	5394.5	8632.8	7357.0	8606.3	3637.9	39032.9
General Purpose	10168.8	9589.3	11833.4	18424.8	34190.3	9350.2	93556.8
Unknown	50.6	6.1	—	—	—	—	56.7
TOTAL	40782.8	43347.1	63014.4	70279.6	109341.6	48062.2	374827.7

(b) Percentage Distribution

	1974	1975	1976	1977	1978	1979 1st half	1974 to June 1979
Bank & Finance	19.6	21.34	21.47	22.49	19.81	26.04	21.55
Transport	9.07	6.72	4.31	3.91	4.16	5.89	5.19
Public Utilities	11.25	9.66	15.83	9.09	11.18	13.89	11.75
Petroleum & Natural Gas	6.06	6.65	6.74	8.42	8.42	7.26	7.53
Natural Resources	1.27	1.82	2.57	1.06	1.15	1.36	1.49
Industry	12.66	18.84	14.80	15.39	14.85	16.79	15.41
Public & Community Services	1.77	0.40	1.80	2.95	1.28	1.75	1.69
International Organizations	13.25	12.44	13.70	10.47	7.87	7.57	10.41
General Purpose	24.93	22.12	18.78	26.22	31.27	19.45	24.96
Unknown	0.12	0.01	—	—	—	—	0.02
TOTAL	100.00	100.00	100.00	100.00	100.00	100.00	100.00

*Made up of foreign bonds and international bonds & Eurocurrency credits.
SOURCES: World Bank, *Borrowing in International Capital Markets*, Dec. 1977 and Oct. 1979.

TABLE 8.4

CURRENCY DISTRIBUTION OF EXTERNAL BOND OFFERINGS IN %

Currency Market Country	International Bonds					
	1973-1975		1976-1977		1978-1979	
	All Issues	Issues by developing countries	All Issues	Issues by developing countries	All Issues	Issues by developing countries
U.S. dollar	55.2	66.0	64.1	34.4	55.1	43.2
Deutsche mark	24.4	14.2	23.1	40.9	32.9	39.6
Netherlands guilder	6.1	2.1	2.4	0.9	2.0	1.6
Kuwaiti dinar	1.1	10.6	1.2	9.8	2.6	12.4
Saudi ryal	0.7	3.5	0.3	2.9	0.3	2.2
Other OPEC currencies	—	—	0.8	7.5	0.1	0.5
Other currencies	12.5	3.6	8.1	3.6	7.0	0.5
Total	100.0	100.0	100.0	100.0	100.0	100.0
	Foreign Bonds					
United States	46.8	50.0	54.3	47.2	25.9	8.7
Switzerland	23.4	8.2	29.3	27.3	40.5	24.0
Japan	4.8	15.5	4.7	25.1	16.9	64.9
Kuwait	1.3	16.6	—	—	—	—
Other OPEC countries	11.3	8.5	2.8	—	0.7	2.4
Other countries	12.4	1.2	8.9	0.4	16.0	—
Total	100.0	100.0	100.0	100.0	100.0	100.0

TABLE 8.5

WORLD BANK LENDING FOR ENERGY AND POWER, 1960–79
(US $ millions/fiscal years[1])

REGIONS OF BORROWERS	Annual Average 1960–70	Annual Average 1971–75	1976	1977	1978	1979
A. ENERGY						
1. Eastern Africa	—	4.0	—	—	—	—
2. Western Africa	—	—	—	—	—	—
3. East Asia & Pacific	—	—	—	—	—	4.9
4. South Asia	3.8	12.0	—	150.0	—	30.0
5. Europe, Middle East & N. Africa	—	18.3	49.0	—	—	77.5
6. Latin America & the Caribbean	—	—	—	—	—	—
7. Subtotal	3.8	34.3	49.0	150.0	—	112.4
B. POWER						
1. Eastern Africa	16.1	57.1	63.0	55.0	48.0	9.0
2. Western Africa	8.4	18.1	1.8	57.0	18.2	1.1
3. East Asia & Pacific	59.1	95.2	125.0	196.0	259.0	255.0
4. South Asia	13.1	37.8	283.0	150.0	305.0	467.8
5. Europe, Middle East & N. Africa	21.4	163.5	258.5	142.5	118.0	276.0
6. Latin America & the Caribbean	234.5	152.4	218.0	351.0	398.0	346.0
7. Subtotal	352.6	524.1	949.3	951.5	1,146.2	1,354.9
C. ALL SECTORS						
TOTAL FOR ALL REGIONS	1,435.5	3,817.8	6,632.4	7,066.8	8,410.7	10,010.5
Lending for Energy as % Total	0.3	0.9	0.7	2.1	0	1.1
Lending for Power as % Total	24.6	13.7	14.3	13.5	13.6	13.5

[1]The fiscal years of the World Bank run from July 1 to June 30.
SOURCE: World Bank, *1979 Annual Report*.

TABLE 8.6

INVESTMENT IN OIL AND GAS BY NON-OPEC DEVELOPING COUNTRIES:
Estimated Requirements, 1976–85
(1977 US $ million)

	Oil[a]	Gas[b]	Annual Average Oil[a]	Gas[b]
Developing Countries with per capita income in 1976 of:				
$1051 and above				
Net oil exporters	10,000	4,500	1,000	450
Net oil importers	15,750	2,250	1,575	225
	25,750	6,750	2,575	675
$626–1050				
Net oil exporters	2,000	1,520	200	152
Net oil importers	7,500	1,000	750	100
	9,500	2,520	950	252
$251–625				
Net oil exporters	9,300	500	930	50
Net oil importers	4,200	1,000	420	100
	13,500	1,500	1,350	150
Below $250				
Net oil exporters	1,000	100	100	10
Net oil importers	6,500	1,380	650	138
	7,500	1,480	750	148
Subtotal: Net oil exporters	22,300	6,620	2,230	662
Subtotal: Net oil importers	33,950	5,625	3,395	563
Grand total	56,250	12,250	5,625	1,225

[a]Includes investment requirements in oil and gas exploration, development of oil, production of oil and associated gas, and crude-oil pipelines in all non-OPEC developing countries. The exploration stage is assumed to account for 25 to 30% of total investment requirements in the upstream phase. The relative costs of the various exploration activities are approximately 5 to 10% for geological surveys, 15 to 30% for geophysical prospecting, and 60 to 75% for drilling.
[b]Refers only to investment in development of nonassociated gas and gas pipelines: excludes investment in liquefied natural gas (LNG) projects except in Malaysia.
NOTE: Investment requirements for oil relate to the projected output in the non-OPEC developing countries of 8.40 mbdoe (of which 2.85 mbdoe in oil-importing developing countries by 1985).
SOURCE: *Petroleum and Gas in Non-OPEC Developing Countries: 1976–1985.* World Bank Staff Working Paper No. 289, April 1978.

TABLE 8.7

TOTAL GROSS AMOUNTS RAISED BY DEVELOPING COUNTRIES ON
INTERNATIONAL FINANCIAL MARKETS

	International Bond Issues	Foreign Bond Issues	Medium and Long Term Syndicated Bank Credits	Total
(a) in million US dollars				
1973	471.9	282.5	7,271.3	8,025.7
1974	96.2	233.8	8,029.6	8,359.6
1975	240.5	305.0	10,972.3	11,517.8
1976	1,046.4	587.1	14,226.1	15,859.6
1977	2,473.4	1,328.5	17,803.5	21,605.4
1978	2,919.3	1,940.0	31,802.4	36,661.7
1979	1,691.9	1,242.6	44,677.0	47,611.5
(b) as percentage of total market borrowing				
1973	10.0	5.3	34.8	26.0
1974	2.1	3.0	28.1	20.5
1975	2.3	2.5	53.3	26.5
1976	6.8	3.1	52.7	25.5
1977	12.7	8.0	52.4	30.9
1978	18.3	9.0	48.2	35.4
1979	9.4	6.4	57.0	40.6
(c) as percentage of total LDC borrowing				
1973	5.9	3.5	90.6	100.0
1974	1.2	2.8	96.0	100.0
1975	2.1	2.6	95.3	100.0
1976	6.6	3.7	89.7	100.0
1977	11.5	6.1	86.7	100.0
1978	8.0	5.3	86.7	100.0
1979	3.5	2.6	93.9	100.0

TABLE 8.8

GEOPHYSICAL SURVEY COSTS FOR PETROLEUM EXPLORATION, 1977

Area	Average miles per crew-month	Average Cost per month U.S. $000	Average Cost per mile U.S. $000
I. *Seismic Reflection Surveys*			
(a) *Land Surveys*			
Latin America	56	142.7	2.5
Africa	64	165.9	2.6
Middle East	*44*	*126.7*	*2.9*
Far East	*51*	*101.3*	*2.0*
(b) *Marine surveys*			
Latin America	837	244.8	0.29
Africa	595	226.2	0.38
Middle East	*898*	*246.5*	*0.27*
Far East	*714*	*205.5*	*0.29*
II. *Airborne Surveys* $^{2}/_{3}1$	4,000	100.0	0.025

[1] Extrapolated averages.

REPRESENTATIVE PETROLEUM EXPLORATION COSTS
(in millions of U.S. $)

		Good Conditions	Bad Conditions
(a)	On Land		
	Geological and geophysical surveys	2.0– 3.0	6.0–10.0
	Drill 3 wells to 10,000 feet (3,000 meters)	4.0– 5.0	10.0–15.0
	Overhead, miscellaneous, and contingencies	1.5– 2.0	4.5– 6.0
	Total	7.5–10.0	20.5–31.0
(b)	Offshore		
	Geophysical surveys	1.0– 2.0	2.0– 3.0
	Drill 3 wells to 10,000 feet (3,000 meters)	9.0–12.0	20.0–30.0
	Overhead, miscellaneous, and contingencies	3.0– 5.0	5.0–10.0
	Total	13.0–19.0	27.0–43.0

SOURCE: D. G. Fallen-Bailey and T. A. Byer, *Energy Options and Policy Issues in Developing Countries*, World Bank Staff Working Paper No. 350, August 1979.

TABLE 8.9

ANNUAL PETROLEUM EXPLORATION EXPENDITURE[a]

Developing Countries	1976 Actual ($ m.)	%	Desirable (mid-80s)		%
			1976 $ m.	1985 $ m.	
Oil exporters[b]	1,150	16	2,000	3,333	17
Oil-importers: producers	600	8	1,200	2,000	10
nonproducers	300	4	800	1,333	7
Subtotal	2,050	28	4,000	6,666	33
Industrialized countries	5,250	72	8,000	13,334	67
Total	7,300	100	12,000	20,000	100

[a]Excludes centrally planned economies.
[b]Includes OPEC and non-OPEC exporters.
SOURCE: World Bank, *A Program to Accelerate Petroleum Production in the Developing Countries,* January 1979.

TABLE 8.10

OIL EXPLORATION DRILLING DENSITY, 1976

	Petroleum Prospective Area (million sq. miles)	Drilling Density (no. of wells per thousand sq. miles of petroleum prospective area)
World[1]	30.5	109
(of which U.S.)	(3.1)	(780)
Non-OPEC Developing Countries	12.9	7
(of which Oil-Importing)	(8.6)	(5)
OPEC Countries[2]	4	20

[1]Does not include centrally planned economies.
[2]The relatively low density in OPEC countries is due to the very favorable geological conditions, i.e., large individual fields, which do not apply elsewhere.
SOURCE: *Energy Options and Policy Issues in Developing Countries,* World Bank Staff Working Paper No. 350, August 1979.

Notes

1. United Nations Population Project, Spring 1979.
2. The official name is the Independent Commission on International Development Issues. Besides Brandt its members are: Abdullatif Hamad, director of the Kuwait Fund for Arab Economic Development; Rodrigo Botero Montoya, former minister of finance for Colombia; Antoine Kipsa Dakouré, adviser to the president of Upper Volta; Eduardo Frei Montaiva, former president of Chile; Katherine Graham, chairman of the board of the Washington Post Company; Edward Heath, former British prime minister; Amir H. Jamal, Tanzanian minister of finance and planning; Lakshmi Kant Jha, former Indian ambassador to the United States; Khatijah Ahmad, Malaysian economist and banker; Adam Malik, vice-president of Indonesia; Haruki Mori, former Japanese ambassador to Britain; Joe Morris, president emeritus of the Canadian Labor Congress; Olof Palme, former prime minister of Sweden; Peter G. Peterson, former U.S. secretary of commerce; French senator Edgard Pisani; Shridath Ramphal, secretary-general of the British Commonwealth; and Layachi Yaker, Algerian ambassador to Moscow.
3. Declaration of the Venice Economic Summit Meeting, attended by President Jimmy Carter, Prime Minister Margaret Thatcher of England, Prime Minister Francesco Cossiga of Italy, President Giscard D'Estaing of France, Chancellor Helmut Schmidt of West Germany, Prime Minister Pierre Elliot Trudeau of Canada, and Foreign Minister Okida of Japan.
4. Sandy Fenstel, "African Minerals and American Foreign Policy," *Africa Report* (September–October 1978).
5. Report of the Group of Eminent Persons on Multinational Corporations and World Development, No. 8, 1973.
6. *Foreign Affairs*, "North-South Policy" (Summer 1980).
7. *Finance and Development* 7 (September 1970).
8. Economic Planning Council, Taiwan Statistical Data Book, 1977.
9. Ibid.
10. *International Quarterly*, "The China Academy" (Winter 1979).
11. Euromoney, *Special Survey on Korea* (April 1977).
12. Louis J. Walinsky, *Economic Development in Burma, 1951–60* (New York: The Twentieth-Century Fund, 1962), p. 77.
13. Ibid.
14. Hugh Tinker, *The Union of Burma: A Study of the First Years of Independence* (New York: Oxford University Press, 1959), p. 126.
15. A. C. Campos, Eulabank, London, 1975.
16. Address by José Alfredo Martinez de Hoz, Minister of the Economy, before the 20th Annual Meeting of the Board of Governors of the Inter-American Development Bank, May 1979, p. 5.
17. *Forbes*, February 4, 1980.
18. *Journal of Commerce*, February 25, 1980.
19. *Wall Street Journal*, "Communist Congo, Capitalist Zaire," July 2, 1980.
20. Ibid.
21. Report to the Second World Scientific Banking Meeting in Dubrovnik, May 1980.
22. *Wall Street Journal*, July 9, 1980.
23. Ibid.
24. *World Bank*, World Debt Tables, December 28, 1979.
25. Adam Parkin, *Euromoney* (March 1980).
26. Bibiano F. Osorio-Tafall, Director General of the Center for the Studies of the Third World, manuscript presented to the Second World Scientific Banking Meeting, May 1980.
27. The International Bank for Reconstruction and Development Report for 1979, September 1980.
28. *New York Times*, September 22, 1980.
29. Hearing before the Subcommittee on International Development Institutions and Finance of the Committee on Banking, House of Representatives, April 1979.
30. U. S. Department of State, Current Policy No. 182, May 15, 1980.
31. For further information, see the reports of UNCTAD conferences; also the State Department, Bureau of Public Affairs statements, May 15, 1980.

Index

Acme-Cleveland Corporation, 204
Addison, Joseph, 27
Afghanistan, 28
Africa, 274ff
Algeria, 55
American Association for the Advancement of Science, 178
American Productivity Center, 184
Anti-Boycott Act, 136
Argentina, 268ff
Arms Export Control Act, 127ff
Aron, Raymond, 215
Atomic Energy Act of 1954, 128

Balance of goods and services, U.S., 1977–78, 41
Balance of payments: current-payments account, 37, 39, 267; problems of, 27ff; surpluses, 51; world figures, 1971, 1976–78, 63
Banks: foreign in U.S., 77; international network of, 68; U.S. in Brazil, 272; U.S. in Caribbean and U.K., 43
Beaconsfield, Lord, 120
Becton, Dickinson and Company, 9
Belgium, tax situation in, 156ff
Bell, Daniel, 215
Bentsen, Senator Lloyd, 186
Bergsten, Fred J., 54
Bingham, Jonathan B., 137
Boeing Corporation, 203
Brandt, Willy, 242, 248
Brazil, 270ff
Bretton Woods System, 38, 47ff
Brinner, Roger E., 190
Bronson, Jack, 192
Brookings Institution: effects of DFI on U.S. jobs, 78
Bucy, J. Fred, Jr., 205
Burke, Edmund, 144
Burke-Hartke Bill, 148
Burma, 264ff

Canada: direct investment in U.S. by, 19; Automotive Agreement with U.S., 89, 92ff; impact on taxation in, 165
Capital: access to, 51; expenditures for research and development, 199ff; inputs and productivity in, 181; investments in, 185; markets, 31; ratio and definition of, 199
"Carter Notes," 40ff
Carter, James Earl, 106–7, 178, 194, 232, 242
Catherwood, Frederick, 136
Center for American Business, Washington University, 200
China, trade embargo with, 33
Chrysler Corporation, 194ff
Church, Senator Frank, 49
Churchill, Winston, 17
Clark, Colin, 187
Compania Vale do Rio Doce (CVRD), 72
Controlled foreign corporations (CFCs), U.S. taxes on, 151
Cooper, W. Paul, 204
Council of Economic Advisors, 183
Cuba, trade embargo with, 132
Currency: declining value of the dollar, 55–56, 73, 91, 106; devaluation of pound sterling, 64; exchange-rate devaluation, 255; parity changes in, 48; recycling of petrodollars, 52; relative appreciation of, 44; relative values of, 34, 38
Current accounts: balances in, 37ff; international transactions, 39

Defense Science Board on Export, 205
de Gaulle, Charles, 31, 193
Denison, Edward, 182, 188, 190
Developing nations: 22, 53; and in-

dustrialization, 254ff; conflict with developed nations, 247ff; debt servicing of, 282ff; explained concept of, 243; exports of, 284; external financing needs of, 285; imports of, 242; investment in petroleum, 202ff; licensing agreements in technology with, 226–27, 232; per capita national income and, 244; prospects in technology of, 225ff; raw material exports of, 250ff; recommendation for closing the gap between rich and poor nations, 248ff; technology transfer and, 217ff

Dickinson, Fairleigh S., Jr., 17
Disraeli, Benjamin, 88
Dollar: depreciation and effects in U.S., 42ff; stability, 56
Domestic International Sales Corporation (DISC): establishment of, 148; impact of, 166ff

Economic Development Board, 257
Energy Act, 1975, 129
Exchange rate: systems of comparison, 46
Export: Export Administration Act, 127ff; 1977 Amendment, 130; Export Credit Insurance, 81; hindrances to, 100ff; licensing problems of, 138; merchandise, 29; national programs of the trading partners of U.S. regarding, 145; tax-related incentive system in, 145
Export-Import Bank: 71, 101, 122–25; Act, 125–26, 131; cargo preference, 137

Fairleigh Dickinson University, 9, 17
Fatemi, Nasrollah S., 9
Federal Reserve Board, monetary policy of, 43
Federal Trade Commission, 184
Fielding, John, 88
Foreign aid, relation to balance of payments, 20
Foreign Assistance Act, 81
Foreign Corrupt Practice Act, 107, 133
Foreign Direct Investment. *See* Investment
Foreign tax credit, 153ff

France: direct investment by, 19; tax incentives in, 158ff
Franklin, Benjamin, 27

Gabon, 35
Garfield, James A., 64
General Accounting Office (GAO), study of farm purchase, 80
General Agreements on Tariffs and Trade (GATT), 20, 145, 252; controversy over the taxes, 165ff
General Assembly Resolution, 220
General Electric Company, 203, 208
General Motors, 193, 200
Germany. *See* West Germany
Giarini, Orio, 184
Gladstone, William, 64
Glick, Norman, 109
Gold: outflow, 30, 32; price of, 29, 31; standard abolished, 33; suspension of dollar conversion, 48, 90
Goodyear, 193
Grant, James, 245
Gross national product (GNP), world population growth and, 245ff
Group of Seventy-seven, 252ff
Grüner, Martin, 106

Harbridge House, Inc., 199
Herrick, Robert, 144
Hickenlooper Amendment, 81
Hoffmeyer, Erik, 234
Hong Kong, 255
Horst, Thomas, 78
Human Rights Act, 130

Income Distribution, technology transfer and, 235
Industry: patterns of ownership in developing countries, 225ff
Inflation, causes of, 17, 21, 47
Institut für Weltwirtschaft, 231
Interest-equalization tax, 32, 48
Internal Revenue Code, 81
International Association for Risk and Insurance Economics Research, 184
International Banking Act (PL 95-369), 82
International Bank for Settlements, report of 1979, 45ff
International Business Machines

(IBM), 10; cross-licensing agreement and, 235
International Fund for Agricultural Development, 286
International Machinists' Union, 235
International Monetary Fund (IMF): 52, 55, 56, 252; dollars held by, 30ff; meeting of Oct. 1979, 47
International Monetary Reserve, 48
Investment: foreign direct in U.S., 19, 63–65, 73ff; results of, 78ff; U.S. direct abroad, 64–65, 68ff; U.S. direct in low-technology industries, 201
Iran, 280
Ivory Coast, 275ff

Japan: defense expenditures of, 28, 49; direct foreign investment strategy of, 79ff; direct investment of in U.S., 79; payment surplus of, 51; real trade surplus of, 37; tax incentives in, 157ff; to U.S. exports of, 89
Johnson, Lyndon B., 32ff
Johnson, Samuel, 120
Joint ventures, problems of, 72

Keiser, Norman F., 27
Kendrick, John, 183
Kennedy, John F., recommendation to Congress, 29
Klein, Burton H., 187
Kuwait, 52
Kuwait International Investment Co., 54

Labor, composition of, 182ff
Land, Edwin H., 10
LeVesque, Rene, 71
Libya, 52, 55
Logan, Patricia, 196
Lundberg, Erick, 187

Machiavelli, Niccolò, 221
Mansfield, Edwin, 154, 216
Mansfield, Senator Mike, 32
Marshall Plan, 64ff
McLaughlin, Glen, 178, 186
Mexico, 273ff
Meyer, Peter, 120
Michelin, 193
Middendorf, William J., 53

Military Assistance Authorization Bill, 140
Monetary-reserve assets, 17, 30; U.S. gold stock, 32
Montesquieu, 144
More, Hannah, 27
Morgan, Dan, 193
Most-favored-nation status, 131ff
Multinational corporations: 17; income, 237; in Ivory Coast, 276; interdependence with developing nations and, 226; investment in developing countries by, 226; measures of technology transfer by, 230ff; oil and, 68ff; production and sales of, 224; resource cost of technology transfer system defined, 229; technology transfer and, 218; trade erosion and, 234; trade with Latin America and, 252
Mutual Defense Assistance Control Act, 217

Nathan Associates, report of, 145
National Center for Productivity and the Quality of Working Life, 199
National Commission on Productivity, 183
National Commission on Technology, Automation, and Economic Progress, 233
National Science Foundation, 185, 190
Natural resources, as political tool, 248ff
Netherlands: direct investment of, 19; tax incentives in, 163ff
New Economic Order, 22
New York Times, 47, 65
Nigeria, 55, 274
Nixon, Richard M., new economic policy of, 95
North Atlantic Treaty Organization (NATO), 95
Norway, taxation of foreign source of income in, 164
Nuclear Nonproliferation Act of 1978, 128

Office of Management and Budget (OMB), 186
Oil: crisis of 1973, 242; exporters of, 53; investments in, 202; multina-

tionals and, 68ff; North Sea reserve of, 238; pattern of ownership and production of, 225ff; price of, 44, 47, 51–52, 95, 253; producing countries, 279ff; production of, 55; research in, 197; reserves of U.S. in, 188; surplus of, 50; U.S. purchases of, 141
Organization for Economic Cooperation and Development (OECD), 18, 197, 245
Organization of Petroleum Exporting Countries (OPEC): aggregate current-account transactions of, 62; aid provided by, 54; Argentina and, 270; assistance to developing countries, 286; current-payments surplus, 36–37, 52ff; direct investment by, 73; Mexico and, 273; Nigeria and, 274; pattern of petroleum industry ownership in countries of, 225; petrochemical industry of, 281; price hike by, 90ff

Patents: by non-U.S. inventors, 198; cost of, to developing countries, 221; cost of, to domestic corporations, 184
Paulus, Amelias, 13
Perry, George, 182
P.L. 480 (cargo preference), 137
Population growth, GNP and, 245ff
Porter, Dwight J., 129
Productivity: capacity utilization of, 41; decline in, 178ff; definition of, 181; effects of U.S. government regulation on, 185ff; effects on U.S. economy, 178ff; percentage share of, 22; process innovation and, 216, 231; unit labor cost in Europe, 77; unit labor cost in U.S. and abroad, 179ff; unit labor cost in U.S manufacturing, 41
Pyidawtha Conference, 265

RCA, 193
Renshay, Edward F., 188
Republic of Korea, 261ff; Trade Promotion Corporation of, 262
Research & Development: by U.S. corporations, 189–98, 230ff; of U.S. compared with Europe and Japan, 232

Rodenstock, M., 163
Rural industrialization, technology transfer and expansion of, 217

Saint-Phalle, Thibaut de, 9
Saint-Simon, 215
Saudi Arabia, 52, 280
Saudi Arabian Monetary Agency (SAMA), 53
Scherer, F. M., 184
Schreiber, Servan, 9
Securities and Exchange Commission, 133
Senate Budget Committee, report of, 18
Senate Subcommittee on Finance, 20, 206
Senate Subcommittee on International Trade and Finance: survey of, 122ff
Sherman Antitrust Act, 130ff
Singapore, 256ff
Smith, Floyd, 235
Smithsonian Institution Agreement, 48
Soviet Union: trade embargo with, 28; trade with, 132
Special Drawing Rights (SDRs), 48
Steel, production of U.S. vs. foreign, 93, 203
Stobaugh, Robert B., 237
Switzerland: direct investment of, 19; payment surplus of, 51

Taiwan, 259ff
Taxation: deferral in, 148, 153; European value-added, 168; foreign-source income, 146; impact of on international trade, 144ff; incentives of other nations, 155ff
Tax Reform Act of 1976, 130, 147
Technology: choice of proper, 219ff; definition of, 215ff; definition of change in, 216; effects of income distribution with the transfer of, 235ff; effects of transfer of, 215; environmental problems of, 222; international transfer of, 218; labor-intensive industries and transfer of, 236; multinational investments in 251; prospects for

Index

developing nations in, 225ff; transfer of, 21, 216ff
Tessar, Delbert, 185
Thompson Houston Company, 238
Trade: bribery and, 134ff; deficit in, 17, 27, 34–35, 89; distortions to, 144; embargoes in, 103; flow of and technology transfer in, 233ff; government controls in, 127ff; international theory of comparative advantage, 234; surplus in, 88
Trade Act of 1974, 131
Trans-Alaskan Pipeline Authorization Act, 129
Triffin, Robert, 48

Underdevelopment: dualistic nature of industrial and agricultural sectors, and the problems of, 217
United Arab Emirates, 52
United Kingdom: direct investment by, 19; impact of taxation in, 164ff
United Nations: UNCTAD II and IV, 293; Conference on International Economic Cooperation, 286; report of technological changes, 200, 217
United Nations Advisory Committee, 218ff
United States: balance of payments of, 18–40, 58, 62; commercial cargo preference, 137; Department of Treasury, 52, 81; direct foreign investment and fear of nationalization, 71, 81; exports of 33, 91–92, 96ff; export competitiveness of, 125ff; export of jobs, 71, 235; foreign aid to Korea, 263; government restrictions on exports, 120–21, 128ff; GNP of, 192; impact on international trade, 144; import-export balance of, 35; international trade of, 88ff; International Trade Commission of, 234ff; lack of export strategy, 100ff; licensing requirements for exports, 138; loans to oil exporters, 53; loans to developing countries, 53, 288ff; military expenditures of, 19, 30, 45, 49, 141, 197–98, 259; monetary policy of, 190; policy on direct foreign investment by U.S. firms, 80ff; policy on direct foreign investment by foreign firms in U.S., 82–83, 85; productivity of, 20ff; protectionist barriers abroad on exports, 101ff; restrictive credit practices by the government of, 122ff; suggestion for improvement of deficit, 141ff; tariffs, 107; tax policy of 185ff; technology, 184ff; "technological gap," 228ff; technological research effort index, 190; trade embargoes, 132; U.S. Tariff Commission, 234
United States industries: aerospace, 196; atomic power, 195; autos, 194, 232; joint ventures of, 203; manufacturing, 201; nonmanufacturing, 201; steel, 203–4, 232; tires, 193, 232
United States Steel Corporation: capital expenditures, 203; tax issues, 168
United Steel Workers of America, 184
University of Michigan, 183

Venice Economic Summit, 249ff
Vietnam: expenditures in, 32; War and inflation, 47; War and productivity, 186
Volcker, Paul, 56

Wall Street Journal, 47, 134ff
Weil, Frank, 109, 133
West Germany: current-account surplus of, 104; defense expenditures of, 28, 49; direct investment of, 19; payment surplus of, 51; research and development support of, 105; tax incentives in, 161ff
Westinghouse Electric Co., 129
World Bank: 47, 52, 274, 283, 287ff; cofinancing of, 290ff

Zaire: 275ff; debt rescheduling, 54
Zenith Radio Corporation: productivity comparison, 193; tax issues, 168